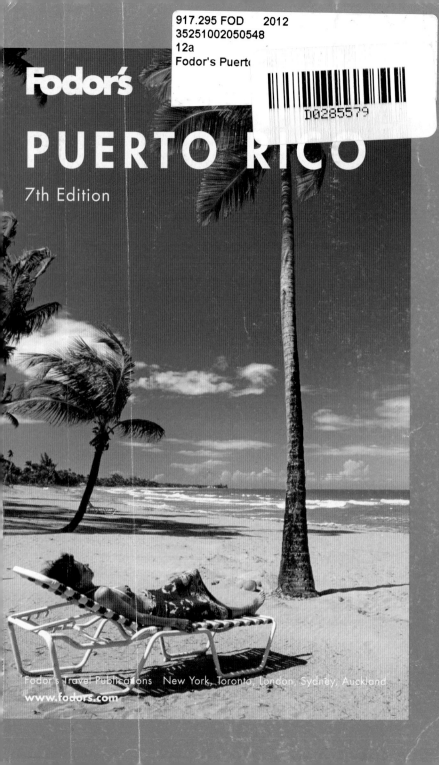

# Fodor's

# PUERTO RICO

7th Edition

Fodor's Travel Publications   New York, Toronto, London, Sydney, Auckland

www.fodors.com

**FODOR'S PUERTO RICO**

**Writers:** Marlise Kast, Marie Elena Martinez, Heather Rodino

**Editors:** Mark Sullivan, Eric B. Wechter

**Production Editor:** Carrie Parker
**Maps & Illustrations:** Henry Colomb and Mark Stroud, Moon Street Cartography; David Lindroth, Inc., *cartographers;* Rebecca Baer, *map editor;* William Wu, *information graphics*
**Design:** Fabrizio La Rocca, *creative director;* Tina Malaney, Chie Ushio, Jessica Walsh, *designers;* Melanie Marin, *associate director of photography;* Jennifer Romains, *photo research*
**Cover Photo:** (Houses on Recinto Sur Street in Old San Juan): Massimo Borchi/ Atlantide Phototravel/Corbis
**Production Manager:** Angela L. McLean

7th Edition

ISBN 978-0-307-92924-2

ISSN 1531–0396

**SPECIAL SALES**
This book is available at special discounts for bulk purchases for sales promotions or premiums. Special editions, including personalized covers, excerpts of existing books, and corporate imprints, can be created in large quantities for special needs. For more information, write to Special Markets/Premium Sales, 1745 Broadway, MD 3-1, New York, NY 10019, or e-mail specialmarkets@randomhouse.com.

**AN IMPORTANT TIP & AN INVITATION**
Although all prices, opening times, and other details in this book are based on information supplied to us at press time, changes occur all the time in the travel world, and Fodor's cannot accept responsibility for facts that become outdated or for inadvertent errors or omissions. So **always confirm information when it matters,** especially if you're making a detour to visit a specific place. Your experiences—positive and negative—matter to us. If we have missed or misstated something, **please write to us.** Share your opinion instantly through our online feedback center at fodors.com/contact-us.

PRINTED IN CHINA

10 9 8 7 6 5 4 3 2 1

# CONTENTS

**1 EXPERIENCE PUERTO RICO....7**

What's Where . . . . . . . . . . . . . . 8
Puerto Rico Planner . . . . . . . . . .10
Puerto Rico Top Attractions. . . . . .12
History You Can See . . . . . . . . . .14
Cruising to Puerto Rico . . . . . . . .16
Weddings and Honeymoons . . . . .18
Gay Puerto Rico. . . . . . . . . . . . .19
State of the Arts in Puerto Rico . . .20
Flavors of Puerto Rico . . . . . . . . .22
Great Itineraries. . . . . . . . . . . . .26
Kids and Family . . . . . . . . . . . .30

**2 SAN JUAN. . . . . . . . . . . . . . .31**

Welcome to San Juan . . . . . . . .32
Beaches of San Juan. . . . . . . . .34
Exploring San Juan . . . . . . . . . .40
Where to Eat. . . . . . . . . . . . . .64
Best Bets for San Juan Dining . . . .66
Where to Stay . . . . . . . . . . . . .83
Best Bets for San Juan Lodging . . .88
Nightlife and the Arts . . . . . . . .95
Shopping . . . . . . . . . . . . . . .106
Sports and the Outdoors . . . . . .112

**3 EL YUNQUE AND
THE NORTHEAST. . . . . . . . . .117**

Welcome to El Yunque
and the Northeast . . . . . . . . . .118
El Yunque National Forest. . . . . .120
Beaches of the Northeast. . . . . .124
The Northeastern Coast . . . . . . .129
The Eastern Coast. . . . . . . . . . .154

**4 VIEQUES AND CULEBRA . . . .159**

Welcome to Vieques
and Culebra . . . . . . . . . . . . . .160
Beaches of Vieques
and Culebra . . . . . . . . . . . . . .162

Walking Old San Juan . . . . . . . . . . . . . . 51
Salsa. . . . . . . . . . . . . . . . . . . . . . . . . . 97
Bioluminescent Bays . . . . . . . . . . . . . . 175
Surfing Puerto Rico . . . . . . . . . . . . . . 261

Vieques . . . . . . . . . . . . . . . . .167
Culebra . . . . . . . . . . . . . . . . .188

**5 PONCE AND THE
PORTA CARIBE . . . . . . . . . . .197**

Welcome to Ponce
and the Porta Caribe. . . . . . . . .198
Beaches of Ponce and
the Porta Caribe. . . . . . . . . . . .200
Masks of Puerto Rico. . . . . . . . .202
Ponce . . . . . . . . . . . . . . . . . .207
The Southeastern Coast . . . . . . .221
The Southwestern Coast. . . . . . .226

**6 RINCÓN AND THE
PORTA DEL SOL . . . . . . . . . .239**

Welcome to Rincón
and the Porta del Sol . . . . . . . .240
Beaches of Rincón
and the Porto del Sol . . . . . . . .242
Rincón. . . . . . . . . . . . . . . . . .248
Mayagüez . . . . . . . . . . . . . . .267

Cabo Rojo. . . . . . . . . . . . . . .270
The Northwestern Coast. . . . . . .277

7 **RUTA PANORÁMICA** . . . . . . .285
Yabucoa to Aibonito . . . . . . . .289
Aibonito to Adjuntas . . . . . . . .291
Adjuntas to Mayagüez . . . . . . .295

**TRAVEL SMART
PUERTO RICO** . . . . . . . . . . .299
Getting Here and Around . . . . . .300
Essentials. . . . . . . . . . . . . . .304

**INDEX** . . . . . . . . . . . . . . . . .312

**ABOUT OUR WRITERS**. . . . . . . 328

The Northeast and the
Eastern Coast . . . . . . . . . . . .130
El Yunque. . . . . . . . . . . . . . .141
Vieques . . . . . . . . . . . . . . . .168
Culebra . . . . . . . . . . . . . . . .189
Ponce Centro. . . . . . . . . . . . .210
Greater Ponce . . . . . . . . . . . .213
Southeast Coast. . . . . . . . . . .222
Porta Caribe . . . . . . . . . . . . .227
San Germán . . . . . . . . . . . . .235
Rincón & the Porta del Sol . . . . .249
Where to Eat and
Stay in Rincon . . . . . . . . . . . .254
Ruta Panorámica . . . . . . . . . .288
Yabucoa to Aibonito . . . . . . . .290
Aibonito to Adjuntas Drive . . . . .292
Adjuntas to Mayagüez Drive . . . .296

## MAPS

Exploring Old San Juan . . . . . 46–47
Exploring Greater San Juan. . . 58–59
Where to Eat and Stay
in Old San Juan . . . . . . . . . . 68–69
Where to Eat and Stay
in Greater San Juan. . . . . . . . 76–77

# ABOUT THIS BOOK

## Our Ratings

At Fodor's, we spend considerable time choosing the best places in a destination so you don't have to. By default, anything we recommend in this book is worth visiting. But some sights, properties, and experiences are so great that we've recognized them with additional accolades. Orange **Fodor's Choice** stars indicate our top recommendations; black stars highlight places we deem **Highly Recommended**; and **Best Bets** call attention to top properties in various categories. Disagree with any of our choices? Care to nominate a new place? Visit our feedback center at www.fodors.com/feedback.

## Hotels

Hotels have private bath, phone, TV, and air-conditioning, and do not offer meals unless we specify that in the review. We always list facilities but not whether you'll be charged an extra fee to use them.

## Restaurants

Unless we state otherwise, restaurants are open for lunch and dinner daily. We mention dress only when there's a specific requirement and reservations only when they're essential or not accepted—it's always best to book ahead.

## Credit Cards

We assume that restaurants and hotels accept credit cards. If not, we'll note it in the review.

## Budget Well

Hotel and restaurant price categories from $ to $$$$ are defined in the opening pages of the respective chapters. For attractions, we always give standard adult admission fees; reductions are usually available for children, students, and senior citizens.

| Listings | | | Hotels & Restaurants | | Outdoors | |
|---|---|---|---|---|---|---|
| ★ | Fodor's Choice | ✎ E-mail | 🏨 | Hotel | 🏌 | Golf |
| ★ | Highly recommended | 🎟 Admission fee | ⤴ | Number of rooms | ⛺ | Camping |
| ⊠ | Physical address | ☉ Open/closed times | ♨ | Facilities | **Other** | |
| ✛ | Directions or Map coordinates | Ⓜ Metro stations | 🍴 | Meal plans | ☕ | Family-friendly |
| 🏠 | Mailing address | ▭ No credit cards | ✕ | Restaurant | ⇨ | See also |
| ☎ | Telephone | | ⚭ | Reservations | ⊠ | Branch address |
| 📠 | Fax | | 🏛 | Dress code | ☞ | Take note |
| ⊕ | On the Web | | ⤡ | Smoking | | |

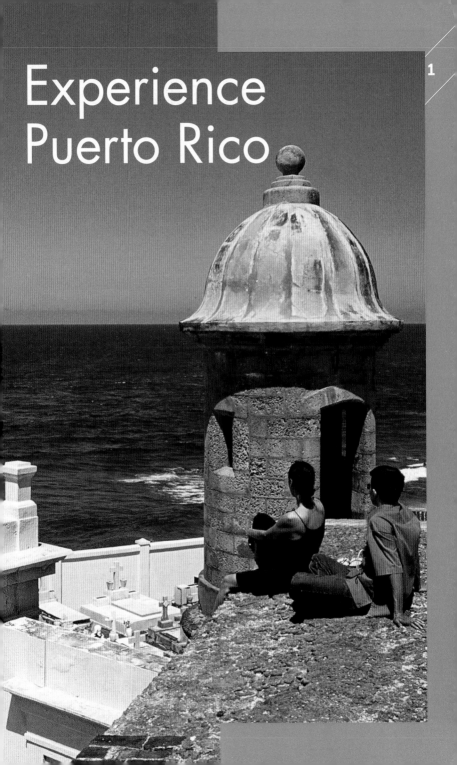

# Experience
# Puerto Rico

# WHAT'S WHERE

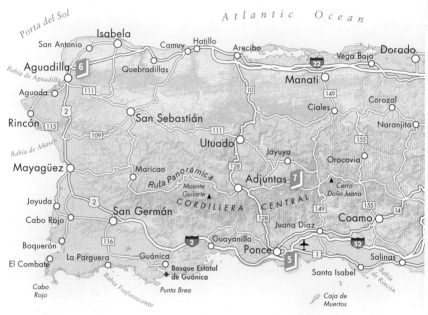

Porta del Sol · Isabela · San Antonio · Camuy · Hatillo · Arecibo · Vega Baja · Dorado · Atlantic Ocean · 22 · Aguadilla 6 · Quebradillas · Manati · Bahía de Aguadilla · Aguada · 111 · 10 · 149 · Corozal · 2 · Ciales · Rincón · 115 · San Sebastián · Naranjito · 109 · Utuado · 155 · Bahía de Añasco · Jayuya · Orocovia · Mayagüez · Maricao · Ruta Panorámica · 128 · Adjuntas 7 · Cerro Doña Juana · Mounte Guilarte · CORDILLERA CENTRAL · 149 · 155 · 14 · Joyuda · 2 · San Germán · 128 · Coamo · Cabo Rojo · Juana Díaz · 116 · Guayanilla · 52 · Boquerón · La Parguera · 2 · Guánica · Ponce · 5 · Salinas · El Combate · Bosque Estatal de Guánica · Santa Isabel · 1 · Bahía de Rincón · Cabo Rojo · Bahía Fosforescente · Punta Brea · Caja de Muertos

*The following numbers refer to chapters.*

**2 San Juan.** Old San Juan's a visual delight of cobbled streets, cathedrals, forts, and convents dating back centuries. Hotels concentrate in the beach-lined Condado and Isla Verde districts, where the nightlife sizzles. San Juan has tremendous museums, a vivacious bar scene, restaurants from earthy to trendy, plus fabulous boutiques and galleries.

**3 El Yunque and the Northeast.** El Yunque is the most popular day trip from San Juan: hiking trails that snake through this tropical rain forest lead to hidden pools and mountaintop miradores (lookouts). Luquillo has one of the island's best-known beaches, the Balneario de Luquillo. Westward, Reserva Natural las Cabezas de San Juan teems with wildlife in mangrove lagoons. Fajardo is a base for exploring the Islas Palominos—exquisite offshore cays.

**4 Vieques and Culebra.** Once used by the U.S. armed forces for military exercises, this pair of sand-fringed isles is now famous for their jaw-dropping beaches. Boutique hotels and trendy eateries have popped up alongside earthy bars. And ecotourism is big, highlighted by snorkeling, diving, kayaking, and visits to the stunning bioluminescent bay in Vieques.

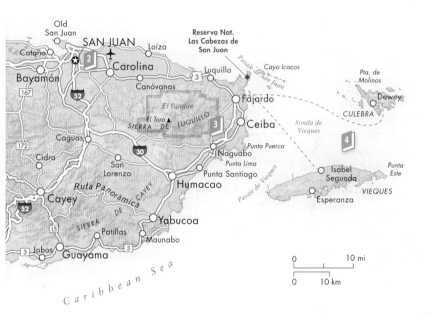

**5** **Ponce and the Porta Caribe.** Puerto Rico's southern coast is studded with tropical dry forests, such as Bosque Estatal de Guánica, a destination for hikers and birders. Be sure to explore the colonial center of Ponce, which has one of the finest art museums in the Caribbean. Offshore, "The Wall" gives scuba divers raptures of the deep.

**6** **Rincón and the Porta del Sol.** The jagged coastline of the southwest is renowned for world-class surfing centered on Rincón, where dozens of beaches beckon those who like to hang 10. Cabo Rojo offers great birding. Architecture buffs appreciate the grandeur of downtown Mayagüez and the charms of San Germán, a colonial hilltop town.

**7** **The Ruta Panorámica.** The rugged mountain spine that runs the width of the isle is festooned with forest. The roads of the scenic Panoramic Route wend through this tangled, lush terrain, linking yesteryear towns and indigenous sites. Several nature reserves along this rewarding drive provide delightful hiking jaunts.

# PUERTO RICO PLANNER

## Health

Few visitors experience health problems, and inoculations aren't required. There's no malaria, but as a precaution against dengue fever, a mosquito-borne disease, use an insect repellent with DEET and wear clothing that covers your arms and legs.

Tap water on the island is generally fine for drinking, but avoid it after storms (when the water supply can become mixed with sewage). Thoroughly wash or peel produce you buy in markets.

Health care is among the best in the Caribbean. All medical centers have English-speaking medical staff, and many large hotels have an English-speaking doctor on call.

## Safety

San Juan, Mayagüez, and Ponce, like most other big cities, have their share of crime, so guard your wallet or purse in crowded areas; handbags should be worn bandolier style (across one shoulder and your chest). Avoid walking anywhere alone at night. Always lock your car, and do not leave any valuables in sight.

## When to Go

Puerto Rico is a tropical island, so temperatures don't vary much. When considering what time of year to visit, think about the "dry" and "rainy" seasons. Dry season runs from mid-December through mid-April. Hotel rates can be as much as 25% higher than the rest of the year, and hotels tend to be packed. This doesn't mean that rooms won't be available, but if you plan to beat that winter sleet in Duluth, make arrangements for flights and accommodations as far in advance as possible. A less expensive time to visit is during the "shoulder" seasons of fall and spring, when discount rates may be available, the weather is still perfect, and the tourist crush is less intense.

The best bargains are in the slower summer season, when temperatures are hotter, it's rainier, and hurricanes are a slim possibility. Puerto Rico can be an excellent hurricane-season option for the Caribbean for last-minute flight and hotel deals, when you'll be able to watch the weather report and know a storm isn't about to strike.

However, business travel—not to mention the fact that San Juan serves as a major hub for connecting flights to the rest of the Caribbean—keeps the flights to Puerto Rico fairly full on weekdays all year long.

## Climate

Puerto Rico's weather is moderate and tropical year-round, with an average temperature of about 82°F (26°C). There are no big seasonal changes, although winter sees cooling (not cold) breezes from the north, and temperatures in higher elevations drop by as much as 20 degrees. The rainier summer months are hurricane season in the Caribbean, which runs July through November. (Historically, August and September present the greatest risk for hurricanes.) The southwest is relatively dry year-round, while the region around El Yunque can be deluged at any time of year, feeding the lush rain forest.

## Festivals and Events

**January: Fiestas de la Calle San Sebastián** (*San Sebastián Street Festival*). The annual Fiestas de la Calle San Sebastián features several nights of live music as well as food festivals and *cabezudos* parades, where folk legends are caricatured in oversize masks.

**February–early March: Carnival.** In the days preceding Lent, Ponce celebrates Carnival with flamboyant costumes, parades, and music.

**Casals Festival.** San Juan's annual Casals Festival honors the world-renowned cellist Pablo Casals, who lived in Puerto Rico for several decades until his death. The 10 days of classical-music performances feature the Puerto Rico Symphony Orchestra, as well as soloists from the island and around the world.

**April: Saborea Puerto Rico.** Puerto Rico's largest culinary event, Saborea Puerto Rico is a three-day extravaganza held at Escambrón Beach in San Juan. It includes presentations by island and international chefs, and food from local restaurants, as well as beer, wine, and rum tastings.

**May: Puerto Rico Restaurant Week.** For two weeks, dozens of restaurants offer a three-course prix-fixe menu, giving diners the chance to sample the island's latest culinary innovations.

**June: SoFo Culinary Festival.** For several days in both June and December, Old San Juan's Calle Fortaleza is closed to traffic for the SoFo Culinary Festival, when many restaurants set up shop on the cobblestone street.

**Heineken JazzFest.** The annual Heineken JazzFest attracts some 15,000 aficionados to San Juan for four days of outdoor concerts by the likes of Spyro Gyra and George Benson.

**Late June–early July: Aibonito Flower Festival.** This popular festival displays incredible tropical foliage, including countless varieties of colorful orchids and ginger plants. There's also plenty of food and music.

**September: Puerto Rico Symphony Orchestra.** The annual season of the Puerto Rico Symphony Orchestra begins in San Juan with classical and pop performances by the island's finest orchestra.

**December: Festival de los Máscaras.** The annual Festival de los Máscaras honors the mask-making traditions of Hatillo, where colorful masks used in religious processions have been crafted for centuries.

## What to Pack

Although "casual" is the operative word for vacation clothes, Puerto Ricans dress up to go out, particularly in the cities. Pack some dressy-casual slacks and shirts, summer skirts for women, casual clothes for the resort, at least two bathing suits, and sturdy shoes for walking. A light sweater or jacket is also a good idea. If you're planning on visiting nature reserves, pack long-sleeve shirts and long pants to guard against mosquitoes.

## Visitor Information

In addition to the Puerto Rico Tourism Company's ¡*Qué Pasa!*, pick up the Puerto Rico Hotel and Tourism Association's *Bienvenidos* and *Places to Go* for information about the island and its activities. All are free and available at tourism offices and hotel desks. The Puerto Rico Tourism Company has information centers at the airport, Old San Juan, Ponce, Aguadilla, and Cabo Rojo. Most towns also have a tourism office, usually in the city hall.

**Contacts Puerto Rico Tourism Company** ⌂ *La Princesa Bldg., Paseo de la Princesa, Old San Juan, San Juan 00902* ☎ *800/866–7827, 787/721–2400* ⊕ *www.seepuertorico.com* ✉ *135 W. 50th St., 22nd fl., New York, New York, USA10020* ☎ *800/223–6530* ✉ *3575 W. Cahuenga Blvd., Suite 560, Los Angeles, California, USA90068* ☎ *800/874–1230.*

# PUERTO RICO
# TOP ATTRACTIONS

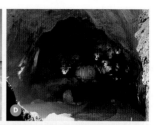

### San Juan National Historic Site

**(A)** The U.S. National Park Service maintains this huge colonial military complex, which includes Castillo San Felipe del Morro and Castillo San Cristóbal. A visit to Old San Juan is not complete without exploring these twin fortresses. Park rangers offer fascinating tours of the tunnels, cannon batteries, and barracks, which today feature museum pieces recalling a once-glorious past.

### El Yunque National Forest

**(B)** Pack your raingear and hike the crown jewel of Puerto Rico's national parks—carpeting the slopes of the rugged Luquillo Mountain Range. From the El Portal Visitor Center, the Sendero El Yunque climbs 1,365 feet through an eerie cloud forest. This 2.6-mile trail puts you atop the summit at 3,496 feet. When it's clear, the 360-degree views are spectacular. Add a twist to your return hike by diverting along Forest Road 10 to the Mt.

Britton observation tower, resembling a castle turret. A spiral staircase leads to a viewing platform.

### Playa Flamenco

**(C)** Puerto Rico's best beach? Ask the thousands of *sanjuaneros* who fly or ferry out to the isle of Culebra on weekends and holidays. Long and broad enough to absorb the masses, this visual stunner tempts disbelief with its bright white sands and waters of Maxfield Parrish blues and greens. Snorkeling is tops thanks to an offshore reef, and when the wind is up surfers are thrilled by the action.

### Parque de las Cavernas del Rio Camuy

**(D)** Puerto Rico has some of the deepest and longest caves in the world, and it's a special thrill to rappel down a cliff face to enter Cueva Camuy. Donned in life jacket and lamped helmet, you'll never forget the 250-foot rope descent, Spider-Man style, into the gaping mouth of the

Angeles cavern. Dripstone formations take on surreal forms in the cool, moist depths, where you slide down mud chutes and body raft in the care of experienced guides. Aventuras Tierra Adento offers trips. Less adventurous travelers can take a tram tour of the caves.

### Bioluminescent Bay, Vieques

**(E)** A remarkable natural wonder, Vieques's world-famous Puerto Mosquito bay's surreal glowing waters inspire childlike delight in all who visit. Microscopic organisms that live in the lagoon light up around your kayak, enveloping you in a neonlike spectral glow. Choose a moonless pitch-black night for best effect. The experience is well worth the journey to Vieques, even if you do nothing else here. Several operators on the island offer trips.

### Arecibo Observatory

**(F)** If this space-age facility deep in the mountains of northwest Puerto Rico looks like something from a sci-fi movie, it

is. *Contact*, with Jodie Foster, was filmed here. The view over the 1,000-ft.-wide dish (the largest such telescope ever built) is a jaw-dropper. The visitor center doubles as a superb museum on astronomy and the atmosphere.

### The Ruta Panorámica

**(G)** Puerto Rico's interior is a beautiful mountainous region with cooler climes and splendid climbs. The Ruta Panorámica is a network of roads that snakes through the entire region. Some are nicely maintained, others less so. But the "Panoramic Route" lives up to its name, providing eye-catching vistas around every bend of the road. It's an exciting journey that reveals an enthralling vision of Puerto Rico undisclosed to those who don't venture beyond the city and shores.

# HISTORY YOU CAN SEE

### Precolonial Puerto Rico

The Taínos were the indigenous group that populated the island prior to its "discovery" by Christopher Columbus during his second trip to the New World in 1493. The Taínos' name for the island was Borinquen, and even today Puerto Ricans honor their Taíno heritage by referring to themselves as boricuas.

**What to See:** The island's two main ceremonial centers—**Tibes** and **Caguana**—have preserved the limited artifacts of Taíno culture that have been discovered over the years. At Tibes, just north of Ponce, visitors can see reproductions of the *bohíos* in which Taínos lived, as well as fields believed to be the sites of ceremonial events.

Closer to San Juan, those curious to get a window into the Taíno world can visit **La Cueva de María de la Cruz**, a cave in Loíza where archaeologists discovered Taíno artifacts in the mid-20th century. As of this writing, entry to the cave was free; there are no officials on-site.

### Colonial Puerto Rico

Columbus arrived in 1493, and the Spanish crown controlled the island—though with a determinedly laissez-faire approach—until the Spanish American War of 1898 ended with the concession of Puerto Rico to the United States. The first Spanish governor of the island was Juan Ponce de Léon, the explorer famous for his tireless pursuit for the elusive fountain of youth. Spain's Queen Isabella charged de Léon with the task of "compel[ling] and forc[ing] the Indians to work for the Christian inhabitants." According to the late historian and archaeologist Ricardo Alegría, the Taínos were decimated, refusing to resist the Spanish conquistadores because they believed that Spaniards were

immortal; thus, taking up arms against them was futile.

By the 1530s, Africans had been brought to the island for slave labor; they built San Juan's two biggest fortresses, Castillo San Felipe del Morro and Castillo San Cristóbal, massive construction projects that took more than 250 years of intense, arduous labor. Slavery in Puerto Rico was finally abolished in 1873.

**What to See:** Built in 1521, **Casa Blanca** was the intended home of Juan Ponce de Léon, who never actually lived here. His descendants, however, called the Old San Juan property home for 250 years. It's currently under renovation, but you can peek it at it through the gates.

**Castillo San Felipe del Morro** and **Castillo San Cristóbal** aren't San Juan's only forts—there's also Fortín San Gerónimo del Boquerón, located just behind the Caribe Hilton, and the Fortinel Cañuelo on Goat Island, visible across San Juan Bay—but they're certainly the largest and most impressive. Both offer commanding views of the Atlantic from their upper levels.

Built between 1533 and 1540, **La Fortaleza** was intended to serve as a perch from which the Bay of San Juan could be monitored and protected. Its strategic limitations were soon discovered, though, and the UNESCO-recognized structure is home to Puerto Rico's governor, as it has been since the late 16th century. Guided tours allow the public to glimpse how the governor lives.

A predominantly Afro–Puerto Rican town, **Loíza** was founded in 1719 and was populated by escaped slaves. Separated from the mainland by the Río Grande, the town remained geographically and socially isolated until the mid 1970s, allowing many Afro–Puerto

Rican traditions to be preserved. Called the "capital of tradition," Loíza is home to popular *bomba* and *plena* (music and dance) and is famous for coconut masks, or *vejigantes*, used during annual festivals (*see also the "Masks of Puerto Rico" feature in Chapter 5*). Though it's most lively during early July, when the Santiago Apóstol festival is under way, a visit at any other time of year should include a stop at **San Patricio**, one of the island's oldest churches and home to what may be the only black St. Patrick statue in the world.

## The Transition to the Commonwealth

In 1898 Puerto Rico became a U.S. territory. Although few would argue that life was better under the Spanish, many have had misgivings about the transfer. As Puerto Rican historians Kal Wagenheim and Olga Jiménez de Wagenheim remarked, "The invasion of Puerto Rico [by the U.S.] ended four centuries of oppressive Spanish colonial rule, only to replace it with a more subtle brand of colonialism."

Although the island was now part of the U.S., Puerto Ricans were without formal citizenship for more than a decade. The educational system underwent frequent upheavals, as did the structure of the government, as the U.S. imposed policies reflecting evolving defense and economic interests. Even when U.S. citizenship was conferred in the 1917 passage of the Jones–Shafroth Act, the development did little to resolve the ambiguous relationship between Puerto Rico and the U.S. Citizenship for Puerto Ricans was not, after all, conferred with all the rights and privileges enjoyed by mainland citizens. In 1952 the island became a commonwealth (or a "free associated state"), though this did little to change the day-to-day lives of the inhabitants.

Fierce debates continue among Puerto Ricans about the status of the island. Of the three major political parties, one is in favor of statehood, one prefers being a commonwealth, and the third advocates independence.

**What to See:** Built between 1919 and 1929, Puerto Rico's beaux arts–style **Capitolio** building is an often-overlooked site that shouldn't be missed. Its rotunda is inlaid with colorful mosaic tiles depicting the major periods of Puerto Rican history, and the Puerto Rican Constitution is displayed in glass cases. Busts of important Puerto Rican politicians are also on display. Visitors will often encounter protesters on the Capitolio steps; citizens gather here frequently to peacefully protest government policies.

The **Las Mercedes Cemetery**, located in Ponce, is the final resting place of some of Puerto Rico's most important and celebrated politicians, among them Don Luis A. Ferré, former governor and founder of the Museo de Arte in Ponce. The grand tombstones and mausoleums in this cemetery are photo worthy, as are the bones resting within your reach in open crypts at the back of the cemetery. ■TIP➔ Every town has its own culture trolley, offering a historic guided tour of the area's highlights. The trolleys are often free. Stops can generally be found in the town's plaza, in front of the city hall.

# CRUISING TO PUERTO RICO

San Juan is a home base for many cruise ships and a staple of itineraries for cruise ships sailing from Florida. It's an excellent way for first-time visitors to sample Puerto Rico, as most cruise companies offer excursions beyond Old San Juan. Some itineraries begin or end here—a chance for more extensive exploration.

## Arriving in San Juan

Most cruise ships dock within a couple of blocks of Old San Juan; however, there is a second cruise pier across the bay at Isla Grande. If your ship docks here you'll need a taxi to get anywhere on the island. The Paseo de la Princesa, a tree-lined promenade beneath the city wall, is a nice place for a quick stroll—you can admire the local crafts and stop at the refreshment kiosks. Fortunately, major sights in the Old San Juan area are mere steps from the piers. Two major tourist information booths are within one block of the cruise-terminal area.

**Carnival Cruises.** They call themselves "fun ships" for good reason, with lots of entertainment and youthful things to do aboard. Singles, couples, children, and even older folks will enjoy these cruises. In fact, the kids' programs earn rave reviews. ☎ 888/227–6482 ⊕ www.carnival.com

**Celebrity Cruises.** Celebrity's focus is on service, and it shows. Every aspect of your trip has been well thought out. They cater to adults more than children, so this may not be the best line for families. ☎ 800/647–2251 ⊕ www.celebritycruises.com.

**Holland America.** The grande dame of cruise lines, Holland America has a reputation for service and elegance. This company includes San Juan on its itineraries departing from Fort Lauderdale and Tampa. ☎ 877/932–4259 ⊕ www.hollandamerica.com.

**Norwegian Cruise Line.** Billing its relatively relaxed, family-friendly cruises as "freestyle," NCL was one of the earliest companies to specialize in the Caribbean. It boasts the youngest fleet on the planet. ☎ 866/234–7450 ⊕ www.ncl.com.

**Princess Cruises.** Princess strives to offer affordable luxury. Its prices start out a little higher, but you get more bells and whistles (more affordable balcony rooms, nice decor, more restaurants, personalized service). It has a wide range of itineraries departing from Fort Lauderdale and San Juan. It draws a slightly older crowd. ☎ 800/774–6237 ⊕ www.princess.com.

**Regent Seven Seas.** Aiming for the high-end market with deluxe staterooms, noteworthy speakers, and performance troupes, this company's ships are among the most sophisticated afloat. ☎ 877/505–5370 ⊕ www.rssc.com.

**Royal Caribbean.** Royal Caribbean is known for its spacious and stylish megaliners. In keeping with its reputation for being all things for all people, Royal Caribbean offers a huge variety of activities and services on board and more shore excursions than any other cruise line. ☎ 800/521–8611 ⊕ www.royalcaribbean.com.

**Seabourn.** With the most luxurious vessels afloat, Seabourn specializes in intimate service and a tranquil cruise experience for the moneyed crowd, using small ships. ☎ 800/929–9391 ⊕ www.seabourn.com.

**Silversea.** Silversea serves deluxe cruisers with small vessels renowned for exquisite decor and attentive service. Expect classical performers among the entertainers. ☎ 877/276–6816 ⊕ www.silversea.com.

Although Puerto Rico is U.S. territory and no passport is required for U.S. citizens, you'll still need yours for ports of call in other Caribbean islands.

Almost all the ship's shore excursions can be arranged more cheaply with local tour operators. Taxis are also available near the dock. Within the city, metered cabs charge an initial $1.75; after that, it's about 10¢ for each additional 1/19 mi. You can negotiate with taxi drivers for specific trips, and you can hire a taxi for as little as $36 per hour for sightseeing tours. You can also prearrange a rental car if you'd prefer to drive yourself, but be sure you leave plenty of time to return it before your ship sails.

Most mainland cell phones will work in Puerto Rico, but that is not usually the case while at sea. Check with the cruise company before setting out.

## SAN JUAN BEST BETS

**Castillo San Felipe del Morro.** Explore the giant labyrinthine fort.

**El Yunque National Forest.** This rain forest east of San Juan is a great half-day excursion.

**Casa Bacardí.** Rum lovers can jump on the public ferry and then taxi over to the factory.

**Old San Juan.** Walk the cobblestone streets of Old San Juan.

**Shopping.** Within a few blocks of the port there are plenty of factory outlets and boutiques.

# WEDDINGS AND HONEYMOONS

Many other Caribbean destinations make a big pitch as wedding destinations, and Puerto Rico often gets overlooked. But it has all the ingredients of a spectacular place to wed and/or honeymoon. Gorgeous beaches dissolving into warm turquoise waters and a sensual tropical climate induce romance, and many an enamored couple has tied the knot here on the spur of the moment.

## Choosing the Perfect Place

You can be as stylish or as informal as you wish. Although Puerto Rico has fewer ritzy beach resorts than many other islands, there's no shortage of exquisite boutique hotels with just the right ambience to inspire "I do." In San Juan, Villa Herencia and El Convento have just the right romantic style. In Rincón the Horned Dorset Primavera exudes honeymoon chic, and the Hix Island House on Vieques will suit honeymooners seeking a reclusive escape. Also on Vieques, the new W Retreat & Spa has all the hip sophistication perfectly suited to young newlyweds, including sexy rooms and a holistic spa. Also consider Copamarina Beach Resort & Spa, which has a "romance package" that includes a bottle of champagne plus massage. Many larger hotels have their own wedding planners to take care of all arrangements—a distinct advantage over smaller hotels if you're seeking to wed on the island.

## Getting Your Licenses

You must get an application from the Demographic Registry Office. There are no special residency requirements, but U.S. citizens must produce a birth certificate, as well as a driver's license or other state-issued photo identification. Non-U.S. citizens must produce a valid passport for identification purposes. Medical certificates, which can be done by your own doctor and approved by a Puerto Rican one, are required. If either of you was previously married, certified copies of a divorce decree or death certificate must be produced. The filing cost is $20. Blood tests are required and must be done within 10 days of the marriage ceremony. The results must be certified and signed by a doctor or hotel physician in Puerto Rico. The cost for the laboratory test in Puerto Rico is $15 to $25.

Both you and your intended must appear together at the office to purchase a marriage license. A judge or any member of the clergy may then perform your ceremony. The fee is usually between $150 and $350. Most large hotels on the island have marriage coordinators who can explain the necessary paperwork and help you complete it on time for your marriage ceremony.

**Information Demographic Registry Office** ⌂ *Plaza Las Américas, 525 Av. Roosevelt, Hato Rey, San Juan 00918* ☎ *787/ 767–9120.*

# GAY PUERTO RICO

In sophisticated San Juan, gays and lesbians will find it easy to mingle. Many gay-friendly hotels, restaurants, and clubs are scattered throughout the city, and the beaches at Condado and Ocean Park tend to attract a gay crowd. Many guesthouses here are gay owned and operated. The bohemian Old San Juan crowd is particularly friendly and—just as in Ocean Park and Condado—many businesses there are owned by gays or lesbians. However, in recent years the gay energy has moved south to relatively nontouristy but artsy and increasingly lively Santurce district; take a taxi to get there.

San Juan's gay hotspots include Circo Bar and the erotically themed Krash Klub, which has cutting-edge music and occasional live music and even drag shows; go on Wednesday for Krash's happening Latin night. Both spots are in Santurce.

Some clubs and bars also host a weekly "gay night." On the first Sunday in June a gay pride parade takes place in Condado and is preceded by a week of events.

Other welcoming areas include Ponce in the south, Rincón in the west, and the island of Vieques in the east, although the local population here is more conservative and it's the large and bohemian expat crowd that is tolerant. Remember that Puerto Rico is overwhelmingly Catholic, which has a strong affect on how locals view gay people. In rural areas and small towns, overt displays of affection between same-sex couples can cause problems.

## IGLTA TRAVEL AGENT

**Connections Travel.** Frank Fournier of Connections Travel, a member of the International Gay and Lesbian Travel Association, is a reliable local travel agent for the gay and lesbian community. 🖂 P.O. Box 9023877, San Juan 00902 ☎ 800/973-5550 ⊕ www.iglta.org.

# STATE OF THE ARTS IN PUERTO RICO

Puerto Rico's visual arts have long been shaped by the influences of its African, Spanish, and indigenous roots. Though the history of Puerto Rican art can be categorized into several predominant thematic preoccupations, a close examination of seminal Puerto Rican works reveals the persistence of these diverse cultural influences.

The indigenous Taíno people were living on the island at the time of Columbus's arrival in the late 15th century; their art consisted primarily of petroglyphs and daily-use or ceremonial objects made of ceramic or wood. Little survived Spanish colonization, but we know about its existence thanks to written accounts of Spanish priests like Fray Ramón Pané, who described Taíno *cemíes*—ceremonial figures—in extensive detail. The few remaining Taíno objects are largely preserved in private collections, although small collections of representative pieces and some examples of petroglyphs can be seen at the **Parque Ceremonial Indígena de Tibes** (Tibes Indigenous Ceremonial Center) in Ponce and the **Parque Ceremonial Indígena de Caguana** (Caguana Indigenous Ceremonial Center) in Utuado.

The arrival of the Spanish also resulted in the introduction of new art forms. According to art historian Osiris Delgado, much of the art from the early colonial period was religious in nature and function, the most representative example being the *santos*—saint figurines carved of wood, an art form that endures on the island to this day *(see also "Santos" feature in chapter 5)*. It wasn't until the mid- to late-18th century that the "fine" arts began in earnest, the works of José Campeche (1751–1809) being the most representative.

Campeche became known for his exceptional oil portraits of religious figures and the social elite; his renown was particularly noteworthy considering he was a self-taught artist with little formal education. Campeche's seminal works, such as *Dama a caballo* (*Lady on Horseback*), can be seen at the **Museo de Arte in Ponce (MAP)** and at the **Museo de Arte de Puerto Rico (MAPR)** in San Juan.

Campeche was followed by Francisco Oller (1833–1917), a painter who remains a central figure in the narrative of Puerto Rican art. Also working primarily in oils, Oller turned his brush toward a realistic treatment of Puerto Rican life as he observed it. His paintings can be grouped into one of two broad categories: landscapes (*paisajes*) and folkloric images of daily life. *La ceiba de Ponce* (*The Ponce Ceiba Tree*) and *Hacienda Aurora* (*Aurora Hacienda*) are cornerstones in the permanent collection at the MAP and help viewers understand why Oller has been called "a realist of impressionism." *El Velorio* (*The Wake*), his most powerful and enduring work, is on display in the **Museo de Historia, Antropología y Arte**, on the main campus of the University of Puerto Rico.

Oller not only established the subjects and styles that would dominate Puerto Rican art throughout most of the 20th century, but he also played a significant role in creating a community of artists and an artistic culture on the island. He opened Puerto Rico's first gallery in Old San Juan around 1870, exhibiting work of local artists. His influence is visible in the works of many 20th-century artists who are shown alongside Campeche and Oller in the permanent collections at the MAP and the MAPR. An appreciation for rural

landscapes and lifestyles, as well as its signature figure, the *jíbaro*—a poor, humble, hard-working mountain man—became the stamp of Puerto Rican identity.

By the 1940s, the government started supporting the arts, and art institutions began to flourish, with the **Museo de la Universidad de Puerto Rico** opening in 1946.

During the 1950s artists turned their interests toward social justice and the urban proletariat, focusing on slums and poverty. The evolution of these motifs is evident in the work of Ramón Frade and Rafael Tufiño, whose works are on display in San Juan's **Galería Nacional**.

The Instituto de Cultura Puertorriqueña (Institute of Puerto Rican Culture) was established in 1955 to promote Puerto Rican artists; today the agency oversees many of the island's museums and art programs. In 1959 the MAP was founded by former governor, philanthropist, and passionate art collector Luis A. Ferré. MAP houses a private collection of more than 4,000 works from the 14th through 19th centuries, including paintings by El Greco, Goya, Rubens, Cranach, Murillo, and Delacroix. The collection is particularly strong in Italian baroque and Pre-Raphaelite works, with good representation by Latin American and Puerto Rican artists from the 18th century to the present, including Myrna Baéz, Julio Rosado del Valle, and Antonio Martorell.

In the 1960s, as the art world moved away from socially committed art, Puerto Rican artists still struggled with nationalism and identity issues. Locally, this struggle resulted in a battle between abstraction—with artists such as Julio Rosado Del Valle, Olga Albizu, and Luis Hernández Cruz—and avant-garde expressionism that favored figurative and socially minded art considered "genuinely" Puerto Rican.

In the 1980s abstract expressionists and other stylistic experimenters were granted a place at the table of Puerto Rican identity. These years opened art to the irreverent humor of Carmelo Sobrino, to the environmental activism of Carlos Marcial, and to aspects of the fantastic, as in the works of Marta Pérez, Jorge Zeno, and Rafi Trelles. Zeno's whimsical sculptures, often fusing human and animal elements, are on permanent display in front of the Hotel El Convento in Old San Juan.

By 1988 a group of artists, professors, critics, collectors, and other art lovers came together to establish the **Museo de Arte Contemporáneo de Puerto Rico** (Museum of Contemporary Art of Puerto Rico). The collection is composed mostly of works donated by the artists. Private collectors continued to expand their sphere of influence in the art world throughout the late 1980s and into the 1990s. Most notable among them are Diana and Moisés Berezdivin, whose collection became so extensive the museum acquired a space for part of the work and opened it to the public in 2005. Their **Espacio 1414** is dedicated to cultivating the visual arts in Puerto Rico and is one of the most interesting places on the island to see art.

The future is exciting as Puerto Rican art attracts art aficionados from abroad and travels beyond the island. The launch of the first annual **CIRCA Art Fair** in 2006 signaled Puerto Rico's readiness to take its place on the international art stage. Increasingly, Puerto Rican artists are showing their work abroad, engaging audiences in a more nuanced dialogue about what, exactly, Puerto Rican art is and what it's becoming.

# FLAVORS OF PUERTO RICO

Puerto Rican cuisine has been experiencing a boom of sorts, with innovative, gourmet restaurants opening around the island. Today more chefs and restaurateurs are developing menus in the line of a Nuevo Latino cuisine. Joyfully departing from traditional continental and Puerto Rican recipes, these chefs nevertheless include traditional ingredients and update old favorites. Standard meats like chicken, pork, and lamb are given an added zest by sauces made from such tropical fruits as tamarind, mango, or guava. Take your palate out for a few adventures. Puerto Rican cuisine may surprise and delight you with both new and old tastes.

## Cocina Criolla

The origins of contemporary Puerto Rican cuisine can be traced to the Taíno people, who inhabited the island in the 15th century. Taíno staples still used today include yucca, peppers, and corn. The Taíno also are believed to have grown guava, pineapple, and soursop.

*Cocina criolla*—literally, creole cooking—is an aggregate of Caribbean cuisines, sharing basic ingredients common to Cuban, Dominican, and to some extent even Brazilian culinary traditions. Still, it has its own distinct flavorings.

When the Spaniards arrived on the island, they brought olives, eggplant, onion, garlic, rice, and cilantro. Wheat would not grow on the island, so yucca remained a staple, as did rice. Regional culinary specialties from Spain, such as *paellas*, came out of the Spanish-influenced kitchen. These specialties played an important role in the development of Puerto Rican recipes, recognizable today in such dishes as *arroz con pollo*. Lacking olive oil, early Puerto Ricans often used lard as a fat. African slaves brought by the Spanish

from Guinea and the Gold Coast of Africa during the 16th century to toil in the sugar fields also left their mark on the Puerto Rican table. The slaves brought plantains, bananas, pigeon peas, okra, and yams. The Taíno used corn husks to wrap foods, but the Africans replaced them with plantain leaves. The African population developed a variety of coconut-based dishes and preferred frying foods to stewing them.

## Local Seafood

Puerto Rico is home to an abundance of freshwater and saltwater fish, both native and introduced, and the island is readily associated with big-game fishing. Off the coast of Culebra, fishermen catch bonefish, tuna, blue and white marlin, and dolphin fish, otherwise known as mahi-mahi. Surprisingly, however, the commercial fishing industry is small and the catch is unpredictable. San Juan restaurant owners will apologetically explain that it's often difficult for them to find fresh local fish. For that, head to the informal restaurants on the coast, where you can often sit on the waterfront, local beer in hand, and feast inexpensively on octopus-stuffed *mofongo* or fried snapper served with *mojo isleño*, a sauce made with olive oil, onions, pimientos, capers, tomato sauce, and vinegar. The seafood shacks of Joyuda are so well regarded that patrons travel from as far away as Ponce and San Juan. In Boquerón customers line up at pushcarts to sample oysters on the half shell. (Hot sauce is optional.)

## Indigenous Fruits and Vegetables

Tropical fruits often wind up at the table in the form of delicious juices or shakes called batidas. A local favorite is pineapple juice from crops grown in the north of the island. Coconut, mango, papaya, lime,

and tamarind are also popular. Puerto Rico is home to lesser-known fruits that are worth trying if you find them; these include the *caimito* (which is also called a star apple and has a mild, grapelike flavor), *quenepa* (also called a Spanish lime, with a yellow sweet-tart pulp surrounded by a tight, thin skin), and *zapote* (a plum-size fruit that tastes like a combination of peach, avocado, and vanilla). The Plaza del Mercado in the Santurce sector of San Juan is a good place to look for the unusual.

## Spices

Puerto Rican dishes often feature pepper, lime rind, cinnamon, cloves, fresh ginger, garlic, and the juice of the sour orange. Three popular herb seasonings are oregano, cilantro, and culantro (known locally as recao). These ingredients, along with small sweet peppers, called ajíes dulces, are commonly used to flavor soups, beans, and meats. The conventional wisdom says that the real secret of the *cocina criolla* depends on the use of *sofrito* (a sauce that may include tomatoes, onion, garlic, peppers, cumin, and cilantro), *achiote* (the inedible fruit of a small Caribbean shrub whose seeds are sometimes ground as a spice), lard, and the *caldero* (cooking pot).

## Plantains and Mofongo

*Plátanos,* or plantains, are related to bananas but are larger and starchier. They are served mostly as side dishes and may be eaten green (as *tostones,* which are salty) or ripe (as *amarillos,* which are sweet). They can be fried, baked, boiled, or roasted, and served either whole or in slices. Sometimes whole amarillos are served with cinnamon as a dessert. *Pasteles,* similar to tamales, are wrapped in plantain leaves and boiled. Traditionally a Christmas specialty, they can be eaten anytime.

Of all the delicious plantain preparations, one of the tastiest is also the simplest: *mofongo.* Green plantains are mashed with a wooden *pilón (mortar and pestle),* mixed with garlic and other flavorings and fried in a pan. Served plain, it's often a side dish. But when it's stuffed with chicken, beef, or some other meat, mofongo becomes one of Puerto Rico's signature entrées.

In the center of the island it's often made with pork. On the coast, however, mofongo is almost always stuffed with fresh fish or shellfish. Some restaurants are even known for what they put in their plantains. A neon sign outside Tino's, one of a long line of seafood restaurants in Joyuda, touts its signature dish: an earthenware goblet overflowing with plantains and seafood.

## Rice

Rice is omnipresent on the Puerto Rican plate. It can be served "white" with kidney beans, or prepared with *gandules* (pigeon peas) or garbanzos (chickpeas); most often rice is simply served with *habichuelas rosadas or blancas* (pink or white beans). Whatever the case, the accompaniment for rice is almost always some kind of bean, always richly seasoned. Crispy rice stuck to the pot, known as *pegao,* is the most highly prized, full of all the ingredients that have sunk to the bottom.

## Rum

As you enjoy your piña colada—a cocktail served in nearly every bar on the island— lift your glass to Christopher Columbus. Although the explorer didn't invent the fruity cocktail, he did bring sugarcane to the Caribbean on his second voyage in 1493. Sugarcane is native to Southeast Asia, but it was cultivated in Spain at the time, and Columbus thought it would do well in the tropical "New World." Juan Ponce de Léon, the island's first governor, planted vast fields of the stuff. The first sugar mill was opened in 1524, leading to the distillation of what was then called *brebaje*. Although rum was first exported in 1897, it took a bit longer for it to become the massive industry it is today. The Bacardí family, after fleeing Cuba, set up shop near San Juan in 1959. Their company's product, lighter-bodied than those produced by most other distilleries, gained favor around the world. Today Puerto Rico produces more than 35 million gallons of rum a year. You might say it's the national drink.

## ON THE MENU

**Adobo:** a seasoning made of salt, oregano, onion powder, garlic powder, and ground black pepper.

**Ájili-mójili:** a dressing combining garlic and sweet, seeded chili peppers, flavored with vinegar, lime juice, salt, and olive oil.

**Alcapurrias:** yucca croquettes stuffed with beef or pork.

**Amarillos:** fried ripe, yellow plantain slices.

**Arepas:** fried corn or bread cakes.

**Batida:** a tropical fruit-and-milk shake.

**Bacalaítos:** deep-fried salt cod fritters.

**Chimichurri:** an herb sauce of finely chopped cilantro or parsley with garlic, oil, and lemon juice or vinegar.

**Empanadillas:** turnovers, bigger than *pastelillos*, filled with beef, crabmeat, conch, or lobster.

**Lechón:** seasoned, spit-roasted whole pig.

**Mofongo:** a deep-fried mix of plantains mashed with garlic, olive oil, and salt in a *pilón*, the traditional Puerto Rican mortar and pestle.

**Mojo or Mojito Isleño:** a sauce made of olives and olive oil, onions, pimientos, capers, tomato sauce, vinegar, garlic, and bay leaves.

**Pasteles:** yucca or other mashed root vegetable stuffed with various fillings and wrapped in a plantain leaf.

**Pastelillos:** deep-fried cheese and meat turnovers; a popular fast-food snack.

**Picadillo:** spicy ground meat used for stuffing or eaten with rice.

**Pique:** a condiment consisting of hot peppers soaked in vinegar, sometimes with garlic or other spices added.

**Tembleque:** a coconut custard, usually sprinkled with cinnamon or nutmeg.

**Tostones:** sliced and crushed fried green plantains.

## DID YOU KNOW?

Much of El Yunque's forest canopy is dominated by the Puerto Rico royal palm, a relatively short tree (40 to 85 ft [12 to 18 m]) that thrives because it can withstand high, hurricane-force winds.

# GREAT ITINERARIES

## COLONIAL TREASURES

More than almost any other island in the Caribbean except Cuba, Puerto Rico has a trove of well-preserved colonial cities. Old San Juan is the best known, and it's a must-see for anyone interested in the region's rich history. But the southern coast also has some gems, from the graceful square in Coamo to the churches of San Germán to the heady mix of neoclassical and art-deco masterpieces in Ponce.

### Day 1: Old San Juan

If you truly want to experience Old San Juan, make sure you stay within the city walls. El Convento, once a Carmelite convent, is one of Old San Juan's most luxurious lodgings. **Gallery Inn** (⇨ p. 87), whose mascot is a cockatoo named Campeche, has the most personality, while **Da House** (⇨ p. 87) is cheap and funky. After you drop off your suitcases, hit the cobblestone streets. Make sure to stroll along the city walls and visit one of the forts—most people pick **Castillo San Felipe del Morro** (⇨ p. 43), but the nearby **Castillo San Cristóbal** (⇨ p. 43) is equally impressive. Old San Juan isn't just for historical sightseeing, though. When the sun goes down, the streets of the historic district light up, becoming one of the city's nightlife centers. For dinner head to Calle Fortaleza, where you'll find some of the city's best restaurants. Then you can while the night away at one of the happening bars or clubs.

**Logistics:** Believe us when we tell you that you don't want the headache of parking in Old San Juan. At San Juan's Aeropuerto Internacional Luis Muñoz Marín, take a *taxi turístico* (tourist taxi) to your hotel. The streets here were made for walking, and that's just what you'll do. Wait and pick up your car when you're ready to leave town for the countryside.

### Day 2: Coamo

Head south from San Juan, and if you get an early enough start, take a short detour to Guayama, where you'll find the gorgeous **Casa Cautiño** (⇨ p. 225). This 19th-century manor house, transformed into a museum, is one of Puerto Rico's most beautifully restored colonial-era structures. Continue west to Coamo, known for its thermal springs. The best place to stay is the **Coamo Springs Resort** (⇨ p. 223), a rustic retreat with hot and cold pools. On Coamo's lovely main square is the gleaming white **Iglesia Católica San Blás** (⇨ p. 223), one of the island's oldest churches. In terms of distance, Coamo isn't so far from San Juan—only about 60 miles (96 km)—so you don't have to leave at the crack of dawn to have most of a day to explore the town.

**Logistics:** Ponce is reached via Route 52, a toll road that heads south from San Juan. Exit Route 52 and follow Route 15 to Guayama. Then take Route 3 west to Santa Isabel; turn north on Route 53 for Coamo.

### Day 3: Ponce

Your destination on your third day is Ponce, the "Pearl of the South." You'll know you've arrived when you drive through the massive letters spelling the name of the city. The main square, the Plaza de las Delicias, is a delight. Here you'll find the **Catedral de Nuestra Señora de Guadalupe** (⇨ p. 209), a church dating from 1835, and the **Parque de Bombas** (⇨ p. 208), a firehouse from 1882 that is painted in bold red-and-black stripes. There are several museums around the city, but the most interesting is the small **Casa Wiechers-Villaronga** (⇨ p. 208), a house built in 1911. In a city filled with neoclassical confections, this is one of the most elaborate. Strolling the downtown streets, you'll also marvel at neoclassical and art-deco architecture. Don't miss the **Museo de Arte de Ponce** (⇨ *p. 214*), one of the Caribbean's best art museums.

**Logistics:** Ponce is reached by Route 14 from Coamo. To get downtown, take Route 1.

### Day 4: San Germán

Less than an hour west of Ponce is San Germán, a must-see for anyone interested in the colonial era. The best place to start a tour of San Germán is Plazuela Santo Domingo, the small park in the center of the historic district. At the eastern edge of the park is the **Capilla de Porta Coeli** (⇨ *p. 235*). This chapel, at the top of some steep stone steps, is now a museum of religious art. Stroll west past the delightful assemblage of buildings of every architectural style from mission to Victorian. Make sure to see the other gorgeous church, the **Iglesia de San Germán de Auxerre** (⇨ *p. 238*) a few blocks north. The best lodging in the area is the simple **Villa del Rey** (⇨ *p. 238*), a few miles outside of town.

**Logistics:** San Germán is easy to reach—simply take Route 2 west of Ponce. When you reach Route 122, head south.

## TIPS

If you're staying in Old San Juan, pick up your rental car at one of the hotel desks. You'll avoid an expensive taxi ride to the airport.

Pack comfortable shoes for exploring these colonial-era cities. You'll be glad you brought sneakers after a few hours traipsing around on the cobblestone streets.

Old San Juan is hillier than it first appears, and in Ponce avoid walking to Castillo Serallés—a stiff hike through an unsavory area. Take advantage of the free public transportation to the most popular tourist sites in both cities.

### Day 5: San Juan

If you have time on your way back to San Juan, stop for lunch at one of the open-air eateries near Guavate, off Route 52. You can try the famous *lechón*, whole pig roasted on a spit.

**Logistics:** From San Germán, take Route 2 until you reach Ponce. Exit onto Route 52; a toll road takes you all the way to San Juan.

# ISLAND HOPPING

If you have a week for your trip, this itinerary will give you a taste of each of eastern Puerto Rico's highlights. However, if you are short on time, Puerto Rico is still the perfect destination. Nonstop flights from many U.S. cities mean that even a long weekend is a possibility, though after you see the beaches, you may not want to limit yourself to just a night or two on Vieques or Culebra.

### Day 1: El Yunque

East of San Juan is El Yunque, the undulating rain forest that covers much of the eastern edge of the island. It's a highlight of any trip to Puerto Rico, and you can still have a memorable time if you have only one day to spend there. Several of the trails can be done in an hour or less, including one leading to the spectacular waterfalls called the **Cascada La Mina** (⇨ p. 122). Spend the night in Río Grande; our favorite hotel along this stretch of shoreline is the luxurious **St. Regis Bahia Beach Resort** (⇨ p. 137), known for its Robert Trent Jones golf course, beautiful private beach, and first-rate service.

**Logistics:** Take Route 3 east of San Juan; then head south on Route 191, which leads through El Yunque.

### Day 2: Reserva Natural Las Cabezas de San Juan

Head to Fajardo, on the northeastern tip of the island. Drop your stuff off at your hotel—we prefer the smaller ones like the **Fajardo Inn** (⇨ p. 151)—and then head out for a prearranged tour of the mangrove forests of the **Reserva Natural Las Cabezas de San Juan** (⇨ p. 148). However, exploring this area isn't just a daytime experience. You may also want to head out at night to get a very different view of Las

Cabezas; you can paddle through the bioluminescent bay here in a kayak. Companies offer the trips nightly, though your experience will be heightened if there is no moon. In the afternoon, take a boat excursion from Fajardo to the Islas Palominos.

**Logistics:** Take Route 3, which leads all the way to Fajardo, from where Route 987 leads to Cabezas de San Juan.

### Days 3 and 4: Culebra

Culebra has some of the most beautiful, powdery soft beaches that you'll find in all of Puerto Rico. It's a small, quiet island, so you won't find much to do except relax. But then, that's the draw. There are no big hotels or fancy restaurants, only small guesthouses and some villas. If this sounds like too much of a get-away-from-it-all experience for your tastes, then skip Culebra and spend more time on Vieques, which has more resorts and better restaurants, and plenty of eco-focused activities. If you want to visit both islands, you can fly between Culebra and Vieques, but note that there's no ferry link.

**Logistics:** Drop off your rental car in Fajardo (or in Ceiba if you're flying)—you'll want to rent a sturdier four-wheel-drive vehicle once you get to Culebra. Take a 90-minute ferry trip from Fajardo or 10-minute puddle-jumper flight to the island from Ceiba. We recommend taking the plane, as the views are spectacular.

### Days 5 and 6: Vieques

Close—both in terms of atmosphere and geography—to the U.S. Virgin Islands, Vieques has an entirely different feel from the rest of Puerto Rico. If you've never been to Vieques, we strongly recommend you spend at least one night there. The beaches are endless, the snorkeling is remarkable, and the **Puerto Mosquito Bioluminescent Bay** (⇨ p. 173) is one of nature's

best shows. A great way to explore the island is on a bicycle tour arranged by a local operator.

**Logistics:** You'll want to fly between Culebra and Vieques—there are scheduled direct flights between the islands. Otherwise you'll need to return to Fajardo and take a ferry to Vieques.

### Day 7: San Juan

From Vieques, take a puddle-jumper flight back to San Juan (or to Ceiba's airport to pick up your rental car). If you want to spend a day in Old San Juan, take a flight into Aeropuerto Fernando L. Ribas Dominicci, which is a short taxi ride from San Juan's colonial heart. If you are connecting to a flight back home, then all you have to do is switch planes and you'll be on your way.

**Logistics:** If you are connecting to a flight back home, make sure your flight to San Juan is headed to Aeropuerto Internacional Luis Muñoz Marín. If it is going to San Juan's regional airport, Aeropuerto Fernando L. Ribas Dominicci, you'll have to shuttle between the airports.

### TIPS

Don't even think about taking your rental car to Vieques or Culebra—it's not allowed!

Check to see if you have to reserve in advance for certain tours, such as the daily trip to Fajardo's Reserva Natural Las Cabezas de San Juan.

Vieques and Culebra are both popular weekend destinations for Puerto Ricans, so the ferries become very crowded, and it's sometimes difficult to get on. If possible, plan your travel for a weekday.

# KIDS AND FAMILY

Puerto Rico is a family-friendly isle, with no end of fun things for kids to see and do, including cave exploration, snorkeling with marine turtles, and going on nighttime excursions to bioluminescent lagoons. And many resort hotels arrange children's activities, freeing parents for romantic beach strolls and candlelit dinners.

## Choosing a Place to Stay

Resort hotels make a point of catering to family needs. Most offer free rooms to children under 12 and can provide cribs. Here are a few questions to ask to gauge the level of family friendliness.

Are there discounted meals and activities? Do the restaurants have kids' menus? Are there children's programs, and is there an age range? A children's pool?

El Conquistador Resort, near Fajardo, has a long list of facilities for children, including the sensational Coqui Water Park. On the south coast the Copamarina Beach Resort & Spa has two children's pools plus kayaks, pedal boats, tennis, and heaps of other activities.

Condos and vacation rentals offer an inexpensive option, especially for larger families. They typically have multiple bedrooms and you can cook for yourselves. ESJ Towers, in Isla Verde, is right on the best beach in San Juan.

## Things to Do

Vacationing in the Caribbean is all about the outdoors. Kids may even forget video games when they see the options: snorkeling, whale-watching, Boogie boarding, and cave exploring. And the list of great beaches is endless. The wave-action around Rincón can be too rough for youngsters, but Vieques and Culebra have the most fantastic, reef-protected sands good for snorkeling, and kids can go kayaking and fishing. Many beaches have riptides; always play safe and heed any posted warnings, such as red flags.

**Parque Las Cavernas de Río Camuy.** This huge cavern will leave kids wide-eyed. They'll have fun trying to discern imaginary figures in the surreal dripstone formations. Tiny *coquí* (frogs) hop around the cavern entrance, and children can spy for crabs and blind fish in the underground river. Bats flitting about overhead help keep kids enthralled. The tram ride to reach the caverns is icing on the cake.

**Arecibo Lighthouse and Historical Park.** Local families flock to this small theme park built around the Los Morrillos lighthouse. It has a museum on seafaring, including pirates. In winter, kids can spy for whales from the lighthouse observation platform. The playground has a pirate's cave and replica galleon, as well as a Taíno village.

**Zoológico de Puerto Rico.** This is a splendid zoo in Mayagüez, on the west coast. The highlight is an African wildlife park with elephants, giraffes, lions, and rhinos. There are also tigers, big apes, and camel rides.

**Museo del Niño.** While exploring San Juan, head to this small two-level museum in a colonial mansion opposite the cathedral. It's a great learning experience for younger children, with exhibits spanning from hurricanes to human biology, plus interactive displays including those in the NASA Space Place.

# San Juan

## WORD OF MOUTH

"A day of walking in Old San Juan is just perfect. You can start by the Castillo del Morro, which is the biggest of the forts built in San Juan by the Spanish. It is a UNESCO World Heritage Site and is pretty amazing. If you are not much into history it is also a great place to view Old San Juan and the bay."

—ARTORIVS

# WELCOME TO SAN JUAN

## TOP REASONS TO GO

★ **Take a stroll:** Wander the cobblestone streets of Old San Juan—the fortifications and governor's mansion are a UNESCO World Heritage Site.

★ **Climb a battlement:** Explore Castillo San Felipe del Morro, the 16th-century fortress that dominates the waterfront; rangers provide a fascinating insight.

★ **Shop:** Head to Condado's Avenida Ashford, where you'll find most of the city's designer boutiques, including that of Nono Maldonado, one of the island's home-grown design talents.

★ **Catch some rays:** Balneario de Carolina, at the eastern tip of Isla Verde, is San Juan's best beach. Take time to parasail.

★ **Dine on the strip:** Dine at Marmalade, just one of many stellar restaurants along the eastern end of Calle Fortaleza, a strip so trendy that locals call it "SoFo."

**1** **Old San Juan.** Still enclosed by its original forti-fied city walls, this enclave of blue-cobbled streets is superbly preserved with more than 800 structures of historic importance, Many date back to the 16th cen-tury. Many of the city's best restaurants and bars are here, as well as boutiques offering wares from cigars to designer clothing. Laid out in an easy-to-navigate grid, Old San Juan has enough sites and shops to enthrall for days.

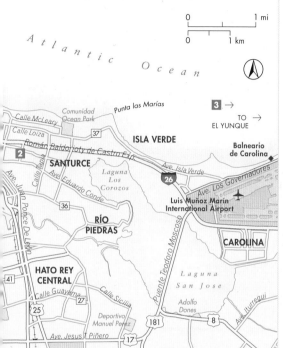

*Atlantic Ocean*

0 — 1 mi
0 — 1 km

Comunidad Ocean Park
Punta las Marías
Calle McLeary
Calle Loíza
Román Baldorioty de Castro Exp.
**ISLA VERDE**
37
2 **SANTURCE**
Calle Isla
Ave. Eduardo Conde
Laguna Los Corozos
Ave. Isla Verde
26
Ave. Los Gobernadores
**Luis Muñoz Marín International Airport**
3 →
TO → EL YUNQUE
**Balneario de Carolina**
Ave. Juan Ponce De León
36
**RÍO PIEDRAS**
**CAROLINA**
**HATO REY CENTRAL**
41
Calle Guayama
27
25
Calle Sicilia
Puente Teodoro Moscoso
Laguna San José
Adolfo Dones
Ave. Iturregui
Deportivo Manuel Pérez
181
8
Ave. Jesús T. Piñero
17

**2 Greater San Juan.** The sprawling modern metropolis opens out like a fan to three sides of Old San Juan. Condado and Isla Verde are superb venues for lazing on the beach by day and living it up by night at casinos and ritzy nightclubs—many associated with the upscale hotels that line the shorefront. Even teetotalers will enjoy an educational tour of the Bacardí rum factory, while culture vultures will delight in the Museo de Arte de Puerto Rico.

**3 San Juan Environs.** White- and golden-sand beaches unspool along the Atlantic shoreline to either side of the city. Several are developed as *balnearios* (public beaches), such as Playa Piñones; others, such as Dorado and Luquillo, boast several world-class hotels. They're popular with *sanjuaneros* on weekends, as is El Yunque National Forest. El Yunque offers fantastic hiking and birding only a one-hour drive, yet a world away, from San Juan.

## GETTING ORIENTED

San Juan wraps around the Bahía de San Juan (San Juan Bay) on the island's northern, Atlantic coast. Old San Juan, the original colonial city, occupies an isle on the northeast side of the bay and is connected by bridges to Condado and, farther east, the districts of Ocean Park and Isla Verde (home of the international airport), which together make up San Juan's hip, touristy, 5-mile-long (8-km-long) coastal strip lined with gorgeous beaches. These districts have the lion's share of hotels, restaurants, entertainment, and sites to see. South of Condado and Ocean Park, Santurce—setting for the city's main art museums—melds into Hato Rey, the city's business and banking district. The greater city fans out from here into suburbs with little touristic appeal.

# BEACHES OF SAN JUAN

Just because you're staying in the city doesn't mean you'll have to forgo time on the *playa*. San Juan's beaches are among the island's best.

Isla Verde beach is a beautiful strand that offers multiple water-sport and dining options or plenty of room to just stretch out and relax.

With 365 different beaches in Puerto Rico, choosing where to spread out your towel might seem like a daunting task. The decision is easier now that seven have been designated with a Blue Flag. Chosen by the Foundation for Environmental Education, a nonprofit agency, Blue Flag beaches have to meet more than 30 criteria, focusing on water quality, the presence of a trained staff, and the availability of facilities such as water fountains and restrooms.

Two beaches on the east side of the island, Seven Seas in Fajardo and Luquillo's Monserrate, made the cut. More surprisingly, two of the beaches are in San Juan: Balneario El Escambrón, in Puerta de Tierra, and Balneario de Carolina, in Isla Verde. A fifth is Punta Salinas in nearby Toa Baja. This means that five of Puerto Rico's finest beaches are within an hour's drive of the capital. The final two Blue Flag beaches are in the west and south: Boquerón in Cabo Rojo and Pelicano Beach in Ponce.

## PUBLIC BEACHES

The government maintains 13 *balnearios* (public beaches), including two in the San Juan metro area. They're gated and equipped with bathrooms, dressing rooms, parking, and, in some cases, lifeguards, picnic tables, playgrounds, and camping facilities. Admission is free; hours are generally daily 9–5 in summer and Tuesday–Sunday 9–5 during the rest of the year.

The city's beaches can get crowded, especially on weekends. There's free access to all of them, but parking can be an issue in the peak sun hours—arriving early or in the late afternoon is a safer bet.

**Balneario de Carolina.** When people talk of a "beautiful Isla Verde beach," this is the one they're talking about. A government-maintained beach, this balneario east of Isla Verde is so close to the airport that the leaves rustle when planes take off. The long stretch of sand, which runs parallel to Avenida Los Gobernadores, is shaded by palms and almond trees. Thanks to an offshore reef, the surf is not as strong as at other nearby beaches, so it's especially good for children and families. There's plenty of room to spread out and lots of amenities: lifeguards, restrooms, changing facilities, picnic tables, and barbecue grills. Although there's a charge for parking, there's not always anyone there to take the money. **Best for:** swimming. ⊠ *Carolina* 🏖 *Parking $3* ⊗ *Daily 8–5.*

**Balneario El Escambrón.** In Puerta de Tierra, this government-run beach is just off Avenida Muñoz Rivera. The patch of honey-colored sand is shaded by coconut palms and has surf that's generally gentle. Favored by families, it has changing rooms, bathrooms, and restaurants. **Best for:** swimming. ⊠ *Puerta de Tierra* 🏖 *Parking $5* ⊗ *Daily 8–5:30.*

**Playa de Ocean Park.** The residential neighborhood east of Condado and west of Isla Verde is home to this 1-mile-long (1½-km-long) stretch of golden sand. The waters are often choppy but still swimmable—take care, however, as there are no lifeguards on duty. Windsurfers say the conditions here are nearly perfect. The tranquil beach is popular with young people, particularly on weekends, as well as gay men. Parking is a bit difficult, as many of the streets are gated and restricted to residents. **Best for:** partiers; windsurfing. ⊠ *Ocean Park* ⊗ *Daily dawn–dusk.*

**Playa del Condado.** East of Old San Juan and west of Ocean Park, this long, wide beach is overshadowed by an unbroken string of hotels and apartment buildings. Beach bars, water-sports outfitters, and chair-rental places abound. You can access the beach from several roads off Avenida Ashford, including Calles Cervantes, Condado, and Candina. The protected water at the small stretch of beach west of the Conrad San Juan Condado Plaza hotel is particularly calm and popular with families; surf elsewhere in Condado can be a bit strong. The stretch of sand near Calle Vendig (behind the Atlantic Beach Hotel) is especially popular with the gay community. If you're driving, on-street parking is your only option. **Best for:** partiers. ⊠ *Condado* ⊗ *Daily dawn–dusk.*

Updated
by Heather
Rodino

If you associate Puerto Rico's capital with the colonial streets of Old San Juan, then you know only part of the picture. San Juan is a major metropolis, radiating out from the bay on the Atlantic Ocean that was discovered by Juan Ponce de León. More than a third of the island's nearly 4 million citizens proudly call themselves *sanjuaneros*. The city may be rooted in the past, but it has its eye on the future. Locals go about their business surrounded by colonial architecture and towering modern structures.

By 1508 the explorer Juan Ponce de León had established a colony in an area now known as Caparra, southeast of present-day San Juan. He later moved the settlement north to a more hospitable peninsular location. In 1521, after he became the first colonial governor, Ponce de León switched the name of the island—which was then called San Juan Bautista in honor of St. John the Baptist—with that of the settlement of Puerto Rico ("rich port").

Defended by the imposing Castillo San Felipe del Morro (El Morro) and Castillo San Cristóbal, Puerto Rico's administrative and population center remained firmly in Spain's hands until 1898, when it came under U.S. control after the Spanish-American War. Centuries of Spanish rule left an indelible imprint on the city, particularly in the walled area now known as Old San Juan. The area is filled with cobblestone streets and brightly painted, colonial-era structures, and its fortifications have been designated a UNESCO World Heritage Site.

Old San Juan is a monument to the past, but most of the rest of the city is planted firmly in the 21st century and draws migrants island-wide and from farther afield to jobs in its businesses and industries. The city captivates residents and visitors alike with its vibrant lifestyle as well as its balmy beaches, pulsing nightclubs, globe-spanning restaurants, and world-class museums. Once you set foot in this city, you may never want to leave.

## IF YOU LIKE

### ARCHITECTURE

San Juan has been under construction for nearly 500 years, which shows in the city's wide range of architectural styles. The Old City's colonial Spanish row houses—brick with plaster fronts painted in pastel blues, oranges, and yellows—line narrow streets and alleys paved with *adoquines* (blue-gray stones originally used as ballast in Spanish ships). Several churches, including the Catedral de San Juan Bautista, were built in the ornate Spanish Gothic style of the 16th century. The massive, white marble El Capitolio, home of Puerto Rico's legislature, was completed in 1929. And firmly rooted in the 20th century are the gleaming high-rise resorts along the beaches in Condado and Isla Verde and the glistening steel-and-glass towers in the business and financial district of Hato Rey.

### MUSIC

Music is a source of Puerto Rican pride and is an inescapable part of nearly every festival, holiday, party, and even political protest. The brash Latin sound is best characterized by the music-dance form salsa, which shares not only its name with the word "sauce" but also its zesty, hot flavor. A fusion of West African percussion, jazz (especially swing and big band), and other Latin beats (mambo, merengue, flamenco, cha-cha, rumba), salsa music is sexy and primal. Dancers are expected to let go of all inhibitions. Most night spots, including restaurants, offer live music several nights a week, especially Fridays and Saturdays.

### NIGHTLIFE

As befits a metropolitan capital city, San Juan has a wide variety of restaurants and bars for people with all sorts of palates and party habits. Old San Juan and Condado, in particular, are big nighttime destinations. Many of the newer establishments have set their tables on terraces, the beach, indoor patios, or streetside to take advantage of the late-night atmosphere. Clubs and bars stay open into the wee hours of morning, closing only when the last patron leaves.

# SAN JUAN PLANNER

### WHEN TO GO

During the high season, mid-December through mid-April, hotels tend to be packed, though rarely full, and rates are a bit higher than in the off-season. Fall and spring are less expensive. The weather's still fantastic, and the tourist crush is less intense. However, a winter visit may allow you to participate in many of San Juan's annual events, particularly the lengthy and lively Christmas season celebrations, which extend through mid-January. The January San Sebastián Street Festival, held in Old San Juan, consists of several nights of live music, food festivals, and *cabezudos* (parades). The Heineken JazzFest, each June, is the Caribbean's showcase for local and international talent.

San Juan's weather is moderate and tropical year-round, with an average temperature of about 82°F (26°C). And although it's true that hurricane season accounts for much of the summer and fall, San Juan's still an attractive destination during those months—hotels charge their lowest rates, restaurant reservations are easier to come by, and fewer tourists roam the streets.

## GETTING HERE

### AIR TRAVEL

**Airports** **Aeropuerto Internacional Luis Muñoz Marín** (*SJU*). Puerto Rico's main aiport serves as the gateway to the Caribbean, with flights from AirTran, American Airlines, Delta, JetBlue, Spirit Air, United, and US Airways. ☎ *787/791–3840.*

International carriers include Air Canada from Toronto, Air France from Paris, British Airways from London, Iberia from Madrid, and Condor from Germany. Air Flamenco and Vieques Air Link offer daily flights from SJU and Isla Grande Airport (SIG) in San Juan to Vieques and Culebra. Cape Air flies between SJU and Vieques.

**Aeropuerto Fernando L. Ribas Dominicci** (*SIG*). Sometimes known as Isla Grande, the Aeropuerto Fernando L. Ribas Dominicci is in Miramar, near the Convention Center. It serves flights to and from Puerto Rico and Caribbean destinations. ☎ *787/729–8711.*

**Airline Contacts** *For airline contact information, see Air Travel in "Travel Smart."*

**Transfers** Before you leave for Puerto Rico, check with your hotel about transfers; many larger hotels provide transport from the airport, free or for a fee, to their guests. Otherwise your best bets are *taxis turísticos* (tourist taxis). Uniformed officials at the airport can help you make arrangements. They will give you a slip with your exact fare written on it to hand to the driver. Rates are based on your destination. A *taxi turístico* to Isla Verde costs $10. It's $15 to Condado and $19 to Old San Juan and the cruise-ship piers. There's a $1 charge for each bag handled by the driver.

The Baldorioty de Castro Expressway (Route 26) runs from the airport into the city. Exits are clearly marked along the way, though you should check with your hotel to determine which one is best for you to take. Plan on 25–40 minutes for the drive from the airport all the way west to Old San Juan.

### FERRY TRAVEL

**Autoridad de Transporte Marítimo.** The Maritime Transport Authority runs passenger ferries from Fajardo to Culebra and Vieques. ☎ *800/981–2005* ⊕ *www.atm.gobierno.pr.*

Service is from the ferry terminal in Fajardo, about a 90-minute drive from San Juan. There are a limited number of seats on the ferries, so get to the terminal in plenty of time. *For schedule information, see Ferry Travel in "Travel Smart."*

## GETTING AROUND

### BUS AND TROLLEY TRAVEL

**AMA** (*Autoridad Metropolitana de Autobuses*). City buses thread through San Juan, running in exclusive lanes on major thoroughfares and stopping at signs marked "Parada." Destinations are indicated above the windshield. AMA bus B-21 runs through Condado all the way to Plaza Las Américas in Hato Rey. Bus A-5 runs from San Juan through

**2**

Santurce and the beach area of Isla Verde. Fares are 75¢ and are paid in exact change upon entering the bus. Most buses are air-conditioned and have wheelchair lifts and lock-downs. ☎ *800/981–0097.*

The Municipio de San Juan operates free trolleys throughout Old San Juan. Trolleys run along three routes beginning at Pier 4, on Calle Gilberto Concepción de Gracia and running to the two forts plus Plaza de Armas.

### CAR TRAVEL

Although car rentals are inexpensive (about $35 a day), we don't recommend that you rent a car if you're staying only in San Juan (at most you might want to rent a car for a day to explore more of the island). Parking is difficult—particularly in Old San Juan—and many hotels charge hefty daily rates; also, traffic can be very heavy. With relatively reasonable taxi rates, it simply doesn't pay to rent a car unless you are leaving the city.

The main highways into San Juan are Route 26 from the east (it becomes the Baldorioty de Castro Expressway after passing the airport), Route 22 (José de Diego Expressway) from the west, and Route 52 (Luis A. Ferré Expressway) from the south.

**Car Rental Contacts Avis** ☎ *800/230–4898.* **Hertz** ☎ *800/654–3131.* **National** ☎ *888/222–9058.* **Thrifty** ☎ *800/847–4389.*

**Local Agencies Charlie Car Rental** ☎ *787/728–2418* ⊕ *www.charliecars.com.* **Vias** ☎ *787/791–4120.*

### TAXI TRAVEL

*Taxis turísticos*, which are painted white and have the *garita* (sentry box) logo, charge set rates based on zones; they run from the airport and the cruise-ship piers to Isla Verde, Condado, Ocean Park, and Old San Juan, with rates ranging from $10 to $20. Make sure to agree on a price before you get inside. City tours start at $36 per hour.

Although you can hail cabs on the street, virtually every San Juan hotel has taxis waiting outside to transport guests; if none are available, have one called. Radioed taxis might charge an extra $1 for the pickup.

**Taxi Contacts Major Taxi** ☎ *787/723–2460, 787/723–1300.* **Metro Taxi** ☎ *787/725–2870, 787/945–5555* ⊕ *www.metrotaxipr.com.*

### VISITOR INFORMATION

You'll find Puerto Rico Tourism Company information officers (identified by their caps and shirts with the tourism company patch) near the baggage-claim areas at Luis Muñoz Marín International Airport.

In Old San Juan the tourism headquarters is at the Old City jail, La Princesa, Its main information bureau is opposite Pier 1 on Calle Tanca at Calle Gilberto Concepción de Gracia. Be sure to pick up a free copy of ¡*Qué Pasa!*, the official visitor guide. Information officers are posted around Old San Juan (near the cruise-ship piers and at the Catedral de San Juan Bautista) during the day.

La Oficina de Turismo del Municipio de San Juan, run by the city, has information bureaus in Old San Juan and in Condado.

Visitor Information **Oficina de Turismo del Municipio de San Juan** ✉ *Calle Tetuán, corner Calle San Justo, Old San Juan* ☎ *787/480–2910* ✉ *Alcaldía, 153 Calle San Francisco, Old San Juan* ☎ *787/480–2548* ✉ *999 Av. Ashford, Condado* ☎ *787/644–7519.* **Puerto Rico Tourism Company** ✉ *500 Ochoa Bldg., Calle Tanca, across from Pier 1, Old San Juan* ☎ *787/721–2400* ⊕ *www. seepuertorico.com* ✉ *Luis Muñoz Marín International Airport* ☎ *787/791–1014.*

# EXPLORING SAN JUAN

San Juan's metro area stretches for 12 miles (19 km) along Puerto Rico's north coast, and defining the city is rather like assembling a puzzle. Neighborhoods are irregular and sometimes overlap—locals disagree, for example, about where Condado ends and Ocean Park begins. The areas most visited by tourists run along the coast.

Farthest west is Old San Juan, the showplace of the island's rich history. On this peninsula you will find some of the city's finest museums and shops, as well as excellent dining and lodging options. To the east is Puerta de Tierra, a narrow strip of land sandwiched between the ocean and the bay. The area is home to a couple of famous hotels and two noteworthy parks, the Parque de Tercer Milenio and the Parque Muñoz Rivera, as well as Escambrón Beach. Beyond Puerta de Tierra is Condado, an upscale older neighborhood that is a mix of beautiful Spanish-style homes, larger apartment buildings, and resort hotels. Here you'll find designer fashions in the boutiques and on the people strolling down the main drag of Avenida Ashford. Ocean Park, to the east of Condado, is mostly residential, but the handful of inns and restaurants here are among the city's best. Beyond Ocean Park is Isla Verde, a more commercial zone and also where you'll find the biggest resorts on the best city beach.

You may want to explore a few other neighborhoods. South of Condado and Ocean Park lies Santurce, a business district with a growing artistic community, thanks to the Museo de Arte de Puerto Rico and the Museo de Arte Contemporáneo. Hato Rey is a busy financial district, where you'll find the large Plaza las Américas Mall. The mostly residential Río Piedras area is home to the Universidad de Puerto Rico.

## OLD SAN JUAN

Old San Juan's 16th-century cobblestone streets, ornate Spanish town houses with wrought-iron balconies, ancient plazas, and eclectic museums are all repositories of the island's colorful history. Founded in 1521 by the Spanish explorer Juan Ponce de León, Old San Juan sits on a islet separated from the "new" parts of the city by a couple of miles and a couple of centuries. Ironically, its culture is youthful and vibrant, reflecting the sensibilities of stylish professionals, a bohemian art crowd, and university students who populate the streets. You'll find more streetfront cafés and innovative restaurants, more contemporary art galleries, more musicians playing in plazas, than anywhere else in San Juan.

Festive street musicians are frequently seen and heard throughout Old San Juan.

Old San Juan slopes north, uphill, to Calle Norzagaray, which runs along the Atlantic shoreline and connects Castillo San Cristóbal to El Morro, the Old City's twin defensive bastions. On the north side of Calle Norzagaray you'll find a small neighborhood tucked beneath the city walls tight up against the ocean—this is La Perla, a rough area that you would be wise to avoid. The west end of the Old City overlooks San Juan Bay, and it's here that the rugged, towering walls of the original city are most evident. On Old San Juan's south side, along Calle Gilberto Concepción de Gracia, you'll find the commercial and cruise-ship piers that jut into San Juan Harbor.

### GETTING AROUND

Don't consider driving in Old San Juan, because you'll just wind up sitting in traffic jams for much of the day, especially on weekends when police change traffic patterns. Old San Juan is a walking city, with narrow, one-way streets, narrower alleys, little parking, and sights and shops packed together in an area hardly larger than one square mile. Some of the streets are steep and many are paved with cobblestones, so wear comfortable shoes as well as a hat and sunscreen—and drink plenty of water.

FERRY  The ferry between Old San Juan and Cataño is operated by the Autoridad de Transporte Marítimo. It costs a mere 50¢ one-way and runs daily every 15 or 30 minutes from 6 am until 10 pm. The ferry, which departs from Pier 2, is the one to take if you wish to visit the Bacardí Rum Factory.

**Information** Autoridad de Transporte Marítimo ☏ 787/788–1155 ⊕ www. atm.gobierno.pr.

PARKING  If you can't avoid taking a car into Old San Juan, park at La Puntilla, at the head of Paseo de la Princesa. It's an outdoor lot with the Old City's cheapest rates (they start at 50¢ an hour). You could also try the Felisa Rincón de Gautier lot on Calle Gilberto Concepción de Gracia or the Frank Santaella lot between Paseo de Covadonga and Calle Gilberto Concepción de Gracia. Parking starts at around $1 or so for the first hour. Many lots open early and close late; some are even open 24 hours a day, like the Felisa Rincón parking garage, known as "Doña Fela" to locals.

TROLLEYS  Free trolleys swing through Old San Juan all day, every day—departing from the main bus terminal area across from Pier 4 and taking three routes through the Old City. One route heads north to Calle Norzagaray, then west to El Morro, dropping you off at the long footpath leading to the fort. Then it retraces its route past Castillo San Cristóbal, west to Plaza de Armas, east on Fortaleza, west on Recinto Sur, and then back along Calle Gilberto Concepción de Gracia (also called Calle la Marina) to the piers. A second route takes you east to the Punta de Tierra district, then via Castillo San Cristóbal to El Morro, then via Calle Norzagaray and Plaza Colón and back to the piers. The third route follows a figure-8 route from Pier 4 north on Tanca, then west along San Francisco and east on Fortaleza, returning via Plaza Colón. The trolleys make regular stops (at 24 signs marked "Parada") on their routes. When you're finished touring, taxis can be found in several spots: in front of Pier 2, near the Catedral de San Juan Bautista, on the Plaza de Armas, or on Calle O'Donnell near the Plaza de Colón. A map of trolley routes is available from the Puerto Rico Tourism Company information offices.

### SAFETY

Old San Juan is generally safe, but keep in mind that pickpockets visit the same places as tourists. Keep money and credit cards out of back pockets, and avoid carrying open handbags. Avoid the Perla district and, if walking, stick to well-policed areas and well-lit streets by night. Women should take licensed taxis at night.

### TIMING

Old San Juan is a small neighborhood, approximately seven city blocks north to south and eight east to west. In strictly geographical terms, it's easily traversed in a day. But to truly appreciate the numerous plazas, museums, boutiques, galleries, and cafés requires two or three days. *For a great half-day itinerary, see "A Stroll Through Old San Juan."*

### TOUR OPTIONS

In Old San Juan free trolleys can take you around, and the tourist board can provide you with a copy of ¡*Qué Pasa!* and an Old San Juan map, which contains a self-guided walking tour.

**Legends of Puerto Rico.** Legends of Puerto Rico has private walking tours of Old San Juan (including food and rum tastings), hop-on-hop-off bus tours, excursions to El Yunque, and special holiday trips that let you experience a local Thanksgiving or Christmas. ☎ *787/605–9060* ⊕ *www.legendsofpr.com.*

**Segway Tours of Puerto Rico.** Segway Tours of Puerto Rico offers group tours of the city's historic district, using Segways for fun and easy transport. ⊠ *Pier 2* 🕾 *787/598–9455* ⊕ *www.segwaytourspr.com.*

★ **Flavors of San Juan.** The friendly, well-infomed guides of Flavors of San Juan can take you on walking tours of Old San Juan, combining visits to restaurants that are off the beaten path with a cultural and historical introduction to the city. ⊠ *Old San Juan* 🕾 *787/964–2447* ⊕ *www. sanjuanfoodtours.com.*

## WHAT TO SEE
### TOP ATTRACTIONS

**Casa Blanca.** The original structure on this site was a wooden house built in 1521 as a home for Ponce de León; he died in Cuba without ever having lived here. His descendants occupied the house's sturdier replacement, a lovely colonial mansion with tile floors and beamed ceilings, for more than 250 years. It was the home of the U.S. Army commander in Puerto Rico from the end of the Spanish-American War in 1898 to 1966. As of this writing, Casa Blanca was closed for a lengthy restoration, but you can still peer in at it through the gates. ⊠ *1 Calle San Sebastián, Old San Juan.*

**Catedral de San Juan Bautista.** The Catholic shrine of Puerto Rico had humble beginnings in the early 1520s as a thatch-roofed, wooden structure. After a hurricane destroyed the church, it was rebuilt in 1540, when it was given a graceful circular staircase and vaulted Gothic ceilings. Most of the work on the present cathedral, however, was done in the 19th century. The remains of Ponce de León are behind a marble tomb in the wall near the transept, on the north side. The trompe-l'oeil work on the inside of the dome is breathtaking. Unfortunately, many of the other frescoes suffer from water damage. ⊠ *151 Calle Cristo, Old San Juan* 🕾 *787/722–0861* ⊕ *www.catedralsanjuan.com* 🖃 *$1 donation suggested* ⊗ *Mon.–Sat. 8–5, Sun. 8–2:30.*

Ⓒ **Castillo San Cristóbal.** This huge stone fortress, built between 1634 and
Fodor's Choice 1790, guarded the city from land attacks from the east. The largest
★ Spanish fortification in the New World, San Cristóbal was known in the 17th and 18th centuries as the Gibraltar of the West Indies. Five freestanding structures divided by dry moats are connected by tunnels. You're free to explore the gun turrets (with cannon in situ), officers' quarters, re-created 18th-century barracks, and gloomy passageways. Along with El Morro, San Cristóbal is a National Historic Site administered by the U.S. Park Service; it's a World Heritage Site as well. Rangers conduct tours in Spanish and English. ⊠ *Calle Norzagaray at Av. Muñoz Rivera, Old San Juan* 🕾 *787/729–6777* ⊕ *www.nps.gov/saju* 🖃 *$3; $5 includes admission to El Morro* ⊗ *Daily 9–6.*

Ⓒ **Castillo San Felipe del Morro** (*El Morro*). At the northwestern tip of the
Fodor's Choice Old City is El Morro ("the promontory"), a fortress built by the Span-
★ iards between 1539 and 1786. Rising 140 feet above the sea, the massive six-level fortress was built to protect the harbor entrance. It is a labyrinth of cannon batteries, ramps, barracks, turrets, towers, and tunnels. Built to protect the port, El Morro has a commanding view of the harbor. You're free to wander throughout. The cannon emplacement walls and the dank secret passageways are a wonder of engineering. The

fort's small but enlightening museum displays ancient Spanish guns and other armaments, military uniforms, and blueprints for Spanish forts in the Americas, although Castillo San Cristóbal has more extensive and impressive exhibits. There's also a gift shop. The fort is a National Historic Site administered by the U.S. Park Service; it's a World Heritage Site as well. Various tours and a video are available in English. ✉ *Calle del Morro, Old San Juan* ☏ *787/729–6960* ⊕ *www.nps.gov/saju* ✉ *$3; $5 includes admission to Castillo San Cristóbal* ⊙ *Daily 9–6.*

**Galería Nacional.** Built by Dominican friars in 1523, this convent—the oldest in Puerto Rico—once served as a shelter during Carib Indian attacks and, more recently, as headquarters for the Antilles command of the U.S. Army. The beautifully restored building contains the Galería Nacional, which showcases the collection of the Institute of Puerto Rican Culture. Arranged chronologically, the museum traces the development of Puerto Rican art over the centuries, from José Campeche and Francisco Oller to Rafael Tufiño and Myrna Báez. You'll also find a good collection of *santos*, traditional wood carvings of saints. ✉ *98 Calle Norzagaray, Old San Juan* ☏ *787/725–2670* ⊕ *www.icp.gobierno. pr* ✉ *$3* ⊙ *Mon.–Sat. 9:30–5.*

**Paseo de la Princesa.** Built in the mid-nineteenth century to honor the Spanish princess of Asturias, this street with a broad pedestrian walkway is spruced up with flowers, trees, benches, and street lamps. Unfurling westward from Plaza del Inmigrante along the base of the fortified city walls, It leads to the Fuente Raíces, a striking fountain depicting the various ethnic groups of Puerto Rico. Take a seat and watch the boats zip across the water. Beyond the fountain is the beginning of Paseo del Morro, a well-paved shoreline path that hugs Old San Juan's walls and leads past the city gate at Calle San Juan and continues to the tip of the headland, beneath El Morro.

## WORTH NOTING

**Alcaldía.** San Juan's city hall was built between 1602 and 1789. In 1841 extensive alterations were made so that it would resemble the city hall in Madrid, with arcades, towers, balconies, and an inner courtyard. Renovations have refreshed the facade of the building and some interior rooms, but the architecture remains true to its colonial style. Only the patios are open to public viewings. A municipal tourist information center and an art gallery with rotating exhibits are in the lobby. ✉ *153 Calle San Francisco, Plaza de Armas, Old San Juan* ☏ *787/480–2548* ✉ *Free* ⊙ *Weekdays 8–4.*

**Capilla del Cristo.** According to legend, in 1753 a young horseman named Baltazar Montañez got carried away during festivities in honor of San Juan Bautista (St. John the Baptist), raced down Calle Cristo, and plunged over its steep precipice. Historical records maintain the man died, but legend contends that he lived. (Another version of the story has it that the horse miraculously stopped before plunging over the cliff.) Regardless, this chapel was built partly to prevent further calamities. Inside is a small silver altar dedicated to the Christ of Miracles. You can peer in through the wrought-iron gates, which are usually closed. ✉ *End of Calle Cristo, Old San Juan* ☏ *No phone* ✉ *Free.*

Hear your footsteps echo throughout Castillo San Felipe's vast network of tunnels, designed to amplify the sounds of approaching enemies.

**Casa de Ramón Power y Giralt.** The restored home of 18th-century naval hero Don Ramón Power y Giralt is now the headquarters of the Conservation Trust of Puerto Rico. On-site are several displays highlighting the physical, cultural, and historical importance of land and properties on the island under the trust's aegis. You'll find a display of musical instruments that you can play, a bird diorama with recorded bird songs, an active beehive, and a seven-minute movie discussing the trust's efforts. Displays are in Spanish; the movie is in English or Spanish. A gift shop sells toys, Puerto Rican candies, and eco-friendly souvenirs. ⊠ *155 Calle Tetuán, Old San Juan* ☎ 787/722–5834 ⛶ *Free* ⊘ *Tues.–Fri. 9–5, Sat. 9–4:30.*

★ **Cementerio Santa María Magdalena de Pazzis.** One of Old San Juan's best-kept secrets, this remarkable cemetery provides a peaceful respite from the bustle of the city. Sandwiched between El Morro and the Perla neighborhood, it offers a panoramic view of the Atlantic Ocean and an enviable resting place for the many notable figures fortunate enough to be buried here. Dating back to the early 1800s, the cemetery was originally administered by Carmelite nuns. Today you can stop by the ornate tombs (many of which are topped with graceful marble sculptures) to pay your respects to an illustrious group of Puerto Rican political figures, intellectuals, artists, and revolutionaries, including José Celso Barbosa, José Ferrer, Pedro Albizu Campos, Rafael Hernández, Ricardo Alegría, and others. △ While a robust police presence has made this area bordering La Perla safer, it's still a good idea to avoid coming after hours or at night. ⊠ *West End of Calle Norzagaray, Old San Juan* ⛶ *Free* ⊘ *Mon.–Fri. 7–3, Sat.–Sun. 7–noon.*

# Exploring
# Old San Juan

Alcaldía ................... **13**

Capilla del Cristo ......... **18**

Casa Blanca ............... **4**

Casa de Ramón
Power y Giralt ............ **20**

Castillo San Cristóbal .... **23**

Castillo San Felipe
del Morro (El Morro) ........ **1**

Catedral de
San Juan Bautista ........ **12**

Cementerio Santa María
Magdalena de Pazzis ....... **2**

Fundación Nacional para
la Cultura Popula ......... **15**

Galería Nacional .......... **7**

Iglesia de San José ......... **5**

La Fortaleza ............... **16**

Museo de las Américas ..... **3**

Museo del Niño ........... **11**

Museo de San Juan ......... **6**

Museo Felisa Rincón
de Gautier ................. **9**

Museo la
Casa del Libro ............ **21**

Parque de las Palomas ... **17**

Paseo de la Princesa ..... **19**

Plaza de Armas ........... **14**

Plaza de Colón ........... **22**

Plazuela de la Rogativa ... **8**

Puerta de San Juan ....... **10**

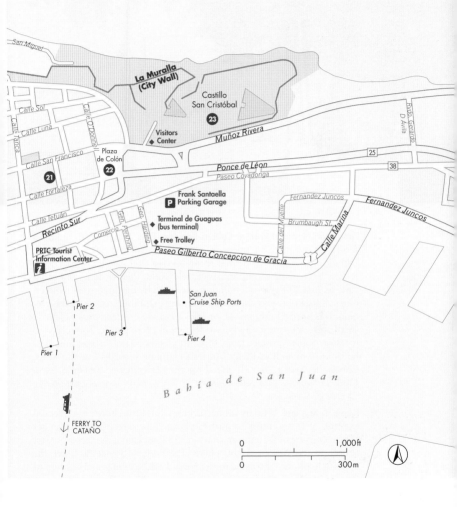

*O c e a n*

San Miguel

La Muralla
(City Wall)

Castillo
San Cristóbal

**23**

Calle Sol

Calle Luna

Calle Blanca

Calle O'Donnell

Visitors
Center

Plaza
de Colón

Calle San Francisco

**22**

Muñoz Rivera

Bvld. Gerardo

D. Ávila

**21**

Calle Fortaleza

Ponce de Léon

Paseo Covadonga

25

38

Calle Tetuán

Frank Santaella
🅿 Parking Garage

Fernandez Juncos

Fernandez Juncos

Recinto Sur

Terminal de Guaguas
(bus terminal)

Brumbaugh St.

Calle del Muelle

Comercio

Gen. Pershing

Gen. Fardina

◆ Free Trolley

PRTC Tourist
Information Center

ℹ

Paseo Gilberto Concepcion de Gracia

1

Calle Marina

Pier 2

San Juan
• Cruise Ship Ports

Pier 3

Pier 4

Pier 1

*B a h í a   d e   S a n   J u a n*

⬇ FERRY TO
CATAÑO

0                 1,000ft

0                 300m

La Muralla, the city wall, towers over the harborside walkway that winds around the Old City.

**Fundación Nacional Para la Cultura Popular.** This nonprofit foundation serves many functions: museum, performance space, dance and music school, and archive dedicated to preserving the contributions Puerto Ricans have made to music, dance, television, theater, film, and other culture. In a 300-year-old building once used by the Spanish as a meterological lookout, you can visit a rotating exhibition, come in the evening to hear live Latin music, or take a *bomba* or *plena* dance class. A small store sells music by Puerto Ricans in every genre, from classical to salsa. Signed posters from El Gran Combo, Tito Puente, and Willie Colon—as well as Ricky Martin's platinum record—line the walls. Check the website or call ahead for the performance schedule. ✉ *56 Calle Fortaleza, Old San Juan* ☎ *787/724-7165* ⊕ *www.prpop.org* 💵 *Free* ⊙ *Weekdays 10–5:30.*

★ **Iglesia de San José.** With its vaulted ceilings, this little church is a splendid example of 16th-century Spanish Gothic architecture. It was built under the supervision of Dominican friars in 1532, making it the second-oldest church in the Western Hemisphere. The body of Ponce de León, the Spanish explorer who came to the New World seeking the Fountain of Youth, was buried here for almost three centuries before being moved to the Catedral de San Juan Bautista in 1909. At this writing, much-needed renovations are under way, so check the website or call for the latest limited visiting schedule. ✉ *Calle San Sebastián, Plaza de San José, Old San Juan* ☎ *787/727-7373* ⊕ *www.iglesiasanjosepr.org.*

**La Fortaleza.** Sitting atop the fortified city walls overlooking the harbor, the Fortaleza was built between 1533 and 1540 as a fortress, but it wasn't a very good one. It was attacked numerous times and was occupied twice, by the British in 1598 and the Dutch in 1625. When El Morro and the city's other fortifications were finished, the Fortaleza became the governor's palace. Numerous changes have been made to the original primitive structure over the past four centuries, resulting in the current eclectic yet eye-pleasing collection of marble and mahogany, medieval towers, and stained-glass galleries. It is still the official residence of the island's governor, and is the Western Hemisphere's oldest executive mansion in continual use. Guided tours are conducted several times a day in English and Spanish; both include a short video presentation. Call ahead to verify the day's schedule, as tours are often canceled because of official functions. Proper attire is required: no sleeveless shirts or very short shorts. The tours begin near the main gate in a yellow building called the Real Audiencia, housing the Oficina Estatal de Preservación Histórica. ⊠ *Western end of Calle Fortaleza, Old San Juan* ☎ *787/721–7000* ⊕ *www.fortaleza.gobierno.pr* ⊇ *$3 suggested donanation* ☉ *Weekdays 9–3:45.*

**Museo de las Américas.** On the second floor of the imposing former military barracks, Cuartel de Ballajá, this museum houses four permanent exhibits covering the native people of the Americas, African heritage in Puerto Rico, conquest and colonization, and popular arts in the Americas. You'll also find a number of temporary exhibitions. ⊠ *Calle Norzagaray and Calle del Morro, Old San Juan* ☎ *787/724–5052* ⊕ *www.museolasamericas.org* ⊇ *$3* ☉ *Tues.–Sat. 9–noon, 1–4; Sun. 11–4.*

**Museo de San Juan.** A bustling marketplace in 1857, this handsome building now houses the small San Juan Museum. You'll find rotating exhibits of Puerto Rican art, plus tableaux and audiovisual shows that present the island's history. Concerts and other cultural events take place in the huge interior courtyard. Stop by on Saturday mornings to check out the small but lively farmer's market. ⊠ *150 Calle Norzagaray, at Calle MacArthur, Old San Juan* ☎ *787/480–3530, 787/480–3547* ⊇ *Free* ☉ *Tues.–Sun. 9–noon; 1–4.*

⟳ **Museo del Niño.** This three-floor, hands-on "museum" is pure fun for kids. There are games to play, clothes for dress-up, a mock plaza with market, and even a barbershop where children can play (no real scissors here). There's also an immense food-groups pyramid, where children can climb to place magnets representing different foods. Older children will appreciate the top-floor garden where bugs and plants are on display, and the little ones can pretend to go shopping or to work at a construction site. For toddlers, there's a playground. Note that when the museum reaches capacity, it stops selling tickets. ⊠ *150 Calle Cristo, Old San Juan* ☎ *787/722–3791* ⊕ *www.museodelninopr.org* ⊇ *$5, $7 children* ☉ *Tues.–Thurs. 10–3:30, Fri. 10–5, weekends noon–5:30.*

**Museo Felisa Rincón de Gautier.** This tiny but fascinating museum honors Felisa Rincón de Gautier, who served as San Juan's mayor from 1946 to 1968. Throughout her life, "Doña Felisa" worked tirelessly on various public causes, including women's voting rights and health care for the poor. Her preschools, known as *Escuelas Maternas*, were used as the model for the United States' Head Start program. Extremely well connected politically both on the island and abroad, she was an egalitarian figure who rose to power at a time when women and politics were not mentioned in the same breath. Even if you have no interest in her story, you can peek inside one of the historic houses of Old San Juan. Guided tours in English or Spanish are available. ⊠ *51 Caleta de San Juan, Old San Juan* ☎ *787/723–1897* ⊕ *www.museofelisarincon.com* ⊠ *Free* ◷ *Weekdays 9–4.*

**Museo la Casa del Libro.** Dedicated to the artistry of the printed word, this museum counts among its holdings approximately 400 books printed before the 15th century—one of the larger such collections in the Western Hemisphere. It also owns two royal decrees from King Ferdinand and Queen Isabella that date back to 1493, the year Columbus first reached Puerto Rico. Because the museum is in a temporary location while long-term restorations to the permanent building are underway, only a small portion of the 6,000-piece collection is on display: you can see a page from the Gutenberg Bible and a 12th-century lunar-cycle calendar, which is impressive and worth a quick look. The gift shop has a terrific collection of posters that draws customers from all over the world. ⊠ *199 Callejón de la Capilla, Old San Juan* ☎ *787/723–0354* ⊕ *www.lacasadellibro.org* ⊠ *Free, but donation appreciated* ◷ *Tues.–Sat. 11–4:30.*

**NEED A BREAK?**

**Ben & Jerry's.** On your hike up hilly Calle Cristo, stop at Ben & Jerry's at the corner of Calle Sol. Savor Vermont ice cream under a palm tree or enjoy fresh fruit smoothies next to a Green Mountain cow. ⊠ *61 Calle Cristo, Old San Juan* ☎ *787/977–6882.*

**Parque de las Palomas.** Never have birds had it so good. The small, shaded park bordering Old San Juan's Capilla del Cristo has a large stone wall with pigeonholes cut into it. Hundreds of *palomas* (pigeons) roost here, and the park is full of cooing local children chasing the well-fed birds. There's a small kiosk where you can buy refreshments and bags of seed to feed the birds. Stop to enjoy the wide views over Paseo de la Princesa and the bay. ⊠ *End of Calle Cristo, Old San Juan.*

**Plaza de Armas.** The Old City's original main square was once used as military drilling grounds. Bordered by Calles San Francisco, Rafael Cordero, San José, and Cruz, it has a fountain with 19th-century statues representing the four seasons as well as a bandstand and a small café. The Alcaldía commands the north side. This is one of the most popular meeting places in Old San Juan, so you're likely to encounter lots of bustle: artists sketching caricatures, pedestrians waiting in line at food carts, and hundreds of pigeons waiting for handouts. ⊠ *Old San Juan.*

**NEED A BREAK?**

**Café 4 Estaciones.** At Café 4 Estaciones tables and chairs sit under a canvas canopy surrounded by potted plants. This tiny kiosk-café is the perfect spot to put down your shopping bags and rest your tired feet. Grab a *café con leche* (coffee with hot milk), an espresso, or cold drink, and watch the children chase the pigeons. It's open 24 hours. ⊠ *Plaza de Armas, Old San Juan.*

**Plaza de Colón.** The tallest statue of Christopher Columbus in the Americas stands atop a soaring column and fountain in this bustling Old San Juan square, kitty-corner to Castillo San Cristóbal. What was once called St. James Square was renamed in 1893 to honor the 400th

*Continued on page 54*

# WALKING OLD SAN JUAN

Old San Juan is Puerto Rico's quintessential colonial neighborhood. Narrow streets and plazas are still enclosed by thick fortress walls, and bougainvillea bowers spill over exquisite facades. A walk along streets paved with slate-blue cobblestones leads past colonial mansions, ancient churches, and intriguing museums and galleries. Vivacious restaurants and bars that teem with life young and old are always nearby, making it easy to refuel and reinvigorate anytime during your stroll.

*by Christopher P. Baker*

left, strolling down Calle del Cristo; top right, a view from El Morro; bottom right, dancers in front of Castillo San Cristóbal

# A STROLL THROUGH OLD SAN JUAN

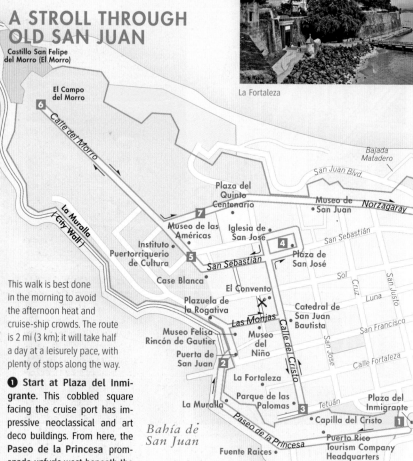

Castillo San Felipe del Morro (El Morro)

El Campo del Morro

**6**

Calle del Morro

La Muralla (City Wall)

La Fortaleza

Bajada Matadero

San Juan Blvd.

Plaza del Quinto Centenario

Museo de San Juan

Norzagaray

**7**

Museo de las Américas

Iglesia de San José

San Sebastián

Instituto Puertorriqueño de Cultura

**5**

San Sebastián

**4**

Plaza de San José

Sol

Cruz

Luna

San Justo

Casa Blanca

El Convento

Plazuela de la Rogativa

Las Monjas

Catedral de San Juan Bautista

San Francisco

Museo Felisa Rincón de Gautier

Museo del Niño

San José

Calle del Cristo

Calle Fortaleza

Puerta de San Juan

**2**

La Fortaleza

Parque de las Palomas

**3**

Tetuán

Plaza del Inmigrante

**1**

La Muralla

Paseo de la Princesa

Capilla del Cristo

Bahía de San Juan

Fuente Raíces

Puerto Rico Tourism Company Headquarters

This walk is best done in the morning to avoid the afternoon heat and cruise-ship crowds. The route is 2 mi (3 km); it will take half a day at a leisurely pace, with plenty of stops along the way.

**1** **Start at Plaza del Inmigrante.** This cobbled square facing the cruise port has impressive neoclassical and art deco buildings. From here, the **Paseo de la Princesa** promenade unfurls west beneath the ancient city wall, **La Muralla.** Artisans set up stalls under the palms on weekends. Midway along the brick-paved walkway, stop to admire the **Fuente**

Puerta de San Juan

Raíces monument and fountain: dolphins cavort at the feet of figures representing Puerto Rico's indigenous, Spanish, and African peoples.

**2** **Pass through the Puerta de San Juan.** This fortified entrance in La Muralla was built in 1520 and still retains its massive wooden gates, creaky on their ancient hinges. Immediately beyond, turn left and ascend to **Plazuela de la Rogativa,** a tiny plaza where a contemporary statue recalls

the torch-lit procession that thwarted an English invasion in 1797. The harbor views are fantastic. Then, walk east one block to reach the **Catedral de San Juan Bautista,** the neoclassical 19th-century cathedral containing the mausoleum of Ponce de León.

**3** **Head south on Calle del Cristo.** Sloping gradually, this lovely street is lined with beautifully restored colonial mansions housing cafés, galleries, and boutiques. Passing Calle

Castillo San Cristóbal

Calle del Cristo

Catedral de San Juan Bautista

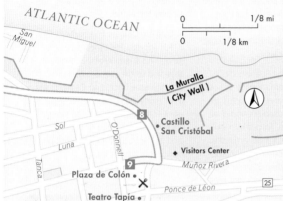

ATLANTIC OCEAN

San Miguel

0        1/8 mi
0        1/8 km

La Muralla (City Wall)

8

Castillo San Cristóbal

Sol

O'Donnell

Luna

Tanca

9

Plaza de Colón

Teatro Tapía

Visitors Center

Muñoz Rivera

Ponce de Léon

25

Castillo San Felipe del Morro

Fortaleza, note **La Fortaleza**, the official residence of the Puerto Rican Governor at the end of the street. Calle del Cristo ends at **Capilla del Cristo**, a chapel adorned within by silver *milagros* (token requests).

❹ Return via Calle del Cristo and continue to Plaza de San José. Catercorner to the cathedral you'll find **El Convento**, a former convent turned hotel, with an excellent tapas bar. At **Plaza de San José** visit the **Iglesia de San José**, a simple

church dating from 1532 that is one of the oldest churches in the Western Hemisphere.

❺ Walk west on Calle San Sebastián. This narrow street with colonial mansions painted in vibrant pastels ends at the gleaming white **Casa Blanca**. The oldest continually occupied residence in the Americas was originally the home of Ponce de León. Today it's a delightful museum furnished with period pieces. The garden is a tranquil spot for contemplation.

❻ Follow Calle del Morro north. One block from Casa Blanca you'll emerge upon a broad grassy headland—the Campo del Morro—popular with kite-flying families. It's skewered by an arrow-straight gravel path that aims at the imposing **Castillo San Felipe del Morro (El Morro)**, guarding the harbor entrance. Allow one-hour to

roam the small museum, turrets, labyrinthine tunnels, and six levels of ramparts soaring 140 feet above the ocean.

❼ Retrace your steps and turn left on Calle Norzagaray. This street runs atop the Atlantic shoreline, offering sweeping ocean vistas. On your right you'll pass the **Plaza del Quinto Centenario**, pinned by an impressive statue: the *Tótem Telúrico*. Beyond, stroll past the Galería Nacional (Convento de los Domínicos) to reach the **Museo de San Juan**. Housed in a former market, it traces the city's history and displays works by Puerto Rico's master painters.

❽ Continue east to Castillo San Cristóbal. Spanning 27 acres, this multitiered fortress was completed in 1771 with mighty bulwarks that protected the city from eastern attack by land. It features superb historical exhibits and reenactments by soldiers in period costumes.

❾ Exit the castle, turn south and walk one block to Plaza de Colón, This leafy square is lined with excellent cafés and restaurants where you can rest your feet and enjoy a great meal.

## Peaceful Music

Cellist Pablo Casals was one of the 20th century's most influential musicians. Born in Catalonia in 1876, he studied in Spain and Belgium, settled for a time in Paris, then returned to Barcelona. Tours in Europe, the United States, and South America brought him artistic and financial success and opportunities to collaborate with other prominent musicians.

By the advent of the Spanish civil war he was an internationally famous musician, teacher, and conductor. He was also an outspoken supporter of a democratic Spain. Forced into exile by Franco's regime, Casals arrived in Puerto Rico, his mother's birthplace, in 1956. Here the then-81-year-old maestro continued to work and teach.

He established the Casals Festival of Classical Music, making the island a home for sublime orchestral and chamber works. During two weeks each June, the Puerto Rico Symphony Orchestra is joined by musicians from all over the world.

In Catalan, Casals's first name is Pau, which appropriately means "peace." He and his friend Albert Schweitzer appealed to the world powers to stop the arms race, and Casals made what many experts say is his greatest work—an oratorio titled *The Manger*—his personal message of peace. Casals died in Puerto Rico in 1973, but his many legacies live on.

—Karen English

anniversary of Columbus's arrival in Puerto Rico. Bronze plaques on the statue's base relate various episodes in the life of the explorer. Local artisans often line the plaza, so it's a good place to stop for souvenirs. ⊠ *Old San Juan.*

**Plazuela de la Rogativa.** According to legend, the British, while laying siege to the city in 1797, mistook the flaming torches of a *rogativa*—religious procession—for Spanish reinforcements and beat a hasty retreat. In this little plaza a monument of a bishop and three women commemorates the legend. The striking contemporary statue was created in 1971 by the artist Lindsay Daen to mark the Old City's 450th anniversary. The fine view of La Fortaleza and the harbor is a bonus. ⊠ *Caleta de las Monjas, Old San Juan.*

**Puerta de San Juan.** Dating back to 1520, this was one of the five original entrances to the city and is the only one still in its original state. The massive gate, painted a brilliant shade of red, gave access from the port. It resembles a tunnel because it passes through La Muralla, the 20-foot-thick city walls. ⊠ *Paseo de la Princesa, Old San Juan.*

## GREATER SAN JUAN

Old San Juan may be Puerto Rico's jewel, but each of the other neighborhoods of San Juan has a distinctive character with its own special attractions. Just east of the Old City is **Puerta de Tierra**, home to a few notable hotels, a nice public beach, and several parks.

For multiple shopping and dining options all within walking distance, look to **Condado**. Home to many of the city's moneyed elite, it's the

The statues of Plaza de Armas's 19th-century fountain represent the four seasons.

most vibrant pedestrian neighborhood outside of Old San Juan. Here you'll find old Spanish-style homes next to sleek, modern apartment buildings and designer shops. The main street, Avenida Ashford, is fun to walk along, but the quieter residential areas are also very attractive. Many hotels are beachfront, though the beach is not as big or alluring as those in Isla Verde.

**Ocean Park** is a partially gated residential community with a laid-back feel. If you've dreamed of staying in a quiet guesthouse on a more secluded beach—away from the crowds—this might be the spot for you.

If you came to work on your tan—and you came to do it on a big, beautiful Caribbean beach—consider staying in **Isla Verde**, home to the nicest beach in the metropolitan area. The main commercial strip is not especially attractive: it's filled with fast-food restaurants and other businesses. You'll also need a car or taxi to get anywhere. That said, the resort-style hotels (many of them beachfront) offer so many amenities and so many restaurants on-site, you may not want—or need—to leave very often.

South of Condado is **Miramar**, home to a few hotels and a handful of the city's top restaurants. Seedy in spots, thriving in others, it's worth a visit if only to see what the innovative chefs are doing. From there you can venture into **Santurce**, a mostly commercial district with a growing artistic community, thanks to the Museo de Arte de Puerto Rico and the Museo de Arte Contemporáneo. You'll also find a thriving nightlife scene there on weekends. **Hato Rey** is a busy financial district, where you'll find the large Plaza las Américas Mall. The mostly residential **Río Piedras** area is home to the Universidad de Puerto Rico.

Plucky pontiff: the bronze bishop of Plazuela de la Rogativa is a monument to the religious procession that, according to legend, repelled British invasion.

## GETTING AROUND

Locals traveling in San Juan often complain about *el tapón* (traffic jam or, more literally, "cork"). A 15-minute drive can easily turn into 45 minutes depending on the road conditions. In addition, drivers can be unpredictable, using the shoulder as a through lane or drifting unpredictably from lane to lane, so be alert. If you choose to rent a car, get a good map. San Juan's roads are well marked, but one-way streets pop up out of nowhere.

Just east of Old San Juan, Avenidas Muñoz Rivera, Ponce de León, and Fernández Juncos are the main thoroughfares that cross Puerta de Tierra, leading to the neighborhoods of Condado, Ocean Park, and Isla Verde. Puente Dos Hermanos, the "Bridge of the Two Brothers," connects Puerta de Tierra with Condado. Avenida Ashford, which splits off into Avenida Magdalena for a few blocks, travels through Condado to Ocean Park. Calle Loíza connects Ocean Park with Isla Verde. These streets can be choked with traffic, so if you are traveling more than a few blocks, consider taking the speedier Route 26.

## TIMING

Depending on what mode of transportation you choose, you can see the Greater San Juan area sights in a day; if you linger in the museums, exploring might require two days. Buses are the least expensive but most time-consuming way to travel. Unfortunately, the beautiful new rapid-transit system, Tren Urbano, does not yet service the main tourist areas; however, if you're traveling to Bayamón, Guaynabo, Río Piedras, or another, more residential suburb, it's an option. Taxis are more convenient and you won't get lost—consider hiring a taxi by the hour and covering your selected sights in a couple of hours. Taxis charge

## GREAT ITINERARIES

### IF YOU HAVE 1 DAY
Many people find themselves with a single day—or even less—to explore San Juan. There should be no question about your destination—head to Old San Juan. Spend the entire day rambling around the cobblestone streets and ducking into the many shops, being sure to save plenty of time for exploring the turrets, towers, and dungeons of **Castillo San Felipe del Morro**, the original fortress on a rocky promontory at the Old City's northwestern tip *(see also "Great Walks: Old San Juan" feature).*

### IF YOU HAVE 3 DAYS
It's only fitting that you spend the first day enjoying a walking tour of Old San Juan. What to see? **Castillo San Felipe del Morro** is at the top of the list. You might want to explore the equally enthralling **Castillo San Cristóbal,** which has underground tunnels and hidden passages, plus cannons and a more impressive museum than San Felipe del Morro. The city's original fortress, the **Fortaleza,** wasn't much protection from marauding pirates, but it does a great job at sheltering the governor and can be toured. And **Casa Blanca,** a home built for Juan Ponce de León, is a wonderful place to explore how the Spanish lived in the colonial days, though at this writing, it was undergoing a lengthy renovation. Day two should be for lazing on a *playa* (beach). Choose from the city's finest at Condado, Ocean Park, or Isla Verde, and park yourself in a rented chair with a good book, a cold drink, and plenty of sunscreen. In the evening, make sure you enjoy the warm weather by dining alfresco. On your third day, hop the ferry across the bay to Cataño for a tour of the **Casa Bacardí Visitor Center.** Return in time for some shopping in the high-end shops and delightful arts-and-crafts galleries along Calle Cristo, then dinner in one of the trendy eateries on Calle Fortaleza.

### IF YOU HAVE 5 DAYS
Follow the itinerary above for your first three days in San Juan. On Day 4 head for the Santurce district. You can immerse yourself in island art at the **Museo de Arte de Puerto Rico** and, nearby, the **Museo de Arte Contemporáneo de Puerto Rico.** Afterward, wander through the produce stalls at the Plaza del Mercado in Santurce, with a fresh papaya or soursop shake in hand, and have your palm read. Be sure to note the giant bronze sculptures of avocados by artist Annex Burgos. On the morning of Day 5, hit the beach once more; then head to Avenida Ashford in Condado for an afternoon of shopping in its ritzy boutiques.

around $36 per hour for city tours, but the rate can be negotiable for long stretches of time.

## WHAT TO SEE
### TOP ATTRACTIONS
**Museo de Arte Contemporáneo de Puerto Rico.** This Georgian-style structure, once a public school, displays a dynamic range of works by both established and up-and-coming Latin American artists. Many of the works on display have strong political messages, including pointed commentaries on Puerto Rico's status as a commonwealth. Only a small part of the more than 900 works in the permanent collection is on display

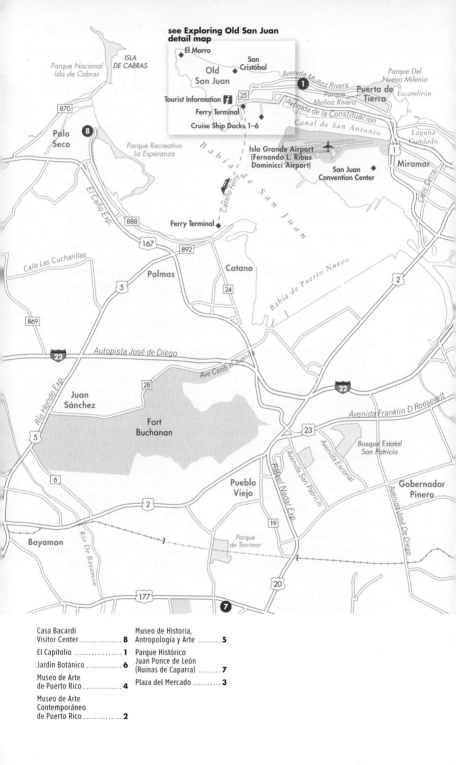

**see Exploring Old San Juan detail map**

El Morro

San Cristóbal

Old San Juan

Tourist Information 🛈

Ferry Terminal

Cruise Ship Docks 1–6

ISLA DE CABRAS

Parque Nacional Isla de Cabras

870

Palo Seco ❽

Parque Recreativo La Esperanza

El Caño Exp.

888

Ferry Terminal

167    892

Palmas

Catano

24

Calle Las Cucharillas

5

869

22

Autopista José de Diego

Ave Central Ivanita

28

Río Hondo Exp.

Juan Sánchez

Fort Buchanan

5

6

Pueblo Viejo

2

Bayamon

Río De Bayamon

2

Parque de Torrimar

177

❼

19

20

23

22

Avenida Franklin D Roosevelt

Bosque Estatal San Patricio

Avenida San Patricio

Rafael Nadal Exp.

Avenida Escorial

Gobernador Pinero

Avenida José De Diego

Avenida Muñoz Rivera ❶

Parque Muñoz Rivera

Puerta de Tierra

Parque Del Nuevo Milenio

Escambrón

Avenida de la Constituación

Canal de San Antonio

Laguna Condado

1

Miramar

Calle Cerra

Isla Grande Airport (Fernando L. Ribas Dominicci Airport)

San Juan Convention Center

Bahía de San Juan

Bahía de Puerto Nuevo

Cataño Ferry

2

25

Casa Bacardí Visitor Center ............... **8**

El Capitolio ................. **1**

Jardín Botánico ............. **6**

Museo de Arte de Puerto Rico ............. **4**

Museo de Arte Contemporáneo de Puerto Rico ............. **2**

Museo de Historia, Antropología y Arte ........ **5**

Parque Histórico Juan Ponce de León (Ruinas de Caparra) ........ **7**

Plaza del Mercado .......... **3**

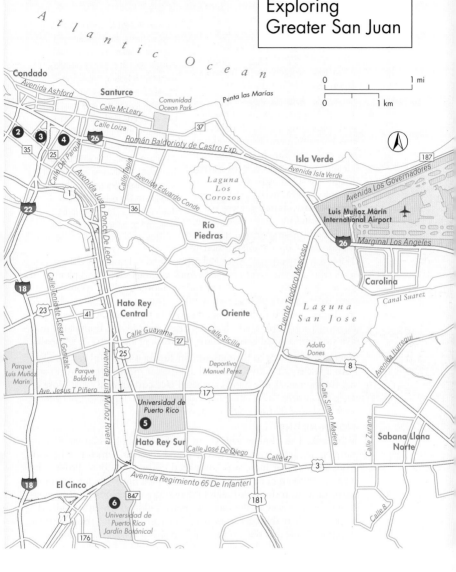

Exploring
Greater San Juan

*Atlantic Ocean*

0       1 mi
0       1 km

Condado
Avenida Ashford
Santurce
Calle McLeary
Comunidad
Ocean Park
Punta las Marías
Calle Loíza
37
2
3
4
26
35
25
Román Balorioty de Castro Exp.
Calle De Parque
Isla Verde
187
Avenida Isla Verde
Avenida Los Governadores
Calle Tapia
Avenida Eduardo Conde
Laguna
Los
Corozos
1
22
Avenida Juan Ponce De León
Luis Muñoz Marín
International Airport
36
Río
Piedras
26
Marginal Los Angeles
18
Carolina
23
41
Calle Teniente Cesar L Gonzale
Hato Rey
Central
Oriente
Canal Suarez
Laguna
San Jose
Puente Teodoro Moscoso
Calle Guayama
27
Calle Sicilia
Parque
Luis Muñoz
Marín
Parque
Baldrich
25
Adolfo
Dones
8
Avenida Iturregui
Ave. Jesus T Piñero
Avenida Luis Muñoz Rivera
17
Calle Simon Madera
Calle Zurana
Sabana Llana
Norte
Universidad de
Puerto Rico
5
Hato Rey Sur
Deportivo
Manuel Perez
Calle José De Diego
Calle 47
3
18
El Cinco
847
181
Calle 8
1
6
Universidad de
Puerto Rico
Jardín Botánico
176
Avenida Regimiento 65 De Infanteri

at any time, but it might be anything from an exhibit of ceramics to a screening of videos. ✉ *1220 Av. Ponce de León, at Av. R.H. Todd, Santurce* ☎ *787/977–4030* ⊕ *www.museocontemporaneopr.org* ✉ *$5 donation suggested* ⊙ *Tues.–Fri. 10–4, Sat. 11–5, Sun. 11–5.*

Fodor'sChoice
★

**Museo de Arte de Puerto Rico.** At 130,000 square feet one of the biggest museums in the Caribbean, this beautiful neoclassical building was once the San Juan Municipal Hospital. The collection of Puerto Rican art starts with works from the colonial era, most of them commissioned for churches. Here you'll find works by José Campeche, the island's first great painter. His *Immaculate Conception*, finished in

1794, is a masterpiece. Also well represented is Francisco Oller y Cestero, who was the first to move beyond religious subjects to paint local scenes. His influence is still felt today: another gallery room is filled with works by artists inspired by Oller. The original building, built in the 1920s, proved to be too small to house the museum's collection of Puerto Rican art by itself: the newer east wing here is dominated by a five-story-tall stained-glass window, the work of local artist Eric Tabales.

There's much more to the museum, including a beautiful garden filled with a variety of native flora and a 400-seat theater that's worth seeing for its remarkable hand-crocheted lace curtain. ✉ *299 Av. José de Diego, Santurce* ☎ *787/977–6277* ⊕ *www.mapr.org* ✉ *$6; free admission Wed. 2–8* ⊙ *Tues.–Sat. 10–5, Sun. 11–6.*

**WORTH NOTING**

**El Capitolio.** The white-marble Capitol, a fine example of Italian Renaissance style, dates from 1929. The grand rotunda, which can be seen from all over San Juan, was completed in the late 1990s. Fronted by eight Corinthian columns, it's a very dignified home for the commonwealth's constitution. Although the Senate and the House of Representatives have offices in the more modern buildings on either side, the Capitol is where the legislators meet. You can also watch the legislature in action—note that the action is in Spanish—when it is in session, most often Monday and Thursday. Guided tours, which last about an hour and include visits to the rotunda and other parts of the building, are by appointment only. ✉ *Av. Constitución, Puerta de Tierra* ☎ *787/724–2030* ⊕ *www.olspr.org* ✉ *Free* ⊙ *Daily 8–5:30.*

**Jardín Botánico** (*Botanical Garden*). This 75-acre forest of more than 200 species of tropical and subtropical vegetation is the Universidad de Puerto Rico's main attraction. Gravel footpaths lead to a graceful lotus lagoon, a bamboo promenade, as well as orchid and palm gardens. Not all plants

## A GOOD TOUR

East of Old San Juan on Avenida Ponce de León you'll find **El Capitolio**, Puerto Rico's magnificent capitol building. Take Avenida Ashford east, branching off onto Avenida Magdalena and then Calle Loíza. At the corner of Avenida Ponce de León is the **Museo de Arte Contemporáneo de Puerto Rico**, with a fine collection of contemporary Latin-American art. If you're hungry, stop for lunch at the nearby **Plaza del Mercado**. Afterward, head east on Avenida Ponce de León, then north on Avenida José de Diego to reach the **Museo de Arte de Puerto Rico**, a former hospital that has been transformed into the island's most ambitious art museum.

From the museum, it's a straight ride south on Avenida Ponce de León (Route 25) to the Río Piedras district, where you'll find the Universidad de Puerto Rico and its **Museo de Historia, Antropología y Arte**. Less than 1 mile (1½ km) to the west, at the junction of Routes 1 and 847, is the 75-acre **Jardín Botánico**.

and trees are labeled, so the garden is more of a tranquil retreat than an opportunity to learn about the vegetation. Trail maps are available at the entrance gate, and groups of 10 or more can arrange guided tours ($25). ✉ *Intersection of Rtes. 1 and 847, at entrance to Barrio Venezuela, Río Piedras* ☎ *787/758–9957* ⊕ *www.upr.edu* 💲 *Free* ☉ *Daily 7–5.*

**Museo de Historia, Antropología y Arte.** The Universidad de Puerto Rico's small Museum of History, Anthropology and Art offers rotating exhibitions in each of these three areas. Its archaeological and historical collection covers the Native American influence on the island and the Caribbean, the colonial era, and the history of slavery. There's also a small collection of Egyptian antiquities. Art holdings include a range of Puerto Rican popular, graphic, folk, and fine art; the museum's prize exhibit is the painting *El Velorio* (*The Wake*), by the 19th-century artist Francisco Oller. If you're looking to see something in particular, call before you go, as only a small portion of the collection is on display at a time. ✉ *Universidad de Puerto Rico, Av. Ponce de León, Río Piedras* ☎ *787/763–3939, 787/764–0000* ⊕ *www.uprrp.edu* 💲 *Free* ☉ *Mon.–Tues. and Thurs.–Fri. 9–4:30, Wed. 9–8:30, Sun. 11:30–4:30.*

**Plaza del Mercado.** Though mostly overlooked by tourists, the Plaza del Mercado is one of the most charming corners of San Juan. At its center is a market hall dating from 1910. Inside you'll find bushels of fruits and vegetables, many of which you probably haven't seen before. Many chefs from the top city restaurants come here to find their produce. If all this food makes you hungry, dozens of storefront restaurants and bars face the central square. These places, mostly serving seafood, are quiet during the week but bustling on weekends, especially in the evening. The area also has many *botánicas,* small shops that sell herbs, candles, and religious items. There may even be an in-house card or palm reader ready to show you your future. The square is between the Museo de Arte de Puerto Rico and the Museo de Arte Contemporáneo de Puerto Rico, making it a good place to stop for lunch if you are museum hopping. ✉ *Calle Dos Hermanos at Calle Capital, Santurce.*

## SAN JUAN ENVIRONS

The suburbs of Cataño, Bayamón, and Guaynabo, west and south of San Juan, are separate municipalities but in many ways are indistinguishable from the city itself. Cataño, bordered by the Bahía de San Juan in the north, is an industrial suburb, perhaps most noted for its distillery belonging to Bacardí. Bayamón can be reached within 15 to 30 minutes from central San Juan; if you come by car, stop by the attractive central park, bordered by historic buildings. Guaynabo is a mix of residential and industrial areas and is worth visiting for its historical importance—Juan Ponce de León established the island's first settlement here in Caparra, and you can visit the ruins of the original fortification.

### GETTING HERE AND AROUND

Avenida Kennedy runs mostly north–south and leads to the suburbs of Bayamón and Guaynabo. The Casa Bacardí Visitor Center is an easy trip from Old San Juan—you simply take a ferry across the harbor. The other sites are a challenge to reach, as you must navigate some of the region's most traffic-clogged streets. Do yourself a favor and take a taxi or book a tour.

### WHAT TO SEE

**Casa Bacardí Visitor Center.** Exiled from Cuba, the Bacardí family built a small rum distillery here in the 1950s. Today it's the world's largest, with the capacity to produce 100,000 gallons of spirits a day and 21 million cases a year. You can hop on a little tram to take an approximately 45-minute tour of the visitor center, though you don't visit the distillery itself. Yes, you'll be offered a sample. If you don't want to drive, you can reach the factory by taking the ferry from Pier 2 for 50¢ each way and then a *público* (public van service) from the ferry pier to the factory for about $2 or $3 per person. ⊠ *Road 165, Rte. 888, Km 2.6, Cataño* ☎ *787/788–1500* ⊕ *www.casabacardi.org* ☑ *Free* ⊙ *Mon.– Sat. 9–6, last tour at 4:30; Sun. 10–5, last tour at 3:45.*

**Parque Histórico Juan Ponce de León (Ruinas de Caparra).** In 1508 Ponce de León established the island's first settlement here. The Caparra Ruins— a few crumbling walls—are what remains of an ancient fort. The small **Museo de la Conquista y Colonización de Puerto Rico** (Museum of the Conquest and Colonization of Puerto Rico) contains historical documents, exhibits, and excavated artifacts, though you can see the museum's contents in less time than it takes to say the name. Both the ruins and the museum are maintained by the Puerto Rican Institute of Culture. ⊠ *Rte. 2, Km 6.4, Guaynabo* ☎ *787/781–4795* ⊕ *www.icp. gobierno.pr* ☑ *Free* ⊙ *Weekdays 8:00–4:30.*

## SIDE TRIP FROM SAN JUAN

About an hour and fifteen minutes (depending on traffic, of course) west of San Juan, off route 22, lies Arecibo, home of the world-famous Arecibo Observatory. If you're in the area visiting the nearby Río Camuy cave park or the Barceloneta outlets—or if you're just an astronomy buff—it's worth a stop to see the massive radio telescope. Once you're out of the metropolitan area, the drive takes you through Puerto Rico's

karst country, with its strangely beautiful limestone formations covered with vegetation.

**Fodor's Choice**
★
**Arecibo Observatory.** Hidden among pine-covered hills, the Arecibo Observatory is home to the world's largest radar-radio telescope. Operated by the National Astronomy and Ionosphere Center of Cornell University, the 20-acre dish lies in a 563-foot-deep sinkhole in the karst landscape. If the 600-ton platform hovering eerily over the dish looks familiar, it may be because it was featured in the movie *Contact*. You can walk around the viewing platform and explore two levels of interactive exhibits on planetary systems, meteors and weather phenomena in the visitor center. There's also a gift shop. Note that the trail leading up to the observatory is extremely steep. For those who have difficulty walking or have a medical condition, ask a staff member at the gate about a van that provides courtesy shuttle service to the observatory entrance. ⊠ *Rte. 625, Km 3.0, Arecibo* ☎ *787/878–2612* ⊕ *www.naic. edu* ✍ *$10 adults; $6 children and seniors* ☉ *Daily 9–4, except closed Mon. and Tues., Jan. 16–May 31, and Aug. 1–Dec. 14.*

# WHERE TO EAT

In cosmopolitan San Juan, European, Asian, Middle Eastern, and chic fusion eateries vie for your attention with family-owned restaurants specializing in seafood or *comida criolla* (creole cooking, or local Puerto Rican food). U.S. chains such as McDonald's and Subway compete with chains like Pollo Tropical and El Mesón, which specialize in local cuisine. Many of the most innovative chefs here have restaurants in the city's large hotels, but don't be shy about venturing into stand-alone establishments—many concentrated in Condado and along Calles Fortaleza and San Sebastián, in Old San Juan. Old San Juan is also home to a number of notable new restaurants and cafés, offering more artisanal-style cuisine—crop-to-cup coffee, rustic homemade pizzas, and creative vegetarian food—at affordable prices. There's a radiant pride in what the local land can provide, and these enthusiastic young restaurateurs are redefining what Puerto Rican food is, bite by tasty bite.

| WHAT IT COSTS IN U.S. DOLLARS | | | | | |
|---|---|---|---|---|---|
| | ¢ | $ | $$ | $$$ | $$$$ |
| At Dinner | under $8 | $8–$12 | $12–$20 | $20–$30 | over $30 |

Prices are per person for a main course at dinner.

Dress codes vary greatly, though a restaurant's price category is a good indicator of its formality. For less expensive places, anything but beachwear is fine. Ritzier spots will expect collared shirts and long pants for men (jacket and tie requirements are rare) and chic attire for women. When in doubt, do as the Puerto Ricans often do and dress up.

For breakfast outside of your hotel, cafés or local bakeries (called panaderías) are your best bet. It's rare for such establishments to close between breakfast and lunch; it's slightly more common for restaurants to close between lunch and dinner. Although some places don't accept reservations, it's always a good idea to make them for dinner whenever possible. This is especially true during the busy season from November through April and on weekends at any time of the year.

## OLD SAN JUAN

*Use the coordinate (✢ 1:A2) at the end of each listing to locate a site on the corresponding "Map 1: Where to Eat and Stay in Old San Juan."*

**$$$** ✕ **Aguaviva.** The name means "jellyfish," which explains why this ultra-
SEAFOOD cool, ultramodern place has dim blue lighting like a tranquil ocean, and lamps shaped like jellyfish floating overhead. Elegantly groomed oysters and clams float on cracked ice along the raw bar. Eating here is like submerging oneself in the ocean. The extensive, regularly changing menu is alive with inventive ceviches, including one with mahimahi, tomato, jicama, and Sriracha hot sauce. For something more filling, try fried snapper stuffed with lobster mofongo, or shrimp in a garlic cream sauce with yuca gnocchi. You could also empty out your wallet for one of the *torres del mar,* or "towers of the sea." This gravity-defying dish comes hot or cold and includes oysters, mussels, shrimp—you name it. Oh, and don't pass up the lobster mashed potatoes. Those alone are worth the trip. ⊠ *364 Calle Fortaleza, Old San Juan* ☎ *787/722–0665* ⊕ *www.oofrestaurants.com* ⊗ *No lunch.* ✢ *1:F4.*

**$$** ✕ **Aureola.** Facing Plaza San José, this colorful restaurant serves solid
MEXICAN Mexican food at a reasonable price. Brightly colored sombreros hang from the walls, cantina music plays overhead, and a bowl of dried chilies decorates your table. It may sound a little cartoonish, but in fact the comfortable seating, friendly service, and pretty back patio all help keep things casually elegant. You won't find anything unexpected here; it's carnitas, burritos, ceviche, tacos, and margaritas all the way. One real standout: the saucy beef enchiladas that you spoon into steaming hot tortillas. ⊠ *106 Calle San Sebastián, Old San Juan* ☎ *787/977–0100* ⊗ *Closed Mon.* ✢ *1:D3.*

**$$$** ✕ **Barú.** A global menu has earned Barú a solid reputation among san-
ECLECTIC juaneros, so this stylishly contemporary restaurant in a 275-year-old colonial townhouse (the tile floor's original) is often crowded. The dishes, some served in medium-size portions so you can order several and share, range from Middle Eastern to Asian to Caribbean. Favorites include almond-crusted goat cheese with mango sauce and yucca chips. More substantial fare includes risotto with shiitake mushrooms and goat cheese, filet mignon with mashed potatoes and red-wine sauce, and pork ribs with a ginger-tamarind glaze. The dining room is dark and mysterious. You can dine on high stools at the bar. Wine pours here are generous. ⊠ *150 Calle San Sebastián, Old San Juan* ☎ *787/977–7107* ⊕ *www.barupr.com* ⊗ *Closed Mon. No lunch* ✢ *1:D3.*

**$$** ✕ **Café Berlin.** A handful of tables spill onto a sidewalk deck lit with
INTERNATIONAL tiny lights at this bohemian and romantic restaurant overlooking Plaza
⟳ Colón. There's something on the international menu for everyone, from a tropical salmon dish with mango and mofongo to a New Orleans–style muffaletta sandwich. There are also quite a few good vegetarian

# BEST BETS FOR SAN JUAN DINING

**Fodor's**Choice★

Cuatro Sombras, ¢, p. 67

Il Mulino New York, $$$$, p. 82

La Fonda del Jibarito, $$, p. 71

Marmalade, $$$, p. 72

Pamela's, $$$, p. 81

Pikayo, $$$$, p. 79

St. Germain Bistro & Café, p. 73

## By Price

**$$**

Aureola, p. 65

Bebo's Cafe, p. 78

Café Berlin, p. 65

Cafetería Mallorca, p. 66

El Patio de Sam, p. 70

La Bombonera, p. 70

La Fonda del Jibarito, p. 71

Kasalta, p. 81

Raices, p. 72

St. Germain Bistro & Café, p. 73

**$$$**

Aguaviva, p. 65

Barú, p. 65

Dragonfly, p. 67

El Picoteo, p. 70

La Cucina de Ivo, p. 70

La Mallorquina, p. 72

Marmalade, p. 72

Parrot Club, p. 72

Sofia, p. 73

Toro Salao, p. 74

**$$$$**

Budatai, p. 78

Carli's Fine Dining & Piano, p. 67

Pikayo, p. 79

Il Mulino New York, p. 82

## By Experience

MOST ROMANTIC

Budatai, p. 78

Marmalade, p. 72

Pamela's, p. 81

BEST LOCAL FOOD

Casa Dante, p. 82

El Pescador, p. 80

La Fonda del Jibarito, p. 71

---

dishes, including tofu in a traditional *salsa criolla*, served with *mamposteao* rice, souped up with extra ingredients. Patrons get a free manjito (a mango mojito) with an entrée order. Breakfast and Sunday brunch are also popular; try the banana and chocolate pancakes. At this writing, the restaurant was at work on adding gluten-free dishes and breads to the menu. ⊠ *407 Calle San Francisco, Old San Juan* ☎ *787/722–5205* ⊕ *www.cafeberlinpr.net* ✛ *1:F3.*

$ ╳ **Cafetería Mallorca.** The specialty at this old-fashioned, 1950s-style
CAFÉ diner is the *mallorca*, a sweet pastry that's buttered, grilled, and then sprinkled with powdered sugar. Wash one down with a terrific cup of café con leche. For something more substantial, try the breakfast mallorca, which has ham and cheese; the menu also includes pancakes, egg dishes, sandwiches, and comida criolla. The waitstaff—all dressed in crisp black uniforms—are friendly and efficient. It gets packed on weekends with locals, who consider it an institution. ⊠ *300 Calle San Francisco, Old San Juan* ☎ *787/724–4607* ⊙ *Closed after 6 pm* ✛ *1:F3.*

$$ ╳ **Caficultura.** One of the best cafés to open in San Juan in recent years,
CAFÉ Caficultura prides itself both on its full coffee-bar menu and its deli-
★ cious *cocina de mercado*. Many ingredients are sourced locally, and the menu changes by the season. For breakfast, try coconut-milk French toast with pineapple jam and coconut shavings. Or for dinner, there's plantain-encrusted chicken in a sauce of Manchego cheese. Numerous

vegetarian options are available, especially at lunch, when you'll also find many delicious gourmet sandwiches on offer. The building is beautifully restored: distressed concrete walls meet an old, Spanish-style wood-beamed ceiling—hanging from it is a magnificent antique chandelier. The customers skew young and intellectual, with students, university professors, and museum-going tourists all part of the mix. The youthful

waitstaff is always friendly, but the downside is that no one seems in a rush to get the food to the table. ⊠ *401 Calle San Francisco, Old San Juan* ☎ *787/723–7731* ✢ *1:F3.*

**$$$**
MEDITERRANEAN
✕ **Carli's Fine Dining & Piano.** As you might guess from the name, the music is as much of a draw as the food at Carli's. The genial owner and host, Carli Muñoz, toured for a number of years with the Beach Boys (note the gold album on the wall) and plays nightly with his jazz trio, often accompanied by singers and musicians who happen to drop in. Inside the skyline-dominating Banco Popular building, this intimate supper-club bistro has elegant tables scattered around the room and a bar made of black Italian granite. Have a seat indoors or on the outdoor patio, and dine on such fusion specialties as New Zealand sautéed green mussels, U.S. filet mignon with wild mushroom sauce, or blackened ahi tuna with Cajun spices. ⊠ *Plazoleta Rafael Carrión, Calle Recinto Sur and Calle San Justo, Old San Juan* ☎ *787/725–4927* ⊕ *www.carlisworld.com* ☉ *Closed Sun. No lunch* ✢ *1:E4.*

**¢**
CAFÉ
**Fodor's**Choice
★
✕ **Cuatro Sombras Torrefacción y Café.** If you want to try locally grown, single-origin, shade-grown coffee, this micro-roastery and café is the place to do it. Owners Pablo Muñoz and Mariana Suárez grow their beans in the mountains of Yauco on a recently revived hacienda that has been in Muñoz family since 1846. After years spent learning the best growing practices, they opened this cafe in early 2011 to take the fruits of their labor from "crop to cup." It's been attracting attention ever since. The wood planks that line the banquette are from repurposed coffee storage pallets, and the red accents that catch your eye throughout the room recall perfectly ripe coffee beans. The name Cuatro Sombras, or "four shades," refers to the four types of trees traditionally used in Puerto Rico to provide shade for coffee plants. And although it's the delicious, medium-bodied brew that steals the show, there's also a small but tasty menu of pastries and sandwiches. ⊠ *259 Calle Recinto Sur, Old San Juan* ☎ *787/724–9955* ⊕ *www.cuatrosombras.com* ☉ *No dinner* ✢ *1:E4.*

**$$$**
ASIAN
✕ **Dragonfly.** Dark and sexy, this popular Latin-Asian restaurant, all done up in Chinese red, feels more like a fashionable after-hours lounge than a restaurant. The romantic ambience, created partly through tightly packed tables and low lighting, is a big draw. The small plates, meant to be shared, come in generous portions. Don't miss the calamari,

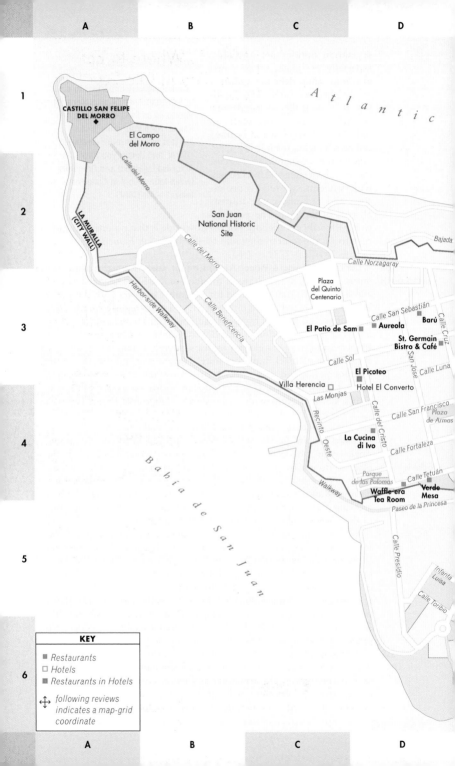

KEY

■ Restaurants
□ Hotels
■ Restaurants in Hotels

⊕ following reviews
indicates a map-grid
coordinate

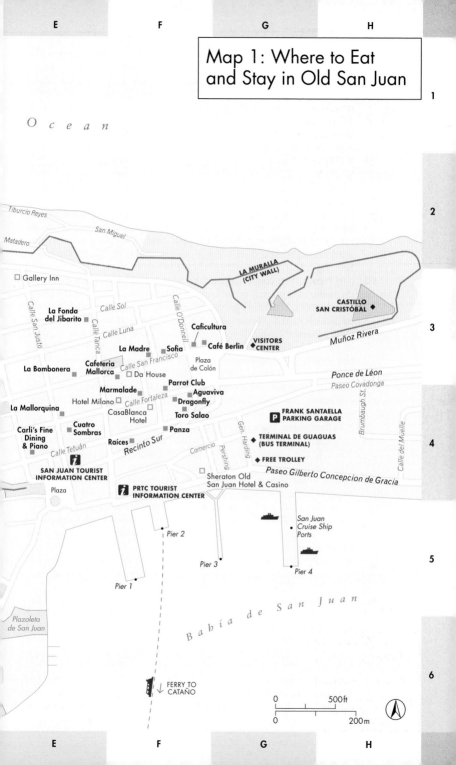

# Map 1: Where to Eat and Stay in Old San Juan

Ocean

Tiburcio Reyes

San Miguel

Matadero

LA MURALLA (CITY WALL)

□ Gallery Inn

Calle Sol

CASTILLO SAN CRISTÓBAL ◆

Calle San Justo

■ La Fonda del Jibarito

Calle Luna

Caficultura ■

Café Berlín ■

VISITORS ◆ CENTER

Muñoz Rivera

Calle Tanca

Calle O'Donnell

La Madre ■

Sofía ■

Cafeteria Mallorca ■

Calle San Francisco

Plaza de Colón

Ponce de Léon

La Bombonera ■

□ Da House

Paseo Covadonga

Marmalade ■

Parrot Club ■

Hotel Milano □

Aguaviva ■

La Mallorquina ■

Calle Fortaleza

Dragonfly ■

CasaBlanca Hotel

Toro Salao ■

FRANK SANTAELLA P PARKING GARAGE

Brumbaugh St.

Carli's Fine Dining & Piano ■

Cuatro Sombras ■

Panza ■

TERMINAL DE GUAGUAS (BUS TERMINAL)

Calle del Muelle

Calle Tetuán

Raíces ■

Recinto Sur

◆ FREE TROLLEY

Gen. Harding

i SAN JUAN TOURIST INFORMATION CENTER

Comercio

Pershing

Paseo Gilberto Concepcion de Gracia

Plaza

i PRTC TOURIST INFORMATION CENTER

Sheraton Old San Juan Hotel & Casino

Pier 2

San Juan Cruise Ship Ports

Pier 3

Pier 4

Plazoleta de San Juan

Bahía de San Juan

Pier 1

FERRY TO CATAÑO

0        500ft

0        200m

E       F       G       H

fried with onions and oyster sauce and tossed with a local cilantro-like herb called *recao*. Tuna sushi is turned on its head and served atop a deep-fried rice cake dressed with spicy mayo and seaweed salad. Make sure to try the inventive cocktails that nicely complement the food. Reservations aren't accepted, but we'll let you in on a secret to save yourself a frustrating wait: you can call ahead and get yourself put on the waiting list. ⊠ *364 Calle Fortaleza, Old San Juan* ☎ *787/977–3886* ⊕ *www.oofrestaurants.com* ⚱ *Reservations not accepted* ☽ *No lunch* ✛ *1:F4.*

**$$**
ECLECTIC

✕ **El Patio de Sam.** A great selection of more than 30 beers, including the locally brewed Medalla, makes this a popular "come as you are" spot, whether at the end of the workweek or after a long day of sightseeing. Just as appealing is the airy courtyard with a skylight that gives the place its name. The menu consists mostly of American and Puerto Rican fare, including what is claimed to be the best burgers in town. Save room for the flan, which melts in your mouth. Night owls can grab grub here until midnight, and there's live music on weekends. ⊠ *102 Calle San Sebastián, Old San Juan* ☎ *787/723–1149* ✛ *1:C3.*

**$$$**
SPANISH

✕ **El Picoteo.** You could make a meal of the small dishes that dominate the menu at this tapas restaurant on a mezzanine balcony at the Hotel El Convento. You won't go wrong ordering the grilled cuttlefish or the pistachio-crusted salmon with a Manchego-cheese sauce and passing them around the table. If you're not into sharing, there are several kinds of paella that arrive on huge plates. There's a long, lively bar inside; one dining area overlooks a pleasant courtyard, and the other looks out onto Calle Cristo. Even if you have dinner plans elsewhere, consider stopping here for a nightcap or a midday pick-me-up. ⊠ *Hotel El Convento, 100 Calle Cristo, Old San Juan* ☎ *787/723–9202* ⊕ *www.elconvento.com* ✛ *1:D3.*

**$$**
CAFÉ

✕ **La Bombonera.** You can't miss the stained glass and gorgeous Moorish-style tilework on the facade of this local café, which was established in 1902. In the window you'll see piles of freshly baked pastries. Inside there's a long counter with salmon-colored stools and a wall lined with booths in the same interesting shade. This local landmark is extremely popular in the morning—particularly on Sunday. It's most famous for its *mallorcas*, a sweet pastry that's grilled and buttered, as well as delicious *café con leche*. The rest of the menu spans from simple sandwiches to hearty local dishes, including *asopao* (a stew with rice and seafood or chicken)—all this even though the food is only average and the seemingly overworked waiters give the appearance of having worked here since the day it opened. ⊠ *259 Calle San Francisco, Old San Juan* ☎ *787/722–0658* ☽ *Closed after 6 pm.* ✛ *1:E3.*

**$$$**
ITALIAN

✕ **La Cucina di Ivo.** A pretty courtyard just steps from the cathedral has been transformed into this traditional trattoria. The staff enters and leaves through leaded-glass doors on either side of the central courtyard that lead to the bar, the wine cellar, and intimate dining rooms. You'll want to dine alfresco, as ceiling fans keep everything cool. A fountain bubbles on one side of the courtyard, and rows of potted fig trees surround the wrought-iron café tables. The place is named for chef Ivo Bignami, and the kitchen turns out specialties of his native Milan. For a lighter meal, or a first course big enough to share with your date,

Hotel El Convento's El Picateo restaurant serves tasty tapas and generous paella.

order the light, fluffy gnocchi. Entrées include a wide range of pasta and risotto dishes, plus such mouthwatering temptations as filet mignon in truffle sauce. For dessert, try the classic and tasty tiramisu. ⊠ *202 Calle Cristo, Old San Juan* ☎ *787/729-7070* ⊕ *www.lacucinadiivo.com* ⊗ *Closed Sun.* ⊹ *1:D4.*

**$$** ✕ **La Fonda del Jibarito.** The menus are handwritten and the tables
PUERTO RICAN wobble, but *sanjuaneros* have favored this casual, no-frills, family-run
**Fodor'sChoice** restaurant—tucked away on a quiet cobbled street—for years. The
★ conch ceviche, goat fricassee, and shredded beef stew are among the specialties on the menu of typical Puerto Rican *comida criolla* dishes. The tiny back porch is filled with plants, and the dining room is filled with fanciful depictions of life on the street outside. Troubadors serenade patrons, including plenty of cruise-ship passengers when ships are in dock. ⊠ *280 Calle Sol, Old San Juan* ☎ *787/725-8375* ⊕ *www. eljibaritopr.com* ⊹ *1:E3.*

**$$** ✕ **La Madre.** La Madre is a new kind of Mexican restaurant for San
MEXICAN Juan, with a stylish young customer base to match. Yes, it covers the standards, including some very tasty fish tacos, but you'll also find innovative, modern interpretations of Mexican cuisine, like a Japanese-style marinated skirt steak with mashed plantains and grilled corn, or pork ribs marinated in beer and served with a chocolate-chili sauce. With well-priced margaritas, you can afford to try several of the unusual flavors, such as cucumber, soursop, Caribbean cherry, and tamarind. The sleek dining room feels artsy and dreamlike, with classic cartoons and old movies projected silently onto a wall. A DJ occasionally spins on weekends. ⊠ *351 Calle San Francisco, Old San Juan* ☎ *787/647-5392* ⊗ *Mon.–Fri. dinner only* ⊹ *1:F3.*

**$$**
PUERTO RICAN

✕ **La Mallorquina.** Dating from 1848, La Mallorquina is thought to be the island's oldest restaurant. It specializes in various versions of *asopao*, a soupy rice dish with chicken or seafood, as well as other Puerto Rican and Spanish-inspired favorites. But it's the old-fashioned atmosphere that really recommends the place. In a room of whirring ceiling fans and antique marble floor tiles, the nattily attired staffers zip between the tables, which are covered in white tablecloths. Note that the restaurant closes during the low-season month of September, and that the servers can be a bit short with tourists. ✉ *207 Calle San Justo, Old San Juan* ☎ *787/722–3261* ⊕ *www.lamallorquinapr.com* ✆ *Closed Sun.* ⊕ *1:E4.*

**$$$**
ECLECTIC
Fodor's Choice
★

✕ **Marmalade.** "Wow!" may well be your first reaction after entering Old San Juan's hippest and finest restaurant. U.S.-born owner-chef Peter Schintler—who apprenticed with Raymond Blanc and Gordon Ramsay—has created a class act that's famous for its ultra-chic lounge bar. The restaurant's sensual and minimalist orange-and-white decor features high-back chairs and cushioned banquettes beneath recessed halogen lights. The menu uses many local, sustainable ingredients prepared California-French fashion, resulting in complex flavors and strong aromas. You might try Kobe beef cheeks with heirloom corn, chanterelles, and barley pilaf, or homemade black truffle tagliatelle with a marsala butter. Schintler also works wonders with vegetables, including the humble parsnip, which is roasted and served with blackberries, Marcona almonds, and an almond milk–rosemary foam. Diners can build their own four- to six-course tasting menu, with or without pairings from the very strong wine list, or order à la carte. In addition, the restaurant is accommodating to vegetarians, those with food allergies, and other dietary restrictions. ✉ *317 Calle Fortaleza, Old San Juan* ☎ *787/724–3969* ⊕ *www.marmaladepr.com* ✆ *No lunch* ⊕ *1:F4.*

**$$$**
LATIN AMERICAN
☾

✕ **The Parrot Club.** Loud and lively, this place is intent on making sure everyone is having a good time. You're likely to strike up a conversation with the bartender as you enjoy the signature passion-fruit cocktail or with a couple at the next table in the covered courtyard. Something about the atmosphere—laid-back Caribbean decor, including murals of palm trees—makes connecting easy. The menu has contemporary variations of Latin classics. You might start with the steak- and cheese–filled empanadas followed by seared shrimp served with a Peruvian-style crab and chorizo fried rice or roasted pork loin with sweet plantain and *arroz mamposteao.* There's also a full kid's menu available and live music, usually on Thursday and Saturday nights. ✉ *363 Calle Fortaleza, Old San Juan* ☎ *787/725–7370* ⊕ *www.oofrestaraunts.com* ⊕ *1:F3.*

**$$**
PUERTO RICAN

✕ **Raíces.** You can't miss this lively restaurant thanks to the waitresses in all-white *campesina* (peasant) dresses. Themed as a country venue, with artsy re-creations of rustic life, the whole atmosphere feels a bit Disneyfied, but it doesn't stop the locals and tourists—who have seen it featured on various TV shows—from packing in for the *criolla* fare. The food is a tad overhyped, but the crowds willing to wait an hour or more for a table seem to disagree. The signature dishes are the giant deep-fried *Kan Kan* pork chop and mofongo with *churrasco* (marinated shirt steak). The garlic shrimp mofongo, served country-style in a *pilón* (pestle), is quite tasty. Drinks come in tin mugs, including

Pineapples, plantains, and coconuts are among the bounty of locally grown produce found in markets and stands throughout the island.

fruity frappes. ✉ *315 Calle Recinto Sur, Old San Juan* ☎ *787/289–2121* ⊕ *www.restauranteraices.com* ☖ *Reservations not accepted* ✥ *1:F4.*

**$$$**
**ITALIAN**
✕ **Sofia Italian Kitchen & Bar.** Ignore the tongue-in-cheek recordings of "That's Amore." Everything else in this red-walled and warmly atmospheric trattoria is the real deal. Start with the squid stuffed with sweet sausage; then move on to the linguine with clams and pancetta or the filet mignon risotto. The plates of pasta are huge, so you might want to consider a generously sized half-order. Pizzas are also available, and the braised osso buco with creamy polenta and baked tomatoes is a house specialty. Save room for—what else?—a tasty tiramisu or chocolate mousse. There's also a small but carefully edited wine list. ✉ *355 Calle San Francisco, Old San Juan* ☎ *787/721–0396* ⊕ *www.ristorantesofia. com* ☽ *No lunch Mon.* ✥ *1:F3.*

**$**
**INTERNATIONAL**
**Fodor's Choice**
★
✕ **St. Germain Bistro & Café.** One of the city's hidden treasures, this charming French-inspired café-restaurant stands on a quiet cobbled street corner. The interior is just as inviting, with rustic white wooden tables and benches. St. Germain delivers exceptionally fresh, made-from-scratch food and friendly service. With an emphasis on seasonal, locally sourced ingredients, the menu leans slightly (but not entirely!) vegetarian and includes gourmet sandwiches, entrée salads, quiches, and pita pizzas. (Its lightness can be a welcome respite after you've been sampling the delicious but often heavy *comida criolla.*) Start with an *agua fresca*, a mildly sweet fruit water that revives you quickly, even on the hottest of days. Then choose from options such as a refreshing mahimahi and shrimp ceviche, hearty lentil soup, or a spinach and mango salad with Dijon vinaigrette. Save room for the just-baked cakes that tempt you

from glass stands on the counter. Sunday brunch is wildly popular, so come early, or stop by later in the evening for crepes and wine. ⊠ *156 Calle Sol, Old San Juan* ☎ *787/725–5830* ⊕ *www.stgermainpr.com* ⚏ *Reservations not accepted* ⊗ *Closed Mon* ✚ *1:D3.*

**$$$**
SPANISH

✕ **Toro Salao.** The name means "Salty Bull," and there's something about this place that makes its moniker entirely appropriate. (And it's not just the bullfighting posters that decorate one of the two-story-high walls.) This popular Spanish-Puerto Rican tapas restaurant was opened by Emilio Figueroa, who helped turn the southern end of Calle Fortaleza into the city's top dining destination. There are plenty of small dishes to share, such as a delicious baked Brie that's served with crostini and topped with a chorizo jam (yes, a sausage jam); crispy mahimahi fritters; and Spanish-style flatbread pizzas, called *cocas*. They also make their own fresh pork sausage. The dining room, with a bar lit up in lusty red, is pleasant enough, but the tables that spill onto the adjacent cobblestone square are even better. Stop by for live music on Thursdays and Saturdays. ⊠ *367 Calle Tetuán, Old San Juan* ☎ *787/722–3330* ⊕ *www.oofrestaurants.com* ⊗ *No lunch July–Oct.* ✚ *1:F4.*

**$$**
VEGETARIAN
★

✕ **Verde Mesa.** For some, the words "healthy," "vegetarian," and "delicious" don't belong in the same sentence, but they all come together at Verde Mesa. With punched-tin ceilings, mason-jar lighting fixtures, and eclectic decor inspired by Versailles' Petit Trianon, the focus at this romantic restaurant is on inspiring beauty and pleasure through the senses. Much of the organic produce used in the regularly changing menu comes from the owners' farm and other local sources. The flavor combinations are anything but accidental. You might try a "potion" drink: one standout is made with tarragon flowers, mixed citrus juices, and ginger. Start with a garlicky "hummus" of local pigeon peas. The signature Verde Mesa rice is a mixture of in-season vegetables and chickpeas that the owners say has turned many a skeptic into further exploring the culinary potential of vegetables. You'll also find quite a few expertly prepared tuna and salmon dishes, if you don't want to go all veggie. ⊠ *254, Calle Tetuán, Old San Juan* ☎ *787/390–4662* ⊗ *Closed Sun.–Mon.* ✚ *1:D4.*

**$**
CAFÉ

✕ **Waffle-era Tea Room.** The only tearoom in Puerto Rico, this breezy spot overlooking San Juan Bay has a sort of neo-Victorian, steam-punk feel. Choose from nearly 30 loose teas, ranging from white and black to fruity blends. But you'll probably be even more curious about the coffee setup, which looks like a mad-science experiment. It's a siphon fire-brewing system, a painstaking process popular in Japan. You can sample premium local coffees and other rare brews, like the famous (or infamous?) Kopi Luwak, one of the world's most expensive coffees (on their way to your cup, the beans pass through—what else?—the digestive track of a civet cat). The menu consists of house-made sweet or savory waffles—or smaller "wafflitos." You might also choose a "waffe-izza" with fresh tomato sauce and blowtorch-melted mozzarella. We're still thinking of the decadent crème brûlée wafflito. ⊠ *Top of Calle Tetuán and Calle Cristo, Old San Juan* ☎ *787/721–1512* ⚏ *Reservations not accepted* ⊗ *Closed Mon.–Wed.* ✚ *1:D4.*

## PUERTA DE TIERRA

*Use the coordinate (✛ 2:A1) at the end of each listing to locate a site on the corresponding "Map 2: Where to Eat and Stay in Greater San Juan."*

**$$$**
ASIAN
✗**Lemongrass.** Whether you sit inside the pagoda-style building or on the large outdoor terrace of this chic restaurant, you'll feel as if you've truly escaped to another world. The dishes are as memorable as the setting. Try the inventive sushi, such as the smoked salmon, Brie, and lingonberry roll. If you're not in the mood for fish, other options include the delicious five-spice short ribs with guava glaze and coconut shrimp; order a side of pancetta fried rice. You might want to leave room for the warm chocolate cake with pistachio sauce and green tea ice cream. ✉ *Caribe Hilton, 1 San Gerónimo Grounds, Puerta de Tierra* ☎ *787/724–5888* ⊕ *www.lemongrasspr.com* ☾ *No lunch* ✛ *2:B2.*

**$$$**
SEAFOOD
✗**Marisquería Atlántica.** This popular restaurant is across from its namesake, so it's no surprise that the seafood is the freshest around. Start with a plate of fried calamari, served lightly breaded and accompanied by a spicy sauce, and then move on to the broiled lobster tail or grilled red snapper in a garlic sauce. Locals swear by the paella, which is loaded with scallops, clams, shrimp, and squid. The restaurant is just west of Playa Escambrón. There's another branch in Isla Verde. ✉ *7 Calle Lugo Viñas, Puerta de Tierra* ☎ *787/722–0890* ⊕ *www.marisqueriaatlantica. com* ☾ *Closed Mon.* ✛ *2:A1.*

## CONDADO

*Use the coordinate (✛ 2:A1) at the end of each listing to locate a site on the corresponding "Map 2: Where to Eat and Stay in Greater San Juan."*

**$$**
MIDDLE EASTERN
✗**Ali Baba.** Tucked discreetly off Ashford Avenue, this newcomer turns out delicious, meticulously prepared Middle Eastern and Mediterranean food, thanks to its Turkish chef-owner. Given how unpretentious this small place is, the presentation is surprisingly elegant. Start with the hummus, served with steaming homemade lavash, or the grilled cheese with fresh herbs and tomatoes. Entrées include an *iskender* kebab drizzled with browned goat butter, and moussaka, which is served warm, beneath a flame. Sandwiches and vegetarian options are also available. ✉ *1214 Av. Ashford, Condado* ☎ *787/722–1176* ⌕ *Reservations not accepted* ☾ *Closed Mon. No lunch Tues.–Thurs.* ✛ *2:C2.*

**$$$$**
EUROPEAN
✗**Augusto's.** Under the direction of noted chef Ariel Rodríguez, this restaurant is one of the more celebrated in the San Juan area and is popular with the city's elite. The formal dining room feels a bit stuffy and uninspired, but is saved somewhat by the local works of art decorating the walls. The cuisine is international, with strong French influences. Some of the dishes commonly served are braised beef short ribs with horseradish mashed potatoes and king salmon wrapped in potato with a chive beurre blanc. A prix fixe menu is also available. A sommelier is usually on hand to help you choose a bottle from the approximately 250 selections on the wine list. ✉ *Courtyard Marriott Miramar, 801 Av. Ponce de León, Miramar* ☎ *787/725–7700* ☾ *Closed Sun.–Mon. No lunch Sat.* ✛ *2:B2.*

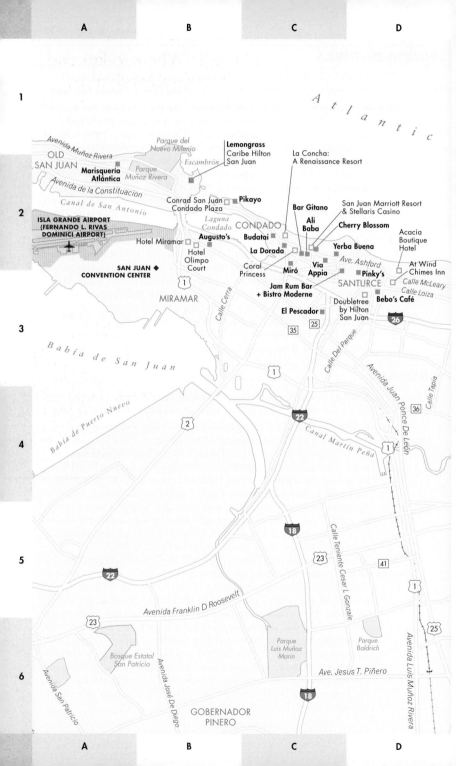

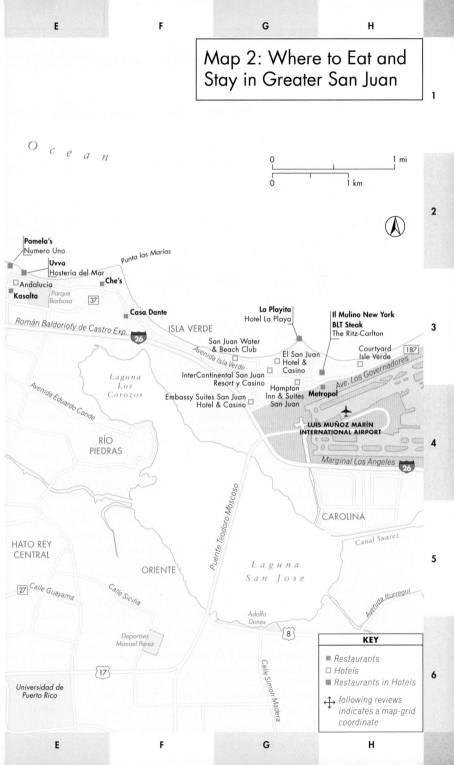

Map 2: Where to Eat and Stay in Greater San Juan

E  F  G  H

1

_O c e a n_

0                    1 mi
0              1 km

2

Pamela's
Numero Uno
Uvva                    Punta las Marías
Hostería del Mar
□ Andalucía      Che's
Kasalta    _Parque_
           _Barbosa_    37

Casa Dante                La Playita       Il Mulino New York
                          Hotel La Playa   BLT Steak
_Román Baldorioty de Castro Exp._  ISLA VERDE            The Ritz-Carlton     3
                    26        _Avenida Isla Verde_
                          San Juan Water              Courtyard
                          & Beach Club     □           Isle Verde    187
                                      El San Juan    □
                          InterContinental San Juan   Hotel &       Ave. Los Governadores
       _Laguna_          Resort y Casino   □ Casino
       _Los_                          Hampton    Metropol
       _Corozos_         Embassy Suites San Juan  Inn & Suites
_Avenida Eduardo Conde_  Hotel & Casino  □  San Juan

                                             LUIS MUÑOZ MARÍN
                                             INTERNATIONAL AIRPORT
       RÍO
       PIEDRAS                                                    4

                                             _Marginal Los Angeles_
                                                            26

                                             CAROLINA

HATO REY                                     _Canal Suarez_
CENTRAL
                                                                 5
                          _Laguna_
27  _Calle Guayama_       _San Jose_
         _Calle Sicilia_                          _Avenida Iturregui_

         _Deportivo_      _Adolfo_
         _Manuel Pérez_   _Dones_
                          8
                          17              ┌─────────────────────┐
                                          │        KEY          │
Universidad de                            │                     │
Puerto Rico                               │ ■ _Restaurants_      │  6
                                          │ □ _Hotels_           │
                                          │ ■ _Restaurants in Hotels_ │
                                          │ ⊕ _following reviews_ │
                                          │   _indicates a map-grid_ │
                                          │   _coordinate_       │
                                          └─────────────────────┘

E  F  G  H

**$$$** ✕ **Bar Gitano.** Themed as a tradi-
SPANISH   tional Andalusian-style *tasca*, this
extremely popular tapas bar is
decorated with artwork created
from Madrid bullfighting photo-
graphs. The marble bar and dark-
wood tables give an impression of
casual elegance. The trendy crowd

is always lively or borderline noisy, especially if there's a soccer match
on. Tapas include blistered padrón peppers with salt and olive oil, dates
wrapped with bacon and stuffed with Valdeón cheese, chargrilled octo-
pus, *jamón Ibérico*, and *cocas* (Spanish flatbread pizzas). You'll also
find paella and other main courses, if small plates aren't what you had
in mind. Stop by for live flamenco Sunday nights. ✉ *1302 Av. Ashford,
C-1, Condado* ☎ *787/294–5513* ☼ *Dinner only Mon.–Sat. Lunch avail-
able Sunday only* ✛ *2:C2.*

**$** ✕ **Bebo's Café.** Huge platters of delicious *comida criolla* are constantly
PUERTO RICAN   streaming out of the kitchen here. Low prices and a family atmosphere
ensure that this longtime local favorite—located near the Doubletree,
on the border of Condado and Santurce—is always packed. The extensive
menu includes everything from grilled skirt steak to seafood-stuffed
mofongo to barbecued ribs, as well as a selection of local desserts,
such as flan and *tres leches* cake. Breakfast is also popular. Note that
the service, while friendly, can sometimes be a bit rushed or distracted.
✉ *1600 Calle Loíza, Santurce* ☎ *787/726–1008* ⊕ *www.beboscafepr.
com* ✛ *2:D3.*

**$$$$** ✕ **Budatai.** You'll feel as if you're entering a secret club when you arrive
ASIAN   at this stylish hotspot in Condado's poshest shopping district. The res-
★   taurant, on the third floor, is decked out in rich, dark colors, with Chi-
nese lanterns that look as if they were designed by Salvador Dalí. The
attentive service and the elegantly dressed crowd, however, never feel
stuffy. The brainchild of one of Puerto Rico's best-known chefs, Roberto
Treviño, it's a seamless mix of Latin-accented pan-Asian food, including
duck fried rice with sweet plantains and halibut sashimi with coconut,
yuzu, and toasted garlic. We couldn't get enough of the calamari, fried
for a few seconds in hot oil and then quickly sautéed with sweet onions.
The upstairs outdoor terrace is a good place for drinks; consider stop-
ping by on the last Sunday evening of the month, when you can enjoy
the jazz concert at Ventana al Mar without the crowds. Sunday brunch
is also served. ✉ *1056 Av. Ashford, Condado* ☎ *787/725–6919* ⊕ *www.
budatai.com* ✛ *2:C2.*

**$$$** ✕ **Cherry Blossom.** It's clear when you walk through the delicately etched
ASIAN   glass doors that this place has a split personality. To the left is a sedate
little sushi bar where you place your order by checking off items on
the menu. (We liked the spicy crab and avocado roll, but people at the
next table seemed happy with their salmon skin roll.) To the right is
a more boisterous dining room where the seating is arranged around
teppanyaki tables. Chefs wearing tall red hats add drama to your meal,
tossing knives and dodging flames as they prepare such dishes as sautéed scallops in ginger sauce or the popular Sunday special, filet mignon

with chicken and shrimp. You can also order from the small but tasty Chinese menu; options include beef stir-fried with scallions and roast duck in savory spices. Wash everything down with a Sapporo beer or a fruity specialty cocktail. ☒ *1309 Av. Ashford, Condado* ☎ *787/723–7300* ⊗ *No lunch Sat.* ✢ *2:C2.*

**$$$**
MEDITERRANEAN
☾

✕ **Jam Rum Bar + Bistro Moderne.** This tucked-away spot may not look like a restaurant from the outside, but inside it's a study in modern design, in whites, oranges, greens, and other bright colors. Though it's only a block from touristy Avenida Ashford, the crowd is mostly locals in on the delicious secret. The menu is Latin-inspired, and you'll find appetizers like plantain-encrusted calamari with a cilantro-anchovy dipping sauce. For the main course, try pan-charred halibut on a bed of black-bean sauce or grilled filet mignon with a roasted poblano pepper and potato gratin. A rum bar showcases close to 70 rums from around the world and some creative rum-based cocktails. Surprisingly enough for a restaurant of this caliber, the place is extremely kid-friendly: there's a playroom if parents want to eat in peace, and kids eat half-price on Sunday. Children can even choose from a special "kidtini" menu of mixed juice drinks. ☒ *Casabella Building, 1400 Av. Magdalena, Condado* ☎ *787/721–5991* ⊗ *No lunch* ✢ *2:D2.*

**$$$**
SPANISH

✕ **Miró.** Like its namesake, the painter Joan Miró, this restaurant draws its inspiration from the Catalan region of Spain, where the cuisine is heavy on seafood and hearty tapas. Start with steamed clams with garlic or braised chorizo and peppers. (If you're here at the right time, you might get to try regional favorites like razor clams or baby octopus.) Main courses include sizzling lamb chops, as well as salmon in a sauce of Cabrales cheese, or *arroz negro* with mixed shellfish. Prints by the artist hang on the walls, adding an authentic touch to the maze of tiny dining rooms. If you prefer, you can also dine on the more casual front terrace. Daily brunch is available, and there's often live Spanish music Thursday through Sunday. ☒ *1214 Av. Ashford, Condado* ☎ *787/723–9593* ⊕ *www.miroseafood.com* ✢ *2:C2.*

**$$$$**
ECLECTIC
Fodor'sChoice
★

✕ **Pikayo.** Celebrity chef and Puerto Rico native Wilo Benet's flagship restaurant makes the most of its elegant surroundings at the Conrad San Juan Condado Plaza hotel. Works from local artists line the walls, and the atmosphere is formal but never hushed. The menu offers a twist on traditional Puerto Rican classics as well as more international flavors. Start with a glass of Benet's own wine, either a simple *tempranillo* (red) or an *albariño* (white). Then try some of the starters; particularly good are the pork belly sliders and the spicy tuna on crispy rice (known here as *pegao*). For main courses, options include lamb chops with wild mushrooms and a Dijon mustard demiglace, and jumbo shrimp with celery-root purée and a chorizo emulsion. Don't be surprised if Benet himself stops by your table to make sure everything is just to your liking. ☒ *Conrad San Juan Condado Plaza, 999 Av. Ashford, Condado* ☎ *787/721–6194* ⊕ *www.wilobenet.com* ⊗ *No lunch* ✢ *2:B2.*

**¢**
CAFÉ
☾
★

✕ **Pinky's.** High school students, tourists, and locals all pack in for some of the freshest gourmet wraps and sandwiches in town at this playful café, where the bustling servers wear cheeky "Eat Me!" T-shirts. You might not need another meal for the rest of the day if you manage to

finish the Drunken Pilot, a breakfast dish that includes four eggs,
spinach, tomato, onion, mush-
room, and goat cheese. (Breakfast
is available all day.) At lunch, try
the popular Surfer, a hot, pressed
sandwich with turkey, mozzarella,
basil, tomato, and pesto mayo.
Finally settling in to its new home
in Condado after previous stints in

Ocean Park and Santurce, Pinky's is also well known for salads, *batidas*
(fruit smoothies), and coffee. It's often nearly impossible to find a seat
at lunchtime, but don't worry: order your food to go, and head to the
beach to enjoy it alfresco. ✉ *1451 Av. Ashford, Suite 100B, Condado*
☎ *787/222–5222* ☜ *Reservations not accepted* ✛ *2:D3.*

$     ✕ **Via Appia.** Popular for decades with everyone from local politicians
PIZZA   and families to sunburned tourists who just dragged themselves off the
☺     beach, this bustling, no-frills restaurant is just as satisfying as its higher-
priced *paisanos*. They're particularly known for their simple Italian
dishes (we usually just stick with the pizza), but during lunch they dish
up some delicious comida criolla, with specials changing every day; try
the *pollo guisado* (chicken stew) on Mondays. The outdoor-seating area
looks out on Condado's busy Ashford Avenue, which makes for good
people-watching. The wine bar next door has a bit more ambience.
✉ *1350 Av. Ashford, Condado* ☎ *787/725–8711* ✛ *2:C2.*

$$$    ✕ **Yerba Buena.** Tables on the terrace are hard to come by at this Cuban
CUBAN   restaurant, one of the busier spots in Condado. That's fine, because
the glassed-in dining room is even more comfortable and has exactly
the same view. Cuban classics such as *ropa vieja* ("old clothes"—meat
cooked so slowly that it becomes tender shreds) seamlessly comple-
ment local dishes served with imaginative presentation. The shrimp
has a coconut-and-ginger sauce; the halibut fillet, one of mango and
orange liqueur. The restaurant claims to use the "original" recipe for
its *mojito*, Cuba's tasty rum, lime, and mint drink. Live Latin music is
played on Monday, Friday, and Saturday nights. ✉ *1350 Av. Ashford,
Condado* ☎ *787/721–5700* ⊕ *www.yerbabuenapr.com* ☾ *No lunch
Mon.–Fri.* ✛ *2:D2.*

## SANTURCE

*Use the coordinate (✛ 2:A1) at the end of each listing to locate a site
on the corresponding "Map 2: Where to Eat and Stay in Greater San
Juan."*

$$          ✕ **El Pescador.** If you want food that's unmistakably Puerto Rican, head
PUERTO RICAN   to Plaza del Mercado. Surrounding a fruit and vegetable market that
dates from 1910 are a few dozen restaurants that are the real deal.
Our favorite is El Pescador, a narrow storefront selling the freshest of
seafood. If you come in the evening it might be cool enough to eat at
one of the handful of tables on the square. If not, settle for the green
polka-dot tables in the dining room. The *chillo entero frito* (fried whole

red snapper) and *camarones al ajillo* (shrimp with garlic) are tasty, but the standout is the *arroz con calamari* (rice with squid). This dramatic inky-black dish draws oohs and aahs from surrounding customers when it arrives at your table. Parking is tough here on weekends, so take a taxi. ✉ *178 Calle Dos Hermanos, Santurce* ☎ *787/721–0995* ⊿ *Reservations not accepted* ⊘ *Closed Mon.* ✛ *2:C3.*

**$$$**
INTERNATIONAL
★
✕ **Laurel Kitchen | Art Bar.** After the popular Chayote closed, its chef-owner, Mario Pagán, moved shop to these elegant new digs in the Museo de Arte. As the host of cooking shows on Latin American television and a contestant on Food Network's *The Next Iron Chef*, Pagán is quite the showman; here he joyfully plays with familiar Puerto Rican ingredients and flavors, using haute-French techniques. His signature Chilean sea bass is served with an impossibly smooth yuca purée, over a port wine and foie gras reduction. Arugula salad with pancetta, papaya, goat cheese, and passion-fruit vinaigrette perfectly balances sour, salty, and sweet flavors. And crispy codfish buñuelos with cilantro-lime aioli recall the favorite Puerto Rican snack, bacalaítos. For dessert, traditional local combinations like cheese and guava paste are incorporated into dishes like a goat cheese tart with guava ice cream. ✉ *Museo de Arte de Puerto Rico, 299 Av. de Diego, Santurce* ☎ *787/522–6444* ⊕ *www.laurelkitchenartbar.com* ⊘ *Closed Sun.–Mon. No lunch Sat.* ✛ *2:D3*

# OCEAN PARK

*Use the coordinate (✛ 2:A1) at the end of each listing to locate a site on the corresponding "Map 2: Where to Eat and Stay in Greater San Juan."*

**$$$**
ARGENTINE
✕ **Che's.** This Argentine-style steak house on the eastern edge of Ocean Park, just before Isla Verde, is worth the trip. If you haven't tried *churrasco*, the marinated skirt steak that locals love, this is the place to do it. Another specialty is the grilled sweetbreads. The hamburgers are huge, and the french fries are fresh. The wine list, which tends toward Spanish and Argentine vintages, is also a winner. ✉ *35 Calle Caoba, Punta Las Marías* ☎ *787/726–7202* ⊕ *www.chesrestaurant.com* ✛ *2:F2.*

**$$**
CAFÉ
✕ **Kasalta.** Those who think coffee can never be too strong should make a beeline to Kasalta, which has an amazing pitch-black brew that will knock your socks off. Make your selection from the display cases full of luscious pastries, particularly the famous *quesito* (cream cheese–filled puff pastry) and other tempting treats. Walk up to the counter and order a sandwich, such as the savory Cubano, or perhaps a octopus salad. For dinner there are fish dishes and other, more substantial fare. Occasionally quality can be uneven, though, and some staff members are curt with tourists. ✉ *1966 Calle McLeary, Ocean Park* ☎ *787/727–7340* ⊕ *www.kasalta.com* ✛ *2:E3.*

**$$$**
CARIBBEAN
Fodor's Choice
★
✕ **Pamela's.** If you've always dreamed of fine dining for two right on the beach, only steps from where crashing waves meet the shore, head to this local favorite in Ocean Park. If you prefer air conditioning, an elegant glassed-in solarium awaits, complete with black cobblestone floors and slow-turning ceiling fans. The menu is a contemporary, creative mix of Caribbean spices and other tropical ingredients. To start, try the

corn fritters with a spicy cilantro aioli. The restaurant prides itself on its fresh seafood, so move on to the rainbow trout, stuffed with crab and coconut and steamed in a banana leaf, or choose the seared salmon served with an *acerola* (Caribbean cherry) chimichurri. ✉ *Numero Uno Guest House, 1 Calle Santa Ana, Ocean Park* ☎ *787/726–5010* ⊕ *www. numero1guesthouse.com* ✛ *2:E2.*

**$$$**
ECLECTIC

✕ **Uvva.** Sit on the deck at this romantic beachfront restaurant, where coconut palms wave in the breeze and the ocean gently laps right in front of you. Start with one of the most well-balanced mojitos we've tried, and then sample the rib eye and caramelized onion dumplings served with a chimichurri mayonnaise. The cuisine tends toward the international, with Mediterranean flavors and a few Asian accents. In season, the restaurant uses local seafood in dishes such as Caribbean spiny lobster risotto or fresh mahimahi served with polenta. ✉ *Hostería del Mar, 1 Calle Tapia, Ocean Park* ☎ *787/727–0631* ⊕ *www.hosteriadelmarpr. com* ✛ *2:E2.*

# ISLA VERDE

*Use the coordinate (✛ 2:A1) at the end of each listing to locate a site on the corresponding "Map 2: Where to Eat and Stay in Greater San Juan."*

**$$$$**
STEAKHOUSE

✕ **BLT Steak.** The sprawling dining room in this branch of Chef Laurent Tourondel's mini-chain invites you to relax: it's stylish and comfortable, with long leather banquettes, warm lighting, and glossy wood tables. Instead of bread, it's BLT's signature warm popovers that arrive at the table. Their version of that usually ho-hum menu standby, tuna tartare, is delicious—super-fresh fish topped with crispy shallots and served over avocado with a soy-lime sauce. As you might expect for a steak house located in a Ritz-Carlton, the prices are not for the faint of heart. Splurge and go for the strip sirloin, weighing in at 22 ounces, or the Japanese Kobe steak, priced per ounce. Not in a carnivorous mood? Try jumbo shrimp in a cilantro and lemon confit. For dessert, there's a densely rich crepe soufflé bathed in passion-fruit sauce. ✉ *The Ritz-Carlton, San Juan, 6991 Av. de los Gobernadores, Isla Verde* ☎ *787/253–1700* ⊕ *www.ritzcarlton.com/sanjuan* ☾ *No lunch* ✛ *2:H3.*

**$$**
PUERTO RICAN

✕ **Casa Dante.** If you're curious about mofongo—green plantains mashed with garlic and pork fat and filled with just about anything imaginable—head here for a stomach- and soul-satisfying version. Casa Dante offers four different types of the Puerto Rican specialty, including a noteworthy pinto version, blending both green and sweet plantains. Customers can then choose from various cuts of chicken, beef, or any combination of seafood. The restaurant's claim to fame is its excellent churrasco with chimichurri, which owner Dante Marini sells 25,000 pounds each year. Vegetarian options are available. ✉ *3022 Av. Isla Verde, Isla Verde* ☎ *787/726–7310* ✛ *2:F3.*

**$$$$**
ITALIAN
Fodor'sChoice
★

✕ **Il Mulino New York.** You'll want for nothing at the San Juan outpost of the famed Manhattan restaurant, where a team of tuxedoed waiters effortlessly coordinates your entire meal experience. The dark-wood-paneled walls and heavy velvet drapes are an odd juxtaposition with the

2

tropical climate, but everything about this place is elegant and tasteful. Garlic bread, fried zucchini, and other antipasti arrive moments after you sit down, though you'll want to pace yourself and leave room for the mammoth entrées to come. Standouts include rigatoni Bolognese, stuffed whole branzino (deboned tableside), and fresh pappardelle with sausage. There's no fusion or haute cuisine here, just solid Italian dishes, painstakingly executed. All this perfection comes at a price, though the shot of homemade grappa they offer at the end might help ease the shock. ⊠ *The Ritz-Carlton, San Juan, 6991 Av. de los Gobernadores, Isla Verde* 🕾 *787/791–8632* ⊕ *www.ilmulino.com* ⌔ *Reservations essential* ☽ *No lunch* ✛ *2:H3.*

$$ ╳ **La Playita.** Unlike some other notable oceanfront restaurants in the
ECLECTIC  metropolitan area, this casual spot doesn't have a price tag as big as the view. Set in a small hotel in Isla Verde, the atmosphere here is laid-back and beachy, and so is the food: you'll find their famous burgers; mofongo with various fillings, including a rare vegetarian option; a local catch of the day; and more creative dishes like mahimahi in a mango-chipotle sauce. All of the seating is outdoors; you can choose the deck and look out for manatees and sea turtles, or relax in a covered section near the bar, where you can try their signature passion-fruit mojitos, or that tropical beach staple, a fresh cold coconut (*coco frío*). The crowd is a fun mix of locals and tourists who have wandered over from nearby hotels to enjoy the breathtaking views. ⊠ *Hotel La Playa, 6 Calle Amapola, Isla Verde* 🕾 *787/791–1115* ⊕ *www.hotellaplaya.com* ✛ *2:G3.*

$$ ╳ **Metropol.** Across the street from a string of major hotels, this casual
CARIBBEAN  restaurant doesn't look like much from the outside, but inside it's decorated in warm, tropical colors, and local art hangs on the wall. (You can shop from your table if you find a painting you like.) The kitchen turns out delicious versions of Cuban and Puerto Rican favorites at reasonable prices. Tasty options include Cornish game hen stuffed with *congri*, a mixture of black beans and rice; perfectly seasoned and tender veal churrasco; and fried chickpeas with ham and chorizo. The crowd is a pleasant mix of tourists and locals, families and groups of friends enjoying a relaxed evening out. The restaurant has several branches around the island, most in the metro area. ⊠ *Av. Isla Verde, Isla Verde* 🕾 *787/791–5585* ⊕ *www.metropolpr.com* ✛ *2:H3.*

# WHERE TO STAY

*For expanded hotel reviews, visit Fodors.com.*

San Juan prides itself on its plentiful clean, comfortable accommodations, and hoteliers, by and large, aim to please. All rooms are now no-smoking. Big hotels and resorts, several with casinos, and a few smaller establishments line the sandy strands along Condado and Isla Verde. If you want to do little but relax on the beach, enjoy ample resort amenities, and partake in lively nightlife, either is a good option. Between these two neighborhoods, the Ocean Park area has homey inns, as do the districts of Miramar and Santurce, although the latter two areas aren't directly on the beach. Independent travelers, artistic types, and anyone who wants to stay a little bit off the beaten tourist

track might prefer these areas. Old San Juan has fewer lodging options, one of which has a casino, but most of the city's best boutique hotels are here. If you're a history or architecture buff or looking for a unique romantic experience, definitely stay in one of these colonial inns; many of the structures date back several

hundred years and will make you feel like you've been transported to another era, even though most have flat-screen televisions and Wi-Fi. (Also consider the Old City if you're in town for a cruise since the ports are within walking distance.) Keep in mind, though, that these buildings are old, and Puerto Rico has a tropical climate, so minor inconveniences like room mustiness or ongoing repairs might be possible.

Staying in a self-catering apartment or condo has advantages over a resort, especially for families. You can cook when and what you want, and you can enjoy considerable autonomy. Several companies represent such properties in San Juan. When booking, be sure to ask about maid service, swimming pools, and any other amenities that are important to you.

### PRICES

The city's rooms aren't inexpensive: for a high-end beach-resort room, expect to pay at least $200 to $300 for a double in high season—roughly mid-November through mid-April. For smaller inns and hotels, doubles start at $100 to $150. As a rule, if your room is less than $50 in high season, then the quality of the hotel might be questionable. Although most hotels operate on the European plan (EP, no meals included), some establishments do include breakfast or offer other meal plans and/or all-inclusive packages; there's only one true all-inclusive hotel in Puerto Rico, and it's not in San Juan.

| WHAT IT COSTS IN U.S. DOLLARS | | | | |
|---|---|---|---|---|
| ¢ | $ | $$ | $$$ | $$$$ |
| For Two People under $80 | $80–$150 | $150–$250 | $250–$350 | over $350 |

Prices are for a double room in high season, excluding 9% tax (11% for hotels with casinos, 7% for paradores) and typical 5%–16% service charge.

### APARTMENT RENTALS

**Caleta 64 Apartments.** Four nicely furnished boutique apartments that are just steps from the cathedral and Calle Cristo are available from Caleta 64. ⊠ *64 Caleta de San Juan, Old San Juan* ☎ *787/667–4926* ⊕ *www.caleta64.com.*

**Puerto Rico Vacation Apartments.** Some 200 properties in Condado and Isla Verde can be rented from this apartment company. ⊠ *Calle Marbella del Caribe Oeste S-5, Isla Verde* ☎ *787/727–1591, 800/266–3639* ⊕ *www.sanjuanvacations.com.*

## OLD SAN JUAN

*Use the coordinate (⊕ 1:A2) at the end of each listing to locate a site on the corresponding "Map 1: Where to Eat and Stay in Old San Juan."*

$    ☷ **CasaBlanca Hotel.** Mere steps away from some of the best dining in town, this boutique hotel adds Moroccan-theme panache to Old San Juan. **Pros:** Exotic decor; close to restaurants and nightclubs. **Cons:** Some rooms dark; noise from street and bars; smallish rooms; no elevator. ✉ *316 Calle Fortaleza, Old San Juan* ☎ *787/725–3436* ⊕ *www. hotelcasablancapr.com* ↰ *26 rooms, 4 suites* ⎙ *In-room: a/c, Internet, Wi-Fi. In-hotel: restaurant, some pets allowed* ⎧⎧ *Multiple meal plans* ⊕ *1:F4.*

HOTEL

¢    ☷ **Da House.** You won't know whether you're checking in to a hotel or an art gallery when you stay at this popular spot, which is in the same building as the fabled Nuyorican Café, a concert hall that many patrons simply refer to as Da House. **Pros:** Hip vibe, artsy types to mingle with; friendly staff; excellent value. **Cons:** Noise from nearby bars; on a steep alley; simple accommodations. ✉ *312 Calle San Francisco(entrance on Callejón de la Capilla), Old San Juan* ☎ *787/977–1180* ⊕ *www. dahousehotelpr.com* ↰ *27 rooms* ⎙ *In-room: a/c, Internet, Wi-Fi. In-hotel: bar, business center* ⎧⎧ *No meals* ⊕ *1:F3.*

B&B/INN
★

$$    ☷ **The Gallery Inn.** Nothing like this rambling, eclectic inn exists anywhere else in San Juan—or Puerto Rico, for that matter. **Pros:** one-of-a-kind lodging; ocean views; wonderful classical music concerts. **Cons:** no elevator; several narrow, winding staircases; an uphill walk from rest of Old San Juan; no sign out front; sometimes raucous pet macaws and cockatoos. ✉ *204–206 Calle Norzagaray, Old San Juan* ☎ *787/722–1808* ⊕ *www.thegalleryinn.com* ↰ *20 rooms, 5 suites* ⎙ *In-room: a/c, Internet, Wi-Fi. In-hotel: restaurant, pool* ⎧⎧ *Breakfast* ⊕ *1:E3.*

B&B/INN

$$$    ☷ **Hotel El Convento.** Carmelite nuns once inhabited this 350-year-old convent, but there's no longer anything austere about it. **Pros:** Lovely building; atmosphere to spare; plenty of nearby dining options. **Cons:** Near some noisy bars; small pool and small bathrooms. ✉ *100 Calle Cristo, Old San Juan* ☎ *787/723–9020* ⊕ *www.elconvento.com* ↰ *63 rooms, 5 suites* ⎙ *In-room: a/c, safe, Internet, Wi-Fi. In-hotel: restaurant, bar, pool, gym, business center, parking* ⎧⎧ *No meals* ⊕ *1:D3.*

HOTEL
Fodor'sChoice
★

$    ☷ **Hotel Milano.** This affordable and conservative hotel is near the best and worst of Old San Juan. **Pros:** Budget-friendly rates; walk to shops and restaurants. **Cons:** A bit staid; on a busy street; noise from nearby bars. ✉ *307 Calle Fortaleza, Old San Juan* ☎ *877/729–9050* ⊕ *www. hotelmilanopr.com* ↰ *30 rooms* ⎙ *In-room: a/c, Internet, Wi-Fi. In-hotel: business center* ⊕ *1:F4.*

HOTEL

$$$    ☷ **Sheraton Old San Juan Hotel & Casino.** This hotel's triangular shape subtly echoes the cruise ships docked nearby. **Pros:** harbor views; near many dining options; good array of room types. **Cons:** motel feel to guest rooms; noise from casino overwhelms lobby and restaurants; Wi-Fi in public areas only. ✉ *100 Calle Brumbaugh, Old San Juan* ☎ *787/721–5100, 866/376–7577* ⊕ *www.sheratonoldsanjuan.com* ↰ *200 rooms, 40 suites* ⎙ *In-room: a/c, safe, Internet. In-hotel: restaurant, bar, pool, gym, business center, parking, some pets allowed* ⎧⎧ *No meals* ⊕ *1:F4.*

HOTEL

# BEST BETS FOR SAN JUAN LODGING

**Fodor's**Choice★

**El San Juan Hotel & Casino**, $$$, p. 92

**Hotel El Convento**, $$$, p. 87

**La Concha—A Renaissance Resort**, $$$, p. 91

**Numero Uno**, $, p. 92

**The Ritz-Carlton, San Juan**, $$$$, p. 94

## By Price

¢

**Da House**, p. 87

$

**Acacia Boutique Hotel**, p. 89

**Andalucía**, p. 91

**CasaBlanca**, p. 87

**Coral Princess**, p. 90

**Hotel Milano**, p. 87

**Numero Uno**, p. 92

**Villa Herencia**, p. 88

$$

**Doubletree by Hilton San Juan**, p. 90

**Gallery Inn**, p. 87

$$$

**Conrad San Juan Condado Plaza**, p. 90

**El San Juan Hotel & Casino**, p. 92

**Hotel El Convento**, p. 87

**San Juan Water & Beach Club**, p. 94

**Sheraton Old San Juan**, p. 87

$$$$

**The Ritz-Carlton, San Juan**, p. 94

## By Experience

BEST FOR ROMANCE

**Hotel El Convento**, p. 87

**Numero Uno**, p. 92

**The Ritz-Carlton, San Juan**, p. 94

**San Juan Water & Beach Club**, p. 94

BEST BEACHFRONT

**El San Juan Hotel & Casino**, p. 92

**The Ritz-Carlton, San Juan**, p. 94

BEST POOL

**Caribe Hilton San Juan**, p. 88

**San Juan Marriott Resort & Stellaris Casino**, p. 91

**The Ritz-Carlton, San Juan**, p. 94

---

$ 　 ☷ **Villa Herencia Hotel.** From the same owners as CasaBlanca Hotel and
B&B/INN 　 Da House, this intimate property transports guests back to the 19th
★ 　 century. **Pros:** delightful furnishings; great for art and architecture lovers; romantic to the max; close to shops and cafés of Calle Cristo. **Cons:**
No in-room phone; no elevator. ⊠ *23 Calle de las Monjas, Old San
Juan* 📞 *787/722–0989* ⊕ *www.villaherencia.com* 📠 *7 rooms, 1 suite*
⊙ *In-room: a/c, Internet, Wi-Fi. In-hotel: some pets allowed* ⦿ *Breakfast* ✛ *1:C4.*

## PUERTA DE TIERRA

*Use the coordinate (✛ 2:A1) at the end of each listing to locate a site on
the corresponding "Map 2: Where to Eat and Stay in Greater San Juan."*

$$$ 　 ☷ **Caribe Hilton San Juan.** Not many hotels can lay claim to their own
RESORT 　 fort, but Fortín San Gerónimo del Boquerón, which once guarded the
☾ 　 entrance to San Juan Bay, is on the grounds of this sprawling resort,
one of the largest on the island. **Pros:** family-friendly atmosphere; private beach; lovely pool area. **Cons:** ongoing renovation; noisy lobby
area; somewhat isolated, with few attractions or restaurants within
walking distance. ⊠ *1 San Gerónimo Grounds, Puerta de Tierra*

The narrow streets and sloping hills of Old San Juan are fantastic for walking. Driving? Not so much.

☎ 787/721–0303, 800/468–8585 ⊕ www.caribehilton.com ↴ 872 rooms, 38 suites ☖ In-room: a/c, safe, kitchen, Internet. In-hotel: restaurant, bar, pool, tennis court, gym, spa, beach, water sports, children's programs, business center, parking ۩۝ No meals ⊕ 2:B2.

## CONDADO

*Use the coordinate (⊕ 2:A1) at the end of each listing to locate a site on the corresponding "Map 2: Where to Eat and Stay in Greater San Juan."*

$ **Acacia Boutique Hotel.** This chic spot, a sister property to At Wind
B&B/INN Chimes Inn, falls somewhere between a boutique hotel and a casual guesthouse. **Pros:** Enormous hot tub with ocean views; good value for the neighborhood; guests can use At Wind Chimes Inn's facilities. **Cons:** Several minutes' walk to most shops and restaurants; some outdated decorations in the rooms. ✉ 8 Calle Taft, Condado ☎ 787/725–0068, 877/725–0668 ⊕ www.acaciaseasideinn.com ↴ 15 rooms, 6 suites ☖ In-room: a/c, safe, Internet, Wi-Fi. In-hotel: restaurant, bar, parking, some pets allowed ۩۝ No meals ⊕ 2:D2.

$ **At Wind Chimes Inn.** Hidden behind a whitewashed wall covered with
B&B/INN bougainvillea, this Spanish-style villa gives the impression of an exclusive retreat. **Pros:** Charming architecture; on the edge of Condado; can use facilities at Acacia Seaside Inn. **Cons:** On a busy street; old-fashioned rooms; only a few rooms have closets. ✉ 1750 Av. McLeary, Condado ☎ 787/727–4153, 800/946–3244 ⊕ www.atwindchimesinn.com ↴ 17 rooms, 5 suites ☖ In-room: a/c, safe, kitchen. In-hotel: pool, parking, some pets allowed ۩۝ No meals ⊕ 2:D2.

**CLOSE UP**

# San Juan Spas

**Olas Spa at the Caribe Hilton.** This full-service spa offers a range of luxurious treatments, including the popular four-hand massage, hydrotherapy, facials, and other body treatments. An Aveda salon is also on site. ✉ *Caribe Hilton, Los Rosales Street, Gerónimo Grounds, Puerta de Tierra* ☎ *787/977–5500, 877/888–6527* ⊕ *www.olasspa.com.*

**The Ritz-Carlton Spa, San Juan.** Popular treatments at this posh spa include stone therapy, the balancing lomilomi massage, and the Ritz-Carlton's signature facial. You can also take private yoga or salsa lessons.

✉ *6961 Av. de los Gobernadores, Isla Verde* ☎ *787/253–1700* ⊕ *www. ritzcarlton.com.*

**Zen Spa.** This family-run spa focuses on wellness, with staff trained in Chinese and Ayurvedic techniques, but all kinds of treatments are available. One facial uses silk fibers to firm and tone skin. You can also get a coffee-infused clay wrap or a lymphatic drainage massage. An attached shop sells Kiehl's and Eminence Organics products, as well the house line, Zendera. ✉ *1054 Av. Ashford, Condado* ☎ *787/722–8433, 866/936–7720* ⊕ *www.zen-spa.com.*

**$$$**
**HOTEL**
🏨 **Conrad San Juan Condado Plaza.** The island's only luxury hotel with both Atlantic and lagoon views is just five minutes from Old San Juan. **Pros:** excellent food at Pikayo; friendly staff; stunning views from some rooms; chic design. **Cons:** hallway noise; no bathtubs; small beach; poor lighting in rooms; no kids' club. ✉ *999 Av. Ashford, Condado* ☎ *787/721–1000* ⊕ *www.condadoplaza.com* ⟿ *509 rooms, 61 suites* ⌂ *In-room: safe, Internet, Wi-Fi. In-hotel: restaurant, bar, pool, tennis court, gym, beach, water sports, laundry facilities, business center, parking* ¶◯¶ *No meals* ✛ *2:B2.*

**$**
**HOTEL**
🏨 **Coral Princess.** This Art Deco building—one of the few left in Condado—has personality to spare. **Pros:** good value; friendly staff; comfortable common areas. **Cons:** not directly on the beach; small pool; Wi-Fi is in lobby only. ✉ *1159 Av. Magdalena, Condado* ☎ *787/977–7700* ⊕ *www.coralpr.com* ⟿ *25 rooms* ⌂ *In-room: a/c, safe, Internet. In-hotel: pool, laundry facilities, parking* ¶◯¶ *Breakfast* ✛ *2:C2.*

**$$**
**HOTEL**
**★**
🏨 **Doubletree by Hilton San Juan.** It's hard to beat this hotel for the price. **Pros:** excellent value for the neighborhood; attractive rooms; good on-site dining options. **Cons:** a bit of a walk to the beach and the main drag in Condado. ✉ *105 Av. de Diego, Condado* ☎ *787/721–1200* ⊕ *www. hilton.com* ⟿ *184 rooms* ⌂ *In-room: a/c, safe, Internet, Wi-Fi. In-hotel: restaurant, bar, pool, gym, spa, laundry facilities, business center, parking* ¶◯¶ *No meals* ✛ *2:D3.*

**$**
**HOTEL**
🏨 **Hotel Olimpo Court.** If you're an independent traveler looking for a clean, inexpensive place to crash, this extremely affordable Miramar hotel will suit just fine. **Pros:** comfortable rooms; good for budget travelers; close to major attractions and convention center. **Cons:** rooms need renovating; neighborhood a little dull; Wi-Fi in lobby only; no sign. ✉ *603 Av. Miramar, Miramar* ☎ *787/724–0600* ⟿ *42 rooms* ⌂ *In-room: a/c, safe. In-hotel: business center, parking* ¶◯¶ *No meals* ✛ *2:B2.*

**$**
HOTEL
**Hotel Miramar.** Catering largely to cruise-ship passengers, this hotel sits in the middle of Miramar, an up-and-coming neighborhood located halfway between Condado and Old San Juan. **Pros:** short drive to Old San Juan and Condado; walk to excellent restaurants; rooftop terrace. **Cons:** simple rooms; not the most interesting neighborhood. ⊠ *606 Av. Ponce de León, Miramar* ☎ *787/977–1000* ⊕ *www.miramarhotelpr.com* ⌁ *50 rooms* ☐ *In-room: a/c, safe, Wi-Fi. In-hotel: restaurant, bar, gym, laundry facilities, business center, parking, some pets allowed* ✥ *2:B2.*

**$$$**
RESORT
Fodor'sChoice
★
**La Concha—A Renaissance Resort.** La Concha—an icon of Tropical Modernist architecture—fits the ideal of a chic Caribbean resort. **Pros:** stunning architecture; numerous on-site social activities; beautiful guestrooms. **Cons:** noisy bar/lobby, particularly when there's live music; beach can be narrow during times of high tide and surf advisories. ⊠ *1077 Av. Ashford, Condado* ☎ *787/721–7500* ⊕ *www. laconcharesort.com* ⌁ *232 rooms, 16 suites; 235 tower suites* ☐ *In-room: a/c, safe, Internet, Wi-Fi. In-hotel: restaurant, bar, pool, gym, beach, business center, parking* ⍾*No meals* ✥ *2:C2.*

**$$$**
RESORT
♻
**San Juan Marriott Resort & Stellaris Casino.** The shape and color of a cardboard box, this lively, popular hotel doesn't add much to the skyline of Condado, but as soon as you step instead the impressive lobby—with its stunning coral sculpture carved from wood, chic spots for lounging, and welcoming bar—you'll feel you've arrived in the Caribbean. **Pros:** on one of the area's best beaches; near dozens of dining options; lots of amenities. **Cons:** uninspired architecture; lots of conventions; overworked staff. ⊠ *1309 Av. Ashford, Condado* ☎ *787/722–7000, 800/465–5005* ⊕ *www.marriottsanjuan.com* ⌁ *513 rooms, 12 suites* ☐ *In-room: a/c, safe, Internet, Wi-Fi. In-hotel: restaurant, bar, pool, tennis court, gym, spa, beach, children's programs, laundry facilities, business center, parking* ⍾*No meals* ✥ *2:C2.*

## OCEAN PARK

*Use the coordinate (✥ 2:A1) at the end of each listing to locate a site on the corresponding "Map 2: Where to Eat and Stay in Greater San Juan."*

**$**
B&B/INN
★
**Andalucía.** In a Spanish-style house, this friendly little inn lives up to its name with such details as hand-painted tiles and ceramic pots filled with greenery. **Pros:** terrific value; helpful hosts; gorgeous courtyard. **Cons:** not right on the beach; some rooms are smaller than others. ⊠ *2011 Calle McLeary, Ocean Park* ☎ *787/309–3373* ⊕ *www. andalucia-puertorico.com* ⌁ *11 rooms* ☐ *In-room: a/c, kitchen, Internet, Wi-Fi. In-hotel: water sports, business center, parking* ⍾*No meals* ✥ *2:E3.*

**$** ⬚ **Hostería del Mar.** A top-to-bottom renovation in 2011 banished this
**B&B/INN** small inn's formerly drab room decor, and in its place are stylish rooms
★ decorated in bright blues and whites, with brand-new mattresses and
plasma-screen televisions. **Pros:** right on the beach; lovely building;
good on-site dining. **Cons:** long walk to other restaurants; no pool;
Wi-Fi in lobby only. ✉ *1 Calle Tapia, Ocean Park* ☎ *787/727–3302*
⊕ *www.hosteriadelmarpr.com* ⬚ *23 rooms, 2 suites* ⬚ *In-room: a/c,
safe, kitchen. In-hotel: restaurant, bar, beach, business center, parking,
some pets allowed* ⊹ *2:E2.*

**$** ⬚ **Numero Uno Guest House.** Although the name refers to the hotel's
**HOTEL** address, Numero Uno is how guests rate this small hotel. **Pros:**
**Fodor'sChoice** friendly atmosphere; great restaurant; right on the beach. **Cons:** a long
★ walk to other restaurants; small pool. ✉ *1 Calle Santa Ana, Ocean
Park* ☎ *787/726–5010, 866/726–5010* ⊕ *www.numero1guesthouse.
com* ⬚ *12 rooms, 4 apartments* ⬚ *In-room: a/c, safe, kitchen, Internet, Wi-Fi. In-hotel: restaurant, bar, pool, beach, some pets allowed*
⦿| *Breakfast* ⊹ *2:E2.*

## ISLA VERDE

*Use the coordinate (⊹ 2:A1) at the end of each listing to locate a site
on the corresponding "Map 2: Where to Eat and Stay in Greater San
Juan."*

**$$** ⬚ **Courtyard by Marriott Isla Verde Beach Resort.** This 12-story resort tries
**RESORT** to be all things to all people—and succeeds to a great degree. **Pros:**
on a great beach; family-friendly environment; good value. **Cons:** you
can hear airport noise from some rooms; noise from lobby. ✉ *7012
Av. Boca de Cangrejos, Isla Verde* ☎ *787/791–0404, 800/791–2553*
⊕ *www.sjcourtyard.com* ⬚ *260 rooms, 33 suites* ⬚ *In-room: a/c, safe,
Internet, Wi-Fi. In-hotel: restaurant, bar, pool, gym, beach, laundry
facilities, business center, parking* ⦿| *No meals* ⊹ *2:H3.*

**$$$** ⬚ **El San Juan Hotel & Casino.** For decades this iconic hotel was the don't-
**RESORT** miss destination in Isla Verde, and a renovation in 2007 has helped keep
♻ everyone's attention. **Pros:** beautiful pool; great dining options in and
**Fodor'sChoice** near hotel; on a fantastic beach. **Cons:** noise in the lobby from bars and
★ casino; self-parking lot is a long walk from the hotel entrance; small
bathrooms. ✉ *6063 Av. Isla Verde, Isla Verde* ☎ *787/791–1000* ⊕ *www.
elsanjuanhotel.com* ⬚ *386 rooms, 57 suites* ⬚ *In-room: safe, kitchen,
Internet, Wi-Fi. In-hotel: restaurant, bar, pool, tennis court, gym, spa,
beach, water sports, children's programs, business center, parking, some
pets allowed* ⦿| *No meals* ⊹ *2:G3.*

**$$$** ⬚ **Embassy Suites San Juan Hotel & Casino.** Overshadowing neighbors with
**HOTEL** more prestigious names, the coral-colored Embassy Suites is one of the
prettiest hotels in Isla Verde. **Pros:** family-friendly place; pretty pool;
full cooked-to-order breakfast and cocktail reception included. **Cons:**
not on beach; chain-hotel feel; highway noise in pool area. ✉ *8000
Calle Tartak, Isla Verde* ☎ *787/791–0505, 888/791–0505* ⊕ *www.
embassysuitessanjuan.com* ⬚ *299 suites* ⬚ *In-room: a/c, safe, Internet,
Wi-Fi. In-hotel: restaurant, bar, pool, gym, laundry facilities, business
center, parking* ⦿| *Breakfast* ⊹ *2:G4.*

El San Juan Hotel & Casino

The Ritz-Carlton, San Juan

El Convento Hotel

**$$**
HOTEL

**⊞ Hampton Inn & Suites San Juan.** If you don't mind a short walk to the beach, you can get a room at this friendly hotel for much less than at many of the competitors across the road. **Pros:** good value; helpful staff; breakfast included. **Cons:** 5 to 10 minute walk to the beach; chain-hotel feel; some highway noise in pool area. ⊠ *6530 Av. Isla Verde, Isla Verde* ☎ *787/791–8777, 800/426–7866* ⊕ *www.hamptoninn.com* ⤵ *147 rooms, 54 suites* ⚒ *In-room: a/c, safe, Internet, Wi-Fi. In-hotel: restaurant, bar, pool, gym, laundry facilities, business center, parking* ❭❐❬ *Breakfast* ✛ *2:H3.*

**$**
HOTEL

**⊞ Hotel La Playa.** As its name suggests, this small, friendly hotel is right on the beach. **Pros:** great value; helpful staff; excellent location; oceanfront restaurant. **Cons:** few on-site amenities; need to drive to most other attractions. ⊠ *6 Calle Amapola, Isla Verde* ☎ *787/791–1115* ⊕ *www.hotellaplaya.com* ⤵ *15 rooms* ⚒ *In-room: a/c, safe, Wi-Fi. In-hotel: restaurant, bar, beach, parking* ❭❐❬ *Breakfast* ✛ *2:G3.*

**$$**
RESORT
⟳

**⊞ InterContinental San Juan Resort & Casino.** Despite its name, this 16-story resort in the heart of Isla Verde is downright dowdy. **Pros:** lovely pool; on one of the city's best beaches; multiple dining options. **Cons:** unattractive facade; cramped lobby. ⊠ *5961 Av. Isla Verde, Isla Verde* ☎ *787/791–6100, 800/443–2009* ⊕ *www.icsanjuanresort.com* ⤵ *376 rooms, 22 suites* ⚒ *In-room: a/c, safe, Internet, Wi-Fi. In-hotel: restaurant, bar, pool, gym, spa, beach, children's programs, business center, parking* ❭❐❬ *No meals* ✛ *2:G3.*

**$$$$**
RESORT
⟳
Fodor's Choice
★

**⊞ The Ritz-Carlton, San Juan.** Elegant marble floors and fountains don't undermine the feeling that this is a true beach getaway. **Pros:** top-notch service; excellent restaurant options; pretty pool area. **Cons:** not much is within walking distance; extremely expensive for San Juan lodging. ⊠ *6961 Av. de los Gobernadores, Isla Verde* ☎ *787/253–1700, 800/241–3333* ⊕ *www.ritzcarlton.com/sanjuan* ⤵ *416 rooms, 11 suites* ⚒ *In-room: a/c, safe, Internet, Wi-Fi. In-hotel: restaurant, bar, pool, tennis court, gym, spa, beach, water sports, children's programs, business center, parking* ❭❐❬ *No meals* ✛ *2:H3.*

**$$$**
HOTEL
★

**⊞ San Juan Water & Beach Club.** Stepping into the elevators decked out in black lights at this boutique hotel is almost like entering a nightclub. **Pros:** fun atmosphere; interesting design; great nightlife option. **Cons:** very dark hallways; small pool. ⊠ *2 Calle Tartak, Isla Verde* ☎ *787/728–3666, 888/265–6699* ⊕ *www.waterbeachclubhotel.com* ⤵ *77 rooms, 4 suites* ⚒ *In-room: safe, Wi-Fi. In-hotel: restaurant, bar, pool, gym, beach, business center, parking, some pets allowed* ✛ *2:G3.*

# NIGHTLIFE AND THE ARTS

Several publications will tell you what's happening in San Juan. ¡*Qué Pasa!*, the official visitors' guide, has current listings of events in the city and out on the island. For more up-to-the-minute information, pick up a copy of the *Puerto Rico Daily Sun*, the island's English-language daily. *Bienvenidos,* published by the Puerto Rico Hotel & Tourism Association, is also helpful.

There are also publications for Spanish-speaking visitors, including the weekend section of the Spanish-language newspaper *El Nuevo Día*; the paper also gives a weekly rundown of events on its website, ⊕ *www. elnuevodia.com*. *Sal!* (⊕ *www.sal.pr*) includes brief restaurant reviews and articles about dining and nightlife. (It's also available as a free downloadable app for iPhone and iPad and can be used in either English or Spanish.)

## NIGHTLIFE

From Thursday through Sunday, it's as if there's a celebration going on nearly everywhere in San Juan. Be sure you dress to party, particularly on Friday and Saturday nights; Puerto Ricans have flair, and both men and women love getting dressed up to go out. Bars are usually casual, but if you have on jeans, sneakers, and a T-shirt, you may be refused entry at nightclubs and discos.

Well-dressed visitors and locals alike often mingle in the lobby bars of large hotels, many of which have bands in the evening. Some hotels also have clubs with shows and/or dancing; admission starts at $10. Casino rules have been relaxed, injecting life into what was once a conservative hotel gaming scene, but you still won't be allowed in if you're wearing a tank top or shorts. There are more games, as well as such gambling perks as free drinks and live music.

In Old San Juan, Calle San Sebastián is lined with bars and restaurants, although the hottest clubs are along and just off Calle Fortaleza. Salsa music blaring from jukeboxes in cut-rate pool halls competes with mellow Latin jazz in top-flight nightspots. The young and the beautiful often socialize in Plaza San José. Mid-January sees the Fiestas de la Calle San Sebastián, one of the Caribbean's best street parties.

Young professionals as well as a slightly older bohemian crowd fill Santurce, San Juan's historical downtown area, until the wee hours. The revitalized Plaza del Mercado (Calle Dos Hermanos at Calle Capital) has structures—many painted in bright colors—dating from the 1930s or earlier. On weekend nights the area's streets are closed to vehicular traffic. You can wander from dive bars to trendy nightspots and sway to music that pours from countless open-air establishments and the marketplace's front plaza.

## BARS

**Barlovento.** Packed on weekends, this chic outdoor bar that's on a breezy plaza is a great place to sip tropical drinks oceanside. It also has a menu if hunger strikes. ⊠ *Plaza Alberto Escudero, 1043 Av. Ashford, Condado* ☎ *787/724–7283.*

**El Barril.** If you stop by this neighborhood bar at, say, 9 or 10 pm, you may find yourself alone with the bartender. It doesn't get going until 11 pm at the earliest, but 1 am is probably better if you want a true taste of San Juan nightlife. It closes, oh, when the last person leaves. There's music most nights, whether live performances or DJs. Although not a sports bar per se, this sister property of Bar Gitano (⇨ *Night Bites, below*) is a good spot to catch an important game, whether Champions League soccer or American football. Several local beers are on tap, and there's also a great passion-fruit–spiked white sangria. Tasty burgers and wings are available, and you can also order from the tapas menu next door. ⊠ *1309 Av. Ashford, C-2, Condado* ☎ *787/723–2517.*

**El Batey.** This legendary hole-in-the-wall bar won't win any prizes for decor, but still it has an irresistibly artsy and welcoming vibe. Add your own message to the graffiti-covered walls (they have a B.Y.O.S, or Bring Your Own Sharpie policy), or put your business card alongside the hundreds that cover the lighting fixtures. The ceiling may leak, but the jukebox has the best selection of oldies in town. Join locals in a game of pool. ⊠ *101 Calle Cristo, Old San Juan* ☎ *No phone.*

**Eternal.** Decorated in the same modern style as the rest of the Condado Plaza hotel, this sleek lounge hosts a range of acts on the weekends, including DJs and live bands, most often salsa, merengue, or Spanish pop. It's a comfortable spot for an evening cocktail during the week as well. ⊠ *Conrad San Juan Condado Plaza, 999 Av. Ashford, Condado* ☎ *787/565–7714* ⊕ *www.eternalpr.com.*

**Jam Rum Bar + Bistro Moderne.** You can come here earlier in the evening to eat a terrific meal, but this hidden spot in the heart of Condado is also a great place for a drink. The bar showcases close to 70 rums from around the world, including all the rums of Puerto Rico. You can try rum flights or one of many inventive rum-based cocktails—in addition to the regular bar. There's live music on Friday and Saturday. ⊠ *Casabella Building, 1400 Av. Magdalena, Condado* ☎ *787/721–5991.*

**Old Harbor Brewery.** Serious beer-lovers know to head to this authentic microbrewery and restaurant close to the harborfront. More clubby than pubby, it packs in locals as well as tourists who come to taste the five delicious German-style beers, brewed in European-style open fermentation tanks. Order the five-beer sampler before making a selection for a pint-glass or liter stein. Jazz buffs should call in on Saturday night for live music. ⊠ *202 Calle Tizol, at Calle Recinto Sur, Old San Juan* ☎ *787/721–2100* ⊕ *www.oldharborbrewery.com.*

**Wet.** On the roof of the San Juan Water & Beach Club Hotel, this sexy spot offers some of the best ocean views anywhere in Isla Verde. On the weekends there's a DJ, and locals pack in to relax at the bar or on the leather beds reserved for bottle service. ⊠ *San Juan Water & Beach Club, 2 Calle Tartak, Isla Verde* ☎ *787/725–4664.*

*Continued on page 101*

# Salsa

## A Guide to Puerto Rico's Favorite Music and Dance

Salsa: its hip-shaking rhythms and sensual moves embody the spirit of the Caribbean and Latin America. The songs and the steps create a language all their own—one that's spoken by passionate dancers and musicians the world over. But it's the Puerto Ricans who are the most fluent. Welcome to the home of salsa! Are you ready to dance?

As the first notes of the song sound, dancers come alive, eager to take their place on the floor with a partner whose skill matches their own. These are the most daring salsa devotees who are found in every corner of the island, dancers who won't quit moving until the music stops. Even as a bystander, it's impossible to stand still.

Salsa isn't a passive rhythm: it's animated, hot, and sensual, a metaphor for the Caribbean itself. In general, the themes of the songs mirror the moves of the dance, with choruses alluding to love, both forbidden and open. In the music and the movement, there's occasional improvisation among those who know the genre. Hips shake to the clave, which marks the basic rhythm, and shoulders shake from one side to the other, fanning the air. It's a democratic form, where experimentation is encouraged . . . you just have to be willing to get out there.

*by Julie Schwietert Collazo*

# SALSA HISTORY

Timbale master Tito Puente

Though salsa has its roots outside Puerto Rico, the island is directly responsible for the rhythm known by this name. As a musical form, the components of salsa can be traced back to Europe and Africa. During the colonial period, Spanish conquistadores arriving from the West Indies brought island rhythms along with them. They also brought the complex, multi-rhythmic riffs of Arabic music, an artifact of the Muslim conquest of the Iberian Peninsula that had become embedded in the music of Spain and Portugal. In Puerto Rico, all of these musical strands came together to create a new rhythm known as bomba.

The emergence of salsa was deeply influenced by musical forms from nearby Cuba and other parts of the Caribbean, as well as musical experimentation by diaspora Puerto Ricans living in New York. Among the most important of these mainland musicians was percussionist and band leader Tito Puente.

The history of salsa is the history of the new world. In salsa, there's evidence of rhythms from past ages, as well as the musical history of our own time. Salsa isn't a "pure" musical form, but represents—like Puerto Rico itself—a mixture of rhythmic elements, adapted by the inhabitants of the new world.

## DID YOU KNOW?

■ The first use of the word "salsa" related to music was in 1937 by Cuban composer Igancio Pineiro in his popular song, "Echale Salsita." It continues to be a frequently recorded song today by artists in and outside Cuba.

■ The song "Oye Como Va" was originally composed by Tito Puente in 1963 and later recorded by Carlos Santana, who made it a number-one hit.

■ The contribution of salsa to jazz music dates from 1940, when Dizzie Gillespie and Stan Kenton incorporated salsa in their tunes, giving birth to "Latin jazz."

■ More than 30 countries celebrate salsa with annual festivals, among them, Poland, Israel, France, Serbia, and Japan.

## SALSA SPEAK

**ABRAZO:** The *abrazo* is the positioning of the partners' hands and arms. The woman's left hand rests lightly on her partner's shoulder, while his right hand is placed on the small of her back to guide her. The abrazo establishes the space each partner maintains during turns.

Abrazo

**VUELTAS:** *Vueltas*, turns, are an important component of salsa. There are numerous styles, and they can occur in both directions, but all are

Vueltas

determined and initiated by the male partner. Turns are spontaneous; their complexity depends upon the skill and experience of the dancers.

**SOLOS:** Solos—a favorite move of experienced dancers—are moments when the partners separate to move independently though still in response to each other. These are often synchronized with the solos of percussion musicians. Solos are also used as a means of rest after a series of complex turns before the pair comes together again for even more intricate turns.

Solos

## SALSA STYLE

Two elements define salsa fashion: comfort and sensuality. Men and women both draw from the best of their wardrobes, with men often dressed in guayabera shirts, linen pants, and two-toned dance shoes. Suede shoes permit optimal movement for men and add a touch of elegance. Women typically wear dresses—often knee length or shorter—and open-toed, medium-heeled dance shoes with ankle support. For both men and women, freedom of movement and maximum ventilation are important elements of a salsa wardrobe.

The dance is an opportunity to show off your elegance and your sensuality, but your clothing should also honor the significance of the event and venue. Many dance organizers impose dress policies, prohibiting running shoes, sleeveless shirts, and overly informal or provocative clothing. Dress to impress.

Salsa dance shoes

# NEXT STEPS

If you're ready to take to the dance floor, here are some of the best places to learn—and then show off—your moves.

## LESSONS

**The Academia de Baile Julie Mayoral.** On the Plaza de las Delicias in Ponce, Mayoral's second floor studio is steaming hot, and her young, enthusiastic instructors will have you doing proper vueltas in no time. For a bit more than $5 for an hour lesson, Mayoral probably offers the best deal in Puerto Rico. Mayoral also has studios in Coamo and Yauco. Call her Ponce studio (☎ 787/843–2830) for information about lessons at any of the three studios.

In San Juan, dancer Paulette Beauchamp offers salsa classes for children and adults on Tuesday. Her studio, **DanzActiva** (☎ 787/775–9438 ⊕ www.danzactiva.com), is in the historic Cuartel de Ballaja building in Old San Juan.

## HOTELS

Locals and tourists alike take to the dance floor at the **San Juan Marriott Resort** and **Stellaris Casino** on weekends, when homegrown musicians provide a soundtrack for the salsa experience. Entry is free, but you'll need to pur-

chase drinks if you decide to rest at one of the tables circling the dance floor.

## CLUBS

Old San Juan's **Nuyorican Café** looks like a dive—and it is—but it's the heart of Puerto Rico's salsa scene. Though the café also hosts jazz and rock groups as well as poetry readings and experimental theatre, its reputation for world-class salsa has expanded far beyond the island. Call ahead for the current schedule (☎ 787/977–1276).

## FESTIVALS

As the home of salsa, Puerto Rico hosts an annual **International Salsa Congress.** It's held in San Juan each July, though the site changes each year. The congress attracts thousands of aficionados from the island and from surprisingly far-flung places, including Japan, Korea, and Norway.

---

(left) A couple prepares for competition at the International Salsa Congress held in San Juan.
(right) Young dancers performing at the International Salsa Congress.

## CASINOS

By law, all casinos are in hotels, and the government keeps a close eye on them. They're allowed to operate 24 hours a day, but individual casinos set their own hours. In addition to slot machines, typical games include blackjack, roulette, craps, Caribbean stud poker (a five-card stud game), and *pai gow* poker (a combination of American poker and the ancient Chinese game of *pai gow*, which employs cards and dice). That said, an easing of gaming regulations has set a more relaxed tone and made such perks as free drinks and live music more common. The range of available games has also greatly expanded. The minimum age is 18. Dress for the larger casinos in San Juan tends to be on the formal side, and the atmosphere is refined. Tank tops or shorts are usually not acceptable attire.

**The Casino at The Ritz-Carlton, San Juan.** With its golden columns, turquoise and bronze walls, and muted lighting, the Ritz casino, the largest in San Juan, stays refined by day or night. There's lots of activity, yet everything is hushed. ⊠ *6991 Av. de los Gobernadores, Isla Verde* ☎ *787/253–1700.*

**Conrad San Juan Condado Plaza Hotel & Casino.** Popular with locals, the casino at the Condado Plaza is probably worth a visit only if you're staying in the hotel or if you're looking for one open 24 hours a day. It's just not as interesting as other options in the city. ⊠ *999 Av. Ashford, Condado* ☎ *787/721–1000.*

**El San Juan Hotel & Casino, The Waldorf Astoria Collection.** Neither the clangs of the slots nor the sounds of the salsa band disrupt the semblance of Old World. The polish continues in the adjacent lobby, with its huge chandeliers and mahogany paneling. ⊠ *6063 Av. Isla Verde, Isla Verde* ☎ *787/791–1000.*

**InterContinental San Juan Resort & Casino.** A blue neon light envelops you as you enter this casino, which underwent a $2 million renovation in 2009, adding a host of new slot machines and more elegant decor. Live music is usually available on Saturday nights. ⊠ *5961 Av. Isla Verde, Isla Verde* ☎ *787/791–6100.*

**San Juan Marriott Resort & Stellaris Casino.** The crowd is casual and the decor tropical and bubbly at this spacious gaming room. Right outside, there's a huge bar, where Latin musicians perform on weekends, and an adjacent café. ⊠ *1309 Av. Ashford, Condado* ☎ *787/722–7000.*

**Sheraton Old San Juan Hotel & Casino.** It's impossible to ignore this ground-floor casino, the only place to gamble in Old San Juan. You can see the gaming room from the hotel's main stairway, the balcony above, and the lobby. Light bounces off the Bahía de San Juan and pours through its many windows; passengers bound off their cruise ships and pour through the many glass doors. ⊠ *101 Calle Brumbaugh, Old San Juan* ☎ *787/721–5100.*

## DANCE CLUBS

**Brava.** A long line of young people can be spotted at the door of this chic club at the El San Juan Hotel. The two-level club, each with its own DJ and dance floor, is one of the best places for dancing. There's a

# The Piña Colada Wars

This mixture of pineapple juice, coconut cream, and liberal amounts of rum, always garnished with a wedge of pineapple and a maraschino cherry, was invented by Ramón Marrero at the Caribe Hilton in 1954 or by Ramón Portas Mingot at the Barranchina Bar in 1963, depending on whom you believe. Was it Marrero, a young bartender who is said to have spent three months on a concoction that would appeal to patrons at the Beachcomber's Bar? (His secret? Using only fresh pineapple juice.) Or was it Mingot, an elderly bartender who was satisfying the whims of patrons at the bar in Old San Juan? (He said his were so frothy because he froze the pineapple juice and coconut cream mixture instead of simply adding crushed ice.)

The two venues have fought over bragging rights for decades. The Caribe Hilton issues press release after press release reminding people that the drink was born in its seaside bar. (If what its public relations department says is true, the drink celebrated its 50th anniversary in 2004.) The Barranchina Bar put up a plaque that tells passersby that it is the true birthplace of the beverage. The Caribe Hilton seems to have the edge. Coco López, the company that makes the coconut cream most often used in the drink, honored Marrero in 1978. In gratitude for his contributions to the "bartending arts," they presented him with a color television set. But the origins of the piña colada—which means "strained pineapple"—remains as unclear as the cocktail itself. You may have to sample several before you make up your own mind.

—Mark Sullivan

different theme party Thursday through Saturday. ✉ *El San Juan Hotel & Casino, 6063 Av. Isla Verde, Isla Verde* ☎ *787/641–3500* ⊕ *www.bravapr.com.*

**Club Lazer.** This multilevel club has spots for quiet conversation, spaces for dancing to loud music, and a landscaped roof deck overlooking San Juan. The crowd changes every night; Saturday is ladies' night, when male strippers sometimes perform. ✉ *251 Calle Cruz, Old San Juan* ☎ *787/725–7581* ⊕ *www.clublazer.com.*

## GAY AND LESBIAN BARS AND CLUBS

With its sophisticated nightlife, San Juan has become a popular destination for gay and lesbian tourists. Condado, perhaps the heart of gay San Juan, is a favorite destination for happy hour. It hosts an annual gay-pride march each June, full of music and dancing, that rivals those in similar cities around the world. Santurce, just south of Condado, has several bars and clubs that cater to men and women of all ages. Most are located on or near Avenida Ponce de León. Stay alert, as parts of this neighborhood can be dangerous at night; consider taking a taxi to your destination rather than walking after dark.

**Atlantic Beach.** The oceanfront-deck bar of this hotel is famed in the gay community for its early-evening happy hours. But the pulsating tropical music, exotic drinks, and ever-pleasant ocean breeze would make it a hit in any case. Good food is also served on deck. ✉ *1 Calle Vendig, Condado* ☎ *787/721–6900.*

**Circo Bar.** Open every evening, this popular gay bar and club in Santurce offers different themed events every night, including karaoke, DJs, and dance parties. If you're coming from Condado, you might want to take a taxi even though it's not that far on foot: the area around the bar can be rough. Free, secured parking is available. ✉ *650 Calle Condado, Santurce* ☎ *787/727–9676* ⊕ *www. circobar.com.*

### REGGAETÓN

If you go out to San Juan's popular dance clubs, you're likely to hear this hip-hop–influenced mix of Jamaican reggae and dance-hall styles along with some Latin rhythms. The music has a strong electronic drum-machine beat, and the lyrics are in Spanish. Many believe the music got its start in Puerto Rico, but its popularity has spread much farther.

**Krash.** A balcony bar overlooks all the drama on the dance floor at this popular club. Most of the time DJs spin house, hip-hop, salsa, and *reggaetón*, but occasionally disco nights send you back to the music of the 1970s and '80s. It's open Wednesday through Saturday. ✉ *1257 Av. Ponce de León, Santurce* ☎ *787/722–1131* ⊕ *www.krashklubpr.com.*

## LATIN MUSIC

★ **Nuyorican Café.** There's something interesting happening at this hipper-than-hip, no-frills, wood-paneled performance space nearly every night, be it an early evening play, poetry reading, or talent show or, later on, a band playing Latin jazz, Cuban *son*, Puerto Rican salsa, or rock. During breaks between performances the youthful, creative crowd chats in an alley outside the front door. It's usually closed on Monday. ✉ *312 Calle San Fransico (entrance on Callejón de la Capilla), Old San Juan* ☎ *787/977–1276* ⊕ *www.nuyoricancafepr.com.*

## NIGHT BITES

San Juan is a cosmopolitan city by Caribbean standards, welcoming to all kinds of visitors, with plenty of late-night places. The establishments listed here are generally open until at least midnight during the week and 2 am on weekends. But many are open much later. Old San Juan's Brickhaus, for example, proudly proclaims that its kitchen doesn't close until 3 am.

**Bar Gitano.** One of the few late-night dining options in Condado, Bar Gitano keeps the tasty tapas and sangria flowing until around midnight during the week, later on weekends. ⇨ *See also Bar Gitano's entry under "Condado" in "Where to Eat."* ✉ *1309 Av. Ashford, C-1, Old San Juan* ☎ *787/294–5513.*

**Brickhaus Sports Bar & Grill.** This friendly bar and sidewalk café on Old San Juan's bustling Plaza Somohano is adjacent to the Teatro Tapia. You can get tasty burgers and wings until 3 am as well as plenty of good conversation. If you eat elsewhere, you might run into your server here, after his or her shift ends. ✉ *359 Calle Tetuán, Old San Juan* ☎ *787/723–1947* ⊕ *www.thebrickhaus.net.*

**El Patio de Sam.** The clientele swears that this Old San Juan institution serves the island's best burgers. Potted plants and strategically placed canopies make the outdoor patio overlooking Plaza San José a fine place to eat in any weather. ✉ *102 Calle San Sebastián, Old San Juan* ☎ *787/723–1149.*

**Señor Frog's.** Latin America's answer to the Hard Rock Cafe, Señor Frog's attracts both hard-partying tourists and the cruise-ship crowd—no surprise, as it's located directly in front of the dock. (Look for the giant inflatable frog.) The just-okay menu is a nod to Mexico, with south-of-the-border favorites like nachos and quesadillas. When it comes to drinks, expect quantity over quality; their signature is the Yard, a tall plastic cup filled with your favorite adult beverage. There's often live music, a ladies' night, or other special events. During the day, it's surprisingly kid-friendly; they make killer balloon animals. ✉ *Paseo Gilberto Concepción de Gracia, corner of Brumbaugh, Old San Juan* ☎ *787/977–4142* ⊕ *www.senorfrogs.com.*

★ **Pirilo.** Brand new in the old city, this diminutive pizza place is turning out some of the finest pizza to be had in San Juan. Owner Eduardo Rubio makes everything from scratch, most notably the pizza crust, which uses a 300-year-old starter as its base. You can have anything from a classic margherita pie to one based on the local *tripleta* sandwich. Given the nightly crowds, it's clear that others are in on the secret. It's always packed, but everyone is having such a good time, you won't mind, especially with more than 50 craft brews available. ✉ *Calles Fortaleza and Tanca, Old San Juan* ☎ *787/721–3322.*

## THE ARTS

San Juan is arguably one of the most important cultural centers of the Caribbean, both for its homegrown culture and the healthy influx of visiting artists that the local population supports. The city hosts the Puerto Rico Symphony Orchestra, the world-renowned Pablo Casals classical-music festival in winter, and an annual series of opera concerts. Many hit plays in New York and other large markets get produced locally, and there are often three or four other local theatrical productions taking place on any given weekend, many of them downright adventurous.

### ISLAND CULTURE

**Le Lo Lai.** The year-round festival called Le Lo Lai celebrates Puerto Rico's Taíno Indian, Spanish, and African heritage. Performances showcasing island music and folklore take place Tuesday and Sunday around Old San Juan. It's sponsored by the Puerto Rico Tourism Company. ☎ *787/721–2400* ⊕ *www.gotopuertorico.com.*

### PERFORMING ARTS

MAJOR EVENTS **The Casals Festival.** The Casals Festival has been bringing some of the most important figures in classical music to San Juan ever since Pablo Casals, the famous cellist, conductor, and composer, started the festival in 1957. Casals went on to direct it until his death in 1973. It has continued to serve as a vibrant stage for top-notch classical performers since then. Most of the shows are held at the Centro de Bellas Artes Luis A.

Ferré, but performances are also at the University of Puerto Rico and other venues. The festival takes place from mid-February through mid-March. Tickets are available at the box office of the Centro de Bellas Artes Luis A Ferré. ☎ *787/721–7727* ⊕ *www.festcasalspr.gobierno.pr.*

**Puerto Rico Heineken Jazzfest.** San Juan is a great place to hear jazz, particularly Latin jazz, and the annual Puerto Rico Heineken Jazzfest, which takes place in early June at the Tito Puente Amphitheater, is one of the best opportunities for it. Each year's festival is dedicated to a particular musician. Honorees have included Chick Corea, Mongo Santamaria, and Dizzy Gillespie. ☎ *866/994–0001, 787/294–0001* ⊕ *www. prheinekenjazz.com.*

TICKETS Two major outlets sell tickets for events throughout Puerto Rico.

**Ticket Center.** With ticket counters available in many of the malls on the island, Ticket Center is a convenient way to score seats to most large-scale events. ☎ *787/792–5000* ⊕ *www.tcpr.com.*

**Ticketpop** ☎ *866/994–0001, 787/294–0001* ⊕ *www.ticketpop.com.*

PERFORMANCE **Anfiteatro Tito Puente** (*Tito Puente Amphitheater*). Surrounded by lagoons VENUES and trees, the open-air theater hosts the annual Heineken Puerto Rico Jazzfest and other musical events. It's named after the late, great musician who is widely credited with bringing salsa to the rest of the world. ✉ *Av. Piñeiro and Expreso Luís A. Ferré, Hato Rey* ☎ *787/792–5000.*

**Centro de Bellas Artes Luis A. Ferré** (*Luis A. Ferré Center for the Performing Arts*). With four different theaters, the largest of which holds up to 1,900 people, this is the largest venue of its kind in the Caribbean. There's something going on nearly every night, from pop or jazz concerts to plays, operas, and ballets. It's also the home of the Puerto Rico Symphony Orchestra. ✉ *Av. Ponce de León, Parada 22½, Santurce* ☎ *787/724–4747, 787/620–4444* ⊕ *www.cba.gobierno.pr.*

**Coliseo de Puerto Rico José Miguel Agrelot.** Seating up to 18,000 people, this relatively new arena, affectionately known as "El Choliseo," is the top venue for international musical events on the island. Previous performers have included Ozzy Osbourne, Paul McCartney, Shakira, Plácido Domingo, and, of course, the hometown favorite, Ricky Martin. ✉ *50 Calle Arterial B, Hato Rey* ☎ *787/294–0001, 866/994–0001* ⊕ *www.coliseodepuertorico.com.*

**Coliseo Roberto Clemente.** The arena has become an important island venue for concerts and fairs in addition to its status as a sports facility. Rap, reggae, salsa, jazz, and pop musicians all play this venue, which holds 8,000 people. ✉ *500 Av. Roosevelt, across from Plaza las Américas, Hato Rey* ☎ *787/781–2586.*

**Fundación Nacional Para la Cultura Popular.** This multifaceted foundation hosts a variety of events, including Latin music and dance performances and classes. Check out the schedule online or call ahead to see what's on. ✉ *56 Calle Fortaleza, Old San Juan* ☎ *787/724–7165* ⊕ *www.PRpop.org.*

**Teatro Tapia.** Named for Puerto Rican playwright Alejandro Tapia y Rivera, the theater hosts traveling and locally produced theatrical and musical productions. Matinee performances with family entertainment are also held here, especially around the holidays. ⊠ *Calle Fortaleza, Plaza Colón, Old San Juan* ☏ *787/480–5004.*

GROUPS    **Orquesta Sinfónica de Puerto Rico** (*Puerto Rico Symphony Orchestra*). Under the direction of conductor Maximiano Valdés, the 80 members of this prominent orchestra perform a full 52-week season that includes classical-music concerts, operas, ballets, and popular-music performances. The orchestra plays most shows at Centro de Bellas Artes Luis A. Ferré, but it also gives outdoor concerts at museums and university campuses around the island, and it has an educational outreach program in island schools. Pablo Casals, the impetus for this group, helped create it in 1956. ☏ *787/721–7727* ⊕ *www.sinfonicapr. gobierno.pr.*

# SHOPPING

In Old San Juan, Calle Fortaleza and Calle San Francisco have everything from T-shirt emporiums to jewelry stores to shops that specialize in made-to-order Panama hats. Running perpendicular to those streets is Calle Cristo, lined with factory-outlet stores, including Coach, Gant, Guess, and Ralph Lauren. On weekends, artisans sell their wares at stalls around Paseo de la Princesa.

With many stores selling luxury items and designer fashions, the shopping spirit in Condado is reminiscent of that in Miami. Avenida Ashford is considered the heart of San Juan's fashion district. High-end chain stores such as Louis Vuitton, Ferragamo, and Gucci are huddled together in what was formerly a derelict shopping strip. They are betting that the newly renovated, luxury hotel La Concha will attract people ready to plunk down their platinum credit cards. A little farther west along Avenida Ashford are the one-of-a-kind clothing retailers that make this a not-to-be-missed neighborhood.

Just as in most other American cities, however, the real shopping occurs in the mall, and the upscale mall here, Plaza Las Américas—the largest in the Caribbean—is not to be missed. Known to locals simply as "Plaza," it's often host to artisan crafts fairs, art exhibitions, antiques shows, live Latin music, and pageants, depending on the time of year.

Thanks to Puerto Rico's vibrant art scene, numerous galleries and studios are opening, and many are doing so in Santurce and other neighborhoods outside the Old City walls. If you prefer shopping in air-conditioned comfort, there are plenty of malls in and just outside San Juan.

## MARKETS AND MALLS

★    **Artesanía Puertorriqueña.** On weekends or when cruise ships are in port, look for vendors selling crafts from around the island at the Artesanía Puertorriqueña, just across from Pier 1. Several vendors also sell handbags, hats, and other items along nearby Paseo de la Princesa. ⊠ *Plaza de la Dársena, Old San Juan* ☏ *787/722–1709.*

★ **Plaza Las Américas.** For a complete shopping experience, head to the massive Plaza Las Américas, which has more than 300 retailers, including the world's largest JCPenney store, Build-A-Bear Workshop, Carolina Herrera, Gap, Sears, Macy's, Sephora, Coach, Forever 21, L'Occitane, and Armani Exchange, as well as multiple restaurants and movie theaters. ⊠ *525 Av. Franklin Delano Roosevelt, Hato Rey* ☎ *787/767–1525* ⊕ *www.plazalasamericas.com.*

## FACTORY OUTLETS

Old San Juan has turned into an open-air duty-free shop for people pouring off the cruise ships. Because they have only a few hours in port, they often pass by more interesting shops and head directly for the factory outlets on and around Calle Cristo. The prices aren't particularly good, but nobody seems to mind.

★ **Belz Factory Outlet World.** Belz Factory Outlet World has more than 135 factory outlet stores, including BCBG, Nautica, Nike, Guess, Gap, and Polo Ralph Lauren. It's in Canóvanas, about 20 minutes east of San Juan. ⊠ *18400 Rte. 3, Km 18.4* ☎ *787/256–7040.*

**Coach.** Stylish, upscale handbags can be purchased at Coach. ⊠ *158 Calle Cristo* ☎ *787/722–6830.*

★ **Puerto Rico Premium Outlets.** About an hour west of San Juan in quiet Barceloneta, Puerto Rico Premium Outlets has around 90 stores, including Banana Republic, Michael Kors, Perry Ellis, Carter's, and Ann Taylor, as well as a movie theater. If you get hungry, the best spot for lunch is the local branch of the tasty Cuban–Puerto Rican restaurant Metropol, which is right across from the outlets. ⊠ *1 Premium Outlets Boulevard, Barceloneta* ☎ *787/846–5300.*

**Ralph Lauren.** Taking up several storefronts, Ralph Lauren has perhaps the best deals around. Stop here toward the end of your trip, as there are plenty of items (e.g., pea coats and scarves) that you won't be wearing until you get home. At this writing, the store was planning to relocate to a space across from Pier 1. ⊠ *Calle Cristo and Calle Fortaleza* ☎ *787/722–2136.*

**Tommy Hilfiger.** There's clothing for men and women at Tommy Hilfiger. The staff is eager to please. ⊠ *206 Calle Cristo* ☎ *787/729–2230.*

## SPECIALTY SHOPS

### ART

★ **Galería Botello.** The very influential Galería Botello displays the works of the late Angel Botelli, who was hailed as the "Caribbean Gauguin" as far back as 1943. His work, which often uses the bright colors of the tropics, usually depicts island scenes. His paintings hang in the Museo de Arte de Puerto Rico. There are works on display here by other prominent local artists as well. ⊠ *208 Calle Cristo, Old San Juan* ☎ *787/723–9987* ⊕ *www.botello.com.*

**Galería San Juan.** Galería San Juan shows sensuous sculptures of faces and bodies by artist Jan D'Esopo. The gallery—a part of the guesthouse

San Juan shopping options include Plaza las Américas, the largest mall in the Caribbean.

she runs—is a work of art in itself. It is a bit hard to find, so look for the busts over the front door. ✉ *204–206 Calle Norzagaray, Old San Juan* ☎ *787/722–1808.*

**Galería Viota.** Galería Viota offers regularly changing works by contemporary Latin American artists. ✉ *793 Av. San Patricio, Las Lomas* ☎ *787/782–1752* ⊕ *www.viotagallery.com.*

## CIGARS

**Cigar House.** The Cigar House has an eclectic selection of local and imported cigars. There's now a lounge and bar, so that you can enjoy your purchase with a glass of your favorite spirits. ✉ *255–257 Calle Fortaleza, Old San Juan* ☎ *787/723–5223* ⊕ *www.thecigarhousepr.com.*

## CLOTHING

MEN'S CLOTHING **Clubman.** With many years spent catering to a primarily local clientele, Clubman remains the classic choice for gentlemen's clothing. ✉ *263 Calle Fortaleza, Old San Juan* ☎ *787/724–5631.*

**El Galpón.** At El Galpón, knowledgeable owners Betsy and Gustavo will fit you with a Panama hat, from $65 to $900. You'll also learn that a genuine Panama hat is made in Ecuador. ✉ *154 Calle Cristo, Old San Juan* ☎ *787/725–3945* ⊕ *www.elgalpon.net.*

**Monsieur.** Sylish casual clothing is what's on offer at Monsieur. ✉ *1126 Av. Ashford, Condado* ☎ *787/722–0918* ⊕ *www.monsieurpuertorico. com.*

**Olé.** Aficionados of the famous Panama hat, made from delicately handwoven straw, should stop at Olé. The shop sells top-of-the-line hats for as much as $1,000. ✉ *105 Calle Fortaleza, Old San Juan* ☎ *787/724–2445.*

**Otto.** In his shop, Otto Bauzá stocks international lines of casual and formal wear for younger men. ✉ *69 Av. Condado, Condado* ☎ *787/722–4609.*

MEN'S AND WOMEN'S CLOTHING

**Abitto.** Hipper than most other Condado boutiques, Abitto carries John Galliano, Alexander McQueen, Roberto Cavalli, and others. ✉ *1124 Av. Ashford, Condado* ☎ *787/724–0303.*

**David Antonio.** Prolific designer David Antonio runs a shop that's small but full of surprises. His joyful creations range from updated versions of the men's classic guayabera to fluid chiffon and silk tunics and dresses for women. ✉ *69 Av. Condado, Condado* ☎ *787/725–0600.*

★ **Nono Maldonado.** Nono Maldonado is well known for his high-end, elegant clothes for men and women, particularly those done in linen. He should know a thing or two about style—he worked for many years as the fashion editor of *Esquire* and presents a periodic couture collection. This second-floor store also serves as the designer's studio. ✉ *1112 Av. Ashford, 2nd floor, Condado* ☎ *787/721–0456.*

WOMEN'S CLOTHING

**Ambar.** Garments by Cambodian-French designer Romyda Keth, whose use of exotic colors and sensuous fabrics meshes perfectly with Puerto Rico's tropical environment, are in the spotlight at Ambar. The store carries only one of each design (of which only eight to ten exist world-wide), ensuring that you're the only one on the entire island who will ever be wearing a particular look. ✉ *69 Av. Condado, Condado* ☎ *787/203–7049.*

★ **Cappalli.** Noted local designer Lisa Cappalli sells her lacy, sensuous designs in this boutique, which specializes in ready-to-wear and custom fashions. ✉ *207 Calle O'Donnell, Old San Juan* ☎ *787/289–6565* ⊕ *www.lisacappalli.net.*

★ **Concalma.** Designer Matilsha Marxuach, who has an eye toward sustainable fashion, has her hip line of fair-trade handbags, messenger bags, and other items made by a local women's cooperative. ✉ *207 Calle San Francisco, Condado* ☎ *787/729–0800* ⊕ *www.concalmalinea.com.*

**E'Leonor.** Head to E'Leonor for bridal apparel, evening gowns, and cocktail dresses as well as more casual attire. There are designs on offer by Missoni, Badgley Mischka, Vera Wang, and St. John. ✉ *1310 Av. Ashford, Condado* ☎ *787/725–3208.*

**Harry Robles.** Head here for the Puerto Rican designer's elegant custom gowns. ✉ *1752 Calle Loíza, Ocean Park* ☎ *787/727–3885.*

**Marella.** This recently opened boutique sells apparel from labels that include Halston Heritage, Diane von Furstenberg, Young Fabulous & Broke, Ramona LaRue, and Alexis. ✉ *1300 Av. Ashford, Condado* ☎ *787/722–0010.*

**Mia.** Mia is the place for youthful, sophisticated outfits that look as if they belong in an art gallery—either on display or on one of the artists. ✉ *1112 Av. Ashford, Condado* ☎ *787/721–5808.*

**Nativa.** The window displays at Nativa are almost as daring as the clothes it sells. ✉ *55 Calle Cervantes, Condado* ☎ *787/724–1396.*

**Piña Colada Club.** A great place to scout out casual resort wear, cover-ups, swimwear, and tropical-inspired jewelry, Piña Colada Club carries its own clothing line, as well as those of Karina Grimaldi, Indah, Maaji, and others. ✉ *1102 Av. Magdalena, Condado* ☎ *787/998–1980.*

**Suola.** As you might expect at a shop named after the Italian word for "sole," the boot-shaped country is the origin of most of the mile-high heels here, which include designs by Alexander McQueen, Christian Louboutin, YSL, and Sergio Rossi. ✉ *1060 Av. Ashford, Condado* ☎☎ *787/723–6653.*

### FURNITURE AND ANTIQUES

★ **El Alcázar.** For nearly three decades, Robert and Sharon Bartos have been selling antiques and objets d'art from all over the world. ✉ *103 Calle San José, Old San Juan* ☎ *787/723–1229* ⊕ *www.elalcazar.com.*

### GIFTS

**Butterfly People.** Exotic *mariposas* cover the walls of Butterfly People. Clear plastic cases hold everything from a pair of common butterflies to dozens of rarer specimens in this serene and lovely shop. The butterflies are gathered only from certified farms once they complete their life spans. ✉ *257 Calle de la Cruz, Old San Juan* ☎ *787/723–2432* ⊕ *www.butterflypeople.com.*

**Spicy Caribbee.** Kitchen items, cookbooks, and many spices and sauces from around the Caribbean are on offer at Spicy Caribbee. ✉ *154 Calle Cristo, Old San Juan* ☎ *888/725–7259* ⊕ *www.spicycaribbee.com.*

### HANDICRAFTS

**Haitian Gallery.** The Haitian Gallery carries Puerto Rican crafts as well as folksy, often inexpensive paintings from around the Caribbean. ✉ *206 Calle Fortaleza, Old San Juan* ☎ *787/721–4362* ⊕ *www.haitiangallerypr.com* ✉ *367 Calle Fortaleza, Old San Juan* ☎ *787/725–0986* ⊕ *www.haitiangallerypr.com.*

**Magia.** The clever shop Magia carries what appear to be traditional crafts, but look more closely. The works, most of which are done by artist-owner Manolo Díaz, are all a bit off. A little wooden shrine, for example, might be sheltering an image of Marilyn Monroe. You can also find vintage costume jewelry. ✉ *99 Calle Cristo, Old San Juan* ☎ *787/368–6164.*

**Mi Pequeño San Juan.** You might manage to find the hotel where you're staying reproduced in plaster at this shop, which specializes in tiny ceramic versions of San Juan doorways. The works, all created by hand right in the shop, make a wonderful souvenir. ✉ *152 Calle Fortaleza, Old San Juan* ☎ *787/977–1636, 787/721–5040* ⊕ *www.mipequenosanjuan.com.*

★ **Mundo Taíno.** Near Old San Juan's main square, Mundo Taíno sells high-quality folk art from around the island. ✉ *151 San José, Old San Juan* ☎ *787/724–2005.*

## CLOSE UP

# Design Lions

Puerto Rico's young fashion designers have opened many a boutique and atelier in metropolitan San Juan during the last few years. Their styles may differ, but these young lions all share an island heritage—complete with a tradition of true craftsmanship—and a level of sophistication acquired after studying and traveling abroad. The result is a fascinating assortment of original, exclusive, high-quality designs.

With all the warmth and sun, it goes without saying that Puerto Rico's designers are most inspired when it comes to creations for the spring and summer seasons. Lacy, flowing creations and lightweight, if not sheer, fabrics dominate designs for women. For men the trend is toward updated linen classics in tropical whites and creams. Whatever you find will be one of a kind, with stylish—if not playful or downright sexy—lines. Some of these designers have their own shops in San Juan.

Which designers should you check out? Lisa Cappalli, a graduate of New York City's Parsons School of Design, favors lace, as lace making is a tradition in her family. David Antonio uses upbeat colors—bold reds and vibrant oranges—in his updated classics. Harry Robles is a bit more established than his peers; he specializes in gowns for women, and his draping designs are often dramatic and always elegant. Each of these young designers has a shop in San Juan.

To see their collections, consider visiting during San Juan Fashion Week, which takes place each year in March and September. The events are full of shows and cocktail parties, all organized by the Puerto Rico Fashion Designers Group under the leadership of island-fashion icons Nono Maldonado and Mirtha Rubio.

—Isabel Abislaimán

**Puerto Rican Arts & Crafts.** For one-of-a-kind *santos*, art, and festival masks, head for Puerto Rican Arts & Crafts. ⊠ *204 Calle Fortaleza, Old San Juan* ☎ *787/725–5596* ⊕ *www.puertoricanart-crafts.com.*

## JEWELRY

**Bared.** For a good selection of watches and jewelry, visit Bared. Look for the massive clock face on the corner. ⊠ *206 San Justo, Old San Juan* ☎ *787/724–4811.*

**Club Jibarito.** Club Jibarito has a fantastic collection of high-end watches by Audemars Piguet, Panerai, Jaeger-LeCoultre, and other designers. ⊠ *202 Calle Cristo, Old San Juan* ☎ *787/724–7797* ⊕ *www. clubjibarito.com.*

**Cristobal.** Cristobal sells glittery pieces in gold and silver that appeal to those with modern tastes. ⊠ *Plaza Ventana al Mar, 1049 Av. Ashford, Condado* ☎ *787/721–8385.*

**Joyería Cátala.** The oldest jewelry store in San Juan, Joyería Cátala is known for its large selection of necklaces made with pearls and semiprecious stones. ⊠ *Plaza de Armas, 152 Calle Rafael Cordero, Old San Juan* ☎ *787/722–3231.*

**N. Barquet Joyero.** N. Barquet Joyero, one of the bigger jewelry stores in Old San Juan, carries Carrera y Carrera, Nanis, and other brands, as well as crystal and watches. Their *coquí* (frog) charms make a nice souvenir. ✉ *201 Calle Fortaleza, Old San Juan* ☎ 787/721–3366 ⊕ *www. nbarquet.com.*

**Portofino.** Portofino has an especially good selection of watches. ✉ *250 Calle San Francisco, Old San Juan* ☎ 787/723–5113.

**Reinhold Jewelers.** Reinhold Jewelers sells designs by Stephen Dweck, David Yurman, and others. ✉ *Plaza Las Américas, 525 Av. Franklin Delano Roosevelt, Hato Rey* ☎ 787/754–0528 ⊕ *www.reinholdjewelers. com* ✉ *El San Juan Hotel & Casino, 6063 Av. Isla Verde, Isla Verde* ☎ 787/791–2521.

# SPORTS AND THE OUTDOORS

Many of San Juan's most enjoyable outdoor activities take place in and around the water. With miles of beach stretching across Isla Verde, Ocean Park, and Condado, there's a full range of water sports, including sailing, kayaking, windsurfing, paddleboarding, kiteboarding, Jet Skiing, deep-sea fishing, scuba diving, and snorkeling.

Land-based activities include biking, tennis, and walking or jogging at local parks. With a bit of effort—meaning a short drive out of the city—you'll discover a world of championship golf courses and rainforest trails perfect for hiking. Baseball is big in Puerto Rico, and the players are world-class; many are recruited from local teams to play in the U.S. major leagues. The season runs from October through February. Games are played in venues around the island.

**Coliseo de Puerto Rico José Miguel Agrelot.** Although primarily a place for music performances and similar cultural events, "El Choliseo" is also used for sporting events from time to time. ✉ *50 Calle Arterial B, across from Plaza las Américas, Hato Rey* ☎ 787/294–0001, 866/994–0001 ⊕ *www.coliseodepuertorico.com.*

## BASEBALL

Does the name Roberto Clemente ring a bell? The late, great star of the Pittsburgh Pirates, who died in a 1972 plane crash delivering supplies to Nicaraguan earthquake victims, was born near San Juan and got his start in the Puerto Rican pro leagues. Many other Puerto Rican stars have played in the U.S. major leagues, including the brothers Roberto Alomar and Sandy Alomar Jr.; and their father, Sandy Alomar. Three players have been inducted into the National Baseball Hall of Fame: Clemente, Roberto Alomar, and Orlando Cepeda.

## BIKING

Most streets don't have bike lanes, and auto traffic makes bike travel somewhat risky; further, all the fumes can be hard to take. That said, recreational bikers are increasingly donning their safety gear and wheeling through the streets, albeit with great care.

San Juan's well-equipped balnearios (public beaches) are among the best on the island.

Your best bet is to look into a bike tour offered by an outfitter. One popular 45-minute trip travels from Old San Juan's cobblestone streets to Condado. It passes El Capitolio and runs through either Parque del Tercer Milenio (oceanside) or Parque Luis Muñoz Rivera, taking you past the Caribe Hilton Hotel and over Puente Dos Hermanos (Dos Hermanos Bridge) onto Avenida Ashford. The truly ambitious can continue east to Ocean Park, Isla Verde, and right on out of town to the eastern community of Piñones and its beachside bike path.

**Rent the Bicycle.** For about $30 a day, this friendly operation offers bicycle rental with free delivery to all major San Juan hotels, in addition to guided tours of Old San Juan, greater San Juan beaches and parks, and Piñones. The bilingual guides are authorized by the National Park Service to give tours of the forts. ⊠ *Pier 6, corner of Av. Fernández Juncos, Old San Juan* ☎ *787/602–9696* ⊕ *www.rentthebicycle.net.*

## DIVING AND SNORKELING

The waters off San Juan aren't the best places to scuba dive, but several outfitters conduct short excursions to where tropical fish, coral, and sea horses are visible at depths of 30 to 60 feet. Escorted half-day dives start around $70 for one or two tanks, including all equipment; in general, double those prices for night dives. Packages that include lunch and other extras start at $100; those that include accommodations are also available.

Snorkeling excursions, which include transportation, equipment rental, and sometimes lunch, start at $55–$60. Equipment rents at beaches for about $10. Avoid unsupervised areas, as rough waters and strong undertows make some places dangerous.

**Eco Action Tours.** Eco Action Tours offers diving trips for all skill levels. ✉ *1035 Av. Ashford, Condado* ☎ *787/791–7509* ⊕ *www. ecoactiontours.com.*

**Ocean Sports.** Ocean Sports offers certified scuba courses; snorkeling excursions; specialty courses in nitrox diving; diving trips; airtank fill-ups; and equipment repairs, sales, and rentals. ✉ *77 Av. Isla Verde, Isla Verde* ☎ *787/723–8513* ⊕ *www.osdivers.com.*

## FISHING

Puerto Rico's waters are home to large game fish such as snook, wahoo, dorado, tuna, and barracuda; as many as 30 world records for catches have been set off the island's shores. Prices for fishing expeditions vary, but they tend to include all your bait and tackle, as well as refreshments, and start at $600 (for a boat with as many as six people) for a half-day trip to around $1,000 for a full day, or around $200 per person for a full day on a split charter.

**Mike Benítez Sport Fishing.** Half-day and full-day excursions as well as split charters can be arranged through Mike Benítez Sport Fishing. From the 45-foot *Sea Born* you can fish for yellowfin tuna, mahimahi, white marlin, blue marlin, and others. ✉ *Club Náutico de San Juan, 480 Av. Fernández Juncos, Puerta de Tierra* ☎ *787/723–2292* ⊕ *www. mikebenitezsportfishing.com.*

## GOLF

Puerto Rico is the birthplace of golf legend and raconteur Chi Chi Rodriguez—and he had to hone his craft somewhere. The island has more than a dozen courses, including some of championship caliber. Several make good day trips from San Juan. Be sure to call ahead for details on reserving tee times; hours vary, and several hotel courses allow only guests to play or give preference to them. Greens fees start at $25 and go as high as $190.

Three golf clubs are within fairly easy striking distance of San Juan. The four 18-hole golf courses at the **Hyatt Hacienda del Mar** are just west of San Juan. *For more information, see "Golf" under "Dorado" in Chapter 6, Rincón and the Porta del Sol.*

There are more options to the east of the city. **Palmas del Mar Country Club** has two good golf courses. *For more information see "Golf" under "Humacao" in Chapter 2, El Yunque and the Northeast.* The spectacular **Rio Mar Beach Resort & Spa** has a clubhouse with a pro shop and two restaurants set between two 18-hole courses. *For more information, see "Golf" under "Río Grande" in Chapter 3, El Yunque and the Northeast.*

# HIKING

El Yunque is the only tropical rain forest within the U.S. National Forest System. The park is officially known as the Bosque Nacional del Caribe (Caribbean National Forest) and is a great day trip from San Juan, about an hour's drive east. *(For more information, see Chapter 3.)*

**Eco Action Tours.** Eco Action Tours organizes a variety of hikes and excursions throughout the island, including in El Yunque. ⊠ *1035 Av. Ashford, Condado* ☎ *787/791–7509* ⊕ *www.ecoactiontours.com.*

# HORSE RACING

**Hípodromo Camarero.** Try your luck with the exactas and quinielas at Hípodromo Camarero, a large Thoroughbred racetrack about 20 minutes east of San Juan. On race days the dining rooms open at 12:30 pm. Post time is at 2:30 pm every day except Tuesday and Thursday. There's an air-conditioned clubhouse and restaurant, as well as a bar where people occasionally dance to live rumba music. Parking and admission to the grandstand and clubhouse are free. ⊠ *Rte. 3, Km 15.3, Canóvanas* ☎ *787/641–6060* ⊕ *www.hipodromo-camarero.com.*

# KAYAKING

The Laguna del Condado is popular for kayaking, especially on weekends. You can simply paddle around it or head out under the Puente Dos Hermanos to the San Gerónimo fort right behind the Caribe Hilton and across from the Conrad San Juan Condado Plaza. Kayaks rent for $25–$35 an hour.

**Iguana Sports.** Iguana Sports rents paddleboards and kayaks for those who want to explore San Juan's peaceful Laguna del Condado. Prices start at $35 per hour. ⊠ *999 Ave. Ashford, Condado Plaza, Conrad* ☎ *787/721–1000.*

# SURFING

★ *See also "Surfing Puerto Rico" feature in Chapter 6.* Although the west-coast beaches around Isabela and Rincón are considered *the* places to surf in Puerto Rico, San Juan was actually the place where the sport got its start on the island. In 1958 legendary surfers Gary Hoyt and José Rodríguez Reyes began surfing at the beach in front of Bus Stop 2½, facing El Capitolio. Although this spot is known for its big waves, the conditions must be nearly perfect to surf here. Today many surfers head to Puerta de Tierra and a spot known as La Ocho (in front of Bus Stop 8). Another, called the Pressure Point, is behind the Caribe Hilton Hotel.

In Condado you can surf La Punta, a reef break behind the Presbyterian Hospital, with either surfboards or Boogie boards. In Isla Verde, white water on the horizon means that the waves are good at Pine Grove, the beach break near the Ritz-Carlton. East of the city, in Piñones, the Caballo has deep-to-shallow-water shelf waves that require a big-wave board known as a "gun." The surf culture frowns upon aficionados who divulge the best spots to outsiders. If you're lucky, though, maybe you'll make a few friends who'll let you in on where to find the best waves.

**Tres Palmas Surf Shop.** At Ocean Park beach, famous surfer Carlos Cabrero, proprietor of Tres Palmas Surf Shop, rents boards (daily rates are $25 for Boogie boards, $30 for short boards, $35 for foam boards, and $40 for long boards), repairs equipment, and sells all sorts of hip beach and surfing gear. ⊠ *1911 Av. McLeary, Ocean Park* ☎ *787/728–3377.*

## TENNIS

If you'd like to use the tennis courts at a property where you aren't a guest, call in advance for information about reservations and fees.

**Club Tennis de Isla Verde.** The four lighted courts of the Club Tennis de Isla Verde are open for nonmember use at $15 per hour for up to four people, daily from 8 am to 10 pm. Reservations are required. ⊠ *Calles Ema and Delta Rodriguez, Isla Verde* ☎ *787/727–6490, 787/642–3208.*

## WINDSURFING AND PADDLEBOARDING

★ The waves can be strong and the surf choppy, but the constant wind makes for good sailing, windsurfing, or paddleboarding, particularly in Ocean Park and Punta Las Marías (between Ocean Park and Isla Verde). In general, you can rent a Windsurfer for about $75 an hour, including a lesson.

**Velauno.** You'll get the best paddleboarding and windsurfing advice and equipment from Jaime Torres at Velauno, a sort of clearinghouse for information on water-sports events throughout the island. The store also sells surfboards and kites and offers repair services and classes. ⊠ *2430 Calle Loíza, Punta Las Marías* ☎ *787/728–8716* ⊕ *www.velaunopaddleboarding.com.*

## YOGA

★ **It's Yoga Puerto Rico.** Husband-and-wife team David Kyle and Elizabeth Sallaberry found the hot, humid climate of Puerto Rico perfect for practicing and teaching ashtanga vinyasa yoga, one of the more vigorous forms of yoga. Their friendly studio, which has a large local following, offers classes ranging from beginner to advanced (most are held in English) as well as workshops from internationally renowned instructors. Be prepared to sweat, as the studio is intentionally not air-conditioned, though there are ceiling fans. The rate is around $17 for a drop-in class, which includes mat rental. ⊠ *1950 Av. McLeary, Ocean Park* ☎ *787/677–7585* ⊕ *www.itsyogapuertorico.com.*

# El Yunque and the Northeast

**WORD OF MOUTH**

"We went to the rain forest, spent about half a day there. Just drove from Luquillo, went to the visitors center and did a couple shorter hikes (one to a waterfall, another that led uphill to an old tower). Both were nice and gave a good taste of the rainforest. The waterfall hike was in the forest the whole time, the other one partly along a road and once at the top gave great views of the forest."

—WhereAreWe

# WELCOME TO EL YUNQUE AND THE NORTHEAST

## TOP REASONS TO GO

★ **Take a hike:** Take in the spectacular waterfalls of El Yunque, the only rain forest within the U.S. National Forest system.

★ **Take a dip:** Relax at the Balneario de Luquillo, one of the prettiest beaches in Puerto Rico and a family favorite.

★ **Take a seat:** Hang with locals at one of the dozens of outdoor seafood shacks on the highway before you get to the Balneario de Luquillo. There are at least 60 to choose from.

★ **Hit the links:** Tee off at the tree-lined fairways of the area's many excellent golf courses, especially those at the St. Regis Bahia Beach and Palmas del Mar resorts.

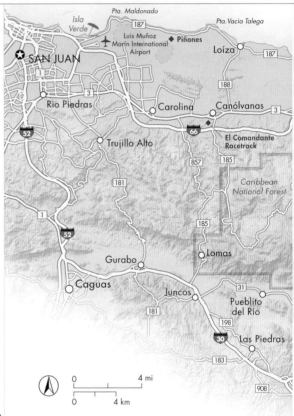

**1 The Northeastern Coast.** Head southeast and inland of San Juan to escape the city crowds and discover Río Grande's natural green land and its long strips of pristine beach. Its closest neighbor is the region's magnificent natural wonder, El Yunque, a park you can explore in the air-conditioned comfort of a car in a few hours or hike for days and still not see all the greenery, waterfalls, and views. Nearby, Balneario de Luquillo (Luquillo Beach), Reserva Natural Las Cabezas de San Juan, and Fajardo are all worth exploring.

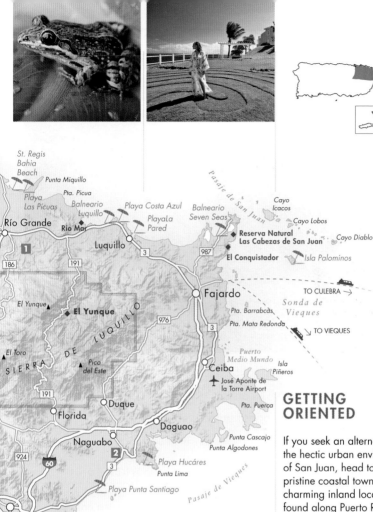

**3**

St. Regis
Bahia
Beach
Punta Miquillo
Pta. Picua
Playa
Las Pícuas
Balneario
Luquillo
Playa Costa Azul
Balneario
Seven Seas
Cayo
Icacos
Cayo Lobos
Río Grande
Rio Mar
Playa La
Pared
Reserva Natural
Las Cabezas de San Juan
Cayo Diablo
Pasaje de San Juan
Luquillo
El Conquistador
Isla Palominos
186
191
3
987
Fajardo
TO CULEBRA →
El Yunque
El Yunque
976
Pta. Barrabás
Sonda de
Vieques
Pta. Mata Redonda
3
TO VIEQUES
El Toro
DE
LUQUILLO
Pico
del Este
Puerto
Medio Mundo
Ceiba
Isla
Piñeros
SIERRA
José Aponte de
la Torre Airport
191
Duque
Pta. Puerca
Florida
Daguao
Punta Cascajo
Naguabo
Punta Algodones
924
60
3
Playa Hucáres
Punta Lima
Playa Punta Santiago
pasaje de Vieques
Humacao
Palmas del Mar

**2 The Eastern Coast.**
Puerto Rico's eastern coast
is home to some of the
island's most popular attractions. Be sure to check out
the beautiful beaches and
crystal-clear snorkeling
conditions of Fajardo before
heading south to Naguabo.
Naguabo is said to be the

birthplace of the *pastelillo
de chapín*, a popular dish
that consists of trunkfish
wrapped inside a deep-
fried flour dough. Farther
south and west, travelers
will stumble upon Humacao,
home of the island's largest
resort, Palmas del Mar.

## GETTING ORIENTED

If you seek an alternative to
the hectic urban environs
of San Juan, head to the
pristine coastal towns and
charming inland locales
found along Puerto Rico's
northeast corridor. Easily
reached by car, El Yunque
and northeast Puerto Rico
are convenient enough for
a quick day trip but beg
exploration of at least two
days. Kayak the lagoon
in Piñones, take a surf les-
son in Luquillo, sunbathe
at Seven Seas Beach in
Fajardo, horseback ride in
the foothills of El Yunque—
the list of exciting and/or
relaxing activities in this
region goes on and on.

# EL YUNQUE NATIONAL FOREST

The more than 100 billion gallons of precipitation that El Yunque receives annually, spawn rushing streams and cascades, outsize impatiens and ferns, and 240 tree species. In the evening millions of inch-long *coquís* (tree frogs) begin their calls. El Yunque is also home to the *cotorra*, Puerto Rico's endangered green parrot, as well as 67 other types of birds.

El Toro Mountain rises more than 3,500 ft (1,070 m), and on a clear day the view from the peak extends to the Atlantic Ocean.

El Yunque is the only tropical rain forest in the U.S. National Forest System, spanning 28,000 acres, reaching an elevation of more than 3,500 ft. and receiving an estimated average of 200–240 inches of rain each year. The forest's 13 hiking trails are extremely well maintained; many of them are easy to navigate and less than 1 mile (1.6 km) long. If you prefer to see the sights from a car, as many people do, simply follow Route 191 as it winds into the mountains and stop at several observation points along the way.

## WHEN TO GO

It's about 73°F year-round, so weather isn't much of a factor for seasonal planning. For easy parking and fewer crowds, be sure to arrive early in the day, although the park rarely gets crowded by U.S. National Park standards. Expect rain nearly every day, but keep eyes peeled post-showers for the best bird-watching.

## PARK HIGHLIGHTS

### FLORA AND FAUNA

Each year more than a million visitors from all over the world come to El Yunque to experience the rain forest's ecological treasures. Rivers and streams provide aquatic habitats for freshwater snails, shrimp, and crabs, while approximately 66 species of migratory birds either winter in or pass through El Yunque. Sonorous *coqui* frogs (endemic tree frogs found only in Puerto Rico), 14 different lizard species, and more than 1,200 insect species ranging from ants to beetles to flies all inhabit the forest.

Four major forest types, roughly stratified by elevation, are home to thousands of native plants including 150 fern species, 240 tree species (88 of these are endemic or rare and 23 are exclusively found in this forest). Two of the islands highest peaks rise out of the forest: El Toro and El Yunque, both more than 3,500 ft (1,070 m).

El Yunque doesn't have bigger wildlife species like monkeys, large cats, and poisonous snakes, but there are hundreds of small creatures that find ecological niches. Many of these species exist nowhere else on the planet, such as the endangered Puerto Rican green parrot, Puerto Rican boa, and Puerto Rican Sharp-Shinned Hawk. If you're interested in bird-watching, pack your binoculars because Puerto Rican Tody, Puerto Rican Lizard Cuckoo, five species of hummingbirds, flycatchers and warblers are commonly spotted.

### VISITOR CENTER

Carve out some time to stop at the cathedral-like **El Portal Visitor Center** (⊠ *$4, Free for children under 15 and senior citizens*). Enter via an elevated walkway that transports visitors across the forest canopy, 60 feet above the ground. Signs identify and explain the birds, animals, and other treasures seen among the treetops.

**STAY THE NIGHT**

If you're thinking about a second day at El Yunque, book a room near the rain forest instead of schlepping back to San Juan. (There is no lodging available within the reserve.) The St. Regis Bahia Beach Resort and Gran Meliá Puerto Rico are both within a 10-minute drive in Río Grande, but the two cottages at Sue's Place in Barrios Sabana, above the town of Luquillo, cannot be beat (www.rainforestrental. com). For a taste of local flavor, visitors leaving the El Yunque area may want to consider stopping off at the *friquitines* (seafood kiosks) that line Route 3 west of the beach turnoff. Frequented by locals and visitors alike, the kiosks are open all day and serve everything from cold drinks to stuffed lobsters, plates of fried fish (head and tail attached) and fritters (usually codfish or corn) to bagels and lox or Spanish-style tapas.

**3**

## BEST ONE-DAY ITINERARY

Start at the **El Portal Rain Forest Center.** Drive about 2½ miles (2.4 km) to **La Coca Falls**—one of the best photo ops in the park. View it from your car or climb up slippery rocks to the base of the falls. Back in the car for about half a mile to **Torre Yokahú** (Yokahú Observation Tower), a lookout with vistas of 1,000-year-old trees, exotic flowers, and birds in flight. The tower has restrooms. Continue just beyond the halfway point to the **Area Pasadías Palma de Sierra.** Rangers here have information on closures, trail conditions, and daily activities. The Center and the next two parking lots, Caimitillo and Palo Colorado, have trailheads to both **El Yunque Summit** (about a half-day adventure) and **La Mina Falls.** Casual hikers should follow the moderate **Big Tree Trail** to reach the falls—about a half-hour hike. Bring a swimsuit for the falls and water shoes or sandals to navigate the slippery rocks. More advanced hikers can follow **La Mina Falls Trail.** It's only .7 miles (1.1 km) long, but climbs to 2,132 ft. Plan 30–45 minutes each way. A little more than a mile up the road is one more trail, **Baño de Oro.**

Below the walkway, find a ground-level nature trail with stunning views of the lower forest and coastal plain. Inside the Center interactive exhibits explain the El Yunque National Forest's history, topography, flora, and fauna. And watch *El Yunque: Journey into a Tropical Rain Forest.* The 15-minute film provides a greater understanding of the ecology, environment, and history of the El Yunque National Forest. The facility also has a well-stocked bookstore and gift shop filled with useful tools for exploring the park, like trail maps printed on recycled plastic paper. (Note: this is the only gift shop in El Yunque that takes credit cards, so plan accordingly.) On a sticky day, the air-conditioning, clean restrooms, and benches overlooking the forest make for a pleasant post-hike respite.

### CASCADA LA COCA
The first spectacular sight you're likely to see in El Yunque is **Cascada La Coca** (La Coca Falls), which plunges 85 feet down a flat sheet of solid rock. The waterfall is inches from the road, so it's visible from your car. The gate to the park, which opens at 7:30 am and closes at 6 pm, is just before the falls. ⊠ *Rte. 191, Km 8.1.*

## BEST WAYS TO EXPLORE

### HITTING THE TRAILS
The 13 official trails throughout El Yunque are quite civilized—paved, well marked, and easy for both beginners and children. The trails on the north side of El Yunque, the park's main tourist hub, tend toward folks with minimal or no hiking experience. There are several short trails (about ½ mile) that are completely paved. On the south side, expect fewer people and moderate to challenging hikes. These trails are not as well maintained as the marked trails found lower in the forest. Regardless of where you go, you'll be immersed in the

sounds, smells, and scenic landscape of the park. For avid outdoor adventurers, it's possible to hike between the north and south sides of El Yunque.

### DRIVING

A leisurely drive-thru may not be as immersive as a hike, but you'll still encounter beautiful waterfalls, hibiscus, banana and orchid plants, lizards, and the occasional vista over the forest and out to the Atlantic Ocean. The main and most direct route to El Yunque, Route 3, is a multilane highway dotted with places to stop for cold drinks and typical Puerto Rican snacks. Obey the speed limit, as rental cars are frequently pulled over. From the highway, hop onto Route 191, the only road through the preserve. When hurricanes and mud slides haven't caused portions of the road to be closed, you can drive straight from the entrance to Km 13, the base of Pico El Yunque. A stop at El Portal Visitor Center will teach you everything you need to know about your majestic surroundings. Make another quick stop to climb the winding stairs of Yokaho Tower for breathtaking views of the rain forest and the island. En route back, stop at El Bosque Encantado, a food *kiosko* with *empanadas*, cold coconut drinks and cliff's-edge views (located on Route 191, Km 7.2). Take note that drivers don't always recognize common road courtesies, such as slow cars to the right, stop signs, and signals.

### ZIPLINING

This adrenaline-fueled, half-day activity enables visitors to take a tree-to-tree canopy tour via a network of platforms, cables, and pulleys.

Step off a platform more than 80 feet in the sky and fly through the air as you take in bird's-eye views of the northern limit of El Yunque National Forest and El Yunque and Este peaks. For more information contact **Yunke Zipline Adventure** (⊕ *yunkezipline.wordpress. com* ☎ 787/242–3368) or **Rain Forest Zip Line Corp** (⊕ *rainforestzipline.com* ☎ 787/370–1010).

## FUN FACTS

The roots of the rain-forest trees do not grow very deep. They find food and water in dead plant parts, fallen tree trunks, and a very thin layer of surface soil.

El Yunque has had many names. President Theodore Roosevelt named it the Luquillo Forest Reserve in 1903, and President Franklin Roosevelt changed its name to the Caribbean National Forest. In 2007 the area officially became El Yunque National Forest.

**3**

## ECO-STAYS

Casa Cubuy Ecolodge is a bit remote, located above Naguabo on the south side of the rain forest, but it's worth the trek. Guests of the tranquil bed-and-breakfast are treated to the sound of nearby waterfalls and are within walking distance of the Cubuy and Icacaos Rivers and jungles of bamboo. Sunbathe on granite slabs and boulders or slip into a natural Jacuzzi. A short uphill trek from the house on a paved road takes you to the El Yunque National Forest recreational facility, where interpretive guides offer forest hikes. At night, the serenading of the *coquis* lulls weary travelers to sleep. The emphasis here is on unplugging—rooms are television- and phone-free—and soaking up nature. Environmentally friendly features of this property include recycled water, solar panels to heat water, composted garbage to fertilize the fruit trees, eco-smart light bulbs, and erosion-prevention techniques for trails.

# BEACHES OF THE NORTHEAST

The Atlantic east coast is edged with sandy, palm-lined shores that are occasionally cut by rugged stretches. Some of these beaches are quiet, isolated escapes. Others—such as Luquillo and Seven Seas near Fajardo—are jammed with water-loving families, especially on weekends and during the Easter holidays.

Playa Luquillo is one of seven beaches in Puerto Rico to be awarded a Blue Flag, a distinction that recognizes superior water quality and accessible facilities.

Known as "La Capital del Sol" (sun capital) and "La Riviera de Puerto Rico" (Puerto Rico's Riviera), Luquillo is beloved for its towering palm trees and shimmering sand. Its public beaches are among the nicest in the San Juan area, making it a popular stop on the coastal highway.

Fajardo has a vibrant boating community with many hotels and inns. Its marina is a prime launching point for day trips to Culebra and Vieques, while snorkelers revel in Fajardo's crystal-clear waters and at night its bioluminescent lagoons. In Piñones you can find solitary coastline. The surf here is strong, and swimming—especially in winter—can be dangerous at some beaches.

## DIVE IN

The waters off eastern Puerto Rico are probably the best for scuba diving and snorkeling and compare favorably to other Caribbean diving destinations. Operators will take you on dives to 65 feet. The east has a good mix of coral, as well as a large variety of marine life. Fine snorkeling and diving spots can be found offshore from Fajardo, and there are many uninhabited islets from which to dive just off the coast.

## PIÑONES

You'll find **Playa de Piñones** right in front of the cluster of food kiosks built by the government for resident cooks. A large barrier reef blocks the strong currents and serves as the foundation for the large bathing pools in front of a sandy beach. ⊠ *Route 187, Km 8.*

## LUQUILLO

★ **Fodor's Choice** Just off Route 3, gentle **Playa Luquillo** (or Balneario La Monserrate) is a magnet for families. It's one of Puerto Rico's distinguished Blue Flag beaches. Lined with colorful lifeguard stations and shaded by soaring palm trees, it's well equipped with restrooms, showers, guarded parking, food stands, picnic areas, and even cocktail kiosks. Lounge chairs and umbrellas are available to rent, as are kayaks and Jet Skis. Its most distinctive facility is the Mar Sin Barreras (Sea Without Barriers), a low-sloped ramp leading into the water that allows wheelchair users to take a dip. The beach is open daily. ⊠ *Off Rte. 3* 🏊 *$4 per car.*

**Playa La Pared**, literally "The Wall Beach," is a surfer haunt. Many local competitions are held here throughout the year, and several surfing shops are close by in case you need a wet suit or a wax for your board. The waves here are medium-range. It's very close to Playa Luquillo but has a separate entrance. There are no facilities. ⊠ *Off Rte. 3.*

## FAJARDO

A long stretch of powdery sand near the Reserva Natural Las Cabezas de San Juan, **Balneario Seven Seas** may turn out to be the best surprise of your trip. Facilities include picnic tables, changing areas, restrooms, and showers. Many restaurants are just outside the gates. Its calm, clear waters are perfect for swimming. Parking is $3. ⊠ *Rte. 987, Las Croabas.*

## HUMACAO

Right beside the Refugio de Vida Silvestre de Humacao, **Playa Punta Santiago** is a long shore with closely planted palm trees that are perfect for stringing up hammocks. There are changing facilities with showers and restrooms, food kiosks, and lifeguard stations. Parking is $3. ⊠ *Rte. 3, northeast of Humacao.*

## NAGUABO

**Playa Húcares.** Playa Húcares is *the* place to be. Though the strip is a little run-down, an authentic vibe permeates the casual outdoor eateries and funky little shops that vie with the water for your attention. Locals sell ice out of trucks, and the heavy base of reggaetón music beats from the windows of passing cars. Two Victorian-style houses anchor one end of the waterfront promenade; a dock with excursion boats anchors the other, and a red, green, and blue bridge connects both sides of the town. ⊠ *Off Rte. 3, south of Naguabo.*

Updated by
Marie Elena
Martinez

Tree frogs, rare parrots, and wild horses only start the list of northeastern Puerto Rico's offerings. The backdrops for encounters with an array of flora and fauna include the 28,000-acre El Yunque tropical rain forest, the seven eco-systems in the Reserva Natural Las Cabezas de San Juan, and Laguna Grande, where tiny sea creatures appear to light up the waters.

As the ocean bends around the northeastern coast, it laps onto beaches of soft sand and palm trees, crashes against high bluffs, and almost magically creates an amazing roster of ecosystems. Beautiful beaches at Luquillo are complemented by more rugged southeastern shores. Inland, green hills roll down toward plains that once held expanses of coconut trees, such as those still surrounding the town of Piñones, or sugarcane, as evidenced by the surviving plantations near Naguabo and Humacao.

The natural beauty and varied terrain continue in the area's other towns as well. Río Grande—which once attracted immigrants from Austria, Spain, and Italy—sits on the island's only navigable river. Naguabo overlooks what were once immense cane fields and Cayo Santiago, where the only residents are monkeys.

You can golf, ride horses, hike marked trails, and plunge into water sports throughout the region. In many places along the coast, green hills cascade down to the ocean. On the edge of the Atlantic, Fajardo serves as a jumping-off point for diving, fishing, and catamaran excursions. Luquillo is the site of a family beach so well equipped that there are even facilities enabling wheelchair users to enter the sea.

## EL YUNQUE AND THE NORTHEAST PLANNER

### WHEN TO GO

In general, the island's northeast coast—preferred by those seeking abandoned beaches and nature reserves rather than casinos and urban glitz—tends to be less in demand than San Juan. The exception is at

Easter and Christmas, when Luquillo and Fajardo become crowded with local sun worshippers, merrymakers, and campers. Island festivals also draw crowds, but planning a trip around one of them will give you a true sense of the region's culture. Be sure to make reservations well in advance if you're visiting during high season, which runs from December 15 through April 15.

## GETTING HERE AND AROUND
### AIR TRAVEL
Air Flamenco, Cape Air, and Vieques Air Link offer several daily flights between San Juan, Fajardo, Vieques, and Culebra. Trips to any of these destinations are between 10 and 20 minutes; the cost ranges from $60 one-way to $180 round-trip.

Information **Air Flamenco** ☏ 787/724–1818 ⊕ www.airflamenco.net. **Cape Air** ☏ 866/CAPE–AIR (227–7747) ⊕ www.capeair.net. **Vieques Air Link** ☏ 787/741–8331, 888/901–9247 ⊕ www.viequesairlink.com.

### BUS TRAVEL
*Públicos* (a cross between a privately owned taxi and a bus) travel between San Juan and Fajardo, stopping en route at the ferry terminal. The full journey can take up to four hours, depending on where you board, frequency of stops, traffic, and where you are dropped off. However, the fare is a huge bargain at about $6 (pay the driver as you board). To get to Fajardo, simply flag down a público anywhere along Route 3.

Within cities and towns, local buses pick up and discharge at marked stops and cost 35¢–50¢. Enter and pay (exact fare required) at the front and exit at the front or the back.

### CAR TRAVEL
Unless you are planning to hop directly onto a ferry to Vieques or Culebra, you should consider renting a car in eastern Puerto Rico. Even the destination resorts are fairly isolated, and you may appreciate the mobility if you want to get out and have a meal away from the resort or explore El Yunque or some of the great beaches. Rates start at about $40 a day, but it may be possible to rent directly from your lodging, so ask about packages.

From San Juan the east coast is accessible via Route 3, or Route 187 if you want to visit Loíza. At Fajardo the road intersects with Route 53, which continues down the coast. Route 3 also continues along the coast, but provides a more scenic, if slower, trip.

### TAXI TRAVEL
You can flag cabs down on the street, but it's faster and safer to have your hotel call one for you. Cabs are usually metered; make sure it's clear whether a flat rate or a meter will determine the fare. Instead of renting a car, consider taking a taxi to Fajardo. The cost from the San Juan area should be about $80 for up to five people.

**Humacao Taxi** ☏ 787/852–6880.

## ABOUT THE RESTAURANTS

Some restaurants carry the tourist board's *meson gastronómico* designation. Such establishments specialize in typical island food. The eastern region has both formal restaurants, where reservations are very necessary, and casual beach-side eateries, where you can walk in unannounced in beach attire and have a fine meal of fresh fish. Bills generally don't include service charges, so a 15% tip is customary and expected. Most restaurants are open for dinner from late afternoon until at least 10 pm.

## ABOUT THE HOTELS

The east coast has a wide variety of lodgings from small lodges in the mountains to large, lavish resorts along the coast. Also available are government-approved *paradores*. Often translated as "country inns," *paradores* offer affordable Puerto Rican hospitality and the cozy comforts of home outside of the San Juan metro area. These small, privately owned properties are usually quite picturesque and found throughout the island's interior and more remote coastal towns. If you wish to get away from it all with a neatly packaged trip, eastern Puerto Rico has some of the island's top resorts: the St. Regis Bahia Beach Resort and the El Conquistador Resort. You'll also find extensive facilities and services at large, self-contained complexes like the Wyndham Rio Mar and the Gran Meliá, making the list of regional offerings more than complete.

| WHAT IT COSTS IN DOLLARS | | | | | |
|---|---|---|---|---|---|
| | ¢ | $ | $$ | $$$ | $$$$ |
| Restaurants | under $8 | $8–$12 | $12–$20 | $20–$30 | over $30 |
| Hotels | under $80 | $80–$150 | $150–$250 | $250–$350 | over $350 |

Restaurant prices are based on the median main course price at dinner. Hotel prices are for a double room in high season, excluding 9% tax (11% for hotels with casinos, 7% for *paradores*) and 5%–12% service charge.

## PACKING FOR EL YUNQUE

When you come to El Yunque, bring binoculars, a camera (preferably with a good zoom function), bottled water, and sunscreen; wear a hat or visor, good walking shoes, and comfortable clothes. Although daytime temperatures rise as high as 80°F (27°C), wear long pants, because some plants can cause skin irritations. There are no poisonous snakes in the forest (or on the island as a whole), but bugs can be ferocious, so a strong repellent is a must. And remember: this is a rain forest, so bring a poncho and be prepared for frequent showers.

## SAFETY

Although crime isn't as high in the island's eastern areas as it is in San Juan, use prudence. Avoid bringing valuables with you to the beach; if you must do so, be sure not to leave them in view in your car. It's best to keep your car locked while driving, and steer clear of out-of-the-way beaches after sunset.

## IF YOU LIKE

### GREAT FOOD

In the east you'll find fine fare of all types. On the traditional side, look for the deep-fried snacks (often stuffed with meat or fish) known as *frituras*, as well as numerous dishes laced with coconut. Plantains are the star ingredient in the hearty *mofongo*, a seafood-stuffed dish, or as *tostones* (fried plantain chips). Fresh fish is commonly prepared with tomatoes, onions, and garlic, or some combination of the three. These days, the island's chefs are experimenting with flavor and texture, putting modern spins on classic dishes. Throughout the island, you'll find a blend of old and new cooking styles and techniques that will suit all palates.

### GOLF

There's something to be said for facing a rolling, palm-tree-lined fairway with the distant ocean at your back. And then there are the ducks, iguanas, and pelicans that congregate in the mangroves near some holes. That's what golf in eastern Puerto Rico is all about. The Arthur Hills–designed course at El Conquistador is one of the island's best. The Flamboyán course, a Rees-Jones creation at Palmas del Mar Country Club, consistently gets raves, as do the courses at the Westin Río Mar. The newest fairway is at the St. Regis Bahía Beach Hotel, where Robert Trent Jones Jr. oversaw construction of an eco-friendly green that overlooks the meeting place of the island's only navigable river, Espíritu Santo, and the Atlantic Ocean.

### VISITOR INFORMATION

The cities usually offer information through offices connected to city hall, and most are open only during business hours on weekdays.

**Information Fajardo Tourism Office** ⊠ *6 Calle Dr. Lopez, Fajardo* ☎ *787/863–4013.* **Naguabo Tourism Office** ⊠ *Naguabo* ☎ *787/874–0169.* **Río Grande Office of Tourism and Culture** ⊠ *Calle San José, Plaza de Recreo, Río Grande* ☎ *787/887–2370* ⊕ *www.riograndepr.org.*

# THE NORTHEASTERN COAST

Just east of San Juan, at the community of Piñones, urban chaos is replaced with the peace of winding, palm-lined roads that are interrupted at intervals by barefoot eateries and dramatic ocean views. Farther southeast and inland is Río Grande, a community that grew by virtue of its location beside the island's only navigable river. The river rises within El Yunque, the short name for El Yunque National Forest, a sprawling blanket of green covering a mountainous region south of Río Grande. Back on the coast, Balneario de Luquillo (Luquillo Beach) has snack kiosks, dressing rooms, showers, and facilities that enable wheelchair users to play in the ocean.

Southeast of Luquillo sits the Reserva Natural Las Cabezas de San Juan, with its restored lighthouse and variety of ecosystems. Anchoring the island's east coast is Fajardo, a lively port city with a large marina, ferry service to the outer islands, and a string of offshore cays. Catamarans

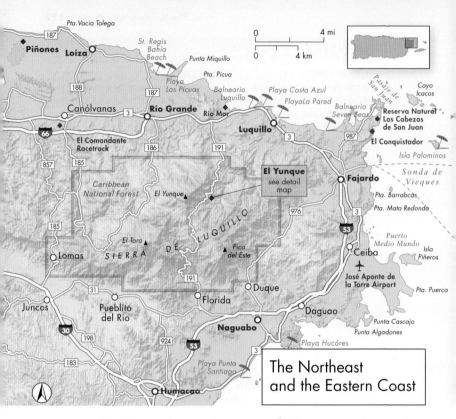

The Northeast
and the Eastern Coast

based here sail to and from great snorkeling spots, yachts stop by to refuel or stock up on supplies, and local fishing craft chug in and out as part of a day's work. ■TIP➔ Leave yourself plenty of time for driving to El Yunque or any of the resorts in the northeast. Route 3, the main route east, is notorious for its bumper-to-bumper traffic.

## PIÑONES

*10 miles (16 km) east of San Juan.*

Funky Piñones is little more than a collection of open-air seaside eateries. Sand floors, barefoot patrons, and tantalizing seafood—traditionally washed down with icy beer—have made it popular with locals, especially on weekend evenings. Chilled *agua de coco* is served right from the coconut. During the day you can rent a bike and follow the marked seaside trail that meanders for 7 miles (11 km) through the mangrove forest and along the northern coastline. It takes about two hours to bike from one end and back, but allow some time to stop and take pictures, grab something to eat, and explore the scenic beach areas.

The area has grown as a nightlife destination, as fancier establishments, some with live music, have opened up. As midafternoon turns into evening and people begin to leave the beach for refreshments, the air

## GREAT ITINERARIES

### IF YOU HAVE 1 DAY

If you have only a day, or even less than a day, to visit eastern Puerto Rico, you should make a beeline to **El Yunque**. Route 3 is the quickest way. This rain forest has hiking trails of various lengths leading to secluded waterfalls and mountaintop towers with spectacular views. It's wonderful to explore even if you never get out of your car. If you are staying overnight, your best bet is nearby **Río Grande**.

### IF YOU HAVE 3 DAYS

If you have a bit more time, you can see much more of the region. To avoid the unrelenting string of strip malls along Route 3, take Route 187 as it winds along the coast. Stop for lunch at one of the seafood shacks that line the beach at **Piñones**. Spend the night in or near **Río Grande**, a town that makes a good base for exploring the region. On your second day, get up early to beat the crowds to **El Yunque**. Make

sure to bring binoculars and watch for the rare Puerto Rican green parrot. On Day 3 you should head to **Luquillo**, which has one of the prettiest beaches on the island. Make sure to stop for lunch in one of the food kiosks on Route 3 just before you reach the town.

### IF YOU HAVE 5 DAYS

*If you have five days, follow the three-day itinerary above.* On Day 4 head east along Route 3 to the coastal city of **Fajardo**, which has plenty of accommodations in every price range. Make sure you have called ahead to reserve a spot on a tour of Reserva Natural Las Cabezas de San Juan. If there's no moon, sign up for a late-night excursion to the reserve's bioluminescent bay. On Day 5 take a snorkeling trip to some of the nearby coral reefs. Many people who travel to Fajardo take advantage of the ferry service or quick flights to the smaller islands of Vieques or Culebra.

is thick with smoke from grilled fish, beef and chicken kabobs, and the kettles of oil used to fry codfish and crab fritters. When the giant orange Caribbean sun starts to fall behind the San Juan skyline, salsa and merengue—not to mention reggae and Latin pop—start to blare out from the jukeboxes and sound systems of the dozens of ramshackle establishments dotting Route 187, the sector's main road. Traffic on the two-lane road into and out of the area is daunting on Friday and Saturday nights, when many of these open-air bars host merengue combos, Brazilian-jazz trios, or reggae bands.

### GETTING HERE AND AROUND

The approach to Piñones from San Juan is simple. Take Route 26 east or Route 37 east, follow signs for the Balneario de Carolina, then go straight on Route 187, and cross Punta Cangrejos. Door to door, the trip should take about 15 minutes. You can also get a taxi out to Piñones or take the bus for about 75¢ (via C45 or B40), but it takes more than an hour. To avoid getting stranded, prearrange a pickup time for your taxi driver to return. Another option is to make Soleil Beach Club your destination. Yes, it's one of the priciest beachfront restaurants in Piñones, but it offers a complimentary shuttle for pickup and drop-off, which helps avoid the risks of drinking and driving.

Taxis **AA American Taxi, Inc.** AA American Taxi, Inc. ☎ *787/982–3466.* **Astro Taxi** ☎ *787/727–8888.*

## EXPLORING

**Paseo Piñones.** One of the most pleasant ways to pass the time is walking along the Paseo Piñones. This 6½-mi (10½-km) boardwalk passes through sand dunes and crosses lagoons and mangrove forests. All the while, a line of coconut palms shades you from the sun. You'll share the path with bikers, joggers, and in-line skaters. Food kiosks abound.

## WHERE TO EAT

$$

PUERTO RICAN

★

✕ **Crispy y Relleno.** Though it looks like your typical roadside shack, grab one of the handful of outdoor tables and prepare your tastebuds for a treat. Many of its neighbors serve fried Puerto Rican fare, but Crispy y Relleno elevates the scene with modern takes on classic dishes. Don't miss specialties like the shrimp in coconut and ginger sauce, plaintain crusted fish, or the braised beef served over a yuca mash. Local ceviches are fresh and flavorful, while arepas and mofongos round out the offerings. The restaurant is set a bit farther away from the chaos that can engulf Route 187's many eateries on the party-heavy weekends, and if you book in advance Chef Fernando Parrilla can create a nine-course tasting menu that will blow you away. ⊠ *Rte. 187, Km 6.4, Piñones* ☎ *787/427–9305* ⊕ *www.crispyyrelleno.com* ☉ *Thurs.–Sun.*

$

SEAFOOD

✕ **The Reef Bar & Grill.** This place has one of the most dazzling views of San Juan, especially in the evening, when the city lights are twinkling. Perched atop a coastal bluff, it's located at the first left once you cross the bridge into Piñones. Grab one of the tables on the deck and order an *ensaladas de mariscos*, a refreshing seafood salad with conch, shrimp, or octopus, or *mofongo relleno*, mofongo stuffed with chicken or your pick of seafood. Cocktails, especially at sunset, are mandatory. ⊠ *Off Rte. 187, Km 1* ☎ *787/791–1973.*

$$$

PUERTO RICAN

✕ **Soleil Beach Club.** A bit more refined than some of its neighbors, this restaurant actually sits on a wooden platform positioned *above* the sand. Even nicer is the upstairs deck that lets you gaze at the ocean instead of the parking lot. The grilled USDA steak served with chimichurri is as good as it gets, and the fresh halibut fillet with beurre blanc and cassava mofongo is equally tasty. Save room for *postres* (dessert)—the coconut ice cream is worth every calorie. There are a couple of bars, and bands playing Latin music set the scene on weekend nights. Call ahead and you can arrange free transportation to and from your hotel—a very good deal. ⊠ *Rte. 187, Km 4.6* ☎ *787/253–1033* ⊕ *www. soleilbeachclub.com.*

### CHIMICHURRI

When you get a steak in Puerto Rico, it usually is served with a little glass jar of a green herb-filled sauce with a small, plastic spoon. This is *chimichurri,* the traditional accompaniment to grilled steak. The sauce, made from finely chopped cilantro or parsley, garlic, lemon, and oil, can be sprinkled liberally or sparingly over the meat to give it a slight kick. You will rarely find steak sauce in Puerto Rico, except at an American chain, though you can frequently get ketchup if *chimichurri* isn't to your liking.

Soft sand and leaning palm trees are hallmarks of Luquillo beaches.

## NIGHTLIFE

Nearly all the restaurants and cafés in Piñones have bands on weekends, mostly playing roof-shaking jazz and island rhythms, and locals go as much for the drinks and live entertainment as for the food. A largely Dominican clientele frequents many of these beachfront dance halls, and you're likely to see some smoking merengue dancing. Couples also twirl to salsa, bounce to *bomba*, or move to the grittier beats of local rap. You'll easily find several open-air establishments drawing weekend crowds for their steamy dance floors inside and smoking barbecue pits outside.

**The Reef Bar & Grill.** The Reef Bar & Grill has pool tables and plenty of live music—or a good juke box for the rare night there isn't a band. ⊠ *Off Rte. 187, Km 1* ☎ *787/791–1973.*

**Soleil Beach Club.** Soleil Beach Club has bars upstairs as well as down, so you never have to go far to order a drink. This bar, the most upscale in Piñones, can get packed on weekends, so go early to claim prime drinking real estate. ⊠ *Rte. 187, Km 4.5* ☎ *787/253–1033.*

## SHOPPING

**Artesanías Castor Ayala.** Just west of Piñones is the town of Loíza, where you'll find Artesanías Castor Ayala, the place to get your authentic coconut *vejigante* masks dubbed "Mona Lisas" because of their elongated smiles. Craftsman Raúl Ayala Carrasquillo has been making these pieces for more than 40 years, following in the footsteps of his late father. Collectors prize these wild masks, most with tentacle-like horns. △ Buyer beware: These masks have been much copied by other artisans, so look for the signature on the back. His one-room shop, in a shack that was painted yellow many years ago, is on the road between Loíza and Río Grande. ⊠ *Rte. 187, Km 6.6, Loíza* ☎ *787/876–1130.*

**Estúdio de Arte Samuel Lind.** At Estúdio de Arte Samuel Lind, located on a short, dusty lane across the street from the Artesanías Castor Ayala, artist Samuel Lind sculpts, paints, and silk-screens images that are quintessentially Loízano. Lind's work is displayed in the two floors of his latticework studio. Of special note are his colorful folk-art posters that are inspired by everyday Puerto Rican life. ⊠ *Rte. 187, Km 6.6, Loíza* ☎ *787/876–1494* ⊕ *samuellind.com.*

## SPORTS AND THE OUTDOORS

Piñones is bordered by a 10-mi (16-km) strip of beaches along the coast, which winds to a bluff called Vacia Talega, a once infamous lovers' lane with a wonderful view of an unspoiled coast lined with dense palm groves and towering sea grapes. The area has some fine surf, and several spots have become favorites of local and visiting surfers. You'll also find good fishing, snorkeling, and scuba opportunities. Away from the coast is Torrecilla Baja, one of the largest mangrove swamps on the island.

BICYCLING   The area's big outdoor attraction is a bike path that follows the swaying coconut palms on a quiet, breezy stretch, sometimes crossing over the main roadway but mostly running parallel to it. Along most of its 7 miles (12 km), it's a wooden boardwalk for bicycles. On weekends and holidays you can rent bikes from several places along Route 187 and explore the path on your own. The going rate is $5 per hour. Many are clustered at the start of the bike trail, at the first left once you cross the bridge into Piñones.

**COPI (Cultural and Ecotouristic Center of Piñones).** Bike rentals are available to explore the Piñones Bicycle Trail in the Piñones State Forest and Nature Reserve. Rentals, including helmets for children and adults, bicycles baby seats, and double-bikes require a donation of $5. Be sure to check your equipment before you set out; some bikes are in better condition than others. ⊠ *Rte. 187, Km 4.2, Piñones* ☎ *787/253–9707* ⊕ *www.copipr.com* ◷ *9–5.*

DIVING AND   Locals go fishing and crabbing right off the coast, and it's likely that the
FISHING TRIPS   crab fritters you eat in any beachfront shack are local as well.

**Cangrejos Yacht Club.** Boating, deep-sea fishing, and scuba-diving trips are run out of the marina right below the bridge from Isla Verde. Cangrejos Yacht Club is open Monday through Saturday from 8 to 5 and Sunday from 10 to 3. ⊠ *Rte. 187, Km 3.8* ☎ *787/791–1015* ⊕ *www. cangrejosyachtclub.com.*

**Puerto Rico Angling.** At Puerto Rico Angling, José Campos and his son run full- and half-day deep-sea fishing trips for up to six people for catch like tuna, wahoo and dorado. They also offer fishing trips through the area's lagoon system. All charters practice tag and release. ☎ *787/724– 2079* ⊕ *www.puertoricofishing.com.*

# RÍO GRANDE

*21 miles (35 km) southeast of San Juan.*

This urban cluster of about 50,000 residents proudly calls itself "The City of El Yunque," as it's the closest community to the rain forest and most of the reserve falls within its district borders. Two images of the rare green parrot, which makes its home in El Yunque, are found on the city's coat of arms; another parrot peeks out at you from the town's flag.

Río Espíritu Santo, which runs through Río Grande, begins in El Yunque's highest elevations and is the island's only navigable river. It was once used to transport lumber, sugar, and coffee from plantations, and immigrants flocked to the region to take advantage of the employment opportunities. Many of today's residents can trace their families to Spain, Austria, and Italy.

## IT'S DA BOMB(A)

The *bomba*—a dance for which the northeastern coast is famous—can be traced to the Kongo people of West Africa. Sometimes wearing a flouncy white dress, the woman of a dancing couple moves in a relatively fixed pattern of steps while her partner improvises to the drumbeat. A lead singer and a choir perform a call-and-response song—recounting a local story or event—while percussionists play maracas, *fuas* (wooden sticks that are smacked against a hard surface), *buleadores* (low-timbre, barrel-shape drums), and *subidores* (higher-pitch drums).

### GETTING HERE

Only 30 minutes from San Juan, in the Northern Coastal Valley, Río Grande is easy to get to. From San Juan, take Road 26 toward Carolina until you reach Road 3. Then take Road 3 towards Fajardo for approximately 20 minutes until you see signs for Río Grande.

**Car Rental Avis** ✉ *St. Regis Bahia Beach Resort, Route 187, Km 4.2* ☎ *787/809–8000* ⊕ *www.avis.com.*

### WHERE TO EAT

**$$**
**PUERTO RICAN**
★

✕**Antojitos Puertorriqueñes.** "*Buen provecho,*" says owner Jorge Martinez as you sit down to an authentic meal at this no-frills spot serving Puerto Rican favorites. Whether you're stopping for breakfast en route to the rain forest, catching the unbeatable $5.50 lunch special—which changes daily and offers choices like fried pork with plantains, grouper in creole sauce, and roasted chicken with beans and rice—or relaxing with a cocktail before dinner, the joint delivers. The premises are equally straightforward—a covered patio with plastic tables and chairs and overhead fans, as well as a soundtrack provided by indigenous coquí frogs. ✉ *160 Río Mar Blvd.* ☎ *787/888–7378.*

**$$$$**
**CARIBBEAN**
**Fodor's Choice**
★

✕**Fern Restaurant.** On the second floor of the St. Regis Bahia Beach's main Plantation House building, this stylish restaurant's indoor/outdoor space is a mix of textures and colors—banquettes with red pillow accents, mesh lamps, metallic-cork wall coverings, recycled kumbok wood tables with tangled brass legs—that create a lush environment for Jean-Georges Vongerichten's Caribbean-Latin inspired menu. An

$82 tasting is available for those interested in sampling the menu's featured dishes, which include a delectable black-pepper octopus laced with indigenous *aji dulce* (sweet chile) for appetizer, and grouper with black beans and marinated beef-tenderloin entrées. Service is impeccable, and the extensive wine list will delight oenophiles. Save room for dessert; the warm apple crumble is irresistible. ⊠ *St. Regis Bahia Beach Resort, Route 187, Km 4.2, Río Grande* ☎ *787/809–8100* ⊕ *www.fernrestaurant.com* ⊛ *Reservations essential.*

**$$$$**
**ITALIAN**
★
✕ **Palio.** Northern Italian dishes, such as fettucine with lobster, shrimp, mussels, and scallops, veal Marsala, and fillet of beef with a carmelized shallot Barolo reduction, are the star attractions at this top-notch restaurant where the staff is attentive and amiable. Specialty coffees are served in mugs engulfed in blue flames, a showstopper that has people at neighboring tables applauding. The dining room, with its black-and-white checkerboard floor and dark-wood paneling, is elegant and refined, and before sunset you can catch a glimpse of the sea through the dramatic floor-to-ceiling windows. ⊠ *Rio Mar Beach Resort & Spa, a Wyndham Grand Resort, 6000 Río Mar Blvd.* ☎ *787/888–6000* ⊕ *www.wyndhamriomar.com* ⊛ *Reservations essential* ⊘ *No lunch.*

**$$$**
**PUERTO RICAN**
✕ **Richie's Café.** Perched on a mountaintop, this restaurant—a convenient option for Wyndham Río Mar guests who don't want to dine on-property but are willing to pay resort prices—has a pair of open-air dining rooms with views to Vieques on a clear day. The atmosphere here is festive; there's often a game playing on one of the big screens or a local band jamming on the weekend. Seafood is the specialty here— try the fried plantains filled with shrimp, conch, octopus, or lobster for an appetizer, and then move on to the whole red snapper or pineapple rice with shrimp, which is served on the pineapple itself. Bring some insect repellent at night, as some readers have mentioned problems with mosquitoes. ⊠ *Route 968, Km 2.0* ☎ *787/887–1435, 787/909–8532* ⊕ *www.richiescafepr.com.*

**WHERE TO STAY**

*For expanded hotel reviews, visit Fodors.com.*

**$$$$**
**RESORT**
🏨 **Gran Meliá Puerto Rico.** This massive resort, on an enviable stretch of pristine coastline, has an open-air lobby with elegant floral displays that resemble a Japanese garden, and the swimming pool's columns call to mind ancient Greece. **Pros:** beautiful setting; lovely pool area; short walk to the beach. **Cons:** parking spots are scarce; facade is blank and uninviting; though Wi-Fi is free in the lobby, in-room Internet is $14/day. ⊠ *200 Coco Beach Boulevard, Rte. 968, Km 5.8, Coco Beach* ☎ *787/809–1770, 877/476–3542* ⊕ *www.gran-melia-puerto-rico.com* ⇥ *363 junior suites, 123 RedLevel suites, 5 oceanfront villas, 1 two-bedroom Oceanfront Presidential Villa* ⚴ *In-room: a/c, safe, Internet. In-hotel: restaurant, bar, golf course, pool, tennis court, gym, spa, beach, water sports, children's programs, parking* ❏❘ *No meals.*

Water-recreation options abound in the enormous pools of the Rio Mar Beach Resort.

**$$$$**
RESORT
 **Rio Mar Beach Resort & Spa, a Wyndham Grand Resort.** Be it for work or play, guests come to this sprawling 500-acre resort to enjoy a host of outdoor activities, including championship golf and tennis, as well as hiking excursions in the nearby rain forest. **Pros:** expansive beachfront; good restaurants in hotel; plenty of outdoor activities. **Cons:** dark and depressing parking garage; long lines at check-in desk; in-room Wi-Fi costs $15/day, worn grounds. ⊠ *6000 Río Mar Blvd.* ☎ *787/888–6000, 888/4–RIO–MAR* ⊕ *www.wyndhamriomar.com* ⤳ *528 rooms, 72 suites, 59 villas* ⌂ *In-room: a/c, safe, Internet, Wi-Fi. In-hotel: restaurant, bar, golf course, pool, tennis court, gym, spa, beach, water sports, children's programs, business center* ¶⊙¶ *No meals.*

**$$$$**
RESORT
Fodor's Choice
★
**St. Regis Bahia Beach Resort.** In the lush foothills of El Yunque rain forest where Río Espíritu Santo meets the Atlantic, this luxurious, environmentally-aware property has raised the bar on lodging in Puerto Rico. **Pros:** Privacy, impeccable service, luxury amenities. **Cons:** Isolated location; daily $60 resort fee; slim off-property restaurant selection. ⊠ *State Road 187, Km 4.2, Río Grande* ☎ *787/809–8000, 866/961–3326* ⊕ *www.stregisbahiabeach.com* ⤳ *104 rooms, 35 suites* ⌂ *In-room: a/c, safe, Wi-Fi. In-hotel: restaurant, bar, golf course, pool, tennis court, gym, spa, beach, water sports, children's programs, business center, parking, some pets allowed.*

### NIGHTLIFE

**Rio Mar Beach Resort & Spa, a Wyndham Grand Resort.** Pick a game—Caribbean stud poker, blackjack, slot machines—and then head to the Las Vegas–style casino at the Rio Mar Beach Resort & Spa. If all that betting makes you thirsty, step into the Players Bar, which is connected to the gaming room. ⊠ *Rio Mar Beach Resort & Spa, 6000 Río Mar Blvd.* ☎ *787/888–6000.*

## SPORTS AND THE OUTDOORS

Activities in the Río Grande region are mostly oriented around the area's resorts, the Rio Mar Beach Resort & Spa, a Wyndham Grand Resort, and the Gran Meliá Puerto Rico, as well as the new St. Regis Bahia Beach Resort.

GOLF   **Berwind Country Club and Golf Course.** The Berwind Country Club and Golf Course has a public 18-hole course known for its tight fairways and demanding greens. It's open to nonmembers Monday through Friday, with greens fees beginning at $25 plus taxes. On Saturdays, nonmembers can play after 12 pm if they make arrangements in advance. ⊠ *Rte. 187, Km 4.7* ☎ *787/876–3056* ⊕ *www.berwindcountryclub.net.*

★   **Río Mar Country Club.** The Río Mar Country Club has a clubhouse with a pro shop, two restaurants between two 18-hole courses, to grab a sit-down lunch or a quick beverage and a bite. The River Course, designed by Greg Norman, has challenging fairways that skirt the Mameyes River. The Ocean Course, designed by Tom and George Fazio, has slightly wider fairways than its sister; iguanas can usually be spotted sunning themselves near its fourth hole. ■TIP➔ If you're not a resort guest, be sure to reserve tee times at least 24 hours in advance. ⊠ *Rio Mar Beach Resort & Spa, a Wyndham Grand Resort, 6000 Río Mar Blvd.* ☎ *787/888–7060* ⊕ *www.wyndhamriomar.com* 🐾. *Greens fees for hotel guests range from $50 (for 9 holes) to $165 (for 18 holes). Fees for walk-ins range from $60 to $180.*

Fodor's Choice   **St. Regis Bahia Beach Resort Golf Course.** Designed by Robert Trent Jones
★   Jr., this tranquil 18-hole course meanders alongside the island's Río Espíritu Santo and overlooks the Atlantic Ocean. Environmentally respectful, this challenging course traipses past scenic lakes, deep-rooted mangroves, and spectacular residences to blend into the area's rain-forest surroundings, while ocean breezes add a degree of difficulty to lush, rolling fairways. Greens fees vary seasonally; rates and times are available on request. ⊠ *State Road 187, Km 4.2, Río Grande* ☎ *787/957–1510.*

**Trump International Golf Course.** The Trump International Golf Course, the former Coco Beach Golf & Country Club, features two 18-hole courses designed by PGA Professional Tom Kite, and is bordered by 100 acres of coastline and outstanding views of El Yunque. ⊠ *Gran Meliá Puerto Rico, 100 Clubhouse Dr., Coco Beach* ☎ *787/657–2000* ⊕ *www.trumpgolfclubpuertorico.com* ⊠ *$120 for the Twilight Rate to $200 for the 18-hole Championship Course.*

HORSEBACK   **Hacienda Carabalí.** Hacienda Carabalí, a family-run operation, is a good
RIDING   place to jump in the saddle and ride one of Puerto Rico's Paso Fino
★   horses. Hour-long rides ($32 adult, $20 kids 3–11) take you around the 600-acre ranch, while two-hour treks take you to a river where you and your horse can take a dip. If you prefer something more high-tech, rent a four-wheeler for an excursion through the foothills of El Yunque. ⊠ *Rte. 992, Km 4* ☎ *787/889–5820* ⊕ *www.haciendacarabalipuertorico.com.*

TENNIS **Peter Burwash International Tennis Center.** The facilities at the Peter Burwash International Tennis Center are the best in the area. Besides the 13 courts with spectacular views, there are lessons for everyone from novices to old pros. ⊠ *Rio Mar Beach Resort & Spa, a Wyndham Grand Resort, 6000 Río Mar Blvd.* ☎ *787/888–6000* ⊕ *www.pbitennis.com* ⌨ *Court rentals start at $25/hour; 1/2 hour private lessons begin at $50.*

WATER **Dragonfly Adventures.** You can rent sea kayaks ($25/hour for single-
SPORTS person kayaks, $35 and $45 for two- and three-person models, respectively) and arrange off-site scuba-diving excursions or full- and half-day snorkeling packages through on-site operator Dragonfly Adventures. Large catamaran snorkeling trips leave from the resort for the calm, crystal-blue seas, beautiful coral reefs, and deserted islands off the coast of northeastern Puerto Rico. Rates begin at $115 per person, including a buffet lunch, limited open bar, and snacks. A Dragonfly Adventures tour desk is also available on-site at the Gran Meliá, also in Río Grande. ⊠ *Rio Mar Beach Resort & Spa, a Wyndham Grand Resort, 6000 Río Mar Blvd.* ☎ *787/888–6000* ⊕ *www.wyndhamriomar.com.*

## SHOPPING

**Treehouse Studio.** The picturesque Treehouse Studio, not far from the rain forest, sells vibrant watercolors by Monica Linville, who also gives workshops. Call for an appointment and directions. ⊠ *Unmarked road off Rte. 3* ☎ *787/436–3153* ⊕ *www.monicalinville.com.*

# EL YUNQUE

Fodor's Choice 7 miles (11 km) southeast of Río Grande; 26 miles (43 km) southeast
★ of San Juan.

*For more information on El Yunque, see the special feature at the beginning of this chapter.*

### GETTING HERE AND AROUND

You can take a taxi from San Juan to El Yunque (metered rates outside San Juan run about $36 per hour), but to get the most out of the rain forest, it's best to rent a car, even if you have only a few hours to explore. From the greater San Juan area, take the Airport Expressway, Highway 26 (Baldorioty de Castro Avenue) and follow signs east to Carolina; once you are on the expressway, follow it to the end (approximately 14 miles [22½ km]). At the final exit (Carolina), stay in the left-hand lane until you merge with Route 3. Continue on Route 3 approximately 13 miles (21 km) until you see the signs for Palmer–El Yunque. Turn right at the traffic signal and follow the road through the village of Palmer until you see the sign for Route 191. Turn left on Route 191 and follow it approximately 2 miles (3 km) until you see the El Yunque National Forest sign. The entrance to the El Portal Rain Forest Center is on your right just after you enter the forest.

### TOUR OPERATORS

Many companies in San Juan offer excursions to El Yunque. A National Forest Service ranger leads one-hour English and Spanish tours from the **Palo Colorado Information Center** along the Caimitillo and Baño de Oro trails (⊗ *11 am–1 pm* ⌐ *$5, seniors and kids 5–12, $3*). Tours are first-come, first-served.

**Eco Action Tours.** Eco Action Tours will pick you up at your hotel and take you to the rain forest, where small groups will hike, swim in the falls, and learn about the flora and fauna. Half-day rates are reasonable, starting at $58 (not including entry free). Full day tours are $68 and can be combined with a stop at Luquillo Beach. ☎ *787/791–7509* ⊕ *www.ecoactiontours.com.*

**Acampa Nature Adventure Tours.** Book a half-day excursion with Acampa Nature Adventure Tours and choose from a moderate hike at lower elevations of the forest to more challenging treks to the El Yunque peak at 3,500 feet. Rates start at $79, with a six-person minimum, and include round-trip transportation to/from your hotel and park fees. ⊠ *1221 Piñero Ave., San Juan* ☎ *787/706–0695* ⊕ *www.acampapr.com* ⊗ *Mon.–Thur.*

**ESSENTIALS**

**Admission Fees.** There is no entrance fee for the El Yunque National Forest itself. There's an optional admission fee for the El Portal Rainforest Center ($4 adults, free for children under 15 and senior citizens).

**Admission Hours.** The road into El Yunque opens daily at 7:30 am and closes at 6 pm. Ranger stations are open 9–5, as is the Welcome Center.

**Emergencies.** If you witness an accident or the commission of an unlawful act or felony, or if you see something happening that looks wrong or suspicious, please contact the Law Enforcement and Investigation Patrol, José Ayala, at 787/888–5675 (office), 787/888–1880 (VHF radio paging), or 787/549–0075 (cellular).

**Restrooms.** There are picnic areas with sheltered tables and bathrooms as well as several basic eateries along the road through the rain forest.

**EXPLORING**

₢ **El Portal Rainforest Center.** Before you begin exploring El Yunque, check out the high-tech, interactive displays—explaining rain forests in general and El Yunque in particular—at El Portal Rainforest Center, the information center near the northern entrance. The beautifully designed facility is where you can pick up a map of the park and talk to rangers about which trails are open. You can stock up on water, snacks, film, and souvenirs at the small gift shop—the only one in the park that accepts credit cards. ⊠ *Rte. 191, Km 4.3, off Rte. 3, Río Grande* ☎ *787/888–1880* ⊕ *www.fs.fed.us/r8/caribbean* ⌐ *$4, free for kids under 15 and seniors.* ⊗ *Daily 9–5.*

**WHERE TO EAT**

₢   ✕ **Muralla.** The rangers at El Yunque swear by this place, a cement-block building painted yellow and green just past Cascada La Coca. You won't find a cheaper meal anywhere in Puerto Rico, that's for sure. *Pasteles* (a local tamale-like snack) with rice and beans are served year-round for $6, and *arroz habichuela con pollo* (fried chicken with rice and beans) is a steal at less than $5. After a long hike, be sure to order one of the fruit shakes to quench your thirst, and take in the unusual artwork in the open-air dining room. Get here early, as the place closes

PUERTO RICAN

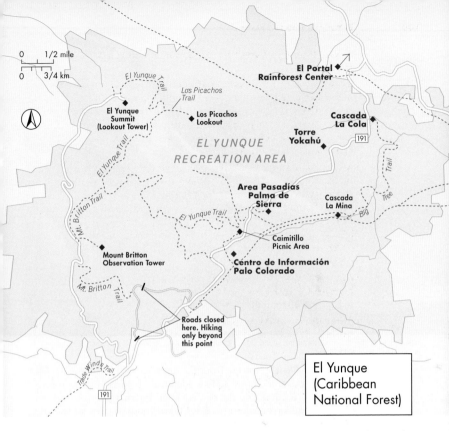

at 5 pm. ☒ *Rte. 191, Km 7.4, El Yunque* ☏ *No phone* ▭ *No credit cards* ⊙ *Closed Thur.*

**$**
**CARIBBEAN**

✕ **Yuquiyú Delights.** Named for the Taíno god of goodness, this open-air dining room will be a sight for sore eyes if you've been hiking all day in the rain forest. The covered terrace is scattered with a few tiled tables further shielded by umbrellas. The chalkboard out front usually lists a few specials like burgers and quesadilla filled with skirt steak. Off the kitchen, there's a little shop where you can stock up on water for the trail or snacks for the ride home. ☒ *Rte. 191, Km 11.3, El Yunque* ☏ *787/396–0970* ⊕ *www.yuquiyudelightspr.com* ▭ *No credit cards* ⊙ *Closed Tues. No dinner.*

## SHOPPING

**El Yunque Gift Shop.** While in El Yunque, buy a recording of the tree frog's song, a video about the endangered green parrot, or a coffee-table book about the rain forest at the large El Yunque Gift Shop in El Portal Visitor Center. Tucked among the rain-forest gifts are other Puerto Rican items, including note cards, maps, soaps, jams, and coffee. ■ **TIP→** This is the only gift shop in El Yunque that accepts credit cards. ☒ *El Portal, Rte. 191, Km 4.3* ☏ *787/888–1880.*

Look closely at the small tree branches along side El Yunque's nature trails and you may spot creatures such as the mountain garden lizard.

★ **Coquí International.** Not far from the entrance to El Yunque are half a dozen souvenir shops selling identical T-shirts and rain-forest tchotchkes. A cut above the rest is Coquí International. A trail with colorful coquís painted on the floor takes you past cubicles featuring local artists' original paintings, handwoven placemats, and one-of-a-kind items of clothing. Interesting jewelry, coconut mobiles shaped like fish, sharks, and insects, handmade soap, and wood carvings cram the space. You'll enjoy exploring this unique boutique where gentle music and incense set shoppers at ease. ⊠ *#54 Calle Principal, El Yunque* ☎ *787/887–0770* ⊕ *www.coquistores.com.*

## LUQUILLO

*8 miles (13 km) northeast of Río Grande; 28 miles (45 km) east of San Juan.*

Known as the Sun Capital of Puerto Rico, Luquillo has one of the island's best-equipped family beaches. It's also a community where fishing traditions are respected. On the east end of Balneario de Luquillo, past the guarded swimming area, fishermen launch small boats and drop nets in open stretches between coral reefs.

Like many other Puerto Rican towns, Luquillo has its signature festival, in this case the Festival de Platos Típicos (Festival of Typical Dishes), a late-November culinary event that revolves around one ingredient: coconut. During the festivities, many of the community's 18,000 residents gather in the main square, Plaza de Recreo, to sample treats rich

## BEST LUQUILLO FOOD KIOSKS

Off Route 3, just before the exit for pristine Luquillo Beach, something of a culinary renaissance is occurring. Here you'll find 60-plus food shacks or kioskos with CIA-trained (Culinary Institute of America) chefs who are cooking everything from burgers to ceviche to stuffed lobsters. Stop in for breakfast, lunch, dinner, or cocktails. These kioskos are turning out some of the island's best eats. Take your time surveying your options at establishments ranging from no-frills takeout counters to full-service restaurants. Once you've chosen, pull up a seat and get ready to feast.

Each kiosk is numbered. Here are a few of our favorites:

**#2, La Parrilla.** Herd here for the original kiosko experience,(see also Where to Eat section), and indulge in a lobster or steak as big as your head.

**#12, El Jefe Burger.** Wrap your hands around stuffed burgers such as the green chile and jalapeño at El Jefe. Don't forget the smothered fries. ⊕ www.eljefeburger.com.

**#13,Tapas 13.** Next door to El Jefe, you'll find Spanish-inspired small plates like the excellent fiery shrimp *ajillo diablo*, and bacon-wrapped dates pair well with house-made sangria. w*www.tapas13.com.*

**#37, New York–style Food Space.** Terrific breakfast sandwiches like "The Belt" (bacon, egg, lettuce, tomato), juicy corned-beef reubens, and massive Italian heroes are popular options here w*www.foodspacepr.com.*

**#38, Ceviche Hut.** Their selection of fresh ceviches and classics like *pescado alo macho,* or fish in Peruvian seafood sauce, are solid choices.

with coconut or coconut milk. There's also plenty of free entertainment, including folk shows, troubador contests, and salsa bands.

**GETTING HERE AND AROUND**

Públicos run between San Juan and Fajardo and will let travelers off at Luquillo (about a 45-minute ride). Driving takes about the same amount of time. From San Juan, head out Route 3, get off at Route 193, and follow signs for Luquillo. If you want to explore the town (it's small but well worth the time), a car is helpful. Take note not to park in places where the curb is painted yellow—it's a parking violation.

**WHERE TO EAT AND STAY**

*For expanded hotel reviews, visit Fodors.com.*

$$$
PUERTO RICAN
✕ **La Parrilla.** There are more than 50 *kioskos,* or food stands, along Highway 3 on the way to Luquillo Beach. This full-service restaurant is one of the originals, and has been elevating the bar for its culinary counterparts. Open every day, usually satisfying at least one rowdy tourist bus, the open-air spot delivers sizzling seafood in generous portions from shrimp, salmon, and red snapper—deboned, stuffed with shrimp and grilled to perfection—to plump lobsters. There are even a couple of steaks on the menu that are guaranteed to satisfy the biggest carnivores. Like all of its neighbors, this place faces the street, but there's a comfortable patio in the rear where you can kick back with an

## DID YOU KNOW?

El Yunque Forest is divided into four forest types according to their elevations. At 2,500 ft. (762 m) above sea level, Cloud Forest is the highest and receives nearly constant rainfall.

## CLOSE UP

## 210 Parrots and Counting

The Taíno Indians called it the *iguaca,* Spanish speakers refer to it as the *cotorra,* and scientists know it as *Amazona vittata.* Whatever moniker it takes, the Puerto Rican green parrot— the only one native to the island—is one of the world's rarest birds. It nests primarily in the upper levels of El Yunque and in the nearby Sierra de Luquillo. The bird is almost entirely green, though there are touches of blue on its wings, white rings around its eyes, and a red band just above its beak. It's only about 12 inches long, and its raucous squawk doesn't match its delicate appearance. The parrots mate for life. In February (the rain forest's driest season), they build nests within tree hollows and lay three to four eggs. Both parents feed the young.

When the Spanish arrived, the parrot population was an estimated 1 million on the main island, Vieques, and Culebra. But deforestation, hurricanes, and parasites have reduced the population (parrot hunting was common before being outlawed in 1940). By 1967 there were only 19 birds; a 1975 count totaled only 13.

But things are looking up, especially with work beginning on a $2.5 million, state-of-the-art breeding facility in El Yunque. At this writing, an estimated total of 300 green parrots were living in both the wild and captivity. Officials are optimistic that the numbers will continue to grow. If you're very observant (and very lucky), you just might spot one.

---

ice-cold beer or sangria and escape the traffic noise. ⊠ *Luquillo Beach, Kiosk #2* ☎ *787/889–0590* ⊕ *www.laparrillapr.com.*

**$$**
MEXICAN
✕ **Lolita's.** When it comes to Mexican food, this place is the real deal. For lunch, grab a few tacos, soft or crispy, for a mere $1.75 each. For dinner, try the *carne tampiqueña* (marinated skirt steak), *enchiladas suizas* (enchiladas in a mild green sauce), or *mole con pollo* (chicken in a spicy sauce laced with chocolate). There's a reason why devoted travelers have been returning for more than a decade. Generous portions are washed down with oversize margaritas. Or choose from a large selection of Mexican beers. The pleasant dining room, decorated with slightly kitschy paintings of simple village life, is on the second floor of a building just east of Luquillo. Very sparse parking can be tricky. ⊠ *Rte. 3, Km 41.3* ☎ *787/889–5770, 787/889–0250.*

**$**
HOTEL
☷ **Yunque Mar.** This cute little hotel is just west of the popular Balneario de Luquillo, but the beach here is nearly as nice and almost always deserted. **Pros:** on a lovely beach; friendly owners; rooms boast only basic amenities but are clean. **Cons:** building is on a crowded street; bland decor; no in-room safe; no elevator. ⊠ *Calle 1 #6 Fortuna Playa* ☎ *787/889–5555, 888/406-0992* ⊕ *www.yunquemarhotel.com* ⇗ *15 rooms, 2 suites* ⚭ *In-room: Wi-Fi. In-hotel: bar, pool, beach, parking* ⍗ *No meals.*

The calm waters of Playa Luquillo are a draw for families and beachgoers looking for a relaxing ocean dip.

## SPORTS AND THE OUTDOORS

SURFING **La Selva Surf Shop.** Not far from Playa La Pared, La Selva Surf Shop has anything a surfer could need, including news about current conditions. Owned by surfer couple Bob and Sue, the shop sells sunglasses, sandals, bathing suits, and other beach necessities. Additionally, Bob can arrange for surfing lessons, and Sue rents out a quaint two-bedroom guesthouse nestled above Luquillo in El Yunque's foothills by the week. ⊠ *250 Calle Fernández Garcia Luquillo* ☎ *787/889–6205* ⊕ *www. rainforestrental.com.*

# FAJARDO

*7 miles (11 km) southeast of Luquillo; 34 miles (55 km) southeast of San Juan.*

Fajardo, founded in 1772, has historical notoriety as a port where pirates stocked up on supplies. It later developed into a fishing community and an area where sugarcane flourished. (There are still cane fields on the city's fringes.) Today it's a hub for the yachts that use its marinas, the divers who head to its good offshore sites, and the day-trippers who travel by catamaran, ferry, or plane to the islands of Culebra and Vieques. With the most significant docking facilities on the island's eastern side, Fajardo is a bustling city of 37,000—so bustling, in fact, that its unremarkable and somewhat battered downtown is often congested and difficult to navigate. Much of the tourist activity in Fajardo centers in the northern reaches of Las Croabas near the gigantic El Conquistador Resort.

## GETTING HERE AND AROUND

Getting around Fajardo is tricky without a car, especially if you plan on visiting several of the sights.

**Travel with Padin.** Travel with Padin will take passengers to and from the San Juan Airport to the ferry for $60 (two people) with prior reservations. ☎ 787/355–6746 *after 6 pm for English, 787/644–3091 8–6, Spanish-only* ⊕ *enchanted-isle.com/padin.*

**Aeropuerto Diego Jiménez Torres.** Fajardo is served by the one-room Aeropuerto Diego Jiménez Torres, just southwest of the city on Route 976, with flight service to Vieques, Culebra, San Juan, St. Thomas, and St. Croix via Air Flamenco, Cape Air, and Vieques Air Link. ☎ 787/ 860–3110.

**Aeropuerto Regional de Humacao.** The landing field at Aeropuerto Regional de Humacao is used mostly by private planes. ☎ 787/852–8188.

**Car Rental Enterprise.** Formerly an Avis, the El Conquistador is now serviced by an on-site Enterprise Car Rental. ⊠ *El Conquistador Resort & Golden Door Spa, 1000 Av. El Conquistador* ☎ *787/801–3722* ⊕ *www.enterprise.com.* **Leaseway of Puerto Rico** ⊠ *Rte. 3, Km 44.4* ☎ *787/860–5000* ⊕ *www.leasewaypr.com.* **Thrifty Car Rental.** In central Fajardo's Marina Puerto Del Rey, Thrifty offers some of the island's most competitive rates. ⊠ *Route 3, Km 51.4, Marina Puerto Del Rey, Fajardo* ☎ *787/860–2030* ⊕ *www.thrifty.com.*

## EXPLORING

Ⓒ **Balneario Seven Seas.** A long stretch of powdery sand near the Reserva Natural Las Cabezas de San Juan, Balneario Seven Seas, one of Puerto Rico's prized Blue Flag beaches, may turn out to be the best surprise of your trip. Facilities include picnic tables, changing areas, restrooms, and showers. Many restaurants are just outside the gates. Its calm, clear waters are perfect for swimming. ⊠ *Rte. 987, Las Croabas.*

**Las Croabas.** A few miles north of Fajardo is this fishing area, where seafood is sold in open-air restaurants along the ocean. In the middle of town is a small park with a lovely waterfront walk, and outfitters for any kind of ocean adventure from kayaking to sailing trips. ⊠ *Rte. 3, Km 51.2* ☎ .

**Marina Puerto Chico.** This lively marina off Route 987 is home to a cadre of glistening fishing boats, the fast-paced Mini-Boat Adventures and Kayaking Puerto Rico offices, and one of the most popular restaurants on the east coast: El Varadero Seaside Grill (⇨ *see Where to Eat*). ⊠ *Rt 987, Barrio Sardinera, Fajardo* ☎ *787/863–0834, 787/860–3721* ⊕ *www.marinapuertochico.com.*

**Marina Puerto del Rey.** Home to 1,100 boats, this is one of the Caribbean's largest marinas. This is the place to hook up with a scuba-diving group, arrange an excursion to Vieques's bioluminescent bay, or charter a fishing boat. The marina, located south of Fajardo, also has several restaurants and boating-supply stores. ⊠ *Rte. 9987, off Rte. 987* ☎ *787/860–1000* ⊕ *www.puertodelrey.com.*

**Reserva Natural Las Cabezas de San Juan.** The 316-acre reserve on a headland north of Fajardo is owned by the nonprofit Conservation Trust of Puerto Rico. You ride in open-air trolleys and wander down boardwalks through seven ecosystems, including lagoons, mangrove swamps, and dry-forest areas. Green iguanas skitter across paths, and guides identify other endangered species. A half-hour hike down a wooden walkway brings you to the mangrove-lined **Laguna Grande,** where bioluminescent microorganisms glow at night. The restored **Fajardo Lighthouse** is the final stop on the tour; its Spanish-colonial tower has been in operation since 1882, making it Puerto Rico's second-oldest lighthouse. The first floor houses ecological displays; a winding staircase leads to an observation deck. The only way to see the reserve is on one of the many guided tours; reservations are required through the Conservation's very comprehensive website. ✉ *Rte. 987, Km 6* ☎ *787/722–5882 weekdays, 787/860–2560 weekends* ⊕ *www.fideicomiso.org.*

**Villa Marina.** The second-largest marina in Fajardo, it's home to charter-fishing boats as well as several catamaran operators who give day tours for swimming and snorkeling to the deserted islands right off Puerto Rico's northeast coast. ✉ *Rte. 987, Km 1.3* ☎ *787/863–5131* ⊕ *www. villamarinapr.com.*

## WHERE TO EAT

**$$$$**
SUSHI
✕ **Blossoms.** Hung with elaborate lanterns, this dining room is a fanciful version of the Far East. The first thing you'll notice is the sound of meats and vegetables sizzling on the large teppanyaki tables. The chefs here know they're on stage and perform with a flourish. Despite the abundance of fresh fish, sushi bars are a rarity in this part of Puerto Rico, but the excellent one here has a seemingly endless array of sushi rolls to satisfy all cravings. Want traditional Chinese fare? Try the "Passion Love Boat" (lobster and shrimp) or "Full Steam Ahead" (steamed fish with scallions and black mushrooms). ✉ *El Conquistador Resort & Golden Door Spa, Rte. 987, Km 3.4* ☎ *787/863–1000* ⊕ *www.elconresort.com* ⌁ *Reservations essential.*

**$$$**
PUERTO RICAN
✕ **Calizo.** There's a string of seafood shacks in the village of Las Croabas, all serving delicious fried fish. This open-air eatery with tables covered by straw-topped umbrellas and anchored by a bustling square bar, takes things up a notch or two. Look for dishes like seafood salad in a spicy vinaigrette, mahimahi with scallops, a rich seafood paella, and chunks of lobster sautéed in cilantro butter. Wash it all down with a cold sangria. It's almost across from the Balneario Seven Seas, making it a great place to refuel after a day at the beach. The only drawback is that it's a bit on the pricey side. ✉ *Rte. 987, Las Croabas* ☎ *787/863–3664.*

**$$**
SEAFOOD
★
✕ **El Varadero Seaside Grill.** El Varadero's tagline says it all—"nothing fancy, just great food"—and at this no-frills seaside spot perched on the docks of pretty Marina Puerto Chico, San Juan native Charlie Barrett has nailed the recipe for success. Simple yet cozy nautical touches serve as the backdrop for grilled fresh tuna, mahimahi, and snapper, as diners while away the hours watching the ships ebb and flow along the docks. An extensive appetizer list rounds out the menu. At lunch be sure to order the two-fisted creole burger, a quintessentially Puerto Rican invention, topped with fried plantains and tangy creole sauce. Kids will love the mahi nuggets, and for those who like fire with their food, this friendly hangout makes five different kinds of hot sauce.

⌧ *Marina Puerto Chico, Route 987, Fajardo* ☎ *787/860* ⊕ *www. elvaraderoseaside.com* ☽ *Closed Mon. & Tue.*

**$$**
BARBECUE
Fodor's Choice
★

✕ **La Estación.** Billing itself as *"Una Parrilla New Yorican,"* this laid-back, reasonably priced, open-air restaurant occupies a former Esso gas station. Elevating Puerto Rican street food to art form, two New Yorkers (one Puerto Rican) who just wanted to live out their dreams of owning a restaurant, are doing it to fabulous result in a prime space outside the El Conquistador Resort. Highlighting products obtained from local fisherman and farmers, then smoking their own meats in an outdoor kitchen, Idalia Garcia and Kevin Roth's awesome joint is one of Puerto Rico's don't miss culinary treats. Settle into one of the mis-matched patio tables—be it made of teak, cedar, or concrete—order up a cocktail like the Don Q-osmo (a passionfruit cosmopolitan made with rum), and get ready to feast. Must-have plates include a side-splitting portion of meaty pork ribs marinated in sofrito, then dry-rubbed in BBQ sauce before smoking, a mixed seafood yuca mofongo (more moist than the plantain variety), a refreshing Puerto Rican green papaya salad with cashews, and some shrimp, shark or pork *pinchos* (Puerto Rican skewers). Don't skip dessert; the carmelized banana *pastelillo* with cin-namon, sugar, and vanilla ice cream is out of this world. ⌧ *Route 987, Km 4, Las Croabas, Fajardo* ☎ *787/863–4481* ⊕ *www.laestacionpr.com* ⌕ *Reservations essential.*

**$$$**
CARIBBEAN

✕ **Pasión por el Fogón.** Pasión por el Fogón is one of Fajardo's most beloved restaurants. Owner Norma Guadaloupe, who will no doubt greet you at the door, promises that the service at this perennial favor-ite can't be beat, while chef Myrta Pérez Toledo possesses a talent for taking traditional dishes and making them into something special. Suc-culent cuts of meat and fish are presented in unexpected ways—witness a perfectly cooked flank steak rolled into a cylinder standing on one end. But what makes this dish remarkable is the slightly sweet tamarind sauce that brings out the meat's earthy flavors. If you're a seafood lover, start with the lime-infused red-snapper ceviche, and then move on to the lobster medallions broiled in butter. For dessert, order the "Caribbean Sun," a version of an ice cream sundae that blends caramel, cinnamon, and chocolate toppings. ⌧ *Rte. 987, Km 2.3* ☎ *787/863–3502* ⊕ *www. pasionporelfogon.net* ⌕ *Reservations essential.*

**$$$$**
SEAFOOD

✕ **Stingray Cafe.** Quieter than the other restaurants at the El Conquista-dor Resort due to its location at the bottom of the property's funicular in the marina, the word "cafe" in the restaurant's name is misleading. An elegant dining establishment with an impressive wine list heavy on New World and California reds, the menu features scallops with figs, a roasted pear salad, and a local pumpkin soup for appetizer while thoughtful entrées like pan-seared cod with a lobster beurre blanc sauce paired with melt-in-your-mouth lobster risotto, and a medium-rare fillet of beef with roasted bacon and shallot sauce beg tasting. Though pricey, the waterfront setting offers a getaway from the hustle and bustle of the main property, and the staff and young chef aim to please the whims and palates of their diners. ⌧ *El Conquistador Resort, 1000 Conquis-tador Avenue, Las Croabas, Fajardo* ☎ *787/863* ⊕ *www.elconresort. com* ⌕ *Reservations essential.*

High on top of a bluff, the El Conquistador Resort has commanding views of the ocean.

## WHERE TO STAY
*For expanded hotel reviews, visit Fodors.com.*

**$**
**B&B/INN**
🖼 **Ceiba Country Inn.** About 5 miles (8 km) south of El Yunque in the the town of Ceiba, colorful birds—the same ones from nearby El Yunque—flutter through Ceibi Country Inn's tropical foliage, and you can catch a glimpse of Culebra off the sunny patio. **Pros:** Gorgeous setting; friendly owners; proximity to El Yunque, free Wi-Fi in public areas. **Cons:** Far from tourist areas; several pets roam the property; no elevator. ✉ *Rte. 977, Km 1.2, Ceiba* ☎ 787/885–0471 ⊕ *www.ceibacountryinn.com* ⇆ *9 rooms* ⚘ *In-room: a/c, no TV. In-hotel: parking, some pets allowed* ⓧ *Breakfast.*

**$$$$**
**RESORT**
★
🖼 **El Conquistador Resort & Golden Door Spa.** Perched on a bluff overlooking the ocean, El Conquistador (The Conqueror) is a sprawling complex that has claimed the northern tip of the island and is one of Puerto Rico's most sought-after destination resorts. **Pros:** bright, spacious rooms; unbeatable views of the nearby islands; good dining options; various meal plans available. **Cons:** must take a boat to reach the beach; long waits at the funicular taking guests between levels; self-parking is far from the hotel entrance; hidden fees like parking ($16/day) and kids club ($70/day). ✉ *1000 Av. El Conquistador* ☎ 787/863–1000, 800/468–0389 ⊕ *www.elconresort.com* ⇆ *750 rooms, 15 suites, 234 villas* ⚘ *In-room: a/c, safe, Wi-Fi. In-hotel: restaurant, bar, golf course, pool, tennis court, gym, spa, water sports, children's programs, parking* ⓧ *Some meals.*

**$**
**HOTEL**
☻
🖼 **Fajardo Inn.** The peach-colored buildings that make up this hilltop hotel offer lovely views of the islands poking out of the Atlantic Ocean. **Pros:** Pretty grounds; family-friendly environment; good value. **Cons:**

Not on the beach; motel-like rooms. ✉ *52 Parcelas, Rte. 195, Beltran Sector* ☎ *787/860–6000, 888/860–6006* ⊕ *www.fajardoinn.com* ⇆ *125 rooms* ⎱ *In-room: a/c, kitchen. In-hotel: restaurant, bar, pool, tennis court, gym, children's programs, laundry facilities, business center, parking* ¶◯| *No meals.*

### NIGHTLIFE

Most of the evening action takes place in El Conquistador Resort's lounges, but there are a few neighborhood bars where locals drink beer.

**El Conquistador Casino.** You can play slots, blackjack, roulette, and Caribbean stud poker at El Conquistador Casino, a typical hotel gambling facility within the resort's lavish grounds. ✉ *El Conquistador Resort & Golden Door Spa, 1000 Av. El Conquistador* ☎ *787/863–1000.*

### SPORTS AND THE OUTDOORS

DAY SAILS   Several reputable catamaran and yacht operators in Fajardo make excursions to the reefs and sparkling blue waters surrounding a handful of small islets just off the coast. Many of the trips include transportation to and from San Juan–area hotels. Whether or not you're staying in Fajardo, if you take a day trip on the water, you'll see classic Caribbean scenes of coral reefs rife with sea life, breathtakingly clear water, and palm-fringed, deserted beaches. The day sails, with stops for snorkeling, include swimming breaks at deserted beaches and picnic lunches. Most of the craft are outfitted for comfort, with quality stereo systems and full-service bars. Many competent operators offer a nearly identical experience, so your selection will probably be based on price and which operators serve your San Juan hotel, or which operate out of the marina in Fajardo that you are visiting. Prices range from $55 to $95; price is affected by whether you join a trip in San Juan or in Fajardo and by what is included in the cost. Ask if extras, such as picnic lunches and a full-service bar, are included. They are quickly becoming standard features.

**East Island Excursions.** At East Island Excursions catamarans ranging in size from 45 feet to 65 feet take you offshore for snorkeling. Two of the catamarans are powered, and this cuts down tremendously on the travel time to outlying islands. Trips include stops at isolated beaches and a lunch buffet, and begin at $89 per person. East Island Excursions can accommodate those who wish to see the bioluminescent bay on Vieques and return the same day. All craft are outfitted with swimming decks, freshwater showers, and full-service bars. These vessels are some of the plushest for day sails in the area. ✉ *Marina Puerto del Rey, Rte. 3, Km 51.4* ☎ *787/860–3434, 877/937–4386* ⊕ *www.eastwindcats.com.*

***Erin Go Bragh.*** The *Erin Go Bragh III* is a 50-foot sailing yacht based in Fajardo that takes groups of six or fewer on tours of the glistening waters and nearby islands. Known for delicious barbecue picnic lunches, snorkel and fishing equipment are provided. Overnight and longer charters are available for groups. Call for rates. ✉ *Marina Puerto del Rey, Rte. 3, Km 51.4* ☎ *787/860–4401, 787/409–2511* ⊕ *www.egbc.net.*

**Fajardo Tours.** Leaving from Villa Marina, Fajardo Tours has a 54-foot sailing catamaran called the *Traveler* that delivers you to pristine coral reefs for an afternoon of snorkeling. There's the usual lunch buffet, a salad bar, and plenty of rum punch). Rates start at $70 for adults, $53 for kids 12 and under. ⊠ *Villa Marina, Rte. 987, Km 1.3* ☎ *787/863–2821* ⊕ *www.travelerpr.com.*

**Spread Eagle II.** The *Spread Eagle II* is a 51-foot catamaran that heads out to isolated beaches on the islands off Fajardo. The trip includes an all-you-can-eat buffet and unlimited piña coladas. To top it off, you get a free snorkel to bring home. Sunset and moonlight cruises are also available. ⊠ *Puerto del Rey Marina, Rte. 3, Km 51.4* ☎ *787/887–8821, 888/523–4511* ⊕ *www.snorkelpr.com.*

DIVING **787 Fishing Puerto Rico.** Sail off on one of Captain Marcos Hanke's 22-ft or 26-ft sportfishing boats for deep-sea, light-tackle, or fly-fishing excursions. Inland, tarpon, snook, bonefish, and kingfish can be caught year-round, while game fish like marlin, sailfish, wahoo, tuna, and mahimahi await just offshore. Half-day (four hours) charters begin at $350, full-days charters (eight hours) on the 26-ft boat price at $800. Sunset fishing charters are also available. ⊠ *Marina Puerto Chico, Slips 4 and 6, Fajardo* ☎ *787/646–2585, 787/FISHING* ⊕ *www.787fishing.com.*

**La Casa del Mar Dive Center.** La Casa del Mar Dive Center focuses its scuba and snorkeling activity on the islets of Palominos, Lobos, and Diablo in Fajardo, but also offers trips to Vieques and Culebra, as well as charters to Vieques' wondrous Puerto Mosquito bioluminescent bay. Full-day St. Thomas, U.S. Virgin Islands, dives are also available for $160, as are PADI certification courses. ⊠ *El Conquistador Resort, 1000 Av. El Conquistador* ☎ *787/863–1000, 787/860–3483* ✎ *www. scubapuertorico.net* ⊠ *Two-tank morning dive $99–$125, depending on equipment needs; single-tank afternoon dive $69–$94; snorkeling $60 per person.*

**Sea Ventures Pro Dive Center.** At Sea Ventures Pro Dive Center you can get your diving certification, arrange dive trips to 20 offshore sites, or organize boating and sailing excursions. ⊠ *Marina Puerto del Rey, Rte. 3, Km 51.4* ☎ *800/739-DIVE* ⊕ *www.divepuertorico.com* ⊠ *Two-tank dive for certified divers, including equipment, $119.*

GOLF **El Conquistador Resort.** The 18-hole, Arthur Hills–designed course at El
★ Conquistador Resort is famous for its 200-foot changes in elevation. From the highest spot, on the 15th hole, you have great views of the surrounding mountains. The trade winds make every shot challenging. Greens fees for resort guests range from $90 to $160 and are even steeper for nonguests. ⊠ *1000 Av. El Conquistador* ☎ *787/863–6784.*

KAYAKING Several tour operators, including some based in San Juan, offer nighttime kayaking tours in the bioluminescent bay at the Reserva Natural Las Cabezas de San Juan, just north of Fajardo.

**Kayaking Puerto Rico.** This adventure outfitter has an excursion for all types of water (and kayak) lovers. They offer a host of day and night trips such as kayaking the glowing waters of Fajardo's bioluminescent lagoon, paddling along Culebra's reefs, snorkeling with local turtles, and piloting an eco-friendly, inflatable speed boat across crystal-clear waters. Rates begin at $45 depending on activity; group rates and specials online. ⊠ *Marina Puerto Chico, Route 987, Fajardo* ☎ *787/435–1665, 787/245–4545* ⊕ *www.kayakingpuertorico.com.*

# THE EASTERN COAST

From Fajardo, a good way to explore the southeast is to travel along the old coastal road, Route 3, as it weaves on and off the shoreline and passes through small towns. The route takes a while to travel but offers terrific beach and mountain scenery.

## NAGUABO

*11 miles (18 km) southwest of Fajardo.*

In this fast-growing municipality's downtown, pastel buildings give the main plaza the look of a child's nursery: a golden-yellow church on one side faces a butter-yellow city hall, and a pink-and-blue amphitheater anchors one corner. It's a good spot for people-watching until the heat drives you to the beach.

Offshore, Cayo Santiago—also known as Monkey Island—is the site of some of the world's most important rhesus-monkey research. A small colony of monkeys was introduced to the island in the late 1930s, and since then scientists have been studying their habits and health, especially as they pertain to the study of diabetes and arthritis. You can't land at Cayo Santiago, but Captain Frank Lopez sails a small tour boat—*La Paseadora*—around it.

### GETTING HERE AND AROUND

To reach Naguabo, it takes about an hour driving from San Juan. It's just south of Fajardo off Route 53, along Route 31. From Route 31, turn down Calle Garzot to reach the town square. Although públicos run to and from Naguabo, public transportation within Naguabo is extremely limited, so a rental car is your best transportation option.

### WHERE TO EAT AND STAY

*For expanded hotel reviews, visit Fodors.com.*

$ ✕**Chumar.** As at the other seafood shacks along Playa Húcares, you
PUERTO RICAN order at the counter and then grab a seat at one of the plastic tables lining the sidewalk. It's right on the ocean, so you are almost guaranteed fresh fish. Paper plates and plastic cutlery accompany the down-home seafood, and the sight of locals nursing beers and shooting the breeze is commonplace. Afterward you can stroll along the waterfront walkway across the street. ⊠ *Rte. 3, Km 66, Playa Húcares* ☎ *787/874–0107.*

$ ▦**Casa Cubuy Ecolodge.** El Yunque's southern edge is the setting for this
B&B/INN eco-friendly hotel where the rooms are simple—no phones or TVs—but comfortable, with tile floors, rattan furniture, and windows that show off one of the island's best views. **Pros:** Spectacular setting; close to some of the island's best hiking trails; doting staff. **Cons:** Basic rooms; up a terrible road; lower-level rooms are small. ⊠ *Rte. 191, Km 22, Barrio Río Blanco* ☎ *787/874–6221* ⊕ *www.casacubuy.com* ↰ *10 rooms* ⌂ *In-room: no a/c, no TV, Wi-Fi. In-hotel: parking* ❢◎❢ *Breakfast.*

### SPORTS AND THE OUTDOORS

*La Paseadora.* For 17 years, Captain Frank Lopez has been sailing visitors from Naguabo's Malecon around Cayo Santiago aboard his boat, *La Paseadora.* Lopez, a charming, well-informed guide, gears

The Palmas del Mar Country Club features the Rees Jones–designed Flamboyán course.

the outings to the group, and over the course of three hours, you can motor around and watch the monkeys at Monkey Island—one of the world's oldest primate colonies. Plan to make some fishing and snorkeling stops in local waters using onboard gear. ⊠ *Playa Húcares dock, Rte. 3, Km 66.6* ☎ *787/850–7881, 787/316-0441.*

# HUMACAO

*9 miles (15 km) southwest of Naguabo; 34 miles (55 km) southeast of San Juan.*

Travelers flock to the Humacao area for one reason: the sprawling resort community called Palmas del Mar and its two world-class golf courses, the Flamboyán and the Palm. Although it's not thought of as a tourist destination, Humacao does have a handful of interesting neocolonial buildings along its traffic-clogged downtown streets. These are worth a peek if you're stuck here on a rainy day.

## GETTING HERE AND AROUND

Huamaco is served by two highways and one toll expressway. Route 30 serves as the main highway coming from points west (Caguas and Las Piedras), while Route 53 serves destinations to the north (Fajardo and Naguabo). Route 3, the main highway bordering the eastern coastline of the island from San Juan, passes through Humacao.

## EXPLORING

**Museo Casa Roig.** The former residence of sugar baron Antonio Roig Torruellas, Museo Casa Roig was built in 1919. Czech architect Antonio Nechodoma designed the facade, unusual for its wide eaves, mosaic work, and stained-glass windows with geometric patterns. This building, which bears more than a passing resemblance to those of Frank Lloyd Wright, was Puerto Rico's first 20th-century building to be included on the register of National Historic Places. The Roig family lived in the home until 1956; it was then abandoned before being turned over to the University of Puerto Rico in 1977. It's currently a museum and cultural center that houses historical photos, furniture, and rotating exhibits of works by contemporary island artists. ⊠ *66 Calle Antonio López* ☎ *787/852–8380* 🖅 *Free* ⊘ *Wed.–Sun. 10–4.*

**Plaza de Humacao.** Plaza de Humacao, downtown's broad square, is anchored by the pale pink Catedral Dulce Nombre de Jesús (Sweet Name of Jesus Cathedral), which dates from 1869. It has a castlelike facade, and even when its grille door is locked, you can peek through to see the sleek altar, polished floors, and stained-glass windows dominated by blues. Across the plaza, four fountains splash under the shade of old trees. People pass through feeding the pigeons, children race down the promenade, and retirees congregate on benches to chat. Look for the little monument with the globe on top; it's a tribute to city sons who died in wars. ⊠ *Av. Font Martel at Calle Ulises Martinez.*

**Refugio de Vida Silvestre de Humacao.** As you travel from Naguabo to Humacao, you'll pass stretches of beach and swaths of undeveloped land, including the swamps, lagoons, and forested areas of the Refugio de Vida Silvestre de Humacao. This nature reserve has an information office, restrooms, and campsites. ⊠ *Rte. 3, Km 74.3* ☎ *787/852–4440* 🖅 *Free* ⊘ *Weekdays 7:30–4:30.*

## WHERE TO EAT AND STAY

*For expanded hotel reviews, visit Fodors.com.*

$
CAFÉ

✕ **Bistro Rico.** Most of Humacao's restaurants are within the bounds of the massive Palmas del Mar, and since you can't eat at Chez Daniel every night, Daniel Vasse opened this casual bistro next door to his original restaurant. The menu is mostly made up of sandwiches that are far from the ordinary. The sliced duck breast with caramelized red onions is simple but satisfying, as is the codfish with slices of hard-boiled eggs or the filet mignon with béarnaise sauce. The handful of entrées includes a smashing quiche Lorraine. The staff is friendly, and the simple decor is livened up with some slightly kitschy seaside murals. ⊠ *Palmas del Mar, Anchor's Village Marina, Rte. 906, Km 86.4* ☎ *787/850–3838* ⊘ *Closed Sun.*

$$$$
FRENCH
Fodor's Choice
★

✕ **Chez Daniel.** When the stars are out, it would be hard to find a more romantic setting than this waterfront eatery in the Anchor's Village Marina. Dozens of gleaming white boats are anchored so close that you could practically hit them with a baguette. The dining room has a chummy atmosphere, probably because many patrons seem to know each other. If you'd prefer alone time, ask for a table on one of the private terraces. Chef Daniel Vasse's French-country-style dishes are some of the best on the island. The exceptional Marseille-style bouillabaisse is full of fresh fish and bursts with the flavor of a white garlic sauce. Something less French, you say? Choose steak or fish simply prepared on the grill, and pair it with a bottle from the extensive wine cellar. Sunday brunch, with its seemingly endless seafood bar, draws people from all over the island, and runs $45 per person with drinks. ⊠ *Palmas del Mar, Anchor's Village Marina, Rte. 906, Km 86.4* ☎ *787/850–3838* ⊕ *www. chezdanielpalmasdelmar.com* ⌦ *Reservations essential* ✆ *Closed Tues.*

**$$**  **Wyndham Garden at Palmas de Mar.** Amid acres and acres of condo
**HOTEL** developments and golf courses, Wyndham Garden, the only hotel in Palmas del Mar, is surprisingly modest in scale, given its opulent surroundings. **Pros:** Access to all the resort's amenities; beautiful pool area; outgoing staff; free Wi-Fi. **Cons:** Uninspired architecture; small casino. ⊠ *170 Candelero Dr.* ☎ *787/850–6000* ⊕ *www.wyndham.com* ⇌ *84 rooms, 9 suites, 14 junior suites* ⌂ *In-room: a/c, safe, Internet, Wi-Fi. In-hotel: restaurant, bar, golf course, pool, tennis court, gym, beach, water sports, business center, parking* ⍾ *No meals.*

### NIGHTLIFE

**Wyndham Garden at Palmas del Mar.** The small casino at the Wyndham Garden at Palmas del Mar Resort offers everything from blackjack to slot machines. The action is liveliest on weekends. ⊠ *170 Candelero Dr.* ☎ *787/850–6000.*

### SPORTS AND THE OUTDOORS

#### FISHING

**Karolette Sport Fishing.** At Karolette Sport Fishing you're in the capable hands of Captain Bill Burleson, who has fished these waters since 1966. He'll take you out for excursions in his bright yellow 46-foot Bertram powerboat. A half day of fishing along the continental shelf costs $680, while a full day (usually more than nine hours) of deep-water fishing costs $1,290. If nobody makes a catch, he'll cut the fee in half. ⊠ *Palmas del Mar, Anchor's Village Marina* ☎ *787/637–7992* ⊕ *www. puertoricodeepseafishing.com.*

**Maragata Charters.** Maragata Charters takes anglers out from Palmas del Mar on a 38-foot power catamaran. Snorkeling and combination trips to Monkey Island, Vieques, and Culebra are also offered. ⊠ *Palmas del Mar, Anchor's Village Marina, Slip #14* ☎ *787/850–7548 Marina, 787/637–1802 Cell* ⊕ *www.maragatacharters.com* ⊠ *Four-hour tours start at $105 per person; eight-hour tours start at $200 per person.*

#### GOLF

★ **Palmas del Mar Country Club.** Palmas del Mar Country Club has two good golf courses: The Rees Jones–designed Flamboyán course, named for the nearly six dozen flamboyant trees that pepper its fairway, has been rated one of the top five courses in the world. The older Gary Player–designed Palm course has a challenging par 5 that scoots around wetlands. ⊠ *Palmas del Mar, Route 906* ☎ *787/656–8548* ⊕ *www. palmaspac.com* ⅃ *Greens fees from $95.*

# Vieques and Culebra

**WORD OF MOUTH**

"Going to Vieques was very easy, but it would be good to have a car there since it was hard to get taxis. We were not allowed to bring our rental car there and I think the car ferry only goes a few days a week so it is best to get a car when you get there. We also tried to go to Culebra but that ferry is much smaller, so get there a few hours early for tickets to Culebra." —AliceL

# WELCOME TO VIEQUES AND CULEBRA

## TOP REASONS TO GO

★ **Puerto Mosquito:** Kayak after dark on the astounding bioluminescent bay on Vieques.

★ **Playa Flamenco:** Catch some rays on this Culebra bay, consistently ranked as one of the world's best white-sand beaches.

★ **Bicycle Refugio Nacional de Vida Silvestre de Vieques:** Explore around the base of Monte Pirata on the western side of the island.

★ **El Resuelve:** Sample real Puerto Rican fare with the locals at this colorful roadside restaurant on Vieques.

★ **Playa Carlos Rosario:** Simply walk into the waters off this deserted Culebra beach to snorkel a fabulous coral reef.

*Pasaje de San Juan*
Cayo Icacos
Cayo Lobos
Cayo Diablo
Isla Palominos
987
Cayo Zancudo
3
Fajardo
976
Pta. Barrabás
Pta. Mata Redonda
3
53
Puerto Medio Mundo
Isla Piñeros
Ceiba
José Aponte de la Torre Airport
Punta Puerca
*Sonda de Vieques*
Punta Cascajo
Punta Algodones
*Pasaje de Vieques*

0      4 mi
0      4 km

Pta. Arenas
Monte Pirata
Green Beach
Esperanza
201
Playa Sun Bay

**1 Vieques.** This wild island, two-thirds of which is now a wildlife refuge, is a fabulous destination for active travelers who like bicycling, kayaking, and fishing. It is fringed by gorgeous beaches, and a visit to the bioluminescent bay is an awesome experience visitors will never forget. Boutique hotels and trendy restaurants have recently begun to open, and the W Resort & Spa and the Malecon House will appeal to urbane fashionistas.

Punta de Molinos

Cayo Lobito

Cayo Lobo

Cayo Norte

Cayo Geniqui

Isla Culebrita

▲ Monte Resaca

251

Cayo de Luis Peña

Dewey ○ *Playa Flamenco*

**2**

*ISLA DE CULEBRA* Punta del Soldado

Isabel Segunda

200

*ISLA DE VIEQUES* Cerro Matias Jalobre ▲

**1**

197

*Blue Beach*

Red Beach

Playa Media Luna

Puerto Mosquito

Pta. Salinas

Pta. Este

# GETTING ORIENTED

Vieques is 21 miles (33½ km) long and 4 miles (6½ km) wide and has two small communities. Isabel Segunda, on the northern shore, is the main town, where the ferry docks. On the southern shore is the village of Esperanza, a string of low-cost bars, restaurants, and hotels along a waterfront promenade that is growing in size. Nearby is the world-famous bioluminescent bay Puerto Mosquito. The bulk of the island is a national park, the Vieques National Wildlife Refuge. Within the park you'll find dozens of beaches with names such as Caracas, Pata Prieta, and Chiva, as well as many more that have no official names, and can be found off unpaved side roads. At 7 miles (11 km) long and 4 miles (6½ km) wide, Culebra is much smaller and less developed than Vieques. There's only one community, the tiny town of Dewey.

**2** Culebra. The island is mostly unspoiled, a quality that brings many people back year after year. People come to Culebra to laze on Playa Flamenco, consistently rated one of the top 10 most beautiful beaches in the world, as well as many lesser-known but sensational expanses of sand. Snorkeling and diving on the cays surrounding Culebra are rated world-class.

4

# BEACHES OF VIEQUES AND CULEBRA

Vieques and Culebra are where you'll find Puerto Rico's most serene shores. Ideal for romantic strolls or family swims, the calm waters and long unspoiled stretches here are what you probably had in mind when you envisioned a Caribbean beach paradise.

Head to the beautiful semicircular shore of Playa Sun Bay on weekdays for less crowds and enjoy a stroll on more than a mile of soft, white sands.

Many of the beaches around Vieques were once named by the U.S. Navy, which assigned them random colors: Red Beach, Blue Beach, and Green Beach. Most beaches have since been renamed in Spanish by locals. Islanders know Sun Bay as Sombé. Those within the Vieques National Wildlife Refuge are open 6 am–sunset. Of Vieques's more than three-dozen beaches, Sun Bay east of Esperanza is easily the most popular. Although both islands' beaches are favored for their comparative isolation, crowds can gather on weekends at the most popular spots such as Culebra's spectacular Playa Flamenco. On weekdays, however, it's not uncommon for large swaths of shore on either island to be sparsely populated.

## WORD OF MOUTH

"Flamenco beach is a must see. White, soft powdery sand, clear water. Water may or may not be calm depending on the time, but there is a shallow, calm area close to the rock pier that is good for kids to play. I recommend MamaCita's for lunch or dinner. [But] if you don't feel like going to town, you can get a decent barbecue chicken/pork-and-rice dish for about $5 at the picnic area at the end of the beach." –bluecow

## VIEQUES

**La Chiva.** Also known as Blue Beach, some consider this the most beautiful beach on Vieques. It has a handful of covered cabañas with individual parking spots so that guests can claim their own personal stretch of sand and gaze onto an expansive, tranquil horizon. Beware of strong surf in some spots, making swimming difficult. ⊠ *Off Rte. 997, 2½ miles (4 km) east of Esperanza.*

**Pata Prieta.** Not so secret Secret Beach is a heavenly cove for those seeking privacy. This tiny yet beautiful horseshoe-shaped stretch of sand, reached via a brambling dirt road, is calm and secluded. You can find yourself completely alone, or one of a few couples embracing in the crystal-clear water. Relish the unadulterated bliss of this perfect spot, an Eden like no other. ⊠ *Off Rte. 997, east of Playa Caracas.*

**Playa Media Luna.** Ideal for families because the water is calm and shallow, this is also a good spot to try your hand at snorkeling. There are no facilities. ⊠ *Off Rte. 997, east of Playa Sun Bay.*

**Playa Sun Bay.** The 1-mile-long (1½-km-long) white sands skirt a crescent-shaped bay. You'll find food kiosks, picnic tables, and changing facilities. It gets packed on holidays and weekends. On weekdays, when the crowds are thin, you might see wild horses grazing among the palm trees. Parking is $3, but

often no one is at the gate to take your money. ⊠ *Rte. 997, east of Esperanza* ☎ *787/741–8198.*

## CULEBRA

★ **Fodor's Choice** **Playa Flamenco.** Consistently ranked one of the most beautiful in the world. Snow-white sands, turquoise waters, and lush hills that rise on all sides make it feel miles away from civilization. During the week it's pleasantly uncrowded; on weekends it fills up fast with day-trippers from the mainland. It's the only beach on Culebra with amenities such as camping, restrooms, showers, and kiosks selling simple fare. ⊠ *Rte. 251, west of the airport.* ☎ *787/742–0700* ☉ *Daily dawn–dusk.*

**Playa Melones.** Just west of Dewey, this is a favorite spot for snorkelers. The reef that runs around the rocky point is easy to reach from shore. Locals swear this is the best place to watch sunsets. To get here, head uphill on the unmarked road behind the church. ⊠ *Camino Vecinal, west of Dewey.*

**Playa Zoni.** On the island's northeastern end, this beach is long and narrow—perfect for afternoon strolls. From the shore you can catch a glimpse of Isla Culebrita, not to mention St. Thomas and St. Croix. Leatherback turtles nest here. ⊠ *At the end of Rte. 250, 7 miles (11 km) northeast of Dewey.*

Updated by
Marie-Elena
Martinez

Although the islands of Vieques and Culebra—known as the "Spanish Virgins"—are only a few miles off the coast of Puerto Rico, they feel like another world. While the rest of the mainland rings with the adrenaline rush of Latin America, this pair of palm-fringed islands has the laid-back vibe of the Caribbean—not surprising, as St. Thomas and St. Croix are clearly visible from the eastern edges of Culebra.

Vieques and Culebra are alike in many ways. Neither has much traffic—in fact, you won't find a single traffic light on either island. High-rise hotels haven't cast a shadow on the beaches. And there are no casinos, fast-food chains, strip malls, or most other trappings of modern life. "Barefoot" is often part of the dress code at the casual restaurants, and the hum you hear in your room more likely comes from a ceiling fan rather than an air conditioner. Things happen here *poco a poco*—slowly, at the islanders' easy pace.

Beautiful beaches abound on both islands. Many of the best stretches of sand on Vieques—Chiva, Caracas, and Green Beach, to name a few—are on land that was once part of a U.S. naval base. This means that development hasn't reared its ugly head. It also means there are few, if any, amenities, so bring plenty of water and a picnic lunch. Most accommodations provide guests with beach chairs, towels, and coolers for the day. Some will even pack guests lunches to take to the beach. The beaches on Culebra are just as unspoiled, as judged by marine turtles, which come ashore to lay eggs.

Wild horses roam Vieques, where two-thirds of the island is a wildlife refuge protecting coastal lagoons, mangrove wetlands, subtropical dry forest, and islands. Ecotourism is a key draw. Fishing in the turquoise flats just offshore is fantastic. And the island is tailor-made for exploring by bicycle and/or kayak. On Culebra several cays delight birders with their colonies of boobies and other seabirds.

Some of the best snorkeling and diving in the Caribbean can be found in the waters surrounding Vieques and Culebra. You can sign up for a half-day or full-day excursion to nearby coral reefs, which are teeming with colorful fish. It's also possible to grab a mask and snorkel, and then simply wade out a few yards to see what you can see. Playa Esperanza, on the southern coast of Vieques, is a good place for beginners. More experienced snorkelers will prefer Blue Beach or Green Beach.

## VIEQUES AND CULEBRA PLANNER

### WHEN TO GO

High season runs roughly from December 15 through April 15. Puerto Ricans flock at Christmas and Easter, when Vieques and Culebra are packed with families enjoying the sun and sand. Be sure to make reservations well in advance if you're visiting during the holidays. The shoulder season, when prices are a bit lower, is a good option. Remember, however, that some restaurants and hotels are open only during the high season. The only time you might want to avoid is late August through late October, when hurricanes can strike the area.

### GETTING HERE AND AROUND

#### AIR TRAVEL

**Air Flamenco.** Air Flamenco flies daily from San Juan's Isla Grande Airport to Vieques and Culebra, and charters from SJU International Airport. ☎ *787/724–1818, 787/724–1105* ⊕ *www.airflamenco.net.*

**Cape Air.** Cape Air flies between SJU International Airport and Vieques. ☎ *866/Cape–Air, 508/771–6944* ⊕ *www.flycapeair.com.*

**Vieques Air Link.** Vieques Air Link flies daily from San Juan's Luis Muñoz International Airport, nearby Isla Grande Airport, and eastern Ceiba to Vieques and Culebra. There is a direct flight between Vieques and Culebra. Round-trip prices range from $60 to $230 depending on season. Charters are also available at higher prices. ☎ *888/901–9247* ⊕ *www.viequesairlink.com.*

These companies also fly from Ceiba (Fajardo). Flights from San Juan are 20 to 30 minutes, and one-way fares are between $65 and $125; flights from Ceiba are about 10 minutes with one-way fares between $30 and $50. Small propeller planes that hold up to nine passengers are used.

Most international travelers fly from San Juan's Aeropuerto Internacional Luis Muñoz Marín (SJU) or nearby Aeropuerto Fernando L. Rivas Dominicci (SIG; more commonly known as Aeropuerto Isla Grande), which is cheaper. Most of the companies that fly from San Juan also fly from Ceiba's Aeropuerto José Aponte de la Torre (RVR) about 7 miles (12 km) south of Fajardo.

#### CAR TRAVEL

It's nearly impossible to see either island without renting a car. Scooters are another option, especially on Culebra, but not if you're headed to the beach. Road conditions and local driving habits are spotty. Both islands have local agencies, including several that specialize in SUVs. Rates are between $40 and $95 a day. It's cheaper to book a hotel-rental car package.

### FERRY TRAVEL

**Puerto Rico Ports Authority.** The Puerto Rico Ports Authority runs passenger ferries from Fajardo to Culebra and Vieques. Service is from the ferry terminal in Fajardo, about 90 minutes' drive from San Juan, and costs approximately $2–$3. ☎ *800/981–2005 ⊕ www.dtop.gov.pr.*

Car ferries also link Fajardo to Vieques and Culebra, but rental agencies won't let you take their vehicles between the mainland and islands. A municipal parking lot next to the ferry costs $5 a day. No ferries link Vieques and Culebra.

There's limited seating, so arrive about an hour ahead of the departure time. The Ports Authority claims to take phone reservations daily from 8 to 11 and 1 to 3, but it's difficult to get anyone to answer this number.

**Fajardo Terminal.** Schedules change often, and ferries are often canceled due to bad weather. Call the Fajardo Terminal to confirm before you plan your trip. ☎ *787/860–2005.*

### ABOUT THE RESTAURANTS

Most of the restaurants on Vieques and Culebra are casual. Because even the most formal restaurants on the islands are on covered terraces or in open-air dining rooms, there's not a single establishment where you'll be frowned on for wearing shorts. Pack a couple of nice shirts and you'll be set.

You'll find seafood at almost every eatery on Vieques and Culebra. The fish is as fresh as you'll find anywhere, since that red snapper was probably splashing around in the Caribbean that very morning. Here you can order your fish in any number of ways. Chefs are experimenting with European and Asian cooking techniques, so you may find your fish smoked or in a sushi roll.

Even if a restaurant focuses on a different type of food, you can be sure that mangos, papayas, and other tropical fruits will make an appearance. Bills often include a service charge; if it isn't included, a 15% tip is customary. Most restaurants are open for dinner from about 6 pm until at least 10 pm.

### ABOUT THE HOTELS

Vieques has a wide variety of lodgings, from surf shacks across from the beach to boutique hotels high up on secluded hillsides. There's something here for everyone. Looking for tropical splendor? Try Hacienda Tamarindo. Sexy sophistication? Head to the W Resort & Spa. Interesting architecture? There's Hix Island House. An intimate inn where you'll meet fellow travelers? Head to Casa de Amistad or Trade Winds.

Culebra has fewer options. Dewey, the island's only town, has a handful of small inns that are easy on the wallet. Scattered around the island are a couple of more luxurious lodgings plus villa rentals. Nothing remotely resembles a chain hotel, and that's how the locals like it.

| WHAT IT COSTS IN U.S. DOLLARS | | | | |
|---|---|---|---|---|
| | ¢ | $ | $$ | $$$ | $$$$ |
| Restaurants | under $8 | $8–$12 | $12–$20 | $20–$30 | over $30 |
| Hotels | under $80 | $80–$150 | $150–$250 | $250–$350 | over $350 |

Prices are for a double room in high season, excluding 9% tax (7% for paradores) and 5%–12% service charge.

### SAFETY

Vieques is relatively crime-free compared with San Juan, although it pays to be on your guard. Avoid bringing valuables to the beach, and don't leave any personal items in your car. Rental agencies advise that you leave your car unlocked when parked at a beach so thieves won't break the windows to get inside. There's very little crime on Culebra.

### WHAT TO PACK

Vieques has a pharmacy and a hospital, and Culebra's small hospital has a prescription-only pharmacy. Stock up on all supplies—such as allergy medications, contact-lens solution, or feminine supplies—before heading to the islands.

### VISITOR INFORMATION

The island's tourism offices are hit and miss when it comes to offering helpful material.

**Vieques Tourism Office.** The Vieques Tourism Office is across the main square in Isabel Segunda. If you need information, ask them to print out a complete list of local businesses. ⊠ *449 Calle Carlos Lebrón, Isabel Segunda, Vieques* ☎ *787/741–0800* ☺ *Mon.–Sat. 8–4:30.*

**Culebra Tourism Office.** The Culebra Tourism Office is near the ferry dock in front of Banco Popular. The staffers will help you as best they can, even recommending restaurants that are off the beaten path. The office is open weekdays 8–4:30. ⊠ *250 Calle Pedro Marquez, Dewey, Culebra* ☎ *787/742–1033.*

# VIEQUES

*8 miles (13 km) southeast of Fajardo.*

Looking for a place to play Robinson Crusoe? Then head to Vieques, where you can wander along almost any stretch of sand and never see another soul. You can while away the hours underneath coconut palms, wade in the warm water, or get a mask and snorkel and explore the coral reefs that ring the island.

For many years the island was known mostly for the conflict between angry islanders and aloof federal officials. Over the course of six decades, the U.S. Navy used two-thirds of Vieques, mostly on the island's eastern side, as a bombing range, and the western tip as an ammunition dump. After an April 1999 bombing accident took the life of one resident, waves of protests brought the maneuvers to a standstill, and political pressure from the island's governor helped force the military to leave on May 1, 2003.

# Vieques

**KEY**
1 Restaurants
1 Hotels

*Sonda de Vieques*

ISLA DE
VIEQUES

TO
FAJARDO

Sonda de Vieques

Punta Salinas
Punta Este

Bahía Salina del Sur

Purple Beach

Cerro Matías

Vieques National Wildlife Refuge

Cayo Jalova

Ensenada Honda

Playa Chiva (Blue Beach)

El Fortín Conde de Mirasol

El Faro Punta Mulas

Sidhia Hutchinson Fine Art Studio & Gallery

Isabel Segunda

Playa Caracas

Puerto Ferro

200

201

996

200

201

997

995

Gringo Beach

Antonio R. Rodríguez Airport

Mosquito

Puerto Mosquito

Playa Sun Bay

Playa Media Luna

Esperanza

Malecón

Vieques Conservation & Historical Trust

Monte Pirata

Vieques National Wildlife Refuge

Punta Arenas

Playa Plata (Green Beach)

Pasaje de Vieques

3 mi

3 km

**Restaurants**

| | |
|---|---|
| Bananas | 8 |
| Bilí | 7 |
| Carambola | 5 |
| Chez Shack | 3 |
| Conuco | 1 |
| Duffy's | 6 |
| El Quenepo | 9 |
| El Resuelve | 10 |
| Mix on the Beach | 2 |
| Next Course | 4 |

**Hotels**

| | |
|---|---|
| Bravo Beach Hotel | 1 |
| Casa de Amistad | 2 |
| Hacienda Tamarindo | 6 |
| Hector's | 8 |
| Hix Island House | 4 |
| Inn on the Blue Horizon | 7 |
| La Finca Caribe | 5 |
| Malecon House | 10 |
| Seagate Hotel | 11 |
| Trade Winds | 9 |
| W Retreat & Spa | 3 |

Ironically, the military's presence helped to keep the island pristine by keeping resort developers away. Today, the military's former holdings have been turned into the Vieques National Wildlife Refuge. The woodsy western end of the island is laced by trails that offer fabulous cycling around the base of Monte Pirata, the island's highest peak. More and more of the eastern part of the island is being opened every year, granting access to stupendous beaches shelving into calm turquoise waters. The park also protects Puerto Mosquito, a flask-shaped bay populated by microscopic organisms that glow when disturbed at night—a thrilling experience for kayakers *(see also Bioluminescent Bays feature in this chapter)*.

**GETTING HERE AND AROUND**
Isabel Segunda is the transportation hub of Vieques. The ferry drops off passengers at the town's dock, and propeller planes deposit passengers at Aeropuerto Antonio Rivera Rodríguez (VQS), which is a 10-minute cab ride from Isabel Segunda or a 15-minute taxi ride from Esperanza. Route 200 leads from the airport to Isabel Segunda, and Route 997 leads from Isabel Segunda to Esperanza. There's also a longer, more scenic route between the two towns: from Isabel Segunda, take Route 200 west to Route 201 south. After about 1 mile (1½ km), take Route 996 to Esperanza.

If you want to rent a car or gas up the one you already have, you need to make a trip to Isabel Segunda. Try Vieques Car Rental, Maritza Car Rental, or Martineau Car Rental.

You can flag down taxis on the street, but it's faster and safer to have your hotel call one for you. Either way, agree on how much the trip will cost before you get inside the taxi, as many drivers are prone to rip off tourists with exorbitant fares. ■TIP→ If you plan to rent a car on Vieques or Culebra, make sure you reserve it in advance, especially when visiting during high season. The rental agencies have a limited number of vehicles, and when they are gone you're out of luck.

**Airport Information Aeropuerto Antonio Rivera Rodríguez** ⊠ *Route 200, Km 2.6, Vieques* ☎ *787/741–0515.*

**Car Rental Avis—W Retreat and Spa** ⊠ *W Retreat & Spa, KM 3.2, Rte 200, Vieques* ☎ *787/741–4100* ⊕ *www.avis.com.* **Vieques Car Rental** ⊠ *KM 1, Route 200, Monti Santo, Vieques* ☎ *787/435–1323* ⊕ *viequescarrental.com.* **Maritza's Car Rental** ⊠ *Rte. 201, Vieques* ☎ *787/741–0078* ⊕ *www.maritzascarrental. com.* **Martineau Car Rental** ⊠ *Rte. 200, Km 3.4, Vieques* ☎ *787/741–0087* ⊕ *www.martineaucarrental.com.*

**Ferry Terminal Vieques Terminal** ☎ *787/741–5018* ⊕ *www.dtop.gov.pr.*

**Taxis Lolo Felix Tours** ⊠ *Vieques* ☎ *787/485–5447.*

# EXPLORING VIEQUES

Just because Vieques is sleepy doesn't mean there's nothing to do besides hit the beach. There are two communities—Isabel Segunda and Esperanza—where you can dine at a variety of excellent restaurants, stock up

## GREAT ITINERARIES

### IF YOU HAVE 1 DAY

If you are headed to one of the islands for an overnight excursion, your best bet is **Vieques**. Get here by plane, either from San Juan or Fajardo, to maximize your time on the island. Spend the day exploring the beaches, especially the half-moon-shaped Sun Bay. In the evening you can dine at one of the oceanfront restaurants in Esperanza, then head off for an excursion to **Puerto Mosquito**, a bay filled with glow-in-the-dark dinoflagellates. Spend the night in Esperanza or Isabel Segunda.

### IF YOU HAVE 3 DAYS

If you have a few days, you can see most of Vieques. Start your first day in Isabel Segunda, where you can take a few snapshots of **El Faro Punta Mulas**, and then explore the hilltop **El Fortín Conde de Mirasol**. Head off for an afternoon by the ocean, perhaps at Green Beach or one of the delightfully deserted beaches on the northern part of the island. Enjoy happy hour at Lazy Jack's, a favorite hangout for expats, in Esperanza. In the cool of the evening, have dinner in one of the chic eateries nearby. On your second day, go for an early-morning mountain-bike ride in the western portion of the

Vieques National Wildlife Refuge, a swath of wilderness that was once a naval base. Head for lunch at El Resuelve, or pack a picnic and head off to Playa Media Luna or another of the beautiful beaches along the southern coast. After dinner, make sure to book a tour of **Puerto Mosquito**. Spend your third day kayaking, snorkeling, and/or fishing. In the evening, head to W Retreat & Spa for a spa treatment, cocktails, and fine dining at Mix on the Beach.

### IF YOU HAVE 5 DAYS

If you have a few more days, you can see both Vieques and Culebra. *After following the itinerary above,* head to Culebra on your fourth day. (A 10-minute flight between the islands is the only way to travel between them.) Your destination should be Playa Flamenco, a long, curving beach of talcum-white sands and turquoise waters. The mountains beyond make a striking backdrop. Dine that evening at Susie's in the only town, diminutive Dewey. On your last day, try snorkeling in **Refugio Nacional de Vida Silvestre de Culebra**, the island's lovely nature preserve. One of the best places for a morning boat trip is **Isla Culebrita**, an islet dominated by a deserted lighthouse.

on supplies, or book a trip to the astonishing Puerto Mosquito, perhaps the world's most luminous bioluminescent bay.

**Playa Caracas.** Also known as Red Beach, Playa Caracas is the first beach reached after turning off of Route 997. This beach is well maintained and boasts covered cabañas for lounging away from the sun. Less rustic than some of the nearby beaches, this spot is good for snorkeling and sheltered from waves. ⊠ *1 mile off Route 997, Vieques.*

## ISABEL SEGUNDA

*18 miles (29 km) southeast of Fajardo by ferry.*

Isabel Segunda (or Isabel II, as it's often labeled on maps) has charms that are not immediately apparent. There's a lovely lighthouse on the

El Faro Punta Mulas, a lighthouse built in 1895, is now a small museum exhibiting Vieques historical items.

coast just east of the ferry dock, and on the hill above town you'll find the last fort the Spanish constructed in the New World. You can also find some of the best restaurants and a great bar here, as well as lodgings ranging from funky to fancy.

**El Faro Punta Mulas.** El Faro Punta Mulas, a Spanish-built lighthouse above the ferry dock in Isabel Segunda, dates from 1895. It was built to guide vessels into the harbor, which is surrounded by a chain of dangerous reefs. Its red light is rumored to be seen from as far away as St. Croix and St. Thomas. In 1992 the elegant structure was carefully restored and transformed into a maritime museum that traced much of the island's history, including the visit by South American liberation leader Simón Bolívar. The tiny museum is open weekdays, but the lighthouse itself is worth a look on any day. ⊠ *At end of Rte. 200, Isabel Segunda, Vieques* ☎ *787/741–0060* ✉ *Free* ☺ *Weekdays 8–3.*

**El Fortín Conde de Mirasol** (*Count of Mirasol Fort*). On a hilltop overlooking Isabel Segunda is El Fortín Conde de Mirasol, the last military structure built by the Spanish in the New World. It was erected on Vieques's northern coast in 1840 at the order of Count Mirasol, then governor of Puerto Rico. Although it's tiny, it took more than a decade to complete, which meant Mirasol had to repeatedly ask for more money. (Queen Isabel, on being petitioned yet again, asked Mirasol whether the walls were made of gold.) The fort helped solidify Spanish control of the area, keeping British, French, Dutch, and Danish colonists away and dissuading pirates from attacking Isabel Segunda. After sitting empty for several decades, it was transformed into a museum in 1991. The museum has an impressive collection of artifacts from the Taíno Indians and other

Popular with local fisherman, the gentle waters of Esperanza Beach are ideal for small boats.

cultures that thrived on this and nearby islands before the arrival of the Spanish. It also has an impressive collection of small arms, plus exhibits on the island's years as a sugar plantation and its occupation by the U.S. Navy. On occasion, it presents temporary exhibitions of contemporary artists. ⊠ *Calle El Fuerte, Isabel Segunda, Vieques* ☎ *787/741–1717* ⊕ *www.icp.gobierno.pr* ✉ *$2* ☉ *Wed.–Sun. 9–5:30.*

## ESPERANZA

*6 miles (10 km) south of Isabel Segunda.*

The only time there's a traffic jam in Esperanza is when one of the wild horses frequently seen on the nearby beaches wanders into the road. This community, once a down-at-the-heels fishing village, now hosts a string of bars, restaurants, and small hotels on the waterfront drag. All of them overlook Playa Esperanza, a shallow stretch of sand made all the more picturesque by the presence of a tiny islet called Cayo Afuera.

**Malecón.** In the evening, there's not a better way to enjoy the sunset than a stroll along Esperanza's 200-yard-long Malecón, a waterfront walkway running the length of the beach. ⊠ *Esperanza, Vieques.*

**Vieques Conservation & Historical Trust.** The Vieques Conservation & Historical Trust was established to help save Puerto Mosquito, one of the last remaining bioluminescent bays in the world. The small museum, located on the main drag in Esperanza, was recently upgraded and has interesting information about the bay, as well as the island's flora and fauna and history. A little pool lets kids get acquainted with starfish, sea urchins, and other denizens of the not-so-deep. There's also a tiny gift shop where the profits are funneled back into the foundation. Call ahead if you're coming at lunchtime, as the place is sometimes closed for an hour or more. ✉ *138 Calle Flamboyán, Esperanza, Vieques* 🕾 *787/741–8850* ⊕ *www.vcht.org* ✉ *Free* ☉ *Tues.–Sun. 11–4.*

### ELSEWHERE ON VIEQUES

Isabel Segunda and Esperanza are just a tiny portion of Vieques. Most of the island—more than two-thirds of it, in fact—was commandeered by the military until 2003. It's now a nature preserve that draws thousands of visitors each year.

Fodor's Choice
★

**Puerto Mosquito Bioluminescent Bay.** East of Esperanza, Puerto Mosquito Bioluminescent Bay is one of the world's best spots to have a glow-in-the-dark experience with undersea dinoflagellates. Local tour operators like Abe's offer kayak trips or excursions on nonpolluting boats to see the bay's microorganisms, which appear to light up when the water around them is agitated. Look behind your boat, and you'll see a twinkling wake. Even the fish that swim through and jump from the water will bear an eerie glow. The high concentration of dinoflagellates sets the bay apart from the other spots around the world (including others in Puerto Rico) that are home to these algae. The bay is at its best when there's little or no moonlight; rainy nights are beautiful, too, because the raindrops splashing in the water produce ricochet sparkles that shimmer like diamonds. *See also the Bioluminescent Bays feature in this chapter.* ✉ *Reach via unpaved roads off Rte. 997, Vieques.*

**Vieques National Wildlife Refuge.** A portion of the west and the entire eastern end of the island is administered by the U.S. Fish & Wildlife Service as the Vieques National Wildlife Refuge, comprising 18,000 acres—about 14,900 acres on the eastern end and 3,100 acres on the west—making it the biggest protected natural reserve in Puerto Rico. The 900-acre bombing range is permanently closed off, a consequence of its contamination by the ammunition shot over its 60-year existence. But most of the rest of eastern Vieques is pristine nature, astonishingly beautiful and well forested, with a hilly center region overlooking powder-white sandy beaches and a coral-ringed coastline; it served mainly as a buffer zone between the military maneuvers and civilian population. The vast majority of this acreage remains off-limits to visitors as authorities carry out a search for unexploded munitions and contaminants. Nonetheless, many of the beaches on the northern and southern coasts are open to the public; in 2009 a new asphalt road opened up six southern beaches. ⌂ *Box 1527, Vieques 00765* 🕾 *787/741–2138* ⊕ *www.fws.gov.*

## WHERE TO EAT

$
CARIBBEAN

✗ **Bananas.** This longtime open-air favorite with playful rain-forest murals climbing the walls in a prime spot in Esperanza that ogles the Caribbean is geared toward gringos. If you're looking for authentic island food, this isn't your place. But they certainly serve up some good Puerto Rican fare. Claim a spot at one of the curvy red concrete tables or under an umbrella-shade out front and order the red-snapper sandwich (popular at lunchtime), or the jerk chicken. Salads are excellent, including the *caribeño* (fresh greens with curried chicken), but be sure to save room for the namesake dish—deep-fried bananas with finger-lickin' hot honey sauce. When the sun goes down, Bananas is one of the hot spots on this side of the island. With new breakfast items and smoothies on the menu, you can spend the night at the attached no-frills guesthouse and stay through dawn. ⊠ *142 Calle Flamboyán, Esperanza, Vieques* ☎ *787/741–8700* ⊕ *www.bananasguesthouse.com.*

**$$** ✕ **Bilí.** Next door to Bananas, this airy and colorful Mediterranean-
CARIBBEAN style tapas restaurant deserves better than the overflow from its more established neighbor. It has the same view, sleeker decor, and more authentic food, prepared by Eva Bolívar, former private chef to a Puerto Rican governor. For lunch, order a tasty sandwich such as dorado wrap with caramelized onions, plantains, and roasted peppers. For something heartier, try seafood paella—the house specialty. Stop by for a beer in the evening and you won't have to shout to be heard. ⊠ *144 Calle Flamboyán, Esperanza, Vieques* ☎ *787/741–1382* ⊕ *enchanted-isle.com/amapola.*

**$$$** ✕ **Carambola.** It's hard to imagine a more romantic setting than this
CARIBBEAN dining room with unbeatable views of the ocean. Indoors is a long wooden table, surrounded by chairs upholstered in a delectable shade of chocolate brown. Through the open doors are smaller tables scattered around the open-air terrace. The service is formal, and so are the meals. The former five- or seven-course set meals have been replaced by an à la carte menu featuring such main courses as lamb chops with a lentil balsamic salad or the mofongo special with jumbo shrimps. In low season, dining is sometimes restricted to the less elegant terrace. ⊠ *Inn on the Blue Horizon, Rte. 996, Km 4.2, Esperanza, Vieques* ☎ *787/741–3318* ⊕ *www.innonthebluehorizon.com.*

**$$** ✕ **Chez Shack.** Owned by one of the more eccentric personalities on the
ECLECTIC island, the original Duffy (of Duffy's in Esperanza), this restaurant is not exactly a shack—but it's close. Whether it will be open or closed on any given night during high season is anyone's guess, as Duffy himself is well into his 80's. If you're lucky enough to experience the joint, it's set in a delightfully ramshackle wooden building off the beaten track on Route 995, off Route 201—a road that winds through Vieques's tropical hills. The dining room is inches from the pavement, but it's unlikely a single car will pass by while you're enjoying your meal. Chicken, beef, and seafood such as baked crab are prepared to tender perfection, but the menu changes according to whim. It's famous for its weekly barbecue night with a steel band (schedule changes from week to week); on other nights good jazz or island rhythms usually flow from the sound system. ⊠ *Rte. 995, Km 1.8, Vieques* ☎ *787/741–2175* ⌨ *Reservations essential* ⏱ *Closed in the off-season.*

**$$** ✕ **Conuco.** A mix of locals and gringos frequents excellent newcomer
PUERTO RICAN Conuco, soft-spoken Puerto Rico native Rebecca Betancourt's homage
Fodor'sChoice to local food with an upscale twist. Barnlike open windows look out
★ onto one of Isabel Segunda's main streets, and within, the airy room is simple but cozy, enhanced by bright yellow walls, seafoam chairs, white table tops, and ceiling fans. A back patio offers alfresco dining. Start with an sangria rum punch, then move onto *any* of the menu's many selections; it's all that wonderful. Piping-hot *arepas V100equenses* are piled high with pepper and octupus salad, while small *tostones rellenos* (fried

*Continued on page 180*

# BIOLUMINESCENT BAYS
*Plankton Pyrotechnics in Puerto Rico*

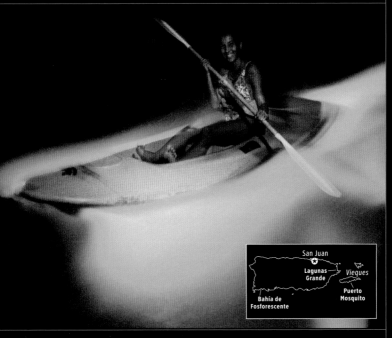

Puerto Rico's bioluminescent bays are beautiful. The slightest stirring of these waters, whether from the swish of a stick or droplets of rain, produces tiny bursts of teal-blue light. The darker the night, the better the bright; a moonless sky affords the most gorgeous marine moments in these wondrous bays.
*by Francesca Drago*

It's estimated that there are only 12 bio bays in the world, but it's difficult to determine exactly because the phenomenon occurs sporadically in warm seas. Puerto Rico has three. **Puerto Mosquito** in Vieques is the most spectacular bay. It won a Guinness World Record for most outstanding bioluminescent bay in the world. **Lagunas Grande** in Fajardo is not as bright, but convenient to see from San Juan. **Bahía de Fosforescente** in La Parquera's deserves an honorable mention even though water pollution, primarily from gas- and diesel-powered tourist boats, has darkened its luster.

Positively glowing! Puerto Rico's bio bays will literally have you beaming with joy.

# WHAT'S IN THE WATER?

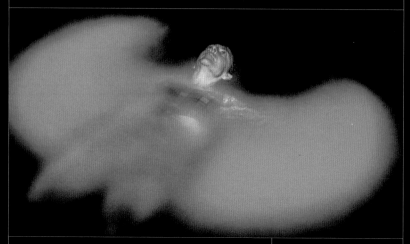

 The undersea shooting stars are produced by microscopic algae called dinoflagellates, or "dinos." They convert chemical energy into light energy and emit tiny flashes when the water is disturbed. Scientists have theorized that their sudden sparks are a defense mechanism—a way to startle and disorient a predator and perhaps attract a larger predator to eat the first one.

A bio bay's brightness is a measure of its health. Dinoflagellates use the energy from sunlight to photosynthesize. Their luminescence is influenced by circadian rhythms, meaning their brightness depends on the light-dark conditions over a 24-hour period. One full day of sunshine and no clouds will result in two nights of plankton brilliance—with the second night brighter than the first. A cloudy day may still produce a bright night, but the following night won't be as spectacular. Artificial and ambient light will disrupt the fragile cycles of these "living lanterns" and erase their natural bioluminescence. Preservation of bio-bay brightness depends on public awareness about the harmful effects of light pollution and thoughtful planning for future land development.

(top) "Glow angel:" a swimmer creates water wings in Puerto Mosquito Bay (bottom) The species of dinoflagellate Pyrodinium Bahamenese, found in Puerto Mosquito, is only 1/500 of an inch

## NEW MOON

Bioluminescence is best experienced on a cloudy or moonless night. The darkest nights occur during the new moon phase, when its face is in shadow. Ask your tour guide what the moon phase will be and when it will rise, because a full moon may not actually appear in the sky until after your planned excursion.

New Moon Calendar, 2013/2014
- Jan 11/Jan 1 & 30
- Feb 10/no new moon
- Mar 11/Mar 1 & 30
- Apr 10/Apr 29
- May 10/May 28
- Jun 8/Jun 27
- Jul 8/Jul 26
- Aug 6/Aug 25
- Sep 5/Sep 24
- Oct 5/Oct 23
- Nov 3/Nov 22
- Dec 3/Dec 22

# PUERTO MOSQUITO: A BAY IN BALANCE

Vieques

Puerto Mosquito Bay

**1**

**2**

**3**

Sun Bay

**4**

Caribbean Sea

Playa Media Luna

Dinoflagellates occur sporadically in tropical waters around the world, but the highest concentration on earth can be found in Puerto Mosquito Bay in Vieques. Billions of dinos dwell here because their habitat is balanced by a number of ecological features and protections.

"Channel surf:" A kayaker paddles the channel leading to Puerto Mosquito Bay

❶ Puerto Mosquito Bay is a **designated wildlife preserve**. This special zoning prevents rampant development, pollution, and destruction of the surrounding forest, which acts as a natural barrier against strong winds and rain.

❷ Salt-tolerant **mangrove trees** are vital for healthy coastal ecosystems. Their pronged roots stabilize the silt-rich shoreline, helping to filter sediments and reduce erosion, while leaves and bark fall into the

water, where they rot and provide food and nutrients essential to the dinos' diet (e.g., vitamin B12). Moreover, the mangroves absorb carbon dioxide and store carbon in their sediments, which makes them a vital resource for reducing greenhouse gasses in the atmosphere.

❸ The long, **narrow channel leading to the ocean** acts as a buffer that minimizes how much seawater flows into the bay daily and limits the amount of dinoflagellates (and nutrients) that are swept out with the tides. This enables the dinos to concentrate in the bay's shallow refuge.

❹ The **channel exit** at the windward end of the bay allows sufficient water exchange with the sea to keep it from overheating or stagnating. The water in Puerto Mosquito remains calm and warm, creating the ideal environment for dinoflagellates to thrive in.

## EXPLORING THE BAYS

Kayaks are an environmentally friendly way to explore the bays.

Seeing your oars glow as they blade through the water is a magical experience. Go with an operator that uses glow sticks to illuminate the stern of each kayak (for minimal light interference) and reviews safety practices at the start. Never book a tour with an operator who is unlicensed or uses gas- or diesel-powered boats. Ask your hotel concierge for assistance. On Vieques all hotels listed in our Where to Stay section will help arrange tours of Puerto Mosquito Bay.

### RECOMMENDED OUTFITTERS

#### IN VIEQUES

**Island Adventures** runs nightly bio bay tours and an educational tour aboard an open-air electric boat. (Prone to motion sickness? Be advised that a 45-minute cruise on a catamaran and 15-minute bus ride on a rough, unpaved road is part of this trip.) **Aqua Frenzy Kayaks** and **Abe's Snorkeling & Bio Bay Tours** both provide sturdy kayaks and knowledgeable guides for day and night trips to Puerto Mosquito.

#### IN FAJARDO

The two-hour night tour at **Las Cabezas Nature Reserve** *(see Exploring, Fajardo, chapter 3)* takes you on a winding boardwalk through mangroves to the water's edge. Strike the dark lagoon with a stick and marvel at the flashing wakes, or stir the water to "draw" with light.

*For more information on recommended outfitters, see Boating & Kayaking in this chapter.*

### KNOW BEFORE YOU GLOW

■ Paddling through the long, dark mangrove channel to reach Mosquito Bay is exciting but also challenging. Kayaking can be strenuous and requires teamwork; book with small groups, if possible, because crowds with varying experience and endurance can lead to exasperation and delay.

■ People with little or no kayak experience, or with small children, may prefer a pontoon trip that provides an easy and safe way to swim in luminescent water.

■ Puerto Mosquito is aptly named. Wear a hat, water shoes, and nylon pants as protection from bites. A lightweight, waterproof windbreaker worn over a bathing suit is ideal.

■ Jellyfish are sometimes present but cannot be seen in the dark water. Look carefully.

■ Bring towels and a change of clothes for the ride home.

In the zone: the forest of Puerto Mosquito is protected land

After the sun sets, the undersea stars shine

Destruction of mangroves, dredging, land development, and overuse of the bays' waters endanger the bio bays. Light pollution is especially harmful, since artificial and ambient light suppress the luminescence of the dinoflagellates. The Vieques Conservation and Historical Trust (VCHT) held its first symposium in the fall of 2008, convening expert scientific and technical authorities to discuss conservation of the bio bays. The goal, said Trust marine expert Mark Martin, was to "involve everybody," including government and the public, and rally commitments and resources to ensure the continuous scientific monitoring of Puerto Mosquito. The VCHT wants to name Puerto Mosquito a UNESCO World

Here's what you can do to help maintain the pristine condition of this precious natural resource:

▓ Book with licensed operators who use kayaks or electric boats only.

▓ Swimming is banned in all the bio bays but Puerto Mosquito. Shun those operators who ignore the law.

▓ Dinoflagellates absorb basic chemicals directly from the water. Bug repellents containing DEET will kill them. Rinse off any remnants of suntan lotion, perfume, and deodorant before swimming.

▓ Do not throw any objects in the water or litter in any way.

▓ Support the conservation efforts of the

## CLOSE UP

# Vieques Libre

For nearly six decades, the U.S. Navy had a stranglehold on Vieques. It controlled the island's eastern half and western end and exerted enormous influence over the destiny of the civilian area in between. Though long protested, the bombing, shelling, and amphibious landings continued. When an off-target bomb killed a civilian on Navy land in April 1999, opposition began to transform the island's placid beaches into political hotbeds.

Protesters camping out on the bombing range kept it shut down from 1999 to 2000. Hundreds of Puerto Rican residents were arrested for trespassing on Navy land during war games. They were joined by celebrity protesters from the United States, including environmental lawyer Robert F. Kennedy Jr. (who gave his baby daughter the middle name Vieques), the wife of Reverend Jesse Jackson, and Reverend Al Sharpton, all of whom were arrested for trespassing on the bombing range. For much of 2000 and 2001, protests were so commonplace that there were semipermanent encampments of opponents. Songs such as "Paz Pa' Vieques" ("Peace for Vieques") began to surface, as did bumper stickers and T-shirts with protest slogans. Latin pop celebrities such as singer-songwriter Robie Draco Rosa (who wrote Ricky Martin's "Livin' la Vida Loca"), actor Edward James Olmos, singer Millie Corejter, protest singer Zoraida Santiago, and

other actors, painters, doctors, and lawyers added to the fanfare when they joined the activities.

President Bill Clinton finally agreed that residents could vote on whether to continue to host the Navy. A nonbinding referendum held in 2001 found that 68% of the island's voters wanted the military to leave immediately. Although some members of Congress argued that the Navy should stay indefinitely—their cries grew louder after September 11, 2001, when even local protesters called for a moratorium on civil disobedience—the administration agreed to withdraw the troops. As a result of the protests, the Navy finally withdrew from its Atlantic Fleet training grounds in May 2002. In 2003 the naval base was officially closed. By the end of 2005, much of the former military base was transformed into the Vieques National Wildlife Refuge. Today, there are concerns that the sustained bombing activity produced high levels of contamination that are linked to health issues such as higher cancer rates among residents. This is widely regarded as a long-term exposure issue that doesn't affect vacationers, but visitors who may be concerned about potential risks associated with travel to the area should check the Centers for Disease Control Web site (⊕ *www.cdc.gov*) for the latest information.

---

plantains) are shaped into cups filled with a citrusy ceviche. *Sorullitos* (cheesy corn fritters) and *bacalaítos* (cod fritters) are reimagined with modern flair. The only thing trumping the flavors of a juicy *churrasco* (skirt steak) with rice and beans and overflowing seafood *mofongo* is the wow-factor of Betancourt's presentations. Elevating cooking to art form, this local spot is one that will have you dreaming about Vieques long after you've left the island. ✉ *110 Luis Muñoz Rivera, Isabel Segunda, Vieques* ☎ *787/741–2500* ⊕ *www.restauranteconuco.com.*

**$**
CARIBBEAN
✕ **Duffy's.** At some point during your time in Vieques, you'll wind up at Duffy's, the island's most popular hangout. Customers crowd around the bar here, which might make you think the food is secondary, and you wouldn't be entirely wrong. You'll find standard burger and fries, but the waterfront restaurant has a chalkboard listing scrawled specials like conch fritters, scallop ceviche, grilled ribeye, and pan-seared pork loin all a step above your usual beach fare. The rest of the menu fills out with wraps, sandwiches, and fried finger food. So why do people ignore the dozen or so tables scattered around the open-air dining room in favor of sitting elbow-to-elbow at the bar? Turns out that owner Michael Duffy, son of the owner of Chez Shack, is a real character. Locals love chewing the fat with him, and you will, too. ✉ *140 Calle Flamboyán, Esperanza, Vieques* ☎ *787/741–7600* ⊕ *www. duffysesperanza.com.*

**$$$**
ECLECTIC
**Fodor's**Choice
★
✕ **El Quenepo.** Elegant yet unpretentious, El Quenepo remains the hottest act in town, adding fine dining and a touch of class to the Esperanza waterfront. Six stable doors on an inviting powder blue building open to expose ocean views. The menu, which changes yearly, features local herbs and fruits such as *quenepas* (limes) and breadfruit in the artfully prepared dishes that owners Scott and Kate Cole call "fun, funky island food." Scott is the chef, known for his seafood specials highlighting the daily catch; Kate is the consummate hostess. Start with the popular grilled Caesar salad followed by sensational *mofongo* stuffed with shrimp and lobster in sweet-and-spicy *criollo* sauce. Oenophiles will appreciate the large wine list, and the sangria is delicious. Lucky walk-ins can grab a seat at the more casual high bar tables, but for the true experience of this gem, make a reservation. ✉ *148 Calle Flamboyán, Esperanza, Vieques* ☎ *787/741–1215* ⌂ *Reservations essential* ⊗ *Closed Mon.*

**¢**
PUERTO RICAN
★
✕ **El Resuelve.** When you hanker for hearty platters of real local fare with real island-born locals, this is the place to be. Bustling at lunch and by night, this open-air *colmado* (grocery-restaurant) presses up against the main Isabel II–Esperanza road. It's barely more than a shack with a counter and shaded aluminum and plastic seating out back. Service is laid-back to the max, but it's worth the wait for *albondigas* (meatballs), crab empanadas, chicken with rice and beans, barbecue ribs, and—for the daring—boiled pigs' ears. Locals sometimes kick up their heels out back, where there's a pool table and slot machine. ✉ *Route 997, Km 1, Isabel Segunda, Vieques* ☎ *787/741–1427* ▭ *No credit cards* ⊗ *Closed Mon. & Tue.*

**$$$**
ECLECTIC
✕ **Mix on the Beach.** Local dining reaches new heights courtesy of celebrated chef Alain Ducasse at Mix on the Beach. The multi-Michelin-decorated restaurant at the W Retreat & Spa—Ducasse's first in the Caribbean—puts a French twist on Caribbean-Latino cuisine. And although it's some of the priciest cuisine on the island, it's worth the splurge. The bi-level dining terraces overlook a sensational swimming-pool complex that at night is delicately lit to perfection. The rollicking ocean provides the soundtrack to some seriously romantic al fresco

dining. To share, the Caribbean paella with local lobster delivers in spades, while server after server can be seen delivering the moist salty cod to neighboring tables. At breakfast, the housemade strawberry jam goes beautifully with flaky, fresh croissants, and for dessert, the Ducasse candy bar–akin to a fancy KitKat–is a must-try. ⊠ *W Retreat & Spa, Route 200, Km 3.2, Isabel Segunda, Vieques* ☎ *787/741–4100* ⊕ *www. wvieques.com/mix* ⌲ *Reservations essential.*

**$$$**  ✕**Next Course.** Warm colors like red, yellow, and orange fill the con-
**ECLECTIC**  sistently packed dining rooms at Next Course, one of the island's lat-
★  est stars. Billed as "cuisine inspired by travel," the space is laced with ethnic nuances like beaded Indian pillows and gold-leaf Buddhas. The menu is an amalgam of flavors from balsamic drizzled mozzarella to sesame-crusted yellowfin tuna with seaweed salad to baby back ribs. This seemingly incongruous assortment comes together beautifully in well-executed dishes by chef Buddy Stone, an Arizona-by-way-of-St. John-transplant who spent two years creating the specials in the kitchen at beloved Duffy's (⇨ *see review*). His fans followed him to Next Course, and judging by the vibe of this buzzing spot, it looks like he's in Vieques to stay. ⊠ *Route 201, Vieques* ☎ *787/741–1028* ⌲ *Reservations essential.*

## WHERE TO STAY

### PRIVATE VILLA RENTALS

One good way to visit Vieques is to rent one of the beautiful vacation homes that have been built in the hilly interior or along the coasts. These are concentrated in three major areas: Bravos de Boston, Esperanza, and Pilón. Several local real-estate agents deal in short-term rentals of at least a week. A popular rental is Bravos House, which has weekly summer rates as low as $900 and in-season rates of $1,500 per week (⊕ *www.viequeshouse.net*).

**Rainbow Realty.** A list of rental properties is available from gay-friendly Rainbow Realty. ⊠ *278 Calle Flamboyán, Esperanza, Vieques* ☎ *787/ 741–4312* ⊕ *www.viequesrainbowrealty.com.*

*For expanded hotel reviews, visit Fodors.com.*

**$$**  🏨**Bravo Beach Hotel.** This completely renovated boutique hotel sev-
**HOTEL**  eral blocks north of the ferry dock in Isabel Segunda feels more suited to swank South Beach than laid-back Vieques. **Pros:** gorgeous build-ing; beautiful pools; friendly new management. **Cons:** out-of-the-way location in residential neighborhood; can't swim on property's beach. ⊠ *North Shore Rd., Isabel Segunda, Vieques* ☎ *787/741–1128* ⊕ *www. bravobeachhotel.com* ➥ *7 rooms, 2 suites, 1 villa* ⌂ *In-room: a/c, safe, Wi-Fi. In-hotel: pool, parking, some age restrictions* ⎩⊙⎨ *Breakfast.*

**¢**  🏨**Casa de Amistad.** If you're looking for a budget-friendly property
**HOTEL**  in the city center, this groovy little guesthouse not far from the ferry
★  dock in Isabel Segunda is the place to be. **Pros:** Gay-friendly; funky furnishings. **Cons:** Drive to beaches; cheaper rooms lack en-suite bath-rooms; no elevator. ⊠ *27 Calle Benito Castaño, Isabel Segunda, Vieques* ☎ *787/741–3758* ⊕ *www.casadeamistad.com* ➥ *7 rooms* ⌂ *In-room: a/c, Wi-Fi. In-hotel: pool, parking* ⎩⊙⎨ *No meals.*

**$$** ▦ **Hacienda Tamarindo.** The 250 year-old tamarind tree rising more than
HOTEL three stories through the center of the main building gives this planta-
★ tion-style house and former dance hall its name. **Pros:** Beautiful views;
nicely designed rooms; excellent breakfasts. **Cons:** Drive to beaches;
small parking lot; no full-service restaurant; no elevator. ⊠ *Rte. 996,
Km 4.5, Esperanza, Vieques* ✉ *Box 1569, Vieques 00765* ☎ *787/741–
8525* ⊕ *www.haciendatamarindo.com* ⤳ *16 rooms, 1 penthouse suite*
⚭ *In-room: a/c, no TV, Wi-Fi. In-hotel: pool, some age restrictions*
†○† *Breakfast.*

**$** ▦ **Hector's.** Reached by a steep and denuded dirt road, this tiny property
HOTEL perches on a bluff overlooking a lovely beach. **Pros:** Hot tub under the
stars; truly marvelous ocean vistas. **Cons:** No credit cards; isolated loca-
tion; meager facilities; maid service every 3–4 days. ⊠ *Rte. 996, Km 4.3,
Esperanza, Vieques* ☎ *787/741–1178* ⊕ *www.hectorsbythesea.com* ⤳ *3
studio-style rooms* ⚭ *In-room: kitchen, no TV. In-hotel: pool, beach,
laundry facilities, parking, some age restrictions* ▭ *No credit cards.*

**$$** ▦ **Hix Island House.** Constructed entirely of concrete and set in the mid-
HOTEL dle of Vieques's tropical forest surroundings, Hix House echoes the
gray granite boulders strewn around Vieques, and the four building
do manage to blend seamlessly with the environment. **Pros:** Acclaimed
architecture; secluded setting; friendly staff. **Cons:** No windows means
bugs (especially pesky mosquitos) in the rooms; damp linens and clothing after tropical showers; no elevator; far from restaurants. ⊠ *Rte.
995, Km 1.5, Vieques* ☎ *787/741–2302* ⊕ *www.hixislandhouse.com*
⤳ *13 rooms* ⚭ *In-room: no a/c, safe, kitchen, no TV. In-hotel: pool,
parking* †○† *Breakfast.*

**$$** ▦ **Inn on the Blue Horizon.** The six Mediterranean-style villas here were
HOTEL the tiny island's first taste of luxury, and it's still a lovely accommoda-
tion, to a large extent because of its perch across sprawling lawns that
overlook breathtaking ocean. **Pros:** eye-popping view; private accom-
modations; spacious grounds; free Wi-Fi in public areas. **Cons:** aloof
staff and inattentive management; no elevator. ⊠ *Rte. 996, Km 4.2,
Esperanza, Vieques* ✉ *Box 1556, Vieques, Vieques 00765* ☎ *787/741–
3318, 877/741–BLUE* ⊕ *www.innonthebluehorizon.com* ⤳ *10 rooms,
1 suite* ⚭ *In-room: safe, no TV. In-hotel: restaurant, bar, pool, ten-
nis court, beach, parking, some pets allowed, some age restrictions*
†○† *Breakfast.*

**$** ▦ **La Finca Caribe.** An edgy, off-beat inn run along the lines of a Berke-
B&B/INN ley, California, commune, this eco-friendly hillside getaway seemingly
miles from anywhere has an irresistible rustic appeal. **Pros:** Communal
hibachi; social informality; nature-focused. **Cons:** Far from island ser-
vices; no a/c, no Wi-Fi. ⊠ *Rte. 995, Km 1.2, Vieques* ☎ *787/741–0495*
⊕ *www.lafinca.com* ⤳ *6 rooms, 2 cabins, 2 houses* ⚭ *In-room: no a/c,
kitchen, no TV. In-hotel: pool, laundry facilities, parking, some pets
allowed.*

**$$** ▦ **Malecón House.** Posh boutique spots like this seaside escape in Espe-
B&B/INN ranza are raising the bar on lodging in Vieques. *105 Calle Flamboyán,*
★ *Esperanza, Vieques* ☎ *787/741–0663* ⊕ *www.maleconhouse.com* ⤳ *9
rooms, 1 suite* ⚭ *In-room: a/c, safe, Wi-Fi. In-hotel: pool, parking*
†○† *Breakfast.*

4

$    🏨 **Seagate Hotel.** Energetic and effusive owner-manager Penny Miller
HOTEL   lavishes attention on guests at her spic-and-span hilltop hotel that overlooks the island's picturesque, historic fort. **Pros:** Friendly and helpful
owner-manager; handy for exploring town. **Cons:** Small rooms; animal presence; no restaurant. ✉ *Barrio Fuerte, Isabel Segunda, Vieques*
☎ *787/741–4661* ⊕ *www.seagatehotel.com* ⤳ *15 rooms* ⌂ *In-room:*
*a/c, kitchen, no TV, Wi-Fi. In-hotel: pool, spa, parking, some pets*
*allowed* ⦿ *Breakfast.*

¢   🏨 **Trade Winds.** The best of a string of inexpensive guesthouses along the
B&B/INN   main road in Esperanza, this place has an unbeatable location across
from the Malecón, or waterfront promenade. **Pros:** Good value; many
nearby dining options. **Cons:** Right on the noisy street; no elevator.
✉ *107 Calle Flamboyán, Esperanza, Vieques* ⊡ *Box 1012, Vieques*
*00770* ☎ *787/741–8666* ⊕ *www.tradewindsvieques.com* ⤳ *11 rooms*
⌂ *In-room: a/c, Wi-Fi. In-hotel: restaurant, bar* ⦿ *Breakfast.*

$$$$   🏨 **W Retreat & Spa.** Hovering over two gorgeous beaches, the über-
RESORT   hip W Retreat & Spa opened in November 2009 as the island's hot
Fodor's Choice   spot for urbane fashionistas. **Pros:** sensational decor; full-service spa;
★   five-minute drive from the airport. **Cons:** high prices even in low season; $60 daily resort fee. ✉ *Rte. 200, Km 3.2, Isabel Segunda, Vieques*
☎ *787/741–4100* ⊕ *www.wvieques.com* ⤳ *156 rooms, 21 suites* ⌂ *In-*
*room: a/c, safe, kitchen, Wi-Fi. In-hotel: restaurant, bar, pool, tennis*
*court, gym, spa, beach, water sports, business center, parking, some*
*pets allowed* ⦿ *No meals.*

## NIGHTLIFE

**Al's Mar Azul.** Not far from the ferry terminal, Al's Mar Azul is the place
to be come sunset. An open-air deck overlooks the ocean, and nautical
decor lines the walls of this popular, spirited bar. Enjoy a game of darts
or pool, lipsync to a song off the jukebox or, on karaoke nights, whip
the crowd into a frenzy with your best Mariah. ✉ *Next to the ferry*
*pier in Isabel Segunda, Calle Plinio Peterson, Isabel Segunda, Vieques*
☎ *787/741–3400.*

**Bananas.** Bananas is the place for burgers and beer—not necessarily in
that order. There's occasional live music and dancing, and on Mondays,
$1.50 bottles of Medalla, the local brew. ✉ *142 Calle Flamboyán, Espe-*
*ranza, Vieques* ☎ *787/741–8700.*

**Club Tumby.** Club Tumby, on the west side of the island in Bunkers, is
an improbably massive state-of-the-art disco on little off-the-beaten-
path Vieques. Wall-to-wall big screens, a bar stretching to the moon,
and a 10,000-square-foot dance floor? Wow! ✉ *Bunkers, Barrio Mos-*
*quito, Barrio Mosquito, Vieques* ☎ *787/231–9966 free phone* ⊕ *www.*
*clubtumby.com.*

**Duffy's.** Hands-down, Duffy's is the most popular bar on the island,
thanks to the jawboning of owner Michael Duffy, live music, daily specials, and a prime location on Esperanza's Malecón. ✉ *140 Calle Flam-*
*boyán, Esperanza, Vieques* ☎ *787/741–7600* ⊕ *www.duffysesperanza.*
*com.*

**La Nasa.** La Nasa is the only establishment on the waterfront side of the street in Esperanza. This simple wooden shack, decorated with strings of Christmas lights the entire year, serves up cheap beer and rum drinks and draws island-born Viequenses rather than expats. Locals congregate on plastic chairs out front to play cards or stare off into the placid Caribbean from an open-air back room. On weekends, the place explodes into a street party of salsa, merengue, and pachanga dancing. ⊠ *Calle Flamboyán, Esperanza, Vieques* ☎ *No phone.*

## SHOPPING

Most residents do their shopping on the mainland, so there are very few shops on Vieques. You'll find mostly clothing stores that lean toward beach attire, as well as a few art galleries.

**4**

**Casa Vieja Gallery.** Casa Vieja Gallery is a small space off Route 201 where several local artists show and sell their work. ⊠ *Rte. 201, Esperanza, Vieques* ☎ *787/741–3581* ⊕ *islavieques.com/galleries.*

**Funky Beehive.** The opening of the W Retreat & Spa has brought new boutiques selling trendy resort wear for men and women to the island. One of the best is Funky Beehive, an eclectic shop full of dresses, tunics, local jewelry, hats, beach bags, home accessories, and soaps. Prices range from $10 to $100. ⊠ *359 Antonio Mellado, Suite 2, Esperanza, Vieques* ☎ *787/741–3192.*

**Kim's Cabin.** Kim's Cabin, which has been in business on Vieques since the late 80s, and was named for the jovial owner's one-time lover, is a local institution. Sparse rooms painted powder blue showcase jewelry and island attire such as cotton sarongs, straw bags, and hats for women. Tunics and button-down short-sleeved shirts for men line the back room. ⊠ *136 Calle Flamboyán, Esperanza, Vieques* ☎ *787/741–3145* ⊕ *islavieques.com/kimscabin.html.*

★ **Siddhia Hutchinson Fine Art Studio & Gallery.** Since the late 80s this gallery has showcased pastel watercolor prints of Caribbean scenes, as well as limited-edition ceramic dinnerware. The gallery is a hip, sophisticated place for Carribean artists to see and be seen, hosting openings of local artists, and it features a number of island artworks. ⊠ *Hotel Carmen, Calle Muñoz Rivera, north of the ferry dock, Isabel Segunda, Vieques* ☎ *787/741–1343* ⊕ *siddhiahutchinsongallery.com* ☉ *Mon.–Sat 10–4.*

Fodor's Choice ★ **Sol Creation.** The carefully cultivated collection at Sol Creation could easily be found in New York's SoHo or L.A.'s Melrose Avenue. The boudoir setting of the pretty boutique opens onto three side rooms—treasure chests of playful, bohemian island duds made from crushed linen, silk, fine cotton, and gauze. Haphazardly strewn chunky leather belts and long, romantic necklaces add character to the neatly hanging garments, and owner Sol Beckedorff, a wonder at styling, is as lovely as her shop. The men's collection is equally lush. Prices range from $35 to $250. ⊠ *Calle Antonio Mellado, Esperanza, Vieques* ☎ *808/280–6223.*

## SPORTS AND THE OUTDOORS

### BIKING

**Vieques Adventure Company.** Garry Lowe at Vieques Adventure Company can set you up with mountain bikes and all the equipment you need starting at $25. They'll even bring the bikes to wherever you are staying. Customized tours of the island—which range from easy rides on country roads to muddy treks into the hills—are $95 half-day to $125 full day. ⊠ *Calle Robles, Esperanza, Vieques* ☎ *787/692–9162* ⊕ *www. viequesadventures.com.*

### BOATING AND KAYAKING

Various outfitters offer trips to Puerto Mosquito, the island's celebrated bioluminescent bay. Most are trips in single-person kayaks, which can be a challenge if you lack experience or endurance. A better option for most people is a boat—an electric-powered model is best, as the gas-powered ones harm the environment.

★ **Abe's Snorkeling and Bio-Bay Tours.** Local boy Abe is one of Vieques's most animated characters, so it's no surprise that his kayaking tours to Puerto Mosquito are the most popular. Over the course of two hours, for $30 per person, guests kayak into the glowing bay for a once-in-a-lifetime experience. For an entire day on the water, Abe's All-in-One Tour involves kayaking through mangrove lagoons, snorkeling coral reefs, watching the sunset on a secluded beach, and visiting the bio bay after dark. Lunch is provided; the tour costs $100 per person. ⊠ *Esperanza, Vieques* ☎ *787/741–2134* ⊕ *www.abessnorkeling.com.*

**Aqua Frenzy Kayaks.** Aqua Frenzy Kayaks also rents sturdy kayaks and arranges comprehensive kayak tours of Puerto Mosquito and other areas if Abe's is booked. Reservations are required for the excursion to the bio bay; the evening kayak trip costs $30. Make reservations at least 24 hours in advance. ⊠ *At dock area below Calle Flamboyán, Esperanza, Vieques* ☎ *787/741–0913* ⊕ *www.aquafrenzy.com.*

**Island Adventures.** If you don't want to ply the waters with a paddle, Island Adventures offers nightly excursions through the glowing waters of Puerto Mosquito aboard an electrically powered double-pontoon boat for $32 per person. ⊠ *Vieques* ☎ *787/741–0720* ⊕ *www.biobay. com.*

**Marauder Sailing Charters.** Marauder Sailing Charters operates the *Marauder,* a 34-foot sailing yacht anchored off Esperanza that can accommodate up to six passengers. It sails around the southern coast, allowing a close-up look at the pristine nature of the island. There's a

Vieques has a number of bays and protected coves that provide calm surf perfect for beginners.

midday stop at a secluded spot for swimming, snorkeling, and sunbathing, followed by a gourmet lunch with open bar. Half-day and full-day trips, sunset cruises, brunch cruises, custom and private charters available. All charters depart from Esperenza. ⌂ *PO Box 355, Vieques 00765* ☎ *787/435–4858* ⊕ *www.maraudersailingcharters.com.*

## DIVING AND SNORKELING

**Black Beard Sports.** If you want to get your own snorkeling or diving equipment, head to this water-sports shop in downtown Isabel Segunda. The team arranges diving trips and PADI certification courses, as well as kayaking, biking, snorkeling, and hiking eco-tours. A second location of Black Beard Sports can be found at the W Retreat & Spa. ⊠ *101 Calle Muñoz Rivera, Isabel Segunda, Vieques* ☎ *787/741–1892,* ⊕ *www.blackbeardsports.com.*

**Nan-Sea SCUBA and Snorkeling Charters.** Nan-Sea Charters is a PADI-certified shop that offers organized dive trips, including shore dives, and snorkeling at Blue Tang Reef and remote offshore isles. The cost for a two-dive trip is $100 per person, not including equipment rental. ⊠ *Esperanza, Vieques* ☎ *787/435–9853* ⊕ *www.nanseacharters.com.*

## FISHING

**Vieques Adventure Company.** Vieques Adventure Company will take you on kayak fly-fishing trips for bonefish and tarpon. "It's extreme fishing," says owner and trip leader Garry Lowe. "When you're in a kayak and have a 50-pound tarpon on the line, you're going to go for a ride!" Rates from $150 per person. ⊠ *Vieques* ☎ *787/692–9162* ⊕ *www.viequesadventures.com.*

**Vieques Sport Fishing.** Captain J. Ferguson has been a charter fisherman since 1989, and off of Vieques's coast he navigates a 26-foot boat into waters laden with tuna, mahimahi, dorado, kingfish, and marlin. Four-hour deep-sea trips begin at $350. ✉ *103 Calle Hucar, Vieques* ☎ *787/450–3744, 787/502–3839* ⊕ *ww.viequessportfishing.com.*

# CULEBRA

*17 miles (28 km) east of Fajardo by ferry.*

Culebra is known around the world for its curvaceous coastline. Playa Flamenco, the tiny island's most famous stretch of sand, is considered one of the top 10 best beaches in the world. If Playa Flamenco gets too crowded, as it often does around Easter or Christmas, many other neighboring beaches will be nearly deserted. And if you crave complete privacy, hire a motorboat to take you to one of the nearby islets such as Isla Culebrita or Cayo Luis Peña. It won't be difficult to find a little cove that you will have all to yourself.

Archaeological evidence shows that Taíno and Carib peoples lived on Culebra long before the arrival of the Spanish in the late 15th century. The Spanish didn't bother laying claim to it until 1886; its dearth of freshwater made it an unattractive location for a settlement. The U.S. Navy and Marine Corps, however, thought it was a very valuable piece of real estate. Although President Theodore Roosevelt created a wildlife refuge in 1909, the military used this island, as well as nearby Vieques, for target practice and amphibious assault training beginning in WWII. Despite their smaller numbers, the residents of Culebra managed to oust the military after staging sit-ins on the beach. The military left Culebra in 1975.

## GETTING HERE AND AROUND

**Aeropuerto Benjamin Rivera Noriega.** Culebra's Aeropuerto Benjamin Rivera Noriega, CPX, is at the intersection of Route 250 and Route 251. The one-room facility has car- and scooter-rental counters. The airport is about three minutes from downtown Dewey. Route 250 leads east and south of the airport. Route 251 leads northeast to Playa Flamenco. ✉ *Culebra* ☎ *787/742–0022.*

Car Rental **Carlos Jeep Rental.** Renting a car or scooter is imperative to get around Culebra. Carlos is a good place to choose a jeep, car, or golf cart. Rates from $56 to $75. ✉ *Aeropuerto Benjamin Rivera Noriega, Culebra* ☎ *787/742–3514* ⊕ *www.carlosjeeprental.com.* **Culebra Scooter Rental.** A fun alternative to renting a full-size car or Jeep. Rates from $35–45. ✉ *Route 250, across from the airport, Culebra* ☎ *787/742.*

Ferry Terminal **Culebra Terminal** ☎ *787/860–2005.*

Taxi **Willy's Taxi.** Willy's Taxi is a full-service operator offering taxi service, Jeep rental, and water taxi trips to Isla Culebrita. ✉ *Culebra* ☎ *787/742–3537.*

# Culebra

← TO
FAJARDO

**KEY**
- ❶ Restaurants
- ①  Hotels

ISLA DE
CULEBRA

Refugio Nacional
de Vida Silvestre
de Culebra

Benjamin Rivera
Noriega Airport

Monte
Resaca

Dewey

Costa
Bonita

Cascaje
Bonita

Sardinas
Bonita

Punta
del Soldado

Mosquite
Beach

Manzanilla Beach

Cabeza de Perro

Isla Culebrita

Lighthouse

Tortuga Beach

Cayo Tiburon

Playa
Zoni

Cayo
Norte

Brava Beach

Playa
Flamenco

Playa Tamarindo

Playa Melones

Cayo
Luis Peña

Piedra Stevens

Punta de Molinos

Cayo Labito

Cayo Lobo

Alcarraza

Los Gemelos

Cayo Yerba

Cayo Raton

Cayo del Auga

Sonda de
Vieques

0          3 mi

0          3 km

**Restaurants**  ▶
Dinghy Dock ............ **4**
El Eden ................... **8**
Heather's Pizza ........ **7**
Juanita Bananas ....... **5**
Mamacita's ............. **3**
Pandeli .................. **1**
Susie's .................. **2**
Zaco's Tacos ........... **6**

**Hotels**  ▶
Bahia Marina ........... **5**
Club Seaborne .......... **4**
Culebra Beach Villas ... **7**
Mamacita's ............. **1**
Posada La Hamaca ..... **2**
Tamarindo Estates ..... **6**
Villa Boheme ........... **3**

4

## EXPLORING CULEBRA

Almost everything about Culebra is diminutive. The island's only community, named in honor of U.S. Admiral George Dewey (island-born locals hate the association and prefer to call the town simply "el pueblo"), is set along a single street leading from the ferry dock. You can explore the few shops along Calle Pedro Márquez in a half hour. The one-room airport is ½ mile (1 km) to the north. Except for one resort, few hotels have more than a dozen rooms.

**Refugio Nacional de Vida Silvestre de Culebra.** Commissioned by President Theodore Roosevelt in 1909, Refugio Nacional de Vida Silvestre de Culebra is one of the nation's oldest wildlife refuges. Some 1,500 acres of the island make up a protected area. It's a lure for hikers and bird-watchers: Culebra teems with seabirds, from laughing gulls and roseate terns to red-billed tropic birds and sooty terns. Maps of trails in the refuge are hard to come by, but you can stop by the U.S. Fish & Wildlife Service office east of the airport to find out about trail conditions and determine whether you're headed to an area that requires a permit. The office also can tell you whether the leatherback turtles are nesting. From mid-April to mid-July, volunteers help to monitor and tag these creatures, which nest on nearby beaches, especially Playa Resaca and Playa Brava. If you'd like to volunteer, you must agree to help out for at least three nights. ⊠ *Rte. 250, north of Dewey, Culebra* ☎ *787/742–0115* ⊕ *www.fws.gov/caribbean/Refuges* ⊠ *Free* ☉ *Daily dawn–dusk.*

**Isla Culebrita.** Part of the Refugio Nacional de Vida Silvestre de Culebra, uninhabited Isla Culebrita is clearly visible from the northeast corner of Culebra. An essential day-trip excursion, this islet is a favorite destination for sunbathers and snorkelers who want to escape the crowds at Playa Flamenco. Isolation set against a palate of crystalline, turquoise waters and dewy, lush greens makes for a one-of-a-kind natural experience. On the northern shore there are several tidal pools; snuggling into one of them is like taking a warm bath. Snorkelers and divers love the fact that they can reach the reef from the shore and carouse with sea turtles, rays, and schools of colorful fish. Bring your sneakers, as you can hike to the peak of the island in about 20–30 minutes where the spectacular ruins of an old lighthouse await. Climb 54 crumbling steps to the top where the views of the surrounding Caribbean are sublime. Be warned; the structure is tumbledown, so enter at your own risk. To get to Culebrita, take a dive boat or hire a water-taxi service like Gammy's Water Tour. ⊠ *Culebra.*

**Cayo Luis Peña.** A kayak is a great way to reach Cayo Luis Peña, an islet just off the western edge of Culebra. There are a handful of protected beaches where you can soak up the sun and not run into a single soul. Cayo Luis Peña is also part of the Refugio Nacional de Vida Silvestre de Culebra. ⊠ *Culebra.*

## WHERE TO EAT

$$ | SEAFOOD — ✕ **Dinghy Dock.** Culebra's version of heavy traffic—the arrival and departure of the water taxi—takes place around the dock that gives this restaurant its name. The menu leans toward grilled meats, from hamburgers and wraps to sirloin steaks. Daily specials often highlight the restaurant's forte: creole-style seafood, including swordfish and yellowtail, as well as lobster. The adjacent open-air bar is usually packed with expats and a cast of local characters. It can get noisy, and the service is anything but doting, so don't expect a quiet dinner for two. ⊠ *Calle Fulladoza, Dewey, Culebra* ☎ *787/742–0233.*

$$$ | ECLECTIC — ✕ **El Eden.** Deli and grocery by day, full-service restaurant by night, the funky El Eden is a little bit of everything when it comes to eating and drinking on Culebra. Set inside a can't-miss trailer trimmed with year-round Christmas lights, what started out as a deli serving sandwiches on fresh baked bread morphed into a liquor store, and now churns out soups, local catch, *churrasco* (skirt steak) platters, pastas, and a signature saffron lobster risotto. Mismatched outdoor furniture, a nautical-themed bar, and friendly owners Richard and Luz only add to the warm feel of the place. Whether you're looking for quality ingredients for a dinner recipe, a bottle of wine, takeout for the beach, or a sit-down meal, El Eden is your spot. ⊠ *Sardinas #3, Culebra* ☎ *787/742–0509.*

$$ | PIZZA — ✕ **Heather's Pizza.** Pizza on the tiny Puerto Rican island of Culebra, you ask? Yep, and pretty good pizza at that. This cute little spot on Dewey's main drag has become something of a hot spot since new owner Willie Vasquez came on the scene last year. Playful blue walls and orange tables front a full bar that stays open until the wee hours, while the oven bakes irresistible pizzas and pastas that keeps diners coming back for more. The Pizza Boricua, topped with mozzarella, ground beef, sweet plantains, and cilantro, is a local favorite, and the spaghetti with meat sauce, at $9, is a heaping plate of undeniable goodness. Chalkboard specials are featured daily and takeout is available. ⊠ *Calle Pedro Marquez 14, Dewey, Culebra* ☎ *787/742–3175.*

$ | SUSHI — ✕ **Juanita Bananas.** This casual spot is one of the most popular eateries on Culebra. Chef Jennifer Daubon uses only the freshest local produce and catch of the day to inspire a menu heavy on appetizers, light bites, and sushi. The menu changes daily—check the chalkboard—but chicken wings at happy hour and a variety of unique sushi rolls are most popular. Order at the bar, and grab a seat inside or on the back patio to witness the the sights of Culebra. ⊠ *Hotel Kokomo, Calle Pedro Marquez, across from the ferry dock, Culebra* ☎ *787/742–1060* ⊕ *www.juanitabananas.com.*

$ | CARIBBEAN — ✕ **Mamacita's.** Pull your dinghy up to the dock and watch the resident iguanas plod past at this simple open-air, tin-roofed restaurant on a rough-plank deck beside the Dewey canal. Tarpon cruise past in the jade waters below, and the to and fro of boaters also keeps patrons amused. Doubling as Culebra's favorite local watering hole and gringo hangout, palm-tree trunks litter the space, which is painted in a rainbow of pink, purple, and green. With a nightly changing menu, Mamacita's down-home dishes play a part in the appeal. The menu is heavy on burgers and sandwiches, but seafood dishes include an excellent mahimahi. ✉ *Calle Castelar, #66, Dewey, Culebra* ☎ *787/742–0322* ⊕ *www.mamacitasguesthouse.com.*

¢ ✕ **Pandeli.** More often than not, when locals go out for breakfast or
CAFÉ lunch they head to this little café on Dewey's main street. The new
mustard-yellow facade is one of the changes of new management, but
the overall experience remains the same. At the counter, you can order
any number of delicious breakfast or lunch sandwiches, some of them
only a few dollars and big enough to share. The Cuban is a favorite, as
are the pastries. It opens before sunrise, but get here early, as the place
closes midafternoon. Service defines "island time," so relax with a gour-
met coffee while you wait. ✉ *Calle Pedro Márquez at Calle Castelar,
Dewey, Culebra* ☎ *787/742–0296* ⊘ *No dinner.*

$$$ ✕ **Susie's.** Hemmed between a gas pump and dry dock, you'd never
ECLECTIC believe this unassuming little establishment could deliver the goods.
★ But what goods! Susie's is truly the island's only upscale restaurant,
yet it's casual and unpretentious. Sanjuanera owner-chef Susie Hebert
learned her culinary skills at San Juan's swank Caribe Hilton and Ritz-
Carlton hotels before settling on Culebra and opening her fine-dining
restaurant, a soothing Zen space filled with banquettes, pillows, and
couches. A lively bar opens onto patio dining off the canal. The Caesar
salad here excels; follow with sautéed jumbo shrimp in ginger-lime and
coconut vinaigrette, Szechuan-style sesame-crusted tuna, or mahimahi
with beurre blanc and scallion-ginger sauce. Feeling carnivorous? The
filet mignon with a simple truffle au jus is divine. ✉ *Off Calle Escudero,
Dewey, Culebra* ☎ *787/742–0574* ⊕ *www.susiesculebra.com* ⚐ *Reservations essential* ⊘ *Closed Thur.*

¢ ✕ **Zaco's Tacos.** After spending years in the kitchen of popular hangout
MEXICAN Mamacita's, chef Zach Sizer decided to open his own joint, a no-frills
**Fodor's**Choice taco spot delivering fresh, flavorful, affordable grub. Good thing he did;
★ Zaco's Tacos is already a runaway success. Arched ceilings are painted
in bright primary colors, lending a warm, festive feel to the cozy space.
An outdoor wood terrace in the back offers open-air dining and Sunday
brunch, though most just prefer to order some delicious beer-battered
fish, *carnitas* (pork), or seared tuna tacos at the bar. For the adventurous, pork belly, beef, and tongue tacos are on the menu, as well as
heartier burritos. Refresh with a light hibiscus tea, or a more obvious
indulgence—one of the many tequila-saturated margaritas. ✉ *21 Calle
Pedro Marquez, Dewey, Culebra* ☎ *787/742–0243* ⊕ *www.zacostacos.
com* ⊘ *Closed Thur.*

## WHERE TO STAY

### VILLA RENTALS
Lovely vacation homes are scattered around Culebra.

**Culebra Island Realty.** Culebra Island Realty has a few dozen properties
for rent, ranging from studios to three-bedroom houses. ✉ *Calle Escudero, Dewey, Culebra* ☎ *787/435–6752* ⊕ *www.culebraislandrealty.
com.*

*For expanded hotel reviews, visit Fodors.com.*

Surfer crossing is often the extent of traffic flow in the town of Dewey, Culebra.

**$**   **🛏 Bahía Marina.** If you're looking for space to spread out or bring the
**HOTEL** family, these one- and two-bedroom villas with sweeping views of
**★** the nearby nature reserve or ocean are made for you. **Pros:** beautiful
setting; good restaurant. **Cons:** feels like an apartment complex; outside of town; no elevator. ⊠ *Calle Fulladoza, Km 1.5, Culebra* ☎ *787/*
*742–0535* ⊕ *www.bahiamarina.net* ↪ *16 one-bedroom suites, 14 two-*
*bedroom villas* ⚬ *In-room: a/c, kitchen, Wi-Fi. In-hotel: restaurant, bar,*
*pool, laundry facilities, parking* ¶⊙| *Breakfast.*

**$$**   **🛏 Club Seaborne.** The most sophisticated place to set down roots in
**HOTEL** Culebra, this cluster of slate-blue plantation-style cottages paints a
**Fodor's Choice** pretty picture on a hilltop overlooking Fulladoza Bay. **Pros:** Lovely
**★** cottages; privacy; lush gardens. **Cons:** Some steps to negotiate; no eleva-
tor; spotty Internet and phone reception. ⊠ *Playa Sardinas Ward II,*
*Fulladoza Bay, Culebra* ⊡ *Box 357, Culebra 00775* ☎ *787/742–3169*
⊕ *www.clubseabourne.com* ↪ *3 rooms, 8 villas, 1 cottage* ⚬ *In-room:*
*a/c, safe, kitchen. In-hotel: restaurant, bar, pool, water sports, parking*
¶⊙| *Breakfast.*

**$**   **🛏 Culebra Beach Villas.** This is the only hotel on Playa Flamenco, or any
**RENTAL** beach in Culebra for that matter, and for that reason alone this place
**☾** is worth your consieration. **Pros:** On the best beach in Puerto Rico;
secluded. **Cons:** Can get noisy with families; inconsistency in units;
management not always available. ⊠ *Playa Flamenco, Off Rte. 251,*
*Culebra* ☎ *787/409–2599* ⊕ *www.culebrabeach.com* ↪ *rooms & 18*
*cabins* ⚬ *In-room: kitchen. In-hotel: bar, beach, water sports, laundry*
*facilities, parking* ¶⊙| *No meals.*

**$**   **🛏 Mamacita's.** The best rooms in Mamacita's venerable wooden mansion
**HOTEL** have balconies overlooking the canal, but this is decidedly a no-frills

establishment befitting budget-minded travelers. **Pros:** Friendly staff; pickup point for water taxis. **Cons:** Basic rooms; no elevator; on a narrow street. ☒ *66 Calle Castelar, Dewey, Culebra* ☎ *787/742–0090* ⊕ *www.mamacitasguesthouse.com* ⤴ *10 rooms, 1 suite* ⚬ *In-room: a/c. In-hotel: restaurant, bar* ⦿ *No meals.*

$ **Posada La Hamaca.** This small bright orange building, which shares
HOTEL Mamacita's mangrove-lined canal, has spic-and-span guest rooms— as simple as they come—with louvered windows and calming color schemes. **Pros:** Walk to shops and restaurants; laid-back atmosphere; cheap rates. **Cons:** Some rooms are small; constant clunking noises from adjacent bridge; no elevator; no parking. ☒ *68 Calle Castelar, Dewey, Culebra* ☎ *787/742–3516* ⊕ *www.posada.com* ⤴ *10 rooms* ⚬ *In-room: a/c, Wi-Fi* ⦿ *No meals.*

$$ **Tamarindo Estates.** On a 60-acre estate hidden away on the western
RENTAL coast of Culebra, this string of one- and two-bedroom beach-apartment cottages is on a long, sandy beach. **Pros:** Peaceful location; pretty pool area. **Cons:** Short walk to the beach; isolated far from dining options; no housekeeping service. ☒ *Off Rte. 251, Culebra* 🖃 *Box 313, Culebra 00775* ☎ *787/742–3343* ⊕ *www.tamarindoestates.com* ⤴ *12 cottages* ⚬ *In-room: a/c, kitchen. In-hotel: pool, beach, parking* ⦿ *No meals.*

$ **Villa Boheme.** Colorful and breeze-swept, this Spanish-style guest-
B&B/INN house, painted baby blue and white, is centrally located next to popular Dinghy Dock. **Pros:** Expansive view of the bay; walk to restaurants and shops. **Cons:** Basic furnishings; no elevator; few on-site amenities. ☒ *Calle Fulladoza, #368, Dewey, Culebra* ☎ *787/742–3508* ⊕ *www. villaboheme.com* ⤴ *12 rooms* ⚬ *In-room: a/c, kitchen* ⦿ *No meals.*

## NIGHTLIFE

**Blue Bar at The Spot.** Blue walls evoke the feeling of the surrounding ocean at this former lunch spot turned late-night hangout and coffee bar. Favorite local bartender Gretchen Costa tends to cocktails here, serving specialty shots with unique Caribbean flair. The must-order drink is the "Drunken Seagull," a refreshing libation that certainly can sneak up on you after a couple of rounds. Shrug off the hangover with a shot of cappucino or espresso. ☒ *Calle Pedro Marquez #14, Dewey, Culebra* ☎ *787/742–0203.*

**Dinghy Dock.** Dinghy Dock is the spot where the island's expat community begins piling into the bar around sunset. It can be a raucous scene, especially when there's a band. The party continues into the wee hours, even during the week. ☒ *Calle Fulladoza, Dewey, Culebra* ☎ *787/742–0233.*

**El Batey.** For a good local scene, head to El Batey, housed in a cement-block building halfway between the airport and the town of Dewey. Popular on the weekends, when locals dance to salsa music, El Batey serves great burgers to help you absorb the booze. ☒ *Calle Escudero, Dewey, Culebra* ☎ *787/742–3828.*

**Mamacita's.** The island's favorite gringo watering hole is always jumping with a daily happy hour from 3 to 6 pm, karaoke Thursdays, and Saturday night's live music featuring local conga band Wiki Sound.

Don't miss the frozen Bushwhacker—a deadly but delicious mix of rum, vodka, Bailey's, amaretto, Kahlua, and coconut. ⊠ *66 Calle Castelar, Culebra* ☎ *787/742–0322.*

## SHOPPING

Culebra is smaller than Vieques but has much better shopping. Dewey has several shops on its main drag that sell trendy jewelry, clothing, and a range of souvenirs from tacky to terrific.

**Butiki.** Butiki is the cream of the crop. You'll find everything from lovely jewelry to original paintings. And co-owner Stephanie Blake is so helpful that the city should shut down the tourism office and send people here. ⊠ *74 Calle Romero, Dewey, Culebra* ☎ *787/267–7284* ⊕ *www. butikiculebra.com.*

**Fango.** In a wooden shack painted vivid shades of yellow and red, Fango is the island's best place for gifts. Local artist Jorge Acevedo paints scenes of island life and Culebra's natural tableau of mangroves and seascapes. The shop—half-studio, half-boutique— is no bigger than a walk-in closet, but you could easily kill an hour browsing among his one-of-a-kind works and original T-shirts. ⊠ *56 Calle Castelar, Dewey, Culebra* ☎ *787/435–6654* ⊕ *www.artefango.com.*

**Island Boutique.** Island Boutique sells local apparel like sarongs, handmade jewelry, and original souvenirs such as windchimes. ⊠ *4 Calle Pedro Marquez, across the ferry depot, Dewey, Culebra* ☎ *787/742–0439.*

**La Cava.** La Cava stocks a little bit of everything. Forgot your snorkel? Left your bathing suit at home? Need a new pair of flip-flops, or a souvenir for your favorite cousin? La Cava is the perfect place to meet all of those needs. ⊠ *138 Calle Escudio, Dewey, Culebra* ☎ *787/742–0566.*

**Paradise.** Paradise is a good spot for souvenirs ranging from wrought-iron iguanas to hand-carved seagulls to plush baby turtles. ⊠ *6 Calle Salisbury, Dewey, Culebra* ☎ *787/742–3569.*

## SPORTS AND THE OUTDOORS

### BIKING

**Culebra Bike Shop.** Because there's very little traffic, biking is a good way to explore the island. You can rent bikes for $15 a day at Culebra Bike Shop. The shop is next door to the Dinghy Dock and also rents kayaks and snorkel gear. ⊠ *Calle Fulladoza, Dewey, Culebra* ☎ *787/742–0589* ⊕ *culebrabikeshop.com.*

### BOATING AND KAYAKING

**Culebra Eco Tours.** Offering a fast-paced alternative to kayaking, Culebra's only Jet-Ski tour offers a way to cruise the crystal-clear waters in a different way. Rates start at $95 per person. ⊠ *Culebra* ☎ *787/902–7928* ⊕ *www.culebraecotours.net.*

**Gammy's Water Tours.** One of the few licensed captains on the island, local boy Gammy Rohlsen is the man to hire for simple water-taxi service or for more comprehensive fishing or snorkeling adventures to

Cayo Luis Peña or Isla Culebrita, St. Thomas, and Vieques. ⊠ *Calle 1, Culebra* ☎ *787/423–2469.*

**Pez Vela Charters.** Operating out of Bahia Marina, sail trips on Captain Bill Penfield's 33-foot catamaran are a true island experience. Most popular is the Picnic Sail, which includes a bit of everything Culebra is known for—a visit to nearby Culebrita and Cayo Norte, snorkeling, deep-sea fishing—and includes breakfast and an end-of-day barbecue with the day's catch. Prices start at $125 per person and include all gear. Custom charters and private excursions can also be arranged. ⊠ *Bahia Marina, Fulladoza Bay, Culebra* ☎ *787/215–3809.*

## DIVING AND SNORKELING

**Aquatic Adventures.** Captain Taz Hamrick takes guests out on snorkeling and PADI-certified scuba trips, as well as charters to the surrounding cayes. ⊠ *Dewey, Culebra* ☎ *787/209–3494* ⊕ *diveculebra.com.*

**Culebra Divers.** Run by Monika and Walter Rieder, Culebra Divers is the island's premiere dive shop catering to those new to scuba and those adept at underwater navigation. Travel to more than 60 local sites on one of the company's 25-foot cabin cruisers and hope to spot wildlife like spotted eagle rays, octopus, moray eels, and turtles. One-tank dives are $70, and two-tank dives are $98; rental equipment is a flat $15. An additional $25 includes an underwater scooter, which propels you through the sea à la James Bond. You can also rent a mask and snorkel to explore on your own. ⊠ *4 Calle Pedro Marquez, Dewey, Culebra* ☎ *787/742–0803* ⊕ *www.culebradivers.com.*

# Ponce and the Porta Caribe

**WORD OF MOUTH**

"Ponce itself is gorgeous, with a world-class art museum . . . You could also visit a coffee plantation around Yauco and go to San Germán, which is a very special place w/ an old cathedral turned into a museum . . . as well as another cathedral off of its second town square."

—cejnyc

# WELCOME TO PONCE AND THE PORTA CARIBE

## TOP REASONS TO GO

★ **Parque de Bombas:** Marvel at a century-old firehouse whose red-and-black color scheme has inspired thousands of photographers.

★ **Bosque Estatal de Guánica:** Hike where the cactus may make you think you're in the American Southwest.

★ **Hacienda Buena Vista:** Sample a cup of the local brew at the historic, beautifully restored coffee plantation outside of Ponce.

★ **San Germán:** Stroll cobblestone streets lined with architectural treasures; then dine on Puerto Rican fusion cuisine high above the main plaza.

★ **Casa Cautiño:** Step back in time to a colonial-era residence in the sleepy community of Guayama.

**1** Ponce. Reminiscent of Old San Juan before the cruise ships arrived, Ponce has a yesteryear charm and increasingly cosmopolitan vibe that delight many visitors. Take a trolley tour of the colonial past, explore some of the best museums on the island, and at night dine at a rooftop restaurant overlooking the famous Parque de Bombas.

**2** The Southeastern Coast. Underexplored and untrammeled, the southeast is one of the least-visited parts of the island. Start with a seaside meal in Salinas, where the famous Mojo Isleño sauce was created; then hop into the hills to relax in the Baños de Coamo, a thermal spring used for hundreds of years.

**5**

**3** **The Southwestern Coast.** Discover the island's first and most inexpensive bioluminescent bay; the university town of San Germán, whose churches and colonial mansions date back as far as five centuries; and the fascinating dry forest at Guánica.

## GETTING ORIENTED

Ponce is the region's dynamic center, with a surrounding metropolitan area that includes a slew of vibrant attractions, sophisticated restaurants, and boutique hotels rivaled only by San Juan. To the southeast the shoreline is rugged and the villages more rural and isolated. Small seaside inns and some of the island's best seafood can be found here. Slightly inland from the coast are the colonial town of Coamo and its thermal baths. In the southwest, dense dry forest, such as the Bosque Estatal de Guánica, and mangroves hide undiscovered bays, inlets, and quaint fishing villages. Here you will also find the beautiful historic city of San Germán, one of Puerto Rico's oldest settlements.

# BEACHES OF PONCE AND THE PORTA CARIBE

South coast beaches are not the typical resort-lined stretches of sand that Puerto Rico is known for. They're more isolated, smaller, and receive fewer visitors. If you're up for a little bit of exploration, you'll be rewarded with unspoiled Caribbean waters that you'll have all to yourself.

Hop a boat for tiny Gilligan's Island and enjoy a tranquil day on this uninhabited cay just off of Guánica.

On Puerto Rico's southern coast you'll find calm bays for swimming and fewer waves than on the northern coast. The closest surfing spot can be found at Playa Inches, just outside Patillas. Ballena Bay, near Guánica, has oft-deserted sandy stretches. Boat operators make trips to such uninhabited cays as Gilligan's Island off the coast of Guánica and Caja de Muertos off Ponce. After the beach, stick around for the evening in La Parguera for Puerto Rico's most inexpensive and original bioluminescent boat tours in the nearby mangroves.

## SEAFOOD BY THE SEASHORE

What the south coast lacks in beach facilities it makes up for with some of the best seafood. The Caribbean warm waters bring everything from mahimahi and red snapper to arrayao and conch. Open-air, waterfront restaurants—many of which are *mesone gastronómicos*—sit in clusters in places such as Salinas, the Playa de Ponce area, and La Parguera.

## PONCE

**Caja de Muertos** *(Coffin Island)*. With a name that comes from its coffinlike shape, Caja de Muertos is a few miles off the coast and has the best beaches in the Ponce area. It is the second-best spot in southern Puerto Rico for snorkeling, after La Parguera. Due to the hawksbill turtles that nest between May and December, the island is protected by the Reserva Natural Caja de Muertos, but you can still swim, snorkel, and dive. There are bathrooms and picnic tables for day use but not much else. ⊠ *Boats leave from La Guancha, at the end of Rte. 14, Ponce.*

**La Guancha.** Ponce's public beach has shallow water nice for children. You'll find bathrooms, a playground, and a few kiosks selling fried food. There's some shade under thatched umbrellas, but bring sunscreen. ⊠ *At the end of Rte. 14, Ponce.*

## GUÁNICA

**Balneario Caña Gorda.** The gentle waters at this beach on Route 333 wash onto a wide swath of sand fringed with palm trees. There is a designated area for swimmers, and lifeguards remain on duty most afternoons. You'll also find picnic tables, restrooms, showers, and changing facilities. During high season there are beach-chair rentals, food vendors, and paid parking. ⊠ *Rte. 333, Km 5.9 west of Copamarina Beach Resort.*

**Playa Jaboncillo.** Rugged cliffs make a dramatic backdrop for this little cove off Route 333, but the water can be rough. The road down to the beach is extremely rocky, so think twice if you don't have a four-wheel-drive vehicle. ⊠ *Rte. 333, west of Copamarina Beach Resort.*

**Playa Santa.** You can rent canoes, kayaks, and pedal boats at this beach at the end of Route 325 in the Ensenada district. This beach is popular with local teens and can get congested, but the mile-long shoreline is kept clean and preserved. ⊠ *Rte. 325, west of Guánica.*

## LA PARGUERA

**Cayo Caracoles.** You can take a 15-minute boat ride to and from this island for $5 per person. There are mangroves to explore as well as plenty of places to swim and snorkel. ⊠ *Boats leave from marina at La Parguera, off Rte. 304.*

**Isla Mata de la Gata.** For about $5 per person, boats will transport you to and from this small island just off the coast for a day of swimming and snorkeling. There are changing rooms and grilling areas. ⊠ *Boats leave from marina at La Parguera, off Rte. 304.*

**Playita Rosada.** The small beach is a convenient place for a quick swim. There's also a square dock built like a picture frame where locals gather to splash in the center of this natural swimming pool. ⊠ *At the end of Calle 7.*

5

# MASKS OF PUERTO RICO

A week before Ash Wednesday, *vejigantes* (pronounced veh-hee-GAN-tays), wearing long, colorful robes and brightly painted horned masks, turn the normally placid city of Ponce into a hotbed of rowdiness. The masked mischief makers prowl city streets, scaring and fascinating anyone in their path.

Red, white, and boo! During festivals *vejigante* masks frighten and delight spectators along parade routes.

Puerto Rico's masks are one of the premier expressions of folk art on the island, a tradition that dates back to Spain in the early 17th century. During the Fiestas de Santiago Apóstol (Saint James Festivals), brightly dressed vejigantes represented the Devil in a holy battle between good and evil. Their costumes consisted of long robes and grotesque masks, and they would wave cow bladders, or *vejigas*, on long sticks at anyone they passed. Parading as devils, their intention was to frighten sinners to compel them to return to church for Lent. Today balloons and plastic bottles have replaced the cow bladders, and the now-more-playful masks have become one of Puerto Rico's most distinguished forms of artistic expression.

## ISLAND ART

The best hand-designed masks in Puerto Rico come from three parts of the island: Ponce, Loíza, and Hatillo. Mask making is a family tradition in these towns, and styles are passed down among generations. For a fine souvenir and a memorable experience, head to one of the local artisans' workshops. Small masks cost $20 or $30; larger ones by well-known makers cost more than $1,000.

## PONCE

Ponce vejigantes masks are made of papier-mâché and are most prominent during the February Carnaval. Many have African and Native American elements; it's even possible to detect influences from ancient Greece and Rome. All masks have at least two horns, but most have several protruding from the forehead, chin, and nose. Some antique masks have more than 100 horns. At the beginning of the 20th century, masks were usually painted red with yellow dots or vice versa, but today they come in every imaginable color and pattern.

**Where to Go:** One of the best-known mask-making families is the Caraballo family from Playa de Ponce near the El Ancla restaurant *(see review in Where to Eat)*. To purchase a mask, show up at the door to their home, and if someone is there, you'll be allowed to browse their workshop. You're most likely to have success in February leading up to Ponce's Carnaval. ⊠ *24 San Tomas, Playa de Ponce* ☎ *No phone.*

## LOÍZA

Loíza Aldea, a palm-fringed town east of San Juan founded by freed and escaped African slaves, is known as the island's Capital of Traditions for its bomba music, traditional Taíno and African cuisine, and distinct culture. Loíza's masks are created from coconut husks and the individual shape of each

determines the face and placement of the nose and lips. The teeth are made of bamboo and the tongue is made out of coconut shell.

**Where to Go:** For generations, the Ayala family, whose workshop sits just east of town, have been the most renowned mask makers in Loíza. Their masks appear during the Saint James Festival of Loíza Aldea each July. ⊠ *Artesanias y Folclorica de la Familia Ayala, Barrio Medianía Alta, Carr. 187 Km 6 Hm 6* ☎ *787/886–1654.*

## HATILLO

Hatillo was founded in 1823 by settlers from the Canary Islands. These *Islenos*, in honor of King Herod's soldiers, the first Christian martyrs or Holy Innocents, would dress head to toe in costumes with a cape, hat, and mask made of fine metallic screening that is meant to resemble the face of a Spaniard. A parade ensues and the masked performers run through surrounding neighborhoods, joined by children, while singing and dancing, eventually ending in the town center. The annual masks festival, Día de las Máscaras, is held every December 28.

**Where to Go:** ⊠ *Puerto Rico Flea Market, Carr. 2, Km 86 Bo. Carrizales* ☎ *No phone.*

Updated by
Marlise Kast

Not as popular as San Juan or Vieques, the south is a region full of underrated attractions, fine food, and a laid-back authentic vibe that is hard to come by elsewhere. From lush tropical mountains to arid seacoast plains, Puerto Rico's southern region lets you sample the island from a local's perspective.

Though rich in history, the area also provides ample opportunities for golf, swimming, hiking, and cave exploration. Snaking roads between major highways reveal a glimpse of how rural Puerto Ricans enjoy life. Every mile or so, you'll see a café or bar, which is the local social center. The only traffic jams you'll likely encounter will be caused by slow-moving farmers taking their goods to the local market.

At the center of everything is Ponce, the "Pearl of the South." Farmers attracted to the rich soil in the area, which was perfect for growing sugarcane, founded Ponce in 1692. Evidence found at the Tibes Indian ceremonial site, just north of the city, suggests that people have been living here since 400 BC. Many residents still carry the last names of the dozens of European pioneer families who settled here during the 19th century. The region's largest city, Ponce is home to some of the island's most interesting architecture, excellent restaurants, and one of its most important art museums. Nearby San Germán, the second-oldest city in Puerto Rico, is known for its two historic main squares, well preserved in a wide variety of architectural styles.

On the coast, Guayama and Patillas show off their splendors as little-known destinations for beachgoers. But the real beach party is at La Parguera, which attracts a young but noisy crowd. If you're willing to explore beyond the casinos, high-rises, and daily traffic congestion of the island's capital, the south is a wise escape from Puerto Rico's usual tourist fare. Don't be surprised by the help many of its residents will offer whether you ask for it or not. Southern *puertorriqueños* are known for their friendliness as well as their hospitality.

## PONCE PLANNER

### WHEN TO GO

The resort towns of Patillas, Guánica, and La Parguera are popular with Puerto Ricans during Easter and Christmas and during summer, when children are out of school and Ponce's spirited pre-Lenten carnival, held the week before Ash Wednesday, draws many visitors. For the rest of the year, much of the south is quiet and receives only a fraction of the number of visitors as other parts of the island, though the weather is equally superb and most facilities remain open. It's not unusual for hotels to close for two weeks to a month during October and November, when tourism slows down. Hotels tend to lower rates from May through November, so check ahead for deals. Some *paradores*—small, government-sponsored inns—and hotels require a minimum two- or three-night stay on weekends.

### GETTING HERE AND AROUND

#### AIR TRAVEL

The only international flights are on JetBlue, which flies from Ponce to Orlando and New York–JFK.

**Transfers:** Taxis at the airport use meters; expect to pay about $6 to get to downtown Ponce. Some hotels have shuttles to and from the airport, but you must make arrangements in advance.

**Airlines JetBlue** ☎ *800/538–2583* ⊕ *www.jetblue.com.*

**Airport Contacts Aeropuerto Mercedita.** The tiny Aeropuerto Mercedita, about 5 miles (8 km) east of Ponce's downtown, has very few amenities. ⊠ *Rte. 506, off Rte. 52, Ponce* ☎ *787/842–6292.*

#### BUS TRAVEL

There's no easy network of buses linking the towns in southern Puerto Rico with San Juan or with each other. Some municipalities and private companies operate buses or *públicos* (usually large vans) that make many stops. Call ahead; although reservations aren't usually required, you'll need to check on schedules, which change frequently. The cost of a público from Ponce to San Juan is about $15–$20; agree on a price beforehand.

**Bus Contacts Choferes Unidos de Ponce** ⊠ *Terminal de Carros Públicos, Calle Vives and Calle Méndez Vigo, Ponce Centro, Ponce* ☎ *787/764–0540.*

#### CAR TRAVEL

Getting around southern Puerto Rico without a car can be quite frustrating. You can rent cars at the Luis Muñoz Marín International Airport and other San Juan locations. There are also car-rental agencies in some of the larger cities along the south coast. Rates run about $35–$65 a day. A road map is essential in southern Puerto Rico. So is patience: allow extra time for twisting mountain roads and wrong turns. Some roads, especially in rural areas, aren't plainly marked.

#### TAXI TRAVEL

In Ponce you can hail taxis in tourist areas and outside hotels. In smaller towns it's best to call a taxi. You can also hire a car service (make arrangements through your hotel); often you can negotiate a lower rate than with a taxi.

## ABOUT THE RESTAURANTS

Not all the culinary hot spots are in San Juan. In fact, people from the capital drive to Ponce or Guánica to see what's new on the horizon. Some of the more ambitious restaurants in this part of Puerto Rico are experimenting with Asian and Latin fusion cuisines, which means you might find pork with tamarind glaze or guava sauce, or snapper in a plantain crust. But what you'll mostly find is open-air eateries serving simple, filling fare. The southern coast is known for seafood, particularly Salinas and Ponce, both of which have a string of popular seaside restaurants. A 15% –20% tip is customary; most restaurants won't include it in the bill, but it's wise to check.

## ABOUT THE HOTELS

Modest, family-oriented establishments near beaches or in small towns and the occasional restored colonial hacienda or mansion are the most typical accommodations. Southern Puerto Rico doesn't have the abundance of luxury hotels and resorts found to the north and east; however, the Hilton Ponce & Casino and the Copamarina Beach Resort are self-contained complexes with a dizzying array of services.

| WHAT IT COSTS IN U.S. DOLLARS | | | | | |
|---|---|---|---|---|---|
| | ¢ | $ | $$ | $$$ | $$$$ |
| Restaurants | under $8 | $8–$12 | $12–$20 | $20–$30 | over $30 |
| Hotels | under $80 | $80–$150 | $150–$250 | $250–$350 | over $350 |

Prices are for a double room in high season, excluding 9% tax (11% for hotels with casinos, 7% for paradores) and 5%–12% service charge.

## SAFETY

For the most part, the south is safe. You won't encounter big-city crime, but you should take a few simple precautions. Don't wear flashy jewelry outside of tourist areas. Keep an eye on your belongings at the beach, and don't leave valuables locked in your car for all to see. Avoid out-of-the-way beach areas after dark.

## TOUR OPTIONS

Alelí Tours and Encantos Ecotours Southwest in La Parguera offer ecological tours of the southwestern area, including two- or three-hour kayak trips that cost about $30. Aventuras Puerto Rico and VIP Tours in Ponce offer city tours, horseback riding, and island-hopping adventures.

**Contacts Alelí Tours** ⊠ Rte. 304, Km 3.2, La Parguera ☎ 787/899–6086 ⊕ www.alelitours.com. **Aventuras Puerto Rico** ☎ 787/380–8481 ⊕ www.aventuraspuertorico.com. **Encantos Ecotours Southwest** ☎ 787/272–0005 ⊕ www.ecotourspr.com. **VIP Tours** ☎ 787/536-4683 ⊕ www.viptourspr.com.

## VISITOR INFORMATION

In Ponce the municipal tourist office is open weekdays from 8 to 4:30, as is the small information desk in the Parque de Bombas. The Puerto Rico Tourism Company's office on Calle Villa is open weekdays from 8 to 4:30. Smaller cities generally have a tourism office in the city hall open weekdays from 8 to noon and 1 to 4.

## IF YOU LIKE

### DIVING AND SNORKELING

Southern Puerto Rico is an undiscovered dive destination, which means unspoiled reefs and lots of fish. You can arrange for dive boats at Caribe Playa Beach Resort in the southeast, Ponce's La Guancha, and in La Parguera and the Copamarina Beach Resort in the southwest. Shore diving and snorkeling are best around islands or cays or along the southwestern coast.

### HIKING

Vegetation in the region is dramatically different from that of the rest of the island. Near Guánica is the 9,900-acre Bosque Estatal de Guánica, a rare dry tropical forest. With more than 100 species of birds, it's known for its excellent bird-watching. There are good trails throughout the area, but printed guides and trail maps are hard to come by. Ask locals for directions to their favorite paths.

**Contacts Ponce Municipal Tourist Office** ✉ *2nd fl. of Citibank, Plaza de las Delicias, Ponce Centro, Ponce* ☎ *787/841–8044* ⊕ *www.visitponce.com.* **Puerto Rico Tourism Company** ✉ *122 Calle Villa, Suite B, Ponce* ☎ *787/290–2911* ⊕ *www.seepuertorico.com.*

# PONCE

*21 miles (34 km) southwest of Coamo.*

"Ponce is Ponce and the rest is parking space" is the adage used by the residents of Puerto Rico's second-largest city (population 194,000) to express their pride in being a *ponceño*. The rivalry with the island's capital began in the 19th century, when European immigrants from England, France, and Spain settled here. Because the city's limits extend from the Caribbean to the foothills of the Cordillera Central, it's a lot hotter in climate than San Juan. Another contrast is the neoclassical architecture of the elegant homes and public buildings that surround the main square.

Many of the 19th-century buildings in Ponce Centro, the downtown area, have been renovated, and the Museo de Arte de Ponce—endowed by its late native son and former governor Luis A. Ferré—is considered one of the Caribbean's finest art museums. Just as famous is Ponce's pre-Lenten carnival. The colorful costumes and *vejigante* (mischief maker) masks worn during the festivities are famous throughout the world *(see special feature in this chapter)*. The best dining in Ponce is just west of town. Seafood restaurants line the highway in an area known as Las Cucharas, named for the spoon-shape bay you'll overlook as you dine.

### GETTING HERE AND AROUND

The fastest route through the region is the Luis A. Ferré Expressway (Route 52), a toll road that runs from San Juan to Ponce, crossing the island's central mountain range. The trip from Condado or Old San Juan takes about two hours. Route 2, also a toll road, connects to San Germán, Mayagüez, and the western part of the island.

Ponce offers a free tour to its major attractions on its "chu chu" train and trolleys. They run daily from 9 to about 5, and leave from Plaza de las Delicias. On Sunday, Guayama has a free trolley that runs to many sights. A trolley tour of San Germán is available by appointment. On weekends there are free horse-and-carriage rides around the plaza, or you could just walk. All the downtown sites are within a few blocks of the main square.

Car rental is typical for most visitors to Ponce and makes exploring the surrounding region considerably easier. Most hotels have parking lots, while metered parking is easy to come by in the center.

**Car Rental Avis** ⊠ *Aeropuerto Mercedita, Rte. 506, off Rte. 52* ☏ *787/842–6154* ⊕ *www.avis.com.* **Budget** ⊠ *Aeropuerto Mercedita, Rte. 506, off Rte. 52* ☏ *787/848–0907* ⊕ *www.budget.com.* **Dollar** ⊠ *Calle Marginal Solar 4, Km 263.2* ☏ *787/843–6940* ⊕ *www.dollar.com.* **Enterprise** ⊠ *1141 Av. Hostos, Ponce Centro* ☏ *787/812–3722.*

**Taxi and Trolley Borinquen Taxi** ☏ *787/843–6000.* **Ponce Trolley and Chu Chu Tren** ⊠ *Plaza de las Delicias, Ponce Centro* ☏ *787/284–3338.*

## EXPLORING PONCE

Plaza de las Delicias (Plaza of Delights), with its trees, benches, and famous lion fountain, is a perfect people-watching square in which to spend an hour or two on a Sunday afternoon. The old red-and-black firehouse is right on the plaza and has a fire-fighting museum on its second floor. Ponce is known for its museums, and has several dedicated to music, art, history, sports, and architecture. Ponceños are proud of their city, nicknamed the "Pearl of the South," and offer all visitors a warm welcome.

### PONCE CENTRO

At the heart of Ponce Centro is the Plaza de las Delicias, with trees, benches, and the famous lion fountain. Several interesting buildings are on this square or the adjacent streets, making the area perfect for a leisurely morning or afternoon stroll.

### TOP ATTRACTIONS

★ **Casa Wiechers-Villaronga.** In a city filled with neoclassical confections, this is one of the most elaborate. Alfredo B. Wiechers, who returned to his native Ponce after studying architecture in Paris, designed the house. Though small in scale, it makes a big impression with details like huge arched windows and a massive rooftop gazebo. No wonder that soon after it was completed in 1911 the Villaronga-Mercado family decided to make it their own. Check out the stained-glass windows and other fanciful touches. Inside, you'll find original furnishings and exhibits on Wiechers and other Ponce architects of his era. The house, restored by the Institute of Puerto Rican Culture, now operates as the Museum of Puerto Rican Architecture. ⊠ *106 Calle Reina, at Calle Méndez Vigo* ☏ *787/843–3363* ⌼ *Free* ⊙ *Wed.–Sun. 8–4:30.*

◔ **Parque de Bombas.** After El Morro in Old San Juan, this distinctive
Fodor'sChoice red-and-black-striped building may be the second-most-photographed
★ structure in Puerto Rico. Built in 1882 as a pavilion for an agricultural

# GREAT ITINERARIES

## IF YOU HAVE 1 DAY

Many residents of San Juan think nothing of a day trip to **Ponce**. If you head south on Route 52 you'll be there in less than two hours. There's plenty to do here, including a tour of the newly renovated Museo de Arte de Ponce. The best way to spend an hour or two is to stroll around the lovely Plaza de las Delicias. Make sure to dine in one of the outstanding restaurants, especially Archipiélago, where you can admire the cityscape from the rooftop.

## IF YOU HAVE 3 DAYS

From San Juan, head south on Route 52 until you reach **Ponce**, the "Pearl of the South." Spend the afternoon strolling around the Plaza de las Delicias, poking into the beautiful Catedral de Nuestra Señora de Guadalupe and the striking Parque de Bombas. On the following day, visit some of the other attractions in and around the city, perhaps the Museo de Arte de Ponce, the Castillo

Serrallés, or Hacienda Buena Vista. Dedicate your final day to **Guánica**, where you'll find wonderful beaches and deserted cays; spend the night here before heading back to San Juan. If you are in the mood for hiking, there's the Bosque Estatal de Guánica.

## IF YOU HAVE 5 DAYS

Make a leisurely trip south from San Juan on Route 52, spending a night in **Coamo**. These hot springs were thought by some to be Ponce de León's Fountain of Youth. Continue on your second day to **Ponce** for two days of exploring. Travel west along the coast and settle at a waterfront hotel in **Guánica**. In the evening you can take a boat trip to the bioluminescent bay at **La Parguera**. On your last day explore the beautifully preserved colonial city of **San Germán**, making sure to see the lovely colonial-era chapel known as the Capilla de Porta Coeli.

**5**

and industrial fair, it was converted the following year into a firehouse. Today it's a museum tracing the history—and glorious feats—of Ponce's fire brigade. Kids love the antique fire truck on the lower level. Short tours in English and Spanish are given on the half hour, and you can sign up for free trolley tours of the historic downtown here. The island's most helpful tourism officials staff a small information desk inside the door. ⊠ *Plaza de las Delicias* ☎ *787/284–3338* ⊕ *www.visitponce.com* ✆ *Free* ☉ *Daily 9–5.*

### WORTH NOTING

**Casa Armstrong-Poventud.** Banker and industrialist Carlos Armstrong and his wife, Eulalia Pou, lived in this neoclassical house designed and built for them in 1901 by Manuel V. Domenech. The building recently underwent a top-to-bottom renovation, and now you can admire the ornate facade, which is chock-full of columns, statues, and intricate moldings. Original furnishings belonging to the family are on display. ⊠ *Calle Unión, across from Catedral de Nuestra Señora de Guadalupe* ☎ *787/290–1530* ✆ *$3* ☉ *Wed.–Sun. 8–4:30.*

**Catedral de Nuestra Señora de Guadalupe.** This pale blue cathedral has always been one of the city's jewels, but it regained much of its luster

Casa
Armstrong-
Poventud .......**2**

Casa
Wiechers-
Villaronga .......**7**

Catedral de
Nuestra
Señora de
Guadalupe .......**1**

Museo de la
Historia de
Ponce ...........**5**

Museo de
la Música
Puertorriqueña ..**6**

Parque de
Bombas ..........**3**

Teatro
La Perla ..........**4**

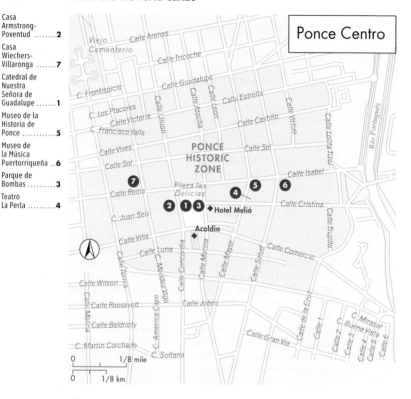

after a complete renovation in 2007. Dedicated to the Virgin of Guadalupe, it is built on the site of a 1670 chapel destroyed by earthquakes. Part of the current structure, where mass is still held, dates from 1835. After another earthquake in 1918, new steeples and a roof were put on and neoclassical embellishments were added to the facade. Inside you'll see stained-glass windows and two alabaster altars. ⊠ *Plaza de las Delicias* ☎ *787/842–0134* ⊙ *Services daily 6 am and 11 am.*

**Museo de la Historia de Ponce.** Housed in two adjoining neoclassical mansions, this museum includes 10 exhibition halls covering the city's residents, from the Taíno Indians to the Spanish settlers to the mix of the present. Hour-long guided tours in English and Spanish give an overview of the city's history. The descriptions are mostly in Spanish, but displays of clothing from different eras are still interesting to see. ⊠ *53 Calle Isabel, at Calle Mayor* ☎ *787/844–7042* ⊠ *Free* ⊙ *Tues.– Sun. 8–4:30.*

**Museo de la Música Puertorriqueña.** At this museum you'll learn how Puerto Rican music has been influenced by African, Spanish, and Native American cultures. On display are dozens of instruments, such as the *triple* (a small string instrument resembling a banjo), as well as memorabilia of local composers and musicians. The small museum takes up several rooms in a neoclassical former residence, which alone is worth

# A GOOD WALK: PONCE CENTRO

Start on the tree-lined Plaza de las Delicias. (You'll find parking nearby on Calle Marina, Calle Isabel, and Calle Reina.) Dominating it is the **Catedral Nuestra Señora de Guadalupe**, dating from 1835. Across the street is the **Casa Armstrong-Poventud**, home of the Institute of Culture's Ponce branch. Leaving Armstrong-Poventud, cross back to the plaza, circle south by the Alcaldía, and continue to the plaza's east side to visit the red-and-black-striped fire station, **Parque de Bombas**.

From the intersection of Calles Marina and Cristina, take Calle Cristina a block east to one of the city's first restoration projects, **Teatro La Perla**, at the corner of Cristina and Mayor. One block north of the theater, at Calles Mayor and Isabel, is a former home that's now the **Museo de la Historia de Ponce**. A block east, at the corner of Calles Salud and Isabel, is the **Museo de la Música Puertorriqueña**. Four blocks west (you will go by Plaza de las Delicias again, and Calle Isabel will turn into Calle Reina) is

the 1911 architectural masterpiece **Casa Wiechers-Villaronga**. For more early-20th-century architecture, continue west on Calle Reina, where you'll see examples of *casas criollas*, wooden homes with the spacious front balconies that were popular in the Caribbean during the early 1900s.

## TIMING

Although it's possible to see Ponce Centro in one morning or afternoon, it's best to devote a full day and evening. Explore the streets and museums during daylight, and then head for the plaza at night, when the lion fountain and street lamps are illuminated and townspeople stroll the plaza. With police officers on nearly every corner, this area is very safe to explore. ■TIP→ Several of the city's most popular museums—Casa Wiechers-Villaronga and the Museo de la Música Puertorriqueña—are not air-conditioned, so they close early when the weather is hot. If you want to see these sites, make sure to arrive before 11 am.

the trip. ⊠ *Calle Isabel and Calle Salud* ☎ *787/848–7016* ⊕ *www.icp. gobierno.pr/myp/museos/m15.htm* 🎟 *Free* ☉ *Wed.–Sun. 8:30–4:30.*

**NEED A BREAK?**

**King's Cream Helados.** An institution for more than 40 years, King's Cream Helados, across from Plaza de las Delicias, is *the* place for ice cream in Ponce. It serves 12 varieties, from tamarind and passion fruit to classics chocolate and vanilla. A bench in the tiny storefront seats three, but most folks take their cups and cones across the street and stake out shady benches around the fountain. King's is open daily from 8 am to midnight. ⊠ *9223 Calle Marina* ☎ *787/843–8520.*

**Teatro La Perla.** This theater was restored in 1941 after an earthquake and fire damaged the original 1864 structure. The striking interior contains seats for 1,047 and has excellent acoustics. It's generally open for a quick peek on weekdays. ⊠ *Calle Mayor and Calle Cristina* ☎ *787/843–4322* 🎟 *Free* ☉ *Weekdays 8–4:30.*

Today it's a museum, but for more than 100 years Parque de Bombas served as Ponce's main firehouse.

## GREATER PONCE

The greater Ponce area has some of Puerto Rico's most notable cultural attractions, including one of the island's finest art museums and its most important archaeological site.

### TOP ATTRACTIONS

**Castillo Serrallés.** This lovely Spanish-style villa—such a massive house that people in the town below referred to it as a castle—was built in the 1930s for Ponce's wealthiest family, the makers of Don Q rum. Guided tours give you a glimpse into the lifestyle of a sugar baron. The dining room is a highlight, with its original hand-carved furnishings. A permanent exhibit explains the area's sugarcane and rum industries. The extensive garden, with sculptured bushes and a shimmering reflection pool, is considered the best kept on the island. ✉ *17 El Vigía, El Vigía* ☎ *787/259–1774* ⊕ *home.coqui.net/castserr* ✉ *$8.50, includes admission to Cruceta El Vigía and Butterfly Garden* ☉ *Thurs.–Sun. 9:30–6:30.*

Fodor's Choice
★

**Hacienda Buena Vista.** Built by Salvador de Vives in 1838, Buena Vista was one of the area's largest coffee plantations. It's a technological marvel—water from the nearby Río Canas was funneled into narrow brick channels that could be diverted to perform any number of tasks, including turning the waterwheel. (Seeing the two-story wheel slowly begin to turn is fascinating, especially for kids.) Nearby is the two-story manor house, filled with furniture that gives a sense of what it was like to live on a coffee plantation nearly 150 years ago. Make sure to take a look in the kitchen, dominated by a massive hearth. In 1987 the plantation was restored by the Puerto Rican Conservation Trust, which leads

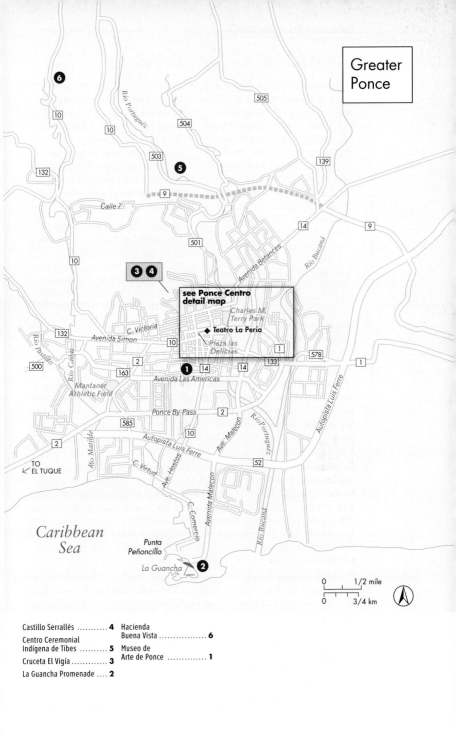

# Greater Ponce

| 6 |
| 10 |
| Río Portugués |
| 505 |
| 10 |
| 504 |
| 503 |
| 132 |
| 5 |
| 139 |
| 9 |
| Calle 7 |
| 14 |
| 9 |
| Río Bucaná |
| 501 |
| 10 |
| Avenida Betances |
| 3 | 4 |

see Ponce Centro
detail map

Charles M.
Terry Park

◆ Teatro La Perla

| C. Victoria |
| 132 | Avenida Simón |
| Río Cañas |
| 10 |
| Plaza las Delicias |
| 1 |
| 578 |
| 1 |
| 500 |
| Río Pastillo |
| 2 |
| 133 |
| 163 |
| 1 | 14 | 14 |
| Avenida Las Américas |
| Mantanet Athletic Field |
| Ponce By-Pass |
| 2 |
| 585 |
| 10 |
| Río Matilde |
| Autopista Luis Ferré |
| Ave. Malecón |
| Río Portugués |
| Autopista Luis Ferré |
| 2 |
| C. Virtud |
| Ave. Hostos |
| 52 |
| Río Bucaná |
| TO
EL TUQUE |
| Avenida Malecón |

## Caribbean Sea

Punta
Peñoncillo

C. Comercio

La Guancha        2

| 0 | 1/2 mile |
| 0 | 3/4 km |

Castillo Serrallés ........... **4**

Centro Ceremonial
Indígena de Tibes .......... **5**

Cruceta El Vigía ............. **3**

La Guancha Promenade .... **2**

Hacienda
Buena Vista ................. **6**

Museo de
Arte de Ponce .............. **1**

## A GOOD TOUR: GREATER PONCE

The **Museo de Arte de Ponce** is on Avenida Las Américas, south of Plaza de las Delicias and not far from the Luis A. Ferré Expressway (Route 52). Anyone with a taste for art can happily while away many hours in its galleries. East of the museum you can pick up Route 14 south to the Caribbean and **La Guancha**, a boardwalk with food kiosks, a playground, and a child-friendly public beach. It's a good place to relax and let the younger generation work off energy. From here, if you retrace your path north past downtown you'll be heading to Calle Bertoly and El Vigía (Vigía Hill), where the **Cruceta El Vigía** towers over the city and the **Castillo Serrallés**, a former sugar baron's villa, is a popular attraction.

Farther north on Route 503 is the **Centro Ceremonial Indígena de Tibes**, which displays native artifacts dating back more than 1,500 years. You'll have to backtrack to reach Route 10, then head north to **Hacienda Buena Vista**, a former coffee plantation that's been restored by the Puerto Rican Conservation Trust. (Call ahead to arrange a tour.)

You can drive to all these sights or hop on the free trolleys or "chu chu" trains that run from Plaza de las Delicias to the museum, La Guancha, and El Vigía. You'll need a car or a cab to reach the Centro Ceremonial Indígena de Tibes or Hacienda Buena Vista.

four tours a day (one in English). The tours are by reservation only, so make sure to call several days ahead. After seeing the plantation, you can buy coffee beans and other souvenirs at the gift shop. Allow yourself an hour to travel the winding road from Ponce. ⊠ *Rte. 123, Km 16.8, Sector Corral Viejo* ☎ *787/722–5882 weekdays, 787/284–7020 weekends* ⌑ *$8* ⊘ *Wed.–Sun., tours at 8:30, 10:30, 1:30 and 3:30.*

Ⓒ **La Guancha Promenade.** Encircling the cove of a working harbor, the seaside boardwalk features a small lookout tower and kiosks where vendors sell local food and drink. The adjacent park has a large children's area filled with playground equipment and, on weekends, live music. The nearby public beach has restrooms, changing areas, a medical post, and plenty of free parking. On Sunday night this place gets packed with locals strolling the boardwalk. ⊠ *End of Rte. 14, La Guancha* ☎ *787/844–3995.*

Fodor'sChoice
★ **Museo de Arte de Ponce.** This building—designed by Edward Durrell Stone, who also designed the original Museum of Modern Art in New York City and the Kennedy Center in Washington, D.C.—is easily identified by the hexagonal galleries on the second story. The museum, which underwent a major renovation in 2010, has one of the best art collections in Latin America, which is why residents of San Juan frequently make the trip down to Ponce. The 3,000-piece collection includes works by famous Puerto Rican artists such as Francisco Oller, represented by a lovely landscape called *Hacienda Aurora*. There are plenty of European works on display as well, including paintings by Peter Paul Rubens and Thomas Gainsborough. The highlight of the

The stately lobby of the Museo de Arte de Ponce.

European collection is the Pre-Raphaelite paintings, particularly the mesmerizing *Flaming June,* by Frederick Leighton, which has become the museum's unofficial symbol. You can take a break in the museum's three sculpture gardens, or relax in Restaurant Al Sur. Watch for special exhibits, such as a recent one examining the work of video artists. ⊠ *2325 Av. Las Américas, Sector Santa María* ☎ *787/840–1510* ⊕ *www.museoarteponce.org* 🖰 *$6* ☯ *Wed-Mon. 10–6.*

### WORTH NOTING

**Centro Ceremonial Indígena de Tibes** (*Tibes Indian Ceremonial Center*). This archaeological site, discovered after flooding from a tropical storm in 1975, is the most important on the island. The ancient ceremonial center dates from AD 300 to 700 and includes nine playing fields used for a ritual ball game that some think was similar to soccer. The fields are bordered by smooth stones, some of which are engraved with petroglyphs that researchers say might have ceremonial or astronomical significance. The most eye-catching part of the site is the Plaza de Estrella, or Plaza of the Star, where the stones are arranged in a pattern that resembles a rising sun. Experts say it might have been used to chart the seasons. A village with several thatched huts has been reconstructed in an original setting. Be sure to visit the small museum before taking a walking tour of the site. ⊠ *Rte. 503, Km 2.5, Barrio Tibes* ☎ *787/840–2255, 787/840–5685* ⊕ *ponce.inter.edu/tibes/tibes. html* 🖰 *$3* ☯ *Tues.–Sun. 8–4:30.*

**Cruceta El Vigía.** At the top of Cerro Vigía—a hill where the Spanish once watched for ships, including those of marauding pirates—is this colossal concrete cross built in 1801. You can climb the stairs or take a glass elevator to the top of the 100-foot cross for a panoramic view across the city. Purchase tickets at nearby Castillo Serrallés. ⊠ *17 El Vigía, across from Castillo Serrallés, El Vigía* ☎ *787/259–3816* ⊕ *www. castilloserralles.org* ✉ *$5.50, $8.50 includes admission to Castillo Serrallés and Butterfly Garden* ☾ *Tues.–Sun. 9–5:30.*

## WHERE TO EAT

**$$$**
LATIN AMERICAN
Fodor's Choice
★

✕ **Archipiélago.** With perhaps the greatest view in all of Puerto Rico, this ambitious restaurant has stepped in to fill the city's culinary vacuum. It sits on the sixth and seventh floors of a building that overlooks the Parque de Bombas and Catedral de Nuestra Señora de Guadalupe. The beautifully designed restaurant and lounge have quickly found their place among the hottest spots in Puerto Rico. Expect a chic crowd that's dressed to impress dining on Puerto Rican fusion dishes as diverse as beer-battered mahimahi, plantain-stuffed pork, or steak topped with lemon chimichurri. A terrace has live jazz on weekends, which pairs well with their renowned mojitos. ⊠ *76 Calle Cristina, 6th Floor, Ponce Centro* ☎ *787/812–8822* ⊕ *www.archipielagopr.com* ☾ *Closed Mon. and Tues.*

**$$**
ECLECTIC
★

✕ **Cabuqui.** On sweltering hot days it takes a lot to make *ponceños* leave their homes. Yet they come out in droves to the tree-shaded courtyard of the Cubuqui. When a breeze shakes the flower-covered branches, things cool down considerably. And if nature doesn't cooperate, there are always the three air-conditioned dining rooms. The menu is extremely well traveled, stopping in Argentina (*churrasco*, or skirt steak, served with homemade chimichurri) and France (veal fillet in a red wine sauce) before heading back to Puerto Rico for such dishes as *masitas de cerdo* (chunks of perfectly seasoned pork). The wine list, which includes many bottles from Spain and Chile, is quite reasonable. There's always live music, whether it's a small band playing jazz or a single accordionist losing himself in a tango. ⊠ *32 Calle Isabel, Ponce Centro* ☎ *787/984–5696* ☾ *Closed Sun.–Tues.*

**$$**
SEAFOOD

✕ **El Ancla.** Families favor this laid-back restaurant, whose dining room sits at the edge of the sea. The kitchen serves generous and affordable plates of fish, crab, and other fresh seafood with *tostones* (fried plantains), french fries, and garlic bread. Try the shrimp in garlic sauce, salmon fillet with capers, or the delectable mofongo stuffed with seafood. Finish your meal with one of the fantastic flans. The piña coladas—with or without rum—are exceptional. ⊠ *805 Av. Hostos Final, Ponce Playa* ☎ *787/840–2450* ⊕ *www.restauranteelancla.com.*

**$$**
ECLECTIC

✕ **Lola.** In the heart of downtown, this trendy bistro has an eclectic menu to match the decor. Grab a seat in a red-velvet booth and start with the sampler of mahimahi nuggets, bruschetta, fried plantains, and egg rolls. The menu ranges from tuna steak to filet mignon to three-cheese risotto. Be sure to ask about the daily specials, which are always worth trying. This is a great place to admire work by local artists and sip on a Lola Martini (grapefruit, cranberry, champagne, lime, and rum). ⊠ *Ramada Inn, Calle Reina and Calle Unión, Ponce Centro* ☎ *787/813–5033* ⊕ *www.lolacuisine.com.*

**$$**
SEAFOOD

✕ **Pito's Seafood.** Choose from the waterfront terrace or one of the enclosed dining rooms at this longtime favorite east of Ponce in Las

The reflection pool is just one highlight of a guided tour through the gardens and villa of Castillo Serrallés.

Cucharas. No matter where you sit, you'll have a view of the ocean. The main attraction is the freshly caught seafood, ranging from lobster and crab to salmon and red snapper. For total indulgence, try the fresh oysters or shrimp wrapped in bacon—both specialties of the house. There's also a wide range of chicken and beef dishes. The plantain cups stuffed with chicken or seafood make an excellent starter. From the expansive wine cellar you can select more than 25 different wines by the glass. Listen to live music on Friday and Sunday night. ⊠ *Rte. 2, Km 218.5, Sector Las Cucharas* ☎ *787/841–4977* ⊕ *www.pitosseafoodpr.com.*

**$$**
STEAKHOUSE
✕ **Rincón Argentina.** Housed in a beautifully restored criollo-style house, Rincón Argentina is one of the city's most popular restaurants. Completely unpretentious, this is the kind of steak house you find all over South America. The specialty of the house is *parrilladas,* meaning just about anything that comes off the grill. Don't pass up the skirt steak, served here with lip-smacking chimichurri, or the mofongo prepared seven different ways. On cool evenings, take a table on the terrace. Otherwise, wander through the maze of dining rooms until you find a table you like. ⊠ *69 Calle Salud, at Calle Isabel, Ponce Centro* ☎ *787/840– 3768* ◿ *Reservations essential.*

**$$**
GREEK FUSION
✕ **Santorini.** The only Greek restaurant in Puerto Rico, this open-air establishment has successfully captured the cuisine and atmosphere of its namesake island. Statues of goddesses line the pathway leading to a dual-level dining area, decorated with 1960s-era movie posters from Greece. Nearly every dish is bathed in olive oil and vinegar, including the salads and sandwiches. You'll also find plenty of Caribbean food and Spanish tapas like conch fritters and stuffed lobster hamburgers. On Friday and Saturday the bar is open late for drinks and dancing.

Request a table on the lower deck, where water gently laps near your table. ⊠ *Rte. 2, Km 220, Sector Las Cucharas* ☎ *939/644–9021* ⊕ *www.santorini-olr.com* ☉ *Closed Mon. and Tues.*

## WHERE TO STAY

*For expanded hotel reviews, visit Fodors.com.*

**$$**
**RESORT**
☺
**☲ Hilton Ponce Golf & Casino Resort.** The south coast's biggest resort sits on a black-sand beach about 4 miles (6 km) south of downtown Ponce. **Pros:** Good golf; large casino; game room and pool for kids. **Cons:** Isolated location; bland rooms. ⊠ *1150 Av. Caribe, La Guancha* ⌑ *Box 741900732* ☎ *787/259–7676, 800/445–8667* ⊕ *www.hiltoncaribbean.com* ⤳ *242 rooms, 13 suites* ⚹ *In-room: a/c, safe, Wi-Fi. In-hotel: restaurant, bar, golf course, pool, tennis court, gym, spa, beach, children's programs, parking* ⦿ *No meals.*

**$**
**HOTEL**
☺
**☲ Holiday Inn.** With all the basic comforts you'd expect from a Holiday Inn, this five-story hotel has a 24-hour casino, a huge pool, and a restaurant and bar where live music can be heard weekends. ⊠ *3315 Ponce Bypass, west of downtown* ☎ *787/844–1200* ⊕ *www.holidayinn.com/ponce* ⤳ *110 rooms, 6 suites* ⚹ *In-room: a/c, safe, Wi-Fi. In-hotel: restaurant, bar, pool, gym, laundry facilities, business center, parking* ⦿ *No meals.*

**¢**
**HOTEL**
**☲ Hotel Bélgica.** Near the central square, this hotel dating from 1872 is both comfortable and economical, with worn yet clean rooms with hardwood floors, high ceilings, and wrought-iron beds. **Pros:** A taste of old Ponce; friendly staff; excellent rates. **Cons:** Front-facing rooms are noisy; some rooms don't have windows; lots of steps and no elevator. ⊠ *122 Calle Villa, Ponce Centro* ☎ *787/844–3255* ⊕ *www.hotelbelgica.com* ⤳ *20 rooms* ⚹ *In-room: a/c, Wi-Fi. In-hotel: business center, some pets allowed* ⦿ *Breakfast.*

**$**
**HOTEL**
**☲ Hotel Meliá.** In the heart of the city, this family-owned hotel has been a local landmark for over a century. **Pros:** Great location on the main square; walking distance to downtown sites; good dining options near hotel. **Cons:** Rooms are somewhat outdated; front rooms are a bit noisy; green carpet and curtains make the rooms rather stuffy. ⊠ *75 Calle Cristina, Ponce Centro* ☎ *787/842–0260, 800/448–8355* ⊕ *www.hotelmeliapr.com* ⤳ *68 rooms, 6 suites* ⚹ *In-room: a/c, Wi-Fi. In-hotel: bar, pool, business center, parking* ⦿ *Breakfast.*

**$**
**HOTEL**
☺
**☲ Howard Johnson.** Two minutes from Mercedita Aeropuerto, this hotel is a good choice if you have an early morning flight. ⊠ *103 Turpó Industrial Park, Airport* ☎ *787/841–1000* ⊕ *www.hojo.com* ⤳ *117 rooms, 3 suites* ⚹ *In-room: a/c, safe, Wi-Fi. In-hotel: restaurant, bar, pool, gym, laundry facilities, business center, parking* ⦿ *No meals.*

**$**
**HOTEL**
**☲ Ramada Inn Ponce.** In a stunningly restored building that dates back to 1882, the Ramada Inn sits right on the main square. **Pros:** Excellent location; lively bar and restaurant. **Cons:** Regular rooms lack charm; small pool gets foot traffic from attached restaurant. ⊠ *Calles Reina and Calle Unión, Ponce Centro* ☎ *787/813–5050* ⊕ *www.ramadaponce.com* ⤳ *70 rooms* ⚹ *In-room: a/c, safe, Internet. In-hotel: restaurant, bar, pool, gym, parking* ⦿ *No meals.*

## NIGHTLIFE AND THE ARTS

### NIGHTLIFE

BARS AND CLUBS **Archipiélago.** Sitting high above the plaza, Archipiélago has an outdoor terrace and upstairs lounge that lure Ponce's glitterati with hip cocktails, live music on weekends, and a dramatic view of the plaza lights below. ⊠ *76 Calle Cristina, Ponce Centro* ☎ *787/812–8822* ⊕ *www.archipielagopr.com* ☾ *Closed Mon. and Tues.*

**Kenepa's Cafe.** On the main square, Kenepa's Cafe has live music and strong drinks. Locals crowd around the bar every night of the week. ⊠ *Edificio Café Plaza, 3 Calle Unión, Ponce Centro* ☎ *787/ 363–6674.*

**TAKE A WALK**

In downtown Ponce people embrace the Spanish tradition of the *paseo,* an evening stroll with family and friends around Plaza de las Delicias, which is spectacular at night when its old-fashioned street lamps glow and the fountain is lit. The boardwalk at La Guancha is also a lively scene with bands playing on weekends. You can buy a bag of sardines and feed seagulls and pelicans right out of your hand.

CASINOS The casinos in Ponce can't hold a candle to their counterparts in San Juan.

**Hilton Ponce Golf & Casino Resort.** Hilton Ponce Golf & Casino Resort has a rather cramped casino that stays open nightly until 4 am. ⊠ *1150 Av. Caribe, La Guancha* ☎ *787/259–7676* ⊕ *www.hiltoncaribbean.com/ ponce.*

**Holiday Inn Ponce.** Holiday Inn Ponce has a small casino with 346 slot machines and 10 tables. ⊠ *3315 Ponce Bypass, El Tuque* ☎ *787/844– 1200* ⊕ *www.holidayinn.com/ponce.*

### THE ARTS

**Museo de Arte de Ponce.** The Museo de Arte de Ponce occasionally sponsors chamber-music concerts and recitals by members of the Puerto Rico Symphony Orchestra. ⊠ *2325 Av. Las Américas, Sector Santa María* ☎ *787/848–0505.*

**Teatro La Perla.** Check for Spanish-language theater productions and concerts at the Teatro La Perla. ⊠ *Calle Mayor and Calle Cristina, Ponce Centro* ☎ *787/843–4322.*

## SHOPPING

On holidays and during festivals, artisans sell wares from booths in Plaza de las Delicias. Souvenir and gift shops are plentiful in the area around the plaza, and Paseo Atocha, a pedestrian mall with shops geared to residents, runs north of it.

**Mi Coquí.** Mi Coquí has shelves filled with carnival masks, colorful hammocks, freshly ground coffee, and bottles and bottles of rum. ⊠ *9227 Calle Marina, Ponce Centro* ☎ *787/841–0216.*

**Plaza del Caribe Mall.** Plaza del Caribe Mall, just outside town, is one of the island's largest malls and has such stores as Sears, Puma, Ann Taylor, and the Gap. ⊠ *Rte. 2, Km 224.9* ☎ *787/259–8989* ⊕ *www.plazadelcaribe.net.*

**Ponce Mall.** Ponce Mall, with more than 30 stores, is an older shopping center, with many local clothing and discount stores. ⊠ *Rte. 2, Km 225.8* ☎ *787/844–6170* ⊕ *www.poncemallpr.com.*

**Utopia.** Utopia sells carnival masks, carved figurines, and other crafts. ⊠ *78 Calle Isabel, Ponce Centro* ☎ *787/848–8742.*

## SPORTS AND THE OUTDOORS

### DIVING AND SNORKELING

You'll see many varieties of coral, parrotfish, angelfish, and grouper in the reefs around the island of Caja de Muertos. Snorkeling around La Guancha and the beach area of the Ponce Hilton is also fairly good.

**Island Venture.** Rafi Vega's Island Venture offers two-tank dive excursions for $65, as well as snorkeling trips for $35. The company also takes day-trippers from La Guancha to Caja de Muertos—a 45-minute boat ride—for a day of relaxing on the beach. ☎ *787/842–8546* ⊕ *www. islandventurepr.com.*

### GOLFING

**Costa Caribe Golf and Country Club.** The Costa Caribe Golf & Country Club, Ponce's only course, has 27 holes, a driving range, and pro shop adjoining the Ponce Hilton. To get here, take Route 12 to Avenida Caribe ⊠ *1150 Av. Caribe, La Guancha* ☎ *787/259–7676* ⊕ *www. costacaribe-resort.com* ⌡ *$89 per round, $40 after 4 pm.*

# THE SOUTHEASTERN COAST

As you cross the Cordillera Central, the scenery becomes drier and more rugged. The Caribbean sparkles in the distance, and the plain between the sea and the mountains, once the heart of the sugarcane industry, is now the domain of cattle. Tucked into the foothills is Coamo, a popular hot-springs resort since the early 1900s. Closer to the coast is Guayama, with a tree-lined square surrounded by many historic buildings.

## COAMO

*21 miles (34 km) northeast of Ponce, 20 miles (33 km) southwest of Cayey, 13 miles (20 km) northwest of Salinas.*

Founded by the Spanish in 1579, Coamo was the third city established in Puerto Rico. It dominated the south of the island until the mid-1880s, when political power shifted to Ponce. Coamo town, however, remained an important outpost; several decisive battles were fought here during the Spanish-American War in 1898.

The thermal springs outside Coamo are believed by some to be the Fountain of Youth for which Ponce de León was searching. In the mid-1800s a fashionable resort was built nearby, and people have been coming to soak in the waters ever since. Coamo is also famous for the San Blas Half-Marathon, which brings competitors and spectators from around the world. The race, held in early February, covers 13 miles (18 km) of the city's hilly streets.

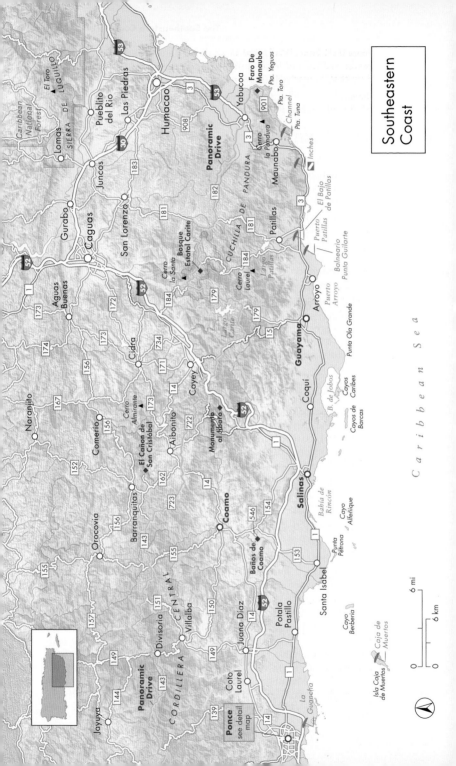

Southeastern Coast

## GETTING HERE AND AROUND

Coamo sits not far from Luis A. Ferré Expressway (Route 52), the toll road that connects San Juan and Ponce; it is about 20 miles northeast of Ponce. You can take the turnoff onto Route 153, though there is also access from several points in the Cordillera. Públicos from Ponce connect with Coamo's town center, though you'll need to flag down a taxi to reach the baths or any of the hotels, which are all a couple of miles away.

## EXPLORING

**Iglesia Católica San Blás.** On Coama's main square, the Iglesia Católica San Blás has a gorgeous neoclassical facade. Dating from 1563, the whitewashed building is one of the oldest churches on the island. ⊠ *Calle Mario Braschetti* ☎ *787/825–1122* ☉ *Daily 6:30–noon.*

**Museo Histórico de Coamo.** Off the main square, the Museo Histórico de Coamo is appropriately housed in the former residence of one of the city's illustrious citizens, Clotilde Santiago, a wealthy farmer and merchant born in 1826. The museum is on the second floor of this sprawling, tangerine-colored building, which dates from 1863. Several rooms are decorated with colonial-style furnishings; photographs of the town and the Santiago family line the walls. ⊠ *29 Calle José I. Quintón* ☎ *787/803–6716* 🖼 *Free* ☉ *Weekdays 8–4:30.*

**Piscinas Aguas Termales.** Outside Coamo you can take a dip at the famous Piscinas Aguas Termales, the thermal springs that are said to have curative powers. Day-trippers can bathe in the steamy modern pool for $3. There's also a changing room at the end of a path. ⊠ *Rte. 546, Km 1.7* ☎ *787/825–6668* 🖼 *$3* ☉ *Daily 7–7.*

## WHERE TO EAT AND STAY

*For expanded hotel reviews, visit Fodors.com.*

$$ ✕ **La Ceiba.** The highway leading to Coama is lined by dozens of fast-
PUERTO RICAN food restaurants. Luckily, there are a few family-owned eateries worth stopping for, one of the best of which is this open-air cantina. You'll find the usual mofongo with chicken or beef, as well as some interesting Puerto Rican dishes like fried pork or red snapper stuffed with seafood. The menu features a variety of fish as well as lobster, shrimp, and octopus. If you are a fan of cheesecake, the chef makes eight different flavors (the pistachio is delicious). World-class margaritas are served at the bar. ⊠ *Rte. 153, Km. 13* ☎ *787/825–2299* ☉ *Closed Mon.*

$ 🏨 **Coamo Springs Resort.** On weekends, musicians wander around the
RESORT central courtyard of this rustic country inn. **Pros:** Relaxing atmosphere; pleasant staff. **Cons:** Uninteresting room decor; pools could be cleaner; overpriced. ⊠ *Rte. 546, Km 1* ☎ *787/825–2186, 787/825–2239* ⮎ *48 rooms* ♿ *In-room: a/c, Wi-Fi. In-hotel: restaurant, bar, pool, spa, parking* ❌ *No meals.*

## SPORTS AND THE OUTDOORS

GOLF **Coamo Springs Golf Club and Resort.** The Coamo Springs Golf Club and Resort is popular for its rugged beauty and affordable greens fees of $40. It's the only 18-hole, par-72 course with Bermuda grass on the island. When it's raining in the capital, sanjuaneros may drive down here for a day of play. The 6,647-yard course, designed by Ferdinand Garbin, is open daily from 7 to 7. ⊠ *Rte. 546, Km. 1* ☎ *787/825–1370* ⊕ *www.coamosprings.com.*

## SALINAS

*27 miles (41 km) east of Ponce.*

Most visitors are familiar with this town only because of seeing its name on an exit sign along Route 52. Islanders, however, know that the road from the expressway exit to Salinas leads to some of Puerto Rico's best seafood restaurants. Most of them are along the seafront in the Playa de Salinas area, reached by heading south on Route 701.

> **SALINAS HAS THE MOJO**
>
> When you stop in Salinas—and you should—be sure to try local seafood with *mojo isleño*, a popular sauce made from tomatoes, onions, and spices, which was created here.

**GETTING HERE AND AROUND**

You can take either the Luis A. Ferré Expressway (Route 52), the toll road that connects San Juan and Ponce, or the more scenic Route 1 along the coast east from Ponce to reach Salinas.

**WHERE TO EAT AND STAY**

*For expanded hotel reviews, visit Fodors.com.*

**$$$**
SEAFOOD
✕ **El Balcón de Capitán.** This *meson gastronómico*, hidden among a string of oceanfront seafood restaurants south of the center in the Playa de Salinas area, is one of the most respected on Puerto Rico's southern coast. Sit in either the open-air patio or air-conditioned dining room and bar and sample specialties like *mofongo relleno de mariscos* (seafood-stuffed plantains) or the many preparations of mahimahi, red snapper, arrayao, octopus, lobster, or conch. The paella with seafood is a house specialty. ✉ *Rte. 701, Playa de Salinas* ☎ *787/824–6210.*

**$$**
PUERTO RICAN
✕ **El Roble.** In operation since 1961, this restaurant is still considered one of the best in town. Don't be surprised to see flapping fish delivered straight off the boats and into the kitchen, where chefs prepare dishes like grouper filet stuffed with seafood. The red snapper is delicious, and like all the fish on the menu it can be prepared fried, buttered, breaded, or with a vinaigrette. There's also a children's menu and a large selection of wines. Be prepared for the collection of fish mounted on the walls. ✉ *Rte.701, Playa de Salinas* ☎ *787/824–2377.*

**$$$$**
INTERNATIONAL
☾
✕ **Piratas del Toro Al' Diente.** Straight out of a scene from *Pirates of the Caribbean*, this place is a must for anyone with children. Housed inside a massive pirate ship, the restaurant is a cross between a carnival and dinner theater. Waiters dressed as swashbucklers serve hearty platters of steak, lobster, chicken, and fish. You can also get your mofongo fix here. From squawking parrots and mechanical bulls to pony rides and an archery range, this place has it all. Although the average plate will run you close to $60, each serves four to five people, making this place quite a bargain. ✉ *Av. Pedro Albizu Campos, 1 mile off Rte. 52* ☎ *787/824-8028* ⊕ *www.toroaldiente.com* ☾ *Closed Mon.–Wed.*

**¢**
HOTEL
☾
🏨 **Manatee Eco Resort.** True to its name, this eco-friendly hotel has energy-efficient lighting, solar-heated water, and its own private well. ✉ *296 Calle A* ☎ *787/824–6688* ⊕ *www.manateeecoresort.com* ⇥ *26 rooms* △ *In-room: a/c, Wi-Fi. In-hotel: restaurant, bar, pool, water sports, parking* ⦿ *Breakfast.*

$   ☐ **Marina de Salinas.** Several different types of mangroves shade this
HOTEL   hotel, and the spacious rooms are cheerfully decorated with tropical
colors, wicker furniture, and paintings of fishing boats. **Pros:** Off-the-
beaten-path vibe, lovely mangrove trees, kayaks for rent. **Cons:** Basic
rooms, no elevator. ☒ *End of Rte. 701* ☎ *787/824–3185, 787/752–
8484* ⊕ *www.marinadesalinas.com* ⤳ *30 rooms; 2 suites* ☐ *In-room:
a/c, Wi-Fi. In-hotel: restaurant, bar, pool, gym, laundry facilities, park-
ing* ⦿| *No meals.*

# GUAYAMA

*18 miles (29 km) east of Salinas, 17 miles (28 km) southeast of Cayey,
31 miles (49 km) southeast of Barranquitas.*

Guayama was founded in 1736, but the city was destroyed by fire in
the early 1800s. It quickly recovered when the sugarcane industry grew
by leaps and bounds, and the wealth that the surrounding plantations
brought to town is evident in the number of striking neoclassical homes
on the streets surrounding the main square. Some have been beautifully
restored, whereas others are crumbling. One of the finest 19th-century
homes, Casa Cautiño, is now a museum.

The nearby countryside is home to Paso Fino horses. Each March at the
Marcelino Blondet Stadium, you can watch these high-stepping show
horses strut their stuff during the Feria Dulce Sueño, a fair named after
one of the island's most famous Thoroughbreds. Folk music and crafts
are part of the festivities.

## GETTING HERE AND AROUND

From the north or west take either Route 53 or the coastal Route 3 to
reach Guayama. On Sunday, Guayama has a free trolley that runs to
many sights.

Information **Guayama Trolley** ☒ *Acaldía de Guayama, Calle Vicente Pales*
☎ *787/864-7765.*

## EXPLORING

★   **Casa Cautiño.** Built for sugar, cattle, and coffee baron Genaro Cautiño
Vázquez and his wife, Genoveva Insúa, Casa Cautiño is an elegant neoclassical home dating from 1887. The painstakingly restored exterior
features a balcony with ornate grillwork. You'll be swept back in time
walking through the home's rooms, which are filled with the original
Victorian-era furnishings. Don't miss the modern-for-its-time bath-
room, complete with a standing shower. The museum is on the main
square. ☒ *1 Calle Palmer, at Calle Vicente Palé Matos* ☎ *787/864–9083*
☒ *Free* ☉ *Tues.–Sat. 9–4:30, Sun. 10–4.*

NEED A
BREAK?   **Rex Cream.** The fruit-flavored ice cream at Rex Cream is hard to pass up.
Flavors vary, depending on what produce is in season, but often include
coconut, lime, pineapple, tamarind, and *guanábana* (soursop). You can
also get milk shakes—the mango is outstanding. ☒ *24 Calle Derkes*
☎ *787/864-1608.*

**Centro de Bellas Artes.** Just a few blocks from the main square, the Centro de Bellas Artes is housed in a beautifully restored neoclassical building. Paintings by local artists fill its 11 rooms. ⊠ *Calle McArthur and Carr. 3* ☎ *787/864–7765* 🔁 *Free* 🕓 *Tues.–Sun. 9–4:30.*

**Iglesia San Antonio de Padua.** One of the prettiest churches on the southern coast, Iglesia San Antonio de Padua was begun in 1827 but not completed until 40 years later. Don't set your watch by the time on the clock; the hand-painted face forever reads 11:30, the time the church was "baptized." The bells in the tower were cast in gold and bronze in 1835. ⊠ *5 Calle Ashford.*

### SPORTS AND THE OUTDOORS

GOLF **Aguirre Golf Club.** Running through an old sugar plantation, the Aguirre Golf Club was built in 1925 for the executives of a local sugar mill. Open daily, the 9-hole course is short but tough. ⊠ *Rte. 705, Km 3, off Rte. 3, Aguirre* ☎ *787/853–4052.*

**El Legado Golf Resort.** The El Legado Golf Resort, designed by golf legend and native son Chi Chi Rodríguez, is one of the island's best courses. The 7,213-yard, 18-hole course has 12 lakes. ⊠ *Rte. 713, off Rte. 53, Cimarrona* ☎ *787/866–8894* ⊕ *www.ellegadogolf.com.*

# THE SOUTHWESTERN COAST

With sandy coves and palm-lined beaches tucked into the coastline's curves, southwestern Puerto Rico fulfills everyone's fantasy of a tropical paradise. The area is popular with local vacationers on weekends and holidays, but many beaches are nearly deserted on weekdays. Villages along the coast are picturesque places where oysters and fresh fish are sold at roadside stands.

## GUÁNICA

*24 miles (38 km) west of Ponce.*

Juan Ponce de León first explored this area in 1508, when he was searching for the elusive Fountain of Youth. Nearly 400 years later, U.S. troops landed first at Guánica during the Spanish-American War in 1898. The event is commemorated with an engraved marker on the city's *malecón,* or jetty. Sugarcane dominated the landscape through much of the 1900s, and the ruins of the old Guánica Central sugar mill, closed in 1980, loom over the town's western area, known as Ensenada. Today most of the action takes place at the beaches and in the forests outside of Guánica.

### GETTING HERE AND AROUND

From Ponce, Route 2 connects with Guánica via Route 116 and extends to San Germán and Mayagüez. The town hugs Guánica bay and runs almost immediately into the neighboring village of Ensenada.

### EXPLORING

**Bosque Estatal de Guánica** (*Guánica State Forest*). The 9,900-acre Bosque Estatal de Guánica, a United Nations Biosphere Reserve, is a great place for hiking expeditions. It's an outstanding example of a tropical dry coastal forest, with some 700 species of plants ranging from the

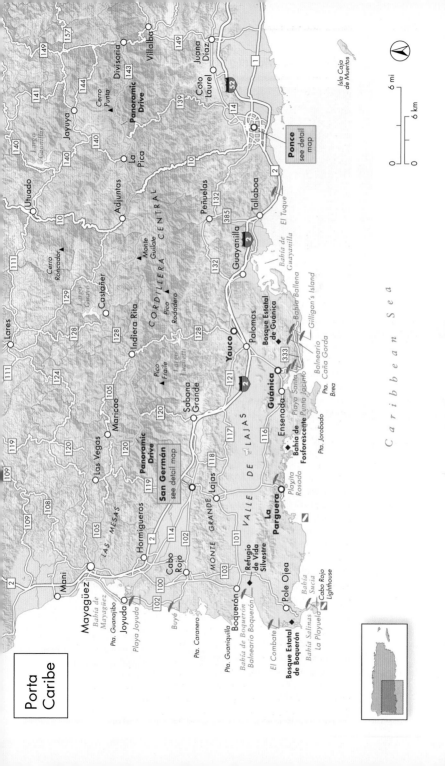

# Porta Caribe

Caribbean Sea

Isla Caja de Muertos

6 mi

6 km

**Mayagüez**
Mani
Bahía de Mayagüez
Pta. Guanajibo
**Joyuda**
Playa Joyuda
Pta. Caranero
Pta. Guaniquilla
**Boquerón**
Bahía de Boquerón
Balneario Boquerón
Buyé
**Cabo Rojo**
Hormigueros
LAS MESAS
Los Vegas
**San Germán**
see detail map
**Panoramic Drive**
Sabana Grande
**Yauco**
CORDILLERA CENTRAL
Adjuntas
Utuado
Lares
Cerro Rondadero
Lago Guayo
Castañer
Indiera Rita
Lago Yauco
Pico Fraile
Pico Rodadero
Monte Guilate
La Pica
Jayuya
Cerro Punta
**Panoramic Drive**
Divisoria
Villalba
Juana Díaz
Coto Laurel
**Ponce**
see detail map
Peñuelas
Tallaboa
El Tuque
Guayanilla
Bahía de Guayanilla
Palomos
**Bosque Estatal de Guánica**
Bahía Ballena
Gilligan's Island
Balneario Caña Gorda
Pta. Brea
Pta. Jacinto
Playa Santa
**Guánica**
Ensenada
Bahía de Fosforescente
Playita Rosada
**La Parguera**
VALLE DE LAJAS
MONTE GRANDE
Lajas
**Refugio de Vida Silvestre**
Pole Ojea
Bahía Sucia
Cabo Rojo Lighthouse
El Combate
**Bosque Estatal de Boquerón**
Bahía Salinas
La Playuela
Pta. Jorobado

Roads: 157, 149, 141, 144, 143, 149, 1, 139, 14, 52, 140, 140, 140, 10, 132, 385, 2, 111, 129, 128, 128, 132, 2, 128, 124, 105, 120, 121, 111, 119, 120, 119, 120, 117, 333, 116, 118, 101, 103, 114, 102, 100, 109, 108, 109, 2, 105

**CLOSE UP**

# A Guide to Puerto Rico's Carved Saints

Hand-carved religious figures, or Santos, are an important part of Puerto Rico's cultural history.

Hand carving wooden *santos* (saints), is one of Puerto Rico's oldest traditional art forms, and the practice has survived for centuries. But you wouldn't know it to walk into one of the local souvenir shops, which often line their shelves with imported pieces. Authentic santos carving thrives today—you just have to know where to find the artisans—and their handiwork.

## HISTORY OF THE SANTOS

Influenced by its African, Spanish, and American roots, as well as its Caribbean neighbors and Latin American ties, Puerto Rico has achieved a unique artistic identity through its continual willingness to integrate many traditions. Its artists have worked hard to preserve their culture, and nowhere is their effort more evident than in their hand-carved santos statues.

The history of the *santo*s is traced back to the arrival of Spanish missionaries in the late 15th and early 16th centuries. The missionaries spread God's word by telling stories animated and illustrated with carved santos. According to carver Miguel Diaz, missionaries left santos behind with prospective converts so they could pray at home. Churches were few and far between, but santos placed on home altars could help keep the spirit of God alive between missionaries' visits. Though missionaries no longer visit homes, and churches are more abundant, santos still enjoy a place of honor in many Puerto Ricans' homes and have become a popular art form, highly prized by collectors on the island and abroad.

## ABOUT THE SAINTS

Santos are not entirely unique to Puerto Rico; just as Spanish missionaries brought them to the island, they also carried them to many other countries. Each country, though, personalized the santos to its own culture over the years. In Puerto Rico the most common figures are the Three Kings, Saint Barbara, Saint Francis, and The Powerful Hand (*La Mano Poderosa*—a member of the Holy Family tops each finger of a hand bearing the stigma). The santos are typically carved in cedar. Once carved, they are brushed with a coat of gesso and then painted. Santos can also be found in ceramic.

CLOSE UP

# (continued)

## WHERE TO FIND THEM

Once you stop looking in souvenir shops, it just takes a little scouting to find santos, as well as the artisans who carve them.

The best place to find santos during business hours in Old San Juan is **Puerto Rican Arts & Crafts** (⊠ *204 Calle Fortaleza, Old San Juan* ☎ *787/725–5596* ⊕ *www. puertoricanart-crafts.com*). The store, which ensures that its entire stock comes from the hands of artisans who live on the island, carries the santos of the late, self-taught carver Domingo Orta, and Antonio Aviles Burgos, who was once recognized as artisan of the year and is the third generation of carvers in his family.

After hours, artisans can often be found working wood and selling their santos during craft fairs held along Old San Juan's Plaza Dársena, located between the cruise piers and Paseo de la Princesa. Friday and Saturday evenings are sure bets, as are Sunday afternoons.

Puerto Rican Arts and Crafts Store

5

Miguel Diaz. If you're interested in visiting an artisan's workshop, carver Miguel Diaz hosts visitors in his studio in Carolina. ☎ *787/392–8857* ✍ *tallertabonuco@gmail.com.*

**Aviles Family.** The Aviles family maintains a museum of its generations of craft work. Visits are by appointment only. ⊠ *Santurce, San Juan* ☎ *787/455–4217.*

## PRICES

As with most art and handicrafts, prices depend on several factors, including the carver's history, the quality of craftsmanship, the setting where the pieces are sold, the amount of decoration or elaboration, and the size of the piece. The average size of a santo is 7 to 8 inches, though some are smaller and many carvers produce larger pieces for commissions and other special occasions.

In general, expect prices for santos to begin at $40 and to go up considerably. Some santos fetch as much as several hundred dollars.

Bargaining is not considered as permissible in Puerto Rico as it is in other Spanish-speaking countries. A carver's stated price is likely the lowest he or she is willing to go.

The Powerful Hand santos

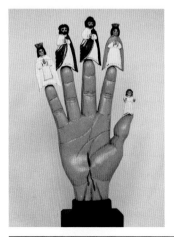

Fish the waters off La Parguera for blue marlin, tuna, or reef fish.

prickly-pear cactus to the gumbo limbo tree. It's also one of the best places on the island for bird-watching, since you can spot more than 100 species, including the pearly-eyed thrasher, the lizard cuckoo, and the nightjar.

One of the most popular hikes is the **Ballena Trail,** which begins at the ranger station on Route 334. This easy 1¼-mi (2-km) walk follows a partially paved road and takes you past a mahogany plantation to a dry plain covered with stunted cactus. A sign reading "Guayacán centenario" leads you to an extraordinary guayacán tree with a trunk that measures 6 feet across. The moderately difficult **Fuerte Trail** takes you on a 3½-mi (5½-km) hike to an old fort built by the Spanish Armada. It was destroyed during the Spanish-American War in 1898, but you can still see the ruins of the old observatory tower.

In addition to going in the main entrance on Route 334, you can enter on Route 333, which skirts the forest's southwestern quadrant. You can also try the less explored western section, off Route 325. ✉ *Enter along Rte. 334, 333, or 325* ☎ *787/821–5706* ✉ *Free* ☉ *Daily 9–5.*

**Gilligan's Island.** Off the southwest coast, near Guánica, is Gilligan's Island, a palm-ringed cay skirted by gorgeous beaches. You'll find picnic tables and restrooms but few other signs of civilization on this tiny island, officially part of the Bosque Estatal de Guánica. Wooden boats line up at the small dock in the San Jacinto section of Guánica, off Route 333 just past the Copamarina Beach Resort. Boats depart every hour from 9 to 5. Round-trip passage is $8. The island is often crowded on weekends and around holidays, but during the week you can find a spot to yourself. Nearby **Isla de Ballena,** reached by the same ferry, is much less crowded. ⊠ *Off Rte. 333* ☎ *787/821–4941* ✆ *Free* ☉ *Daily 9–5.*

## WHERE TO EAT

**$$$**
CARIBBEAN
★

✕ **Alexandra.** Puerto Ricans drive for miles to reach this restaurant in the Copamarina Beach Resort. You won't find such creative cuisine anywhere else west of Ponce. The kitchen makes traditional dishes into something special; take the salmon fillet with a mango and lemon crust served with eggplant and pumpkin lasagna, for example, or the roasted chicken stuffed with prosciutto and Manchego cheese in a marsala sauce. A standout is the lobster with roasted potatoes in butter and thyme. The elegant dining room looks out onto well-tended gardens; if you want to get closer to the flora, ask for a table outside on the terrace. The only disappointment may be noisy children, who tend to run in and out of the pool area. ⊠ *Copamarina Beach Resort, Rte. 333, Km 6.5* ☎ *787/821–0505* ✍ *Reservations essential.*

**$$**
SEAFOOD

✕ **San Jacinto.** Popular with day-trippers to Gilligan's Island, this modest restaurant sits right at the ferry terminal. This doesn't mean, however, that the dining room has views of the Caribbean. For those, grab one of the outside picnic tables, shaded by umbrellas. The menu is almost entirely seafood, running the gamut from fried snapper to broiled lobster. It also serves kid-friendly pizza, burgers, and empanadillas. When it's not high season the menu can be limited to two or three items. Bonus: The place also rents kayaks and snorkel gear. ⊠ *Off Rte. 333* ☎ *787/821–4941.*

## WHERE TO STAY

*For expanded hotel reviews, visit Fodors.com.*

**$$**
RESORT
♻

▦ **Copamarina Beach Resort.** Without a doubt the most beautiful resort on the southern coast, the Copamarina is set on 16 palm-shaded acres facing the Caribbean Sea. **Pros:** Tropical decor; plenty of activities; great dining options. **Cons:** Sand at the beach has a gummy feel; noise from the many kids. ⬧ *Rte. 333, Km 6.5* ☎ *787/821–0505, 800/468–4553* ⊕ *www.copamarina.com* ⬧ *104 rooms, 2 villas* ⬧ *In-room: a/c, safe, Wi-Fi. In-hotel: restaurant, bar, pool, tennis court, gym, spa, beach, water sports, children's programs, laundry facilities* ⵔ *No meals.*

**$**
RENTAL
Fodor'sChoice
★

▦ **Mary Lee's by the Sea.** This meandering cluster of apartments sits upon quiet grounds full of brightly colored flowers. **Pros:** Feels like a home away from home, warm and friendly owner, near pristine beaches and forests. **Cons:** Weekly maid service unless requested daily, no nightlife options, no pool. ⊠ *Rte. 333, Km 6.7* ⬧ *Box 394, Guánica 00653* ☎ *787/821–3600* ⊕ *www.maryleesbythesea.com* ⬧ *10 apartments* ⬧ *In-room: a/c, kitchen, no TV. In-hotel: laundry facilities, some pets allowed* ⵔ *No meals.*

**$**
HOTEL

▦ **Parador Guánica 1929.** This colonial-style building is very pretty, with lovely arches adding more character than you usually find along the southern coast. **Pros:** Historic setting; pretty pool area; basketball and volleyball courts. **Cons:** No beach; slightly off the beaten path. ⊠ *Rte. 3116, Km. 2.5, Ensenada* ☎ *877/784–6835* ⊕ *www.paradorguanica1929pr.com* ⬧ *27 rooms* ⬧ *In-room: a/c, Wi-Fi. In-hotel: restaurant, pool* ⵔ *No meals.*

5

## SPORTS AND THE OUTDOORS

DIVING AND
SNORKELING

Dramatic walls created by the continental shelf provide great diving off the Guánica coast. Shallow gardens around Gilligan's Island and Cayo de Caña Gorda (off Balneario Caña Gorda) also attract snorkelers and divers.

**Dive Copamarina.** Dive Copamarina offers instruction and trips. ⊠ *Copamarina Beach Resort, Rte. 333, Km 6.5* ☎ *787/821–0505.*

HORSEBACK
RIDING

**Gaby's World.** In nearby Yauco, Gaby's World is a 204-acre horse ranch that conducts half-hour, one-hour, and two-hour rides through the hills surrounding Yauco. There are also pony rides and a playground for children. The on-site steak house serves Yauco's specialty, *chuletas can-can.* ⊠ *Rte. 127, Km 5.1, Yauco* ☎ *787/856–2609* ⊕ *www.gabysworld.net.*

# LA PARGUERA

*8 miles (13 km) west of Guánica, 15 miles (24 km) southwest of Yauco.*

La Parguera is best known for its bioluminescent bay. Although it is not nearly as spectacular as the one off the island of Vieques, it's still a beautiful sight on a moonless night. Glass-bottom boats lined up at the town dock depart several times each evening for 45-minute trips across the bay. During the day you can explore the nearby mangrove forest.

The town bursts at the seams with vacationers from other parts of the island on long holiday weekends and all during the summer. The town's dock area feels a bit like Coney Island, and not in a good way. Vendors in makeshift stalls hawk cheap souvenirs, and ear-splitting salsa music pours out of the open-air bars. There are signs warning people not to drink alcoholic beverages in the street, but these are cheerfully ignored.

If you're driving through the area between February and April, keep your eyes open for roadside vendors selling the area's famous pineapples, called *piñas cadezonas.* In late June there's the colorful Fiesta de San Pedro, honoring the patron saint of fishermen.

### GETTING HERE AND AROUND

You can reach La Parguera from Guánica via Route 116, which turns into Route 318 when it heads to San Germán. Públicos depart from the turnoff at Route 304 and head to Lajas, where connections can be made to San Germán.

### EXPLORING

**Bahía de Fosforescente** (*Phosphorescent Bay*). On moonless nights large and small boats line up along the dock to take visitors out to view the Bahía de Fosforescente. Microscopic dinoflagellates glow when disturbed by movement, invading the waves with thousands of starlike points of light. The bay's glow has been diminished substantially by pollution—both light pollution from nearby communities and water pollution from toxic chemicals being dumped into the bay. (And, yes, the smoke-belching boats that take tourists to the bay are doing damage, too.) If you've seen the bioluminescent bay in Vieques (see the feature in Chapter 4), give this one a pass. If not, you may find it mildly interesting. There's no need to make arrangements in advance; just show up at the docks around 7:30 pm to find a boat ($6–$7 per person). ⊠ *Rte 304, Km. 3.5.*

Many of La Parguera's restaurants and shops overlook the bay.

**Bosque Estatal de Boquerón** (*Boquerón State Forest*). The eastern section of the Bosque Estatal de Boquerón is made up of miles of mangrove forests that grow at the water's edge. Boats from the dock in La Parguera can take you on cruises through this important breeding ground for seabirds. You can also organize a kayak trip. ⊠ *Boats leave from marina at La Parguera, off Rte. 304.*

## WHERE TO EAT AND STAY

*For expanded hotel reviews, visit Fodors.com.*

**$$**
SEAFOOD
✕ **La Casita.** The so-called Little House isn't little at all—it's a sizable establishment that sits smack in the middle of the town's main road. Generous portions make this family-run restaurant one of the town's favorites. Try the *asopao*, which is made with shrimp, lobster, or other types of seafood. The mofongo with octopus in garlic source is very flavorful. You can take a table in the rather bland ground-floor dining room or on the second-floor terrace, which has a view of the water. ⊠ *Rte. 304, Km 3.3* ☎ *787/899–1681.*

**$$**
HOTEL
⌂ **Villa Parguera.** The rooms in this gingerbread-trimmed hotel are clustered around small courtyards filled with bright tropical flowers. **Pros:** Family atmosphere; plenty of entertainment options; walking distance to the marina. **Cons:** Bland rooms; pool area gets crowded; noise from nearby bars; no elevator. ⊠ *Rte. 304, Km 3.3* ☎ *787/899–7777* ⊕ *www. villaparguera.net* ⤳ *74 rooms* ⌂ *In-room: a/c, Wi-Fi. In-hotel: restaurant, bar, pool* ⊙ *No meals.*

## NIGHTLIFE AND THE ARTS

La Parguera's dock area heats up after sunset, when crowds come to take excursions to the Bahía de Fosforescente.

**Mar y Tierra.** On weekends Mar y Tierra is the most popular place on the strip. The open-air establishment has a couple of pool tables that are always in use. Pay attention to the sign that tells you not to put your feet on the wall. ⊠ *Rte. 304, Km 3.3* ☏ *787/899–4627.*

**Villa Parguera.** The live floor show on Saturday night includes a buffet. The show changes frequently but includes live music, dancing, and comedy of the seltzer-in-your-pants variety. ⊠ *Villa Parguera, Rte. 304, Km 2.3* ☏ *787/899–7777, 787/899–3975.*

## SHOPPING

Outdoor stands near Bahía Fosforescente sell all kinds of souvenirs, from T-shirts to beaded necklaces.

**Nautilus.** In La Parguera's center there are several small souvenir shops, including Nautilus, that sell posters, mugs, and trinkets made from shells. ⊠ *Rte. 304* ☏ *787/899–4565.*

## SPORTS AND THE OUTDOORS

DIVING & SNORKELING Endangered leatherback turtles, eels, and an occasional manatee can be seen from many of the sites that attract divers and snorkelers from all parts. There are more than 50 shore-dive sites off La Parguera, including the famous Black Wall that starts out at 60 feet and then suddenly drops 200 into a vast canyon.

**Paradise Scuba.** Paradise Scuba offers classes and trips, including night-snorkeling excursions in phosphorescent waters. Divers will enjoy the 150-foot vertical drop at the Black Wall, considered one of the most spectacular dive sites in Puerto Rico. Their most popular package is the sunset snorkel tour, which includes snacks, drinks, and a trip to the phosphorescent bay. ⊠ *Hostal Casa Blanca, Rte. 304, Km 3.5* ☏ *787/899–7611* ⊕ *www.paradisescubasnorkelingpr.com.*

FISHING **Parguera Fishing Charters.** You can spend a day or half day fishing for blue marlin, tuna, or reef fish with Capt. Mickey Amador at Parguera Fishing Charters. Lunch is included in the price. ⊠ *Rte. 304, Km 3.8* ☏ *787/382–4698, 787/899–4698* ⊕ *www.puertoricofishingcharters. com.*

# SAN GERMÁN

*6 miles (10 km) north of La Parguera, 104 miles (166 km) southwest of San Juan.*

During its early years, San Germán was a city on the move. Although debate rages about the first settlement's exact founding date and location, the town is believed to have been established in 1510 near Guánica. Plagued by mosquitoes, the settlers moved north along the west coast, where they encountered French pirates and smugglers. In the 1570s they fled inland to the current location, but they were still harassed. Determined and creative, they dug tunnels and moved beneath the city (the tunnels are now part of the water system). Today San Germán has a population of 39,000, and its intellectual and political activity is anything but underground. It's very much a college town, and students and professors from the Inter-American University often fill the bars and cafés.

Alcaldía
Antigua ..........**5**

Capilla de
Porta Coeli ......**1**

Casa de Lola
Rodríguez
de Tió ...........**8**

Casa Kindy .......**3**

Casa Morales ....**2**

Casa Perichi .....**4**

La Casona .......**6**

Iglesia de
San Germán
de Auxerre .......**7**

Museo de
Arte y Casa
de Estudio .......**9**

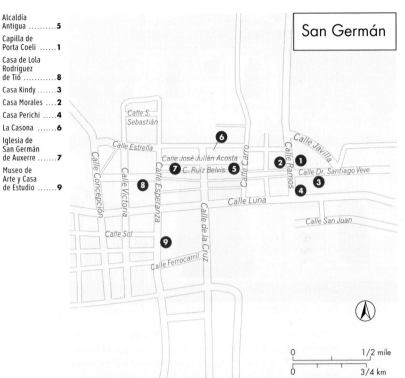

San Germán

Around San Germán's two main squares—Plazuela Santo Domingo and Plaza Francisco Mariano Quiñones (named for an abolitionist)— are buildings done in every conceivable style of architecture found on the island, including mission, Victorian, creole, and Spanish colonial. The city's tourist office offers a free, guided trolley tour. Most of the buildings are private homes; two of them—the Capilla de Porta Coeli and the Museo de Arte y Casa de Estudio—are museums. Strip malls surround the historical center, and the town is hemmed to the south and west by busy seaside resorts.

### GETTING HERE AND AROUND

San Germán sits just off Highway 2 between Ponce and Mayagüez on Route 122. Being a university town, it is a transportation hub with públicos departing to nearby villages such as Mayagüez and Lajas from the intersection of Calle Luna and Route 122. A trolley tour of San Germán is available by appointment.

**San Germán Trolley** ⊠ *Acaldía de San Germán, 136 Calle Luna* ☎ *787/892–3500.*

### TOP ATTRACTIONS

★ **Capilla de Porta Coeli** (*Heaven's Gate Chapel*). One of the oldest religious buildings in the Americas, this mission-style chapel overlooks the long, rectangular Plazuela de Santo Domingo. It's not a grand building, but

Iglesia de San Germán de Auxerre is a 17th-century church that's still in use today.

its position at the top of a stone stairway gives it a noble air. Queen Isabel Segunda decreed that the Dominicans should build a church and monastery in San Germán, so a rudimentary building was built in 1609, replaced in 1692 by the structure that can still be seen today. (Sadly, most of the monastery was demolished in 1866, leaving only a vestige of its facade.) The chapel now functions as a museum of religious art, displaying painted wooden statuary by Latin American and Spanish artists. ⊠ *East end of Plazuela Santo Domingo* ☎ *787/892–5845* ⊕ *www. icp.gobierno.pr* ✉ *$3* ⊙ *Wed.–Sun. 8:30–noon and 1–4.*

**La Casona.** On the north side of Plaza Francisco Mariano Quiñones, this two-story home was built in 1871 for Tomás Agrait. (If you look closely, you can still see his initials in the wrought-iron decorations.) For many years it served as a center of cultural activities in San Germán. Today it holds several shops. ⊠ *Calle José Julien Acosta and Calle Cruz.*

### WORTH NOTING

**Alcaldía Antigua** (*Old Municipal Building*). At the eastern end of Plaza Francisco Mariano Quiñones, this Spanish-colonial-style building served as the town's city hall from 1844 to 1950. Once used as a prison, the building is now the headquarters for the police department. ⊠ *East end of Plaza Francisco Mariano Quiñones.*

**Casa de Lola Rodríguez de Tió.** On the National Registry of Historic Places, this house bears the name of poet and activist Lola Rodríguez de Tió. A plaque claims she lived in this creole-style house, though town officials believe it actually belonged to her sister. Rodríguez, whose mother was a descendant of Ponce de León, was deported several times by Spanish authorities for her revolutionary ideas. She lived in Venezuela and then

# A GOOD TOUR: SAN GERMÁN

The best place to start is Plazuela Santo Domingo, the sun-baked park in the center of the historic district. At the eastern edge of the park is the **Capilla de Porta Coeli**, perched at the top of an imposing set of stairs. From the top you get a good view of the rest of the city. Several historic homes, none of them open to the public, are within a block of the Capilla de Porta Coeli. Across the street is the **Casa Morales**, striking for its Victorian-style gables. It would not look out of place in any New England hamlet. Half a block east on Calle Dr. Santiago Veve are two criollo-style houses, **Casa Kindy** and Casa Acosta y Forés. A block south of the Capilla de Porta Coeli is one of the most beautiful homes in San Germán, **Casa Perichi**.

Head west through Plazuela Santo Domingo. The hulking yellow building you see at the northwest corner of the park is the rear of the **Alcaldía Antigua**. It faces the town's other park, the Plaza Francisco Mariano Quiñones. This park is more popular with locals, as the tree-shaded benches are a pleasant place to watch the world go by. On the park's northern edge is **La Casona**, one of the town's best-preserved criollo-style buildings. The most imposing structure on the park, however, is the **Iglesia de San Germán de Auxerre**.

A block and a half west of the church is the **Casa de Lola Rodríguez de Tió**, on Calle Dr. Santiago Veve. It's one of the best examples of criollo-style architecture in the city. Backtrack to Calle Esperanza and head two blocks south to where you'll find the **Museo de Arte y Casa de Estudio**.

## TIMING
San Germán's historic district is compact, so you can cover all the sights in about an hour. You'll want to budget a bit more time to stroll around the nearby streets. Be sure to wear comfortable shoes, as there will be a lot of walking uphill and downhill on cobbled streets.

in Cuba, where she died in 1924. The museum, which houses Rodríguez's desk and papers, isn't open regular hours; call ahead to schedule a tour. ✉ *13 Calle Dr. Santiago Veve* ☎ *787/892–3500* ⊠ *Free* ⊙ *By appointment only.*

**Casa de los Kindy.** East of the Plazuela de Santo Domingo, this 19th-century home is known for its eclectic architecture, which mixes neoclassical and criollo elements. Note the elegant stained glass over the front windows. It's now a private residence. ✉ *64 Calle Dr. Santiago Veve.*

**Casa Morales.** Facing Plazuela de Santo Domingo, this Victorian-style house was designed in 1913 by architect Pedro Vivoni for his brother, Tomás. The gleaming white structure has numerous towers and gables. The current owners have kept it in mint condition. It is not open to the public. ✉ *38 Calle Ramos.*

**Casa Perichi.** You'll find an excellent example of Puerto Rican ornamental architecture in this elegant mansion, which sits a block south of Plazuela Santo Domingo. This gigantic white home, on the National Register of Historic Places, was built in 1920. Note the sensuous curves of the wraparound balcony and wood trim around the doors. It's not open to the public. ⊠ *94 Calle Luna.*

**Iglesia de San Germán de Auxerre.** Dating from 1739, this neoclassical church has seen many additions over the years. For example, the impressive crystal chandelier imported from Barcelona was added in 1866. Be sure to take a look at the carved-wood ceiling in the nave. This church is still in use, so the only time you can get a look inside is during services. ⊠ *West side of Plaza Francisco Mariano Quiñones* ☎ 787/892–1027 ☉ *Mass Mon.–Sat. at 7 am and 7:30 pm and Sun. at 7, 8:30, 10 am, and 7:30 pm.*

**Museo de Arte y Casa de Estudio.** This early 20th-century home—built in the criollo style with some obvious neoclassical influences—has been turned into a museum. Displays include colonial furnishings, religious art, and artifacts of the indigenous peoples; there are also changing exhibits by local artists. ⊠ *7 Calle Esperanza* ☎ 787/892–8870 ☑ *Free* ☉ *Wed.–Sun. 10–noon and 1–3.*

## WHERE TO EAT AND STAY
*For expanded hotel reviews, visit Fodors.com.*

$ ✕ **Chaparritas.** On San Germán's main drag, this place certainly feels like
MEXICAN a traditional cantina. The Mexican food here is the real deal. Although you'll find some dishes that are more Tex than Mex, such as the cheesy nachos, the kitchen does best with more authentic tacos, burritos, and enchiladas. For something a bit more off the wall, try the shrimp fried in tequila. ⊠ *Calle Luna 171* ☎ 787/892–1078 ☉ *Closed Sun.–Wed.*

¢ ✕ **Tapas Café.** One of the biggest surprises in San Germán is this wonderful
SPANISH little restaurant facing Plaza Santo Domingo. The dining room looks like
★ a Spanish courtyard, complete with blue stars swirling around the ceiling. Don't expect tiny portions just because the eatery serves tapas—several of the dishes, including the medallions of beef topped with a dab of blue cheese, could pass as full entrées anywhere. You'll find old favorites on the menu, including spicy sausage in red wine, but some new creations as well, such as the yam-and-codfish fritters. ⊠ *50 Calle Dr. Santiago Veve* ☎ 787/264–0610 ☉ *Closed Mon.–Tues. No lunch Wed.–Thurs.*

$ ▦ **Villa del Rey.** On a quiet country road, Villa del Rey is set among
B&B/INN banana and papaya trees, and this family-run inn couldn't be simpler, but it's clean and comfortable. **Pros:** Decent pool and authentic ambiance. **Cons:** Could use an all around face-lift; rooms are slightly musty; no Internet; staff doesn't speak English. ⊠ *Rte. 361, Km 0.8, off Rte. 2* ✉ *Box 3033, San Germán 00667* ☎ 787/264–2542, 787/642–2627 ⊕ *www.villadelrey.net* ⤴ *19 rooms, 2 suites* ♿ *In-room: a/c, kitchen. In-hotel: pool* ¶◎¶ *Breakfast.*

# Rincón and the Porta del Sol

**WORD OF MOUTH**

"If your budget is generous, consider the Horned Dorset Primavera in Rincón. On the beach in a fairly rural area, with luxurious villas with private plunge pools on a beautifully landscaped site. My husband and I pre-celebrated our 20th anniversary here."

—Callaloo

# WELCOME TO RINCÓN AND THE PORTA DEL SOL

## TOP REASONS TO GO

★ **Visit El Combate:** Hike to the lighthouse at this peninsula, which juts out into the Caribbean Sea.

★ **Pamper yourself at the Horned Dorset Primavera:** Relax in your private plunge pool at perhaps the most romantic inn in the Caribbean.

★ **Please your palate at the "Golden Mile":** Sample fresh seafood at any of the dozens of oceanfront eateries in Joyuda.

★ **Catch a Wave at Playa Tres Palmas:** Challenge the waves here or at any of Rincón's world-famous surfing spots.

★ **Explore Desecheo Island or Mona Island:** Enjoy snorkeling, diving, or fishing around these spectacular islands.

**1 Rincón.** The first World Surfing Championships in 1968 put Rincón on the map, and its laid-back vibe and epic waves have kept it there. Paddle out to one of the town's 15 surf spots, or experience horseback riding on the beach and fishing in the crystal Caribbean waters. One of Rincón's greatest attractions is the diving and snorkeling at nearby Desecheo Island.

**2 Mayagüez.** Stroll the marble-paved square of Plaza Colón, where a statue of Christopher Colombo commemorates the site where he allegedly disembarked. Visit architectural gems such as Nuestra Señora de la Candelaria Cathedral, built in 1780, or experience an artistic performance at the Teatro Yagüez, which dates back to 1909. Savor the flavor of Mayagüez by sampling traditional *brazo gitano* ("gypsy arm") jelly roll, baked at the century-old Ricomini Bakery.

**3 Cabo Rojo.** Sample the island's freshest catch at Joyuda's Milla de Oro (Golden Mile), a string of more than 15 waterfront restaurants built on stilts. Slurp fresh oysters and clams from one of the many vendor carts lining the fishing town of Boquerón. Hike to the Cabo Rojo Lighthouse at Puerto Rico's southwestern tip.

**4 The Northwestern Coast.** The colorful fishing boats that line Playa Crashboat are a photographer's dream. Relax over a rum punch at an oceanfront bar while watching surfers get barreled at Jobos Beach. Explore the hidden waterfalls at Gozalandia, also known as El Charco de la Leche ("Puddle of Milk") near San Sebastián.

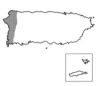

## GETTING ORIENTED

The speedy Highway 22 and the more meandering Highway 2 head west from San Juan and swing around the northwestern part of the island, skirting the beaches of the northern coast. A short 45 minutes from the capital, you'll pass through the resort town of Dorado; after Arecibo, Highway 2 continues along the coast, where the ragged shoreline holds some of the island's best surfing beaches, and a steady contingent of surfers in Aguadilla and Rincón gives the area a laid-back atmosphere. Past Mayagüez, Highway 100 leads to an area known as Cabo Rojo, where you'll find seaside communities like Joyuda, Boquerón, and El Combate.

6

# BEACHES OF RINCÓN AND THE PORTO DEL SOL

The waves of northwestern Puerto Rico have long served as a siren song for traveling surfers. Spared the trade winds that can limit surf in other areas, the northwest's beaches have some of the best waves in the world, especially in winter. But you don't have to be a big-wave rider to enjoy the beaches of the northwest.

Tools of the trade: At nearly all the beaches in Rincón you won't have to look far to find someone with their trusty stick (surfboard) in-hand.

The best beaches north of Rincón are lined up along Route 413 and Route 4413 (the road to the lighthouse). South of town the only beach worth noting is Playa Córcega, off Route 115. As with many other beaches in the Caribbean, there are often urchins, riptides, undertows, and rocky reefs below the surface. Know the area before you head into the water, and never swim alone.

Mayagüez isn't famous for its beaches—you'll find better stretches in Rincón, about 25 minutes north—but Balneario de Añasco, also called Tres Hermanos Beach, is 10 minutes north of town via Highway 2 and Routes 115 and 401. Dotted with palm trees, it's good for swimming and has changing facilities and restrooms.

## GOLDEN MILE

Anyone interested in seafood must visit Milla de Oro del Buen Comer, aka the Gourmet Golden Mile. In the small fishing village of Joyuda, this string of more than 15 restaurants serves the best fish on the island. It spans from Tony's Restaurant at Km 10.9 to Parada los Flamboyanes at Km 16. The seafood here is the freshest—caught daily from the Caribbean Sea or from Laguna Joyuda.

## RINCÓN

**Balneario de Rincón.** Swimmers can enjoy the tranquil waters at this beach. The beautiful facility has a playground, changing areas, restrooms, and a clubhouse. It's within walking distance of the center of town. Parking is free. ✉ *Rte. 115.*

**Domes.** Named for the eerie green domes on a nearby power plant, this beach is extremely popular with surfers. On a good surf day, arrive early if you want a spot on the sand. Although not recommended for swimmers because of the rocks, it's a great whale-watching spot in winter. There are no facilities here, so plan accordingly. ✉ *Rte. 4413, north of the lighthouse.*

**Maria's.** This surf spot, south of Domes, can get crowded when the waves are high. When waves are small, surf lessons are generally taught here. It's popular with locals for its proximity to the Calypso Café. Look for the street sign reading "Surfer crossing." ✉ *Rte. 4413, south of the lighthouse.*

**Playa Córcega.** The long stretch of yellow sand in front of Villa Cofresí is considered one of the best swimming beaches in Rincón. ✉ *Rte. 115, Km 12.0.*

**Steps.** A set of concrete steps sitting mysteriously at the water's edge gives this beach its name. The waves, breaking on a shallow reef, can get huge. On a calm day, the snorkeling here is wonderful. This is also a good place to find

sea glass. It's hard to find—look for the turnoff at a whale-shaped sign indicating "Playa Escalera." ✉ *Rte. 413, north of turnoff for Black Eagle Marina.*

**Tres Palmas.** On a handful of days each year, this epic wave is one of the world's best, drawing surfers from around the globe. On calm days, it's an excellent snorkeling spot and is home to the Tres Palmas Marine Reserve. The clear waters are filled with tropical fish and brain coral. ✉ *Rte. 413, north of turnoff for Black Eagle Marina.*

## BOQUERÓN

**Balneario Boquerón.** The long stretch of sand at this beach off Route 101 is a favorite with islanders, especially on weekends. You'll find changing facilities, cabins, showers, restrooms, picnic tables, a playground, and lifeguards keeping watch over the beach. Parking costs $4. ✉ *Off Rte. 101.*

**Playa Buyé.** The white-sand beach has swaying palm trees and crystal-clear water. There is free parking on the side of the road, and a few picnic tables. Bathrooms (although dirty) are available. ✉ *Rte. 307, north of Boquerón.*

## EL COMBATE

**El Combate Beach.** This great beach draws college students to its rustic waterfront eateries. You can rent small boats and kayaks here, and in summer there are often concerts and festivals. ✉ *At the end of Rte. 3301.*

**La Playuela**. The crescent-shaped strand is the most secluded, and beautiful, of the area's beaches. It's commonly referred to as Bahía Sucia ("Dirty Beach") because of the blankets of seaweed that drift to shore during winter months. The label is rather unfitting for the white sand and turquoise waters that mark the island's southwestern corner. There are no amenities. ☒ *End of Rte. 301, past the vast salt flats.*

### AGUADILLA

**Playa Crashboat**. Here you'll find the colorful fishing boats that are portrayed on postcards all over the island. The sand is soft and sugary, and the water's smooth as glass. There are picnic huts, showers, parking, and restrooms. A food stand run by locals serves the catch of the day with cold beer. ☒ *End of Rte. 458, off Rte. 107.*

### ISABELA

**Playa de Guajataca**. Nearby is El Tunel, part of an old tunnel used by a train that once ran from San Juan to Ponce. Just before El Tunel is El Merendero de Guajataca, a picnic area with cliffside trails. This is not a swimming beach due to strong currents. ☒ *Off Rte. 113.*

**Playa Jobos**. This beach is famous for surfing, especially with beginners. On the same stretch of sand there are a couple of restaurants with oceanfront decks. Down the road, the dunes and long stretches of golden sand are gorgeous for walks or running. ⚠ Next to the large rock formation is a strong riptide that drags people out to sea. The water is only about thigh high, but when the wind changes, the current is like a raging river. There are no lifeguards, no signs, and no roped-off areas, so be sure to stay close to shore. ☒ *Rte. 466.*

**Playa Montones**. Not far from Playa de Jobos, this is a beautiful beach for swimming; it has a protected natural pool perfect for children. ☒ *Rte. 466, in front of Parador Villas del Mar Hau.*

**Playa Shacks**. Known for its surfing and horseback riding, this secluded spot has an area called the Blue Hole that's popular with divers. It is east of Villa Montaña Beach Resort. ☒ *Rte. 4446.*

Updated by
Marlise Kast

The "Gateway to the Sun" is how tourism officials describe the island's western coast. Unlike the area around San Juan, the Porta del Sol is relatively undiscovered. Even around Rincón, which has the lion's share of the lodgings, the beaches are delightfully deserted. And in places like Aguadilla and Isabela, two sleepy towns on the northwestern corner of the island, it's easy to find a stretch of shoreline all to yourself.

Adventurers since the time of Christopher Columbus have been drawn to the jagged coastline of northwestern Puerto Rico. Columbus made his first stop here on his second voyage to the Americas in 1493. His exact landing point is the subject of ongoing dispute: both Aguadilla, on the northernmost tip of the coast, and Aguada, just south of Aguadilla, claim the historic landing, and both have monuments honoring the explorer.

Less than a century ago, western Puerto Rico was still overwhelmingly rural. Some large fruit plantations dotted the coast, while farther inland, coffee was grown on hillside *fincas* (farms). The slow pace of rural life began to change during the mid-20th century. New roads brought development to the once-isolated towns. They also brought international surfers, who were amazed to find some of the world's best waves in Rincón, Isabela, and Aguadilla. Now there are top-notch hotels, interesting natural areas to explore, and almost every kind of water sport imaginable.

## RINCÓN AND THE PORTA DEL SOL PLANNER

### WHEN TO GO

Winter weather is the best and it's the height of the surfing season, so you'll need to book well in advance. Between December and March you might get a glimpse of the humpback whales that winter off the coast. During the summer many family-oriented hotels fill up with *sanjuaneros* escaping the city for the weekend—some hotels require a two-night stay. Larger resorts normally drop their rates in summer by at least 10%. The weather gets hot, especially in August and September.

## GETTING HERE AND AROUND

### AIR TRAVEL

Aguadilla is a convenient gateway to western Puerto Rico, thanks to several daily international flights. Continental Airlines flies from Newark to Aguadilla, and JetBlue has daily service from Orlando or New York–JFK to Aguadilla. American Eagle and Cape Air fly between San Juan and Mayagüez.

**Transfers:** There are no airport shuttles in either Aguadilla or Mayagüez. A taxi from either airport into town is about $10, but if you are going any farther, you should rent a car.

Airlines **American Eagle** ☎ 800/981–4757 ⊕ www.aa.com. **Cape Air** ☎ 800/525–0280 ⊕ www.flycapeair.com. **Continental** ☎ 800/525–0280 ⊕ www.continental.com. **JetBlue** ☎ 800/538–2583 ⊕ www.jetblue.com.

### BUS AND VAN TRAVEL

No easy network of buses links the towns in the Porta del Sol region of northwestern Puerto Rico. Some municipalities and private companies operate buses and large shared vans *(públicos)* that travel from one city to another, but schedules are loose. But if you're adventurous and not easily frustrated, it's possible to arrange for cheap transportation from San Juan to Aguadilla, Rincón, and Mayagüez, among other towns. Prices from terminal to terminal are set, but drivers may go to another destination if arranged beforehand.

Choferes Unidos travels from San Juan to Aguadilla for about $10 per person. Línea Sultana has vans from San Juan to Mayagüez that also drop off passengers along Highway 2 in Aguada, Quebradillas, and Isabela; the price is about $12 per person. Línea Caborrojeña travels between San Juan and Cabo Rojo.

Contacts **Choferes Unidos** ☎ 787/764–0540. **Línea Caborrojeña** ☎ 787/723–9155. **Línea Sultana** ☎ 787/765–9377.

### CAR TRAVEL

You really need a car to see northwestern Puerto Rico, especially the mountain area. The toll road, Highway 22, makes it easy to reach Arecibo from San Juan. Highway 22 turns into Highway 2 just after Arecibo, swings by the northwestern tip of the island, then heads south to Mayagüez. *See also Ruta Panorámica chapter.*

### TAXI TRAVEL

Taxis can be hailed near the main plaza in Mayagüez, but in the smaller towns they may be hard to come by. Check with your hotel or restaurant, and staff there may be able to call one for you.

## ABOUT THE RESTAURANTS

If you like seafood, you're in the right place. Throughout northwestern Puerto Rico you'll find wonderful *criollo* (creole) cuisine. Most local eateries serve deep-fried tapas, commonly called *pinchos* (meaning "spike"), because they are served with toothpicks. Offering a break from fried food are dozens of foreign-owned eateries that serve everything from sushi and hamburgers to vegetarian and Thai cuisine. Farther south along the coast, options are limited, so you may want to ask the chef to grill or sauté your fish. A trip to Puerto Rico is not complete without sampling *mofongo relleno*, a seafood mixture served inside a yuca crust. Simply head to where locals from all over the island go for fresh seafood—Joyuda. In Rincón the Horned Dorset Primavera has a 10-course tasting menu served at one of the most elegant eateries in the Caribbean. When it comes to beverages, locals usually drink rum punch (rum, fruit juice, and grenadine) or Medalla Light, Puerto Rico's most popular and affordable beer. All restaurants are no-smoking. Tips, normally 15%–20%, are usually not included in the bill, but it's always wise to double-check.

## ABOUT THE HOTELS

The western part of the island near Rincón has a variety of hotels, from furnished villas geared toward families to beachfront hotels ideal for honeymooners. Interior design leaves much to be desired, however, as most rooms are decorated with faux wood, sun-bleached photographs, floral bedding, and white linoleum flooring. Fortunately, some of the newer accommodations resemble Spanish villas, a refreshing change from the typical 1970s decor. Surprisingly, the few hotels with Internet access only have it available in the common areas. Smaller beach cottages, especially in Rincón, usually have "adopted" dogs or cats roaming the premises, so guests with allergies may want to inquire ahead.

| WHAT IT COSTS IN U.S. DOLLARS | | | | | |
|---|---|---|---|---|---|
| | ¢ | $ | $$ | $$$ | $$$$ |
| Restaurants | under $8 | $8–$12 | $12–$20 | $20–$30 | over $30 |
| Hotels | under $80 | $80–$150 | $150–$250 | $250–$350 | over $350 |

Restaurant prices are per person for a main course at dinner. Hotel prices are for a double room in high season, excluding 9% tax (11% for hotels with casinos, 7% for paradores) and 5%–12% service charge.

## SAFETY

Unless you're camping in a recreational area, it's best to go to forest reserves during daylight hours only. Outside metro areas there's little crime, but you should take normal precautions: Remember to lock your car, and don't leave valuables unattended.

**For Surfers:** The waves in the Rincón area range from gentle, low waves suitable for novice surfers to expert-only breaks. It's a good idea to talk with other surfers about which beaches would be suitable for your skill level. *See also "Surfing" feature later in this chapter.*

## TOUR OPTIONS

The Mayagüez-based AdvenTours offers bird-watching, biking, and kayaking trips. Rincón Vacations has history tours and outdoor adventures.

Contact **AdvenTours** ✉ *1102 Calle Uroyán, Mayagüez* ☎ *787/530–8311* ⊕ *www.adventourspr.com.* **Rincón Vacations** ✉ *Rte. 414, Km 2, Rincón* ☎ *787/632–2889* ⊕ *www.rinconvacations.com.*

### VISITOR INFORMATION

The Puerto Rico Tourism Company has an office at the airport in Aguadilla. The Cabo Rojo branch is open weekdays from 8 to 4:30. Rincón's tourism office is open weekdays from 9 to 4. Mayagüez has a tourism office in city hall.

Contacts **Cabo Rojo Tourism Office** ✉ *Galleria 100, Calle 100, Km 7.6, Cabo Rojo* ☎ *787/851–7070.* **Isabela Tourism Office** ☎ *787/830–1034.* **Mayagüez City Hall** ✉ *8 McKinley St., Mayagüez* ☎ *787/834–8585.* **Puerto Rico Tourism Company** ✉ *Rafael Hernández Airport, Hwy. 2, Km 148.7, Aguadilla* ☎ *787/890–3315* ⊕ *www.seepuertorico.com.* **Rincón Tourism Office** ✉ *Sunset Village, Rte. 115, Rincón* ☎ *787/823–5024* ⊕ *www.rincon.org.*

# RINCÓN

*93 miles (150 km) southwest of San Juan.*

Jutting out into the ocean along the rugged western coast, Rincón, meaning "corner" in Spanish, may have gotten its name because it's tucked into a bend of the coastline. Some, however, trace the town's name to Gonzalo Rincón, a 16th-century landowner who let poor families live on his land. Whatever the history, the name suits the town, which is like a little world unto itself.

The most famous hotel in the region is the Horned Dorset Primavera—the only Relais & Chateaux property in Puerto Rico. It's one of the most luxurious resorts on the island, not to mention in the Caribbean. A couple of larger hotels, including the Rincón of the Seas and Rincón Beach Resort, have been built, but Rincón remains a laid-back place. The town is still a mecca for wave-seekers, particularly surfers from the East Coast of the United States, who often prefer the relatively quick flight to Aguadilla airport direct from New York–area airports instead of the long haul to the Pacific. The town continues to cater to all sorts of travelers, from budget-conscious surfers to families to honeymoners seeking romance.

The pace picks up from October through April, when the waves are the best, but tourists can be found here year-round, and many American mainlanders have settled here. Budget travelers will most likely find discount accommodations during August and September, when tourism is slow. Hurricane season runs from June through November, bringing in occasional swells for the surf crowd.

### GETTING HERE AND AROUND

Rincón itself is a spread-out labyrinth of unmarked streets without any apparent logic to its layout. Built on a hillside, most streets are narrow and steep, weaving erratically through the intermingled residential-business zones. There are three main routes to keep in mind; Route 115 cuts through the middle of "downtown" (the administrative center) and

# Rincón and Porta del Sol

Playa Shacks
Playa Jobos
Playa Montones
Playa Guajataca
San Antonio
Isabela
Hatillo
Camuy
466
113
Playa Borinquen
Mora
Quebradillas
485
2
130
Playa Wilderness
2
446
119
Playa Gas Chamber
112
Bosque
Estatal
113
Case de Piedra
Playa Crashboat
Aguadilla
110
Guajataca
Bahía de
Aguadilla
CORDILLERA
JAICOA
Largo de
Guajataca
Quebrada
Playa Table Rock
Moca
111
Gozalándia Waterfalls
(El Charco de la Leche)
119
Balneario Pico de Piedra
107
Playa Dome's
Aguada
110
Parque de las Cavernas
del Río Camuy
Pta. Higüero
Rincón
see detail
map
San Sebastián
115
Playa Tres Palmas
109
111
Lares
111
LA CADENA
119
Balneario de Rincón
Córcega
SAN FRANCISCO
Playa Córcega
2
Pta. Cadena
Añasco
109
Balneario
de Añasco
108
Mani
120
124
129
Estación Experimental
de Agricultura Tropical
MONTAÑAS DE UROYAN
Ruta
Panoramica
128
Largo
Guayo
Mayagüez
105
Las Vegas
128
Castañer
Bahía de
Mayagüez
LAS MESAS
Maricao
105
128
Ruta
Panoramica
Joyuda
2
120
Indiera Rita
Hormigueros
119
CORDILLERA
CENTRAL
102
100
Bosque
Estatal de
Maricao
120
Pico
Fraile
Pico
Rodadero
Cabo Rojo
114
San
Germán
102
Sabana
Grande
Largo
Luchetti
128
Pta. Caranero
MONTE
GRANDE
Lajas
118
Playa Buyé
103
117
121
Yauco
Pta. Guaniquilla
Boquerón
101
VALLE
DE
LAJAS
Palomas
Bahía de Boquerón
Balneario Boquerón
Refugio
de Vida
Silvestre
El Combate
301
116
Guánica
Bosque Estatal
de Boquerón
Pole Ojea
La
Parguera
Ensenada
333
Bahía Salinas
Bahía
Sucia
Playita
Rosada
La Playuela
Cabo Rojo
Pta. Jorobado
Pta.
Brea

*Caribbean Sea*

0        6 mi

0        6 km

connects north to Aguadilla airport and south to Mayagüez airport. Route 413 snakes the hillsides, past villas and local restaurants. The smaller Route 4413 parallels the water, past Punta Higüeras Lighthouse, and ends at the Bonus Thermonuclear Energy Plant.

### AIR TRAVEL
San Juan's International Airport is the most commonly used on the island and is approximately two hours from Rincón. The closest airports however, are in Mayagüez and in Aguadilla, only 20 minutes' drive in either direction. A taxi from either airport into town costs around $10, but the best option is to rent a car at the airport.

### BUS AND VAN TRAVEL
Amigos Tours & Travel has private transfers from Aguadilla's airport to Rincón and to most hotels in the Porta del Sol for $80 per van (limit five passengers).

**Amigos Tours & Travel** ☎ 787/826–6418 ⊕ www.amigostours.net.

### CAR TRAVEL
To reach Rincón from San Juan, take Highway 22, which becomes Highway 2 after Arecibo. Follow it past the northwestern tip of the island, just beyond Aguadilla. Take the 115 southwest past Aguada until you reach Rincón's Route 413, "The Road to Happiness."

### TIMING
With a land area of 14 square miles (36 square km), Rincón is easily traversable in an afternoon. However, to fully embrace its laid-back surfer vibe, you'll want to allocate three to five days for surfing, diving, fishing, or just relaxing at the beach.

## EXPLORING RINCÓN

**Desecheo Island.** For divers, Desecheo Island, about 13 miles (20 km) off the coast of Rincón, has abundant reef and fish life. Protected by the U.S. Fish and Wildlife Service, this uninhabited island is home to lizards, rats, and Rhesus monkeys, first introduced in 1967 from Cayo Santiago. The main draw here is "Candy Land," a rocky bottom sloping to 120 feet that rims the island. Here long tunnels and caverns covered with purple hydrocoral distinguish one formation known as Yellow Reef. With visibility of 150 feet, this is also a popular snorkeling spot. There are other sites with plentiful fish and coral in the shallower water just off Rincón's shores.

**Parque Pasivo El Faro.** Surrounding the Punta Higuera Lighthouse, Parque Pasivo El Faro has small kiosks at the water's edge. If you're lucky, you may spot a whale in the distance. (Have patience, though, as it could take days to see one.) You can also glimpse the rusting mint-colored dome of the defunct Bonus Thermonuclear Energy Plant from here; it has been closed since 1968. The park—complete with benches and a refreshment stand—is a nice place to take in sunsets. The lighthouse is closed to the public, but it's hard to walk away without taking a photo of the stately white structure. ⊠ *End of Rte. 413* 🎫 *Free* ⊙ *Daily 8 am–midnight.*

Looking down at Domes Beach from Punta Higüeras Lighthouse in El Faro Park.

OFF THE
BEATEN
PATH
**Gozalandia Waterfalls.** About 45 minutes east of Rincón, just north of San Sebastián, are these hidden waterfalls also known as El Charco de la Leche (The Pool of Milk). Though difficult to find, the tiered swimming holes are worth the effort it takes to get there. The first of the three is generally visited by locals, but a five-minute hike upstream will bring you to a second cascade, where the waters are deep enough for diving. A crude rope swing entices adventurers to mimic Tarzan's antics before plunging into the cool spring. Follow the trail about ½ mile (1 km) farther to reach yet a third oasis. From Rincón, take Route 115 northeast to Route 111 east. Near San Sebastián, take the 446 north and continue ½ mile (1 km). Turn right over the bridge and follow the road up about a mile. On the left you will see two gates. One has "No Parking" signs on it and the other looks like an entrance to a park with a cement paved driveway. Go around the larger gate and follow the driveway down to some mud pathways that will lead you to the waterfalls. ⊠ *Off Rte. 111, San Sebastian.*

## WHERE TO EAT

*Use the coordinate (✛ A1) at the end of each listing to locate a site on the corresponding "Where to Eat and Stay in Rincón" map.*

¢
CAFÉ
✕ **Banana Dang.** "Think, Drink, Link" is the motto of this Internet café, where you can check e-mails while drinking one of the specialty coffees. The fruit smoothies are a local favorite, as are the light breakfasts of veggie panini, bagels with cream cheese, and pastries like cranberry teacake and carrot muffins. As part of their "green initiative," the owners serve

## GREAT ITINERARIES

**IF YOU HAVE 1 DAY**
If you have only a day to spend in the Porta del Sol, make the drive to **Joyuda** for some of Puerto Rico's freshest seafood. You probably won't be the only ones driving from San Juan for this feast.

**IF YOU HAVE 3 DAYS**
If you have a few days to explore the region, start in **Rincón**, where you'll find accommodations for every taste, from compact inns to sprawling resorts. There isn't too much to see, other than the lighthouse at Parque Pasivo El Faro, but you will see plenty of beautiful beaches. Most have been discovered, however. If you crave complete solitude, you're more likely to find empty beaches in the communities of **Aguadilla** or **Isabela**. On Day 2 drive south to the coastal communities in the Cabo Rojo. Your first stop should be **Joyuda**, where you can choose from dozens of seaside restaurants. After

lunch, continue past **Boquerón** to **El Combate**. This is the end of the line, quite literally. The road ends at the lighthouse that once warned sea captains about the treacherous waters around the island's southwestern tip. On Day 3 you can explore more of this windswept landscape, or head offshore for a look at Mona Island.

**IF YOU HAVE 5 DAYS**
After spending three days along the western coast, you may be tempted to set sail to one of the islands off the coast. On Day 4, head out on an overnight trip to **Mona Island**, a 14,000-acre paradise known as the "Galápagos of the Caribbean." You'll have to camp on this deserted island, but the view from the 200-foot cliffs on the northern shore makes it all worth it. Trips to Mona Island must be arranged weeks in advance.

locally grown coffee and utilize compostable cups. ⊠ *Rte. 413, Km 4.1* ☎ *787/823–0963* ⊕ *www.bananadang.com* ⊘ *Closed Tues.* ✛ *B2.*

**$$**
GERMAN
Fodor'sChoice
★

✕ **Das Alpen.** Granted, it's not traditional Puerto Rican fare nor does it have anything to do with the local culture, but the authentic German food at this restaurant will make you feel as if you're on a vacation from your vacation. Owner Jacob Elmstrom—of German descent—has gone to great lengths to re-create the flavors of Deutschland. Everything is homemade, including the *Bratwurst* (sausage), *Sauerbraten* (beef marinated in red wine), and *Kasseler Rippchen* (smoked pork chops). All the classics are served with red cabbage, bread dumplings, or *Spätzle*. The *Schnitzel* (there are three types) are ridiculously flavorful, and there are plenty of imported beers to wash down the goodness. As much as locals love the German cuisine, they also come for the Italian dishes like pumpkin ravioli or sausage tagliatelle, all made from scratch. Of course a meal wouldn't be complete without hot apple strudel. If you happen to be in Rincón during the month of October, Das Alpen holds the biggest *Oktoberfest* in Puerto Rico. Portions are large, so elastic waistbands are recommended. ⊠ *Calle Muñoz Rivera, Corner of Calle Comercio* ☎ *787/233–8009* ⊕ *www.dasalpencafe.com* ⊘ *Closed Tues. and Wed. No lunch* ✛ *B4.*

$    ✕**The English Rose.** Open just for breakfast, this quaint bed-and-
CAFÉ    breakfast has a spectacular view of the valley spilling into the sea.
House specialties such as eggs Benedict are served with homemade
breads and sausages. The latest addition to the menu is the "BBC,"
a toasted croissant topped with organic chicken, cranberry sausage,
poached egg and hollandaise sauce. If terrace seating is not available,
inside dining is equally charming with the walls colorfully decorated
with work by local artisans. Adding to the freshness of the dishes are
the herbs grown on-site. During high season you may wait up to an
hour for a table, but it's worth every minute. ✉ *Rte. 413, Km 2, Barrio
Ensenada* ☎ *787/823–4032* ⊕ *www.larosainglesa.com* ⊗ *Closed Sep.
and Nov. Closed Mon.–Wed. May–Aug.* ⊹ *B2.*

$$$    ✕**Lazy Parrot Restaurant.** This open-air terrace restaurant highlights the
CARIBBEAN    impossibly lush greenery that draws so many people to Rincón. Located
on the second floor of the Lazy Parrot Hotel, it catches a breeze even
when the rest of the island is stifling in the heat. For dinner there are
tropical entrées like Caribbean bouillabaisse, red snapper ceviche, and
coconut-crusted shrimp. Meat lovers will enjoy the grilled rib eye or
roasted chicken, both served with rustic smashed potatoes. For lunch,
head downstairs to the Rum Shack for fish tacos, pork sandwiches, or
chicken burritos—perfect after a day at the beach. ✉ *The Lazy Par-
rot Hotel, Rte. 413, Km 4.1* ☎ *787/823–0101, 787/823–0103* ⊕ *www.
lazyparrot.com* ⊗ *Closed May–Oct.* ⊹ *B2.*

$$    ✕**Pancho Villa Mexican Grill.** Following the success of his first restaurant,
MODERN    Tamboo, owner Javier Quinones opened this festive Tex-Mex cantina
MEXICAN    just off the main square. Setting the scene is Mexican music with colorful ponchos and sombreros adorning the walls. Heat up your palate
with the jalapeño popper starter before trying the sizzling churrasco
fajitas served with tortillas, rice and beans. Other memorable entrées
include mahimahi cooked inside a banana leaf or Mexican salad topped
with zesty cilantro dressing. Save room for their chocolate burrito filled
with hot fudge and vanilla ice cream. This is Rincón's most happening
spot on Tuesdays when locals gather for $1 tequila shots. ✉ *Rincón
Plaza, Plaza de Recreo* ☎ *787/823–8226* ⊕ *www.panchovillarincon.
com* ⊗ *Closed Lunch and Mon.* ⊹ *B4.*

$    ✕**The Pool Bar Sushi.** One of only a few sushi restaurants on the west
JAPANESE    coast, the open-air Pool Bar attracts visitors from as far away as San
Fodor'sChoice    Juan. The menu rivals that of any high-end Japanese restaurant, offer-
★    ing mango tuna rolls, eel maki, dim sum, and wakame seaweed salads. A house favorite is the Starving Surfer Roll of crunchy shrimp
and avocado topped with spicy tuna. The relaxed setting is especially
popular with surfers drawn by the nightly surf flicks projected on the
movie-screen backdrop. Arrive early on Thursday nights to enjoy live
jazz. ✉ *Pools Beach Cabanas, Rte. 413* ☎ *787/823–2583* ⊕ *www.
poolsbeach.com* ⊗ *Closed Tues. No Lunch* ⊹ *A1.*

$$$$    ✕**Restaurant Aaron at the Horned Dorset Primavera.** People come from all
CARIBBEAN    over the island for a meal at this exquisite restaurant. A pair of stone
★    stairways leads up to the elegant dining room, with black-and-white
marble floors, chandeliers with ruby-red shades, and a Steinway piano
dating back to 1901. Dessert and after-dinner drinks are often served

6

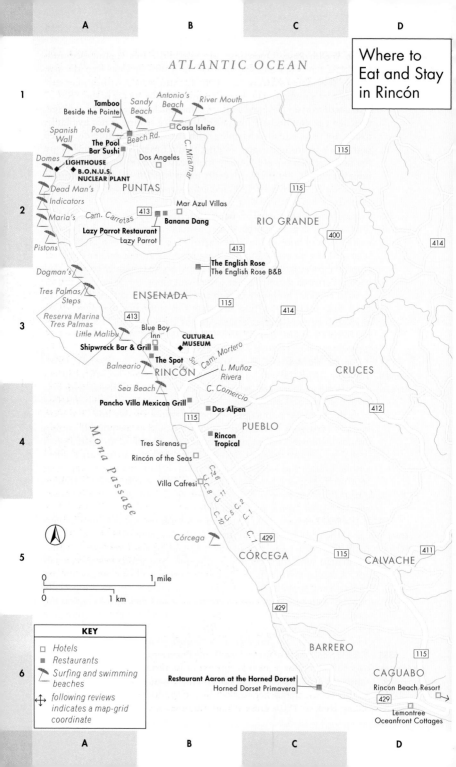

Where to
Eat and Stay
in Rincón

ATLANTIC OCEAN

A   B   C   D

1

**Tamboo**
Beside the Pointe
Sandy Beach
Antonio's Beach
River Mouth
Casa Isleña
*Spanish Wall*
*Pools*
Beach Rd.
**The Pool Bar Sushi**
*Domes*
**LIGHTHOUSE**
**B.O.N.U.S. NUCLEAR PLANT**
Dos Angeles
115

PUNTAS

C. Miramar

2

*Dead Man's*
*Indicators*
Mar Azul Villas
115
RIO GRANDE
*Maria's*
Cam. Carretas
413
**Banana Dang**
400
414
*Pistons*
**Lazy Parrot Restaurant**
Lazy Parrot

*Dogman's*
**The English Rose**
The English Rose B&B

ENSENADA
115
414

*Tres Palmas*
*Steps*

3

*Reserva Marina Tres Palmas*
413
Blue Boy Inn
**CULTURAL MUSEUM**
*Little Malibu*
**Shipwreck Bar & Grill**
**The Spot**
Sol. Cam. Mortero

*Balneario*
RINCÓN
L. Muñoz Rivera
CRUCES

*Sea Beach*
C. Comercio
**Pancho Villa Mexican Grill**
**Das Alpen**
412
115
PUEBLO

4

**Rincon Tropical**
Tres Sirenas
Rincón of the Seas
Mona Passage
Villa Cafresi
C. 14
C. 8
C. 11
C. 10
C. 5
C. 2
C. 1

*Córcega*
C. 1
429
115
411
CÓRCEGA
CALVACHE

5

0        1 mile
0      1 km

429

BARRERO
115

CAGUABO

**KEY**

□ *Hotels*
■ *Restaurants*
⟋ *Surfing and swimming beaches*
↔ *following reviews indicates a map-grid coordinate*

6

**Restaurant Aaron at the Horned Dorset**
Horned Dorset Primavera
Rincon Beach Resort
429
Lemontree
Oceanfront Cottages

A   B   C   D

on the terrace, where you'll hear the constant crash of the waves. The 10-course tasting menu, an extravagant meal with a $125 price tag, might include foie gras with maple berry glaze, pan-seared scallops with asparagus risotto, or poached *chillo* (red snapper) with apricot gnocchi. Adding Caribbean accents to classical French cuisine, the à la carte menu changes weekly but might include roasted rack of lamb and wahoo in a pistachio crust. Dress is formal by island standards, except in the downstairs "Blue Room" dining area, where a similar menu is served. ⊠ *Horned Dorset Primavera, Rte. 429, Km 3* ☎ *787/823–4030* ⊕ *www.horneddorset.com* ✍ *Reservations essential Jacket required* ◷ *Closed Mon.–Wed. Apr.–Nov.* ✛ *C6.*

$ ✕**Rincón Tropical.** Don't be scared off by the cheap plastic tables and
PUERTO RICAN chairs. What you should notice is that they are almost always full of locals enjoying the area's freshest seafood. The kitchen keeps it simple, preparing dishes with the lightest touch. Highlights include mahimahi with onions and peppers as well as fried red snapper with rice and beans. Fried plantains make a nice accompaniment to almost anything. Stop by weekdays for the $5 lunch special. ⊠ *Rte. 115, Km 12* ☎ *787/823–2017* ⊕ *www.rinconpr.com/rincontropical* ✛ *B4.*

$$$ ✕**Shipwreck Bar & Grill.** This pirate-theme restaurant is one of the most
CARIBBEAN popular eateries in town, and it's easy to see why. It has a laid-back vibe and a friendly staff that's always ready with a smile or a joke. Don't be surprised to see local fishermen making their way to the kitchen with their still-flapping catch, attesting to the freshness of the food. Look for four specials a night, as well as their most requested dishes, such as juicy steaks, grilled mahimahi, homemade pastas, and skewered pork. Although portions are enormous, lighter-fare options include various wraps and seared ahi served on a pyramid of mixed greens. Don't miss the daily happy hour from 3 to 7 or the Sunday afternoon pig roast, offered November to April. ⊠ *Black Eagle Marina, Black Eagle Rd., off Rte. 413* ☎ *787/823–0578* ⊕ *www.rinconspipwreck.com* ◷ *No Lunch May–Oct.* ✛ *B3.*

$$ ✕**Tamboo.** Here is a bar and grill that doesn't fall too far into either
CARIBBEAN category. The kitchen prepares a wide range of unique items, from king-crab sandwiches to baby-back ribs brushed with guava sauce. Despite the laid-back atmosphere, the food presentation is fit for a high-end restaurant. The open-air bar serves a mean mojito, recently voted the best on the island. The deck is a great place to watch novice surfers wipe out on the nearby beach. On weekends you can enjoy live music. ⊠ *Beside the Pointe, Rte. 413, Km 4.4* ☎ *787/823–8550* ⊕ *www.besidethepointe.com* ◷ *Closed Sep.* ✛ *A1.*

## WHERE TO STAY

*For expanded hotel reviews, visit Fodors.com.*

*Use the coordinate (✛ A1) at the end of each listing to locate a site on the corresponding "Where to Eat and Stay in Rincón" map.*

$ ⌂**Beside the Pointe.** This perennial favorite sits right on Sandy Beach,
HOTEL where the waves are big but not too large for novice surfers. **Pros:** Social atmosphere; popular restaurant; great views. **Cons:** Noise from

restaurant; not all rooms have ocean views; no elevator. ⊠ *Rte. 413, Km 4.4* ☎ *787/823–8550* ⊕ *www.besidethepointe.com* ⇨ *7 rooms, 2 apartments* ⚅ *In-room: a/c, safe, kitchen. In-hotel: restaurant, bar* ⊗ *closed Sept.* ⦿ *No meals* ✛ *A1.*

**$$**
B&B/INN
🏨 **Blue Boy Inn.** A walled garden that surrounds this little inn makes you think you're miles away from civilization. **Pros:** Gorgeous gardens and pool, use of common kitchen, extremely private. **Cons:** Not on beach, some noise from nearby restaurant, non-animal lovers might consider the owner's roaming cats a nuisance. ⊠ *556 Black Eagle Rd., off Rte. 413* ☎ *787/823–2593* ⊕ *www.blueboyinn.com* ⇨ *8 rooms* ⚅ *In-room: a/c, Wi-Fi. In-hotel: bar, pool, parking* ⊗ *Closed Sept.* ⦿ *Breakfast* ✛ *B3.*

**$$**
B&B/INN
🏨 **Casa Isleña.** With its barrel-tiled roofs, wall-enclosed gardens, and open-air dining room, Casa Isleña might remind well-traveled souls of a villa on the coast of Mexico. **Pros:** Secluded setting; beautiful beach; great tapas bar; daily yoga offered. **Cons:** Hotel closed September and October; books up quickly; management seldom on-site. ⊠ *Rte. 413, Km 4.8, Barrio Puntas* ☎ *787/823–1525, 888/289–7750* ⊕ *www.casaislena.com* ⇨ *9 rooms* ⚅ *In-room: a/c. In-hotel: restaurant, bar, pool, beach, parking* ⦿ *Breakfast* ✛ *B1.*

**$**
B&B/INN
🏨 **Dos Angeles.** On a quiet hillside overlooking the ocean, this no-frills guesthouse is about as clean and comfortable as it gets. **Pros:** friendly staff; great breakfast; peaceful haven. **Cons:** morning rooster crows; uphill climb from the beach. ⊠ *Calle Vista del Mar* ☎ *787/823–1378, 787/431–6057* ⊕ *www.dosangelesdelmar.com* ⇨ *5* ⚅ *In-room: a/c, Wi-Fi. In-hotel: pool, parking* ⦿ *Breakfast* ✛ *B2.*

**$**
B&B/INN
🏨 **The English Rose.** Nestled in the hills of Rincón, this bed-and-breakfast has some of the best views of the Caribbean ocean. **Pros:** Excellent breakfast; peaceful setting; hospitable owners. **Cons:** Somewhat isolated; no beach; restaurant serves breakfast only; closed September and October. ⊠ *Carr. 413, Km 2, Barrio Ensenada* ☎ *787/823–4032* ⊕ *www.larosainglesa.com* ⇨ *3 apartments* ⚅ *In-room: kitchen, Wi-Fi. In-hotel: restaurant, pool, parking* ⊗ *Closed Sept. and Oct.* ⦿ *Breakfast* ✛ *B2.*

**$$$$**
RESORT
**Fodor's Choice**
★
🏨 **Horned Dorset Primavera.** This is, without a doubt, the most luxurious hotel in Puerto Rico. **Pros:** Unabashed luxury; unmatched meals; lovely setting; yoga "treehouse." **Cons:** On a very slender beach; staff is sometimes haughty; morning light floods through small shadeless windows near the ceiling. ⊠ *Rte. 429, Km 3* ☎ *787/823–4030, 800/633–1857* ⊕ *www.horneddorset.com* ⇨ *40 villas* ⚅ *In-room: a/c, safe, kitchen, no TV, Wi-Fi. In-hotel: restaurant, bar, pool, gym, beach, parking, some pets allowed, some age restrictions* ⦿ *Some meals* ✛ *C6.*

**$**
HOTEL
🏨 **Lazy Parrot.** Painted in eye-popping tropical hues, this mountainside hotel doesn't take itself too seriously. **Pros:** Economy rooms available; tropical setting; microwaves in rooms. **Cons:** Not on the beach; stairs to climb, some may consider the whimsical style tacky. ⊠ *Rte. 413, Km 4.1* ☎ *787/823–5654, 800/294–1752* ⊕ *www.lazyparrot.com* ⇨ *21 rooms* ⚅ *In-room: a/c, Wi-Fi. In-hotel: restaurant, bar, pool* ⦿ *Breakfast* ✛ *B2.*

Tres Sirenas

Horned Dorset Primavera

**$$**
HOTEL
⊞ **Lemontree Oceanfront Cottages.** Sitting right on the beach, this pair of lemon-yellow buildings holds six apartments named after such fruits as Mango, Cocoa, Banana, and Piña. **Pros:** Far from the crowds; on-call massage therapist; spacious balconies. **Cons:** Beach is very narrow; must drive to shops and restaurants; no elevator. ⊠ *Rte. 429, Km 4.1* ☎ *787/823–6452* ⊕ *www. lemontreepr.com* ⟿ *6 apartments* ⏚ *In-room: a/c, kitchen, Wi-Fi. In-hotel: beach, parking* ⏀*No meals* ✛ *D6.*

**$**
RENTAL
⊞ **Mar Azul Villas.** Set in a tropical garden behind Mar Azul Surf Shop, these charming little apartments have all the comforts of home. **Pros:** Spotless rooms; friendly owners; walking distance to restaurants, best surf shop in Rincón. **Cons:** Limited ocean view; foot traffic from attached surf shop. ⊠ *Rte. 413, Km 4.4* ☎ *787/214–7224, 787/823–5692* ⊕ *www.puertoricosurfinginfo.com* ⟿ *2 apartments* ⏚ *In-room: a/c, safe, kitchen, Wi-Fi. In-hotel: laundry facilities, parking* ⏀*No meals* ✛ *B2.*

**$$**
RESORT
⊞ **Rincón Beach Resort.** It's a bit off the beaten path, but that's part of the allure of this oceanfront resort. **Pros:** Beautiful pool area; laid-back vibe; children's playground. **Cons:** Far from dining options; lacks Puerto Rican flavor; decor is slightly dated; halls echo. ⊠ *Rte. 115, Km 5.8, Añasco* ☎ *787/589–9000* ⊕ *www.rinconbeach.com* ⟿ *112 rooms* ⏚ *In-room: a/c, safe, kitchen, Wi-Fi. In-hotel: restaurant, bar, pool, gym, beach, water sports, parking* ⏀*No meals* ✛ *D6.*

**$**
HOTEL
☺
⊞ **Rincón of the Seas.** Tucked at the end of a palm-lined drive, this high-rise hotel feels as if it could be in Miami Beach. **Pros:** Lush gardens; gorgeous pool area; Wi-Fi in common areas. **Cons:** On a slender beach; loud music blares from pool area all day. ⊠ *Rte. 115, Km 12.2* ☎ *787/823–7500* ⊕ *www.rinconoftheseas.com* ⟿ *112 rooms* ⏚ *In-room: a/c, safe, Internet. In-hotel: restaurant, bar, pool, beach, parking* ⏀*No meals* ✛ *B4.*

**$$$**
B&B/INN
Fodor's Choice
★
⊞ **Tres Sirenas.** Waves gently lap against the shores at this boutique inn named "Three Mermaids" in honor of the owners' daughters. **Pros:** In-room massages; spotless and tastefully decorated, discounted rates May through October. **Cons:** Usually booked; set breakfast hour; Wi-Fi occasionally drops. ⊠ *26 Seabeach Dr.* ☎ *787/823–0558* ⊕ *www.tressirenas. com* ⟿ *2 rooms, 1 studio, 2 apartments* ⏚ *In-room: a/c, kitchen, Wi-Fi. In-hotel: pool, beach, water sports, laundry facilities, parking, some pets allowed* ⏀*Breakfast* ✛ *B4.*

**$**
HOTEL
⊞ **Villa Cofresí.** On one of the best swimming beaches in town, Villa Confresí is Rincón's oldest hotel, making it extremely popular with Puerto Rican families. **Pros:** Good restaurant; family-friendly environment. **Cons:** Standard rooms lack ocean views; not enough parking; lots

of noise from pool area. ⌧ *Rte. 115, Km 12* ☎ *787/823–2450* ⊕ *www. villacofresi.com* ⤸ *107 rooms* ⚟ *In-room: a/c, kitchen. In-hotel: restaurant, bar, pool, beach* ⎟◯⎢ *Breakfast* ✛ *B4.*

## VILLA RENTALS

Villa rentals are becoming more and more popular in Rincón. Because many people come here for a week or more to surf, find a secluded spot on the beach, or just hang out, renting a villa makes perfect sense. Guests can make the place their own, without worrying about the noise from the kids bothering the people in the next room or leaving sandy shoes outside the door. In the long run, it might also be a money saver for those who cook at home rather than dine out. There are several local chefs who will prepare gourmet dinners for large groups in private villas.

A few things to keep in mind: If you're looking for a secluded location, you won't find it on this crowded part of the coast. It's likely that your neighbor will be within shouting distance. In addition, few villas are actually on the ocean, and the ones that are go for a premium price. Many are within walking distance of the water, but some will require that you drive to reach the shore. If a beachfront location is important to you, make sure to specify. And where you stay will depend on whether or not you're a surfer. Those who like to ride the waves favor the northern coast, while those who want to snorkel, scuba dive, or swim prefer the calmer southern shore.

**Island West Properties & Beach Rentals.** Island West Properties & Beach Rentals can help you rent villas in Rincón by the day, week, or month. The company has been around for years, so it corners the market. ⌧ *Rte. 413, Km 0.7* ☎ *787/823–2323* ⊕ *www.islandwestrentals.com.*

**$$$**  ⛫**Caribbean Paradise.** This two-story house would be great for two
RENTAL  families traveling together, as each floor has plenty of room, and there is a fenced yard where children can play. ⌧ *Calle 8, Corsega Beach* ☎ *787/823–2323* ⊕ *www.islandwestrentals.com* ⤸ *4 rooms, 3 baths* ⚟ *In-room: a/c, kitchen. In-hotel: beach, laundry facilities.*

**$$$$**  ⛫**Rincón Ocean Villa.** This 10-bedroom villa has served as a vacation
RENTAL  home for the rich and famous, including country star Shania Twain. **Pros:** beautiful pool; sleeps 26 guests; private bath in each room; wait-staff included. **Cons:** small gym; only one TV in lounge area; courtyard marble gets slippery with rain; this public beach might see weekend traffic. ⌧ *Carr. 429, Km 1.4* ☎ *787/925–6600* ⊕ *www.rinconoceanvilla. com* ⤸ *10* ⚟ *In-room: a/c, safe, kitchen, Wi-Fi. In-hotel: pool, gym, beach, parking.*

**$$$$**  ⛫**Villa Tres Palmas.** Not all beach houses are created equal, as Villas Tres
RENTAL  Palmas makes clear. ⌧ *Off Rte. 413, Playa Tres Palmas* ☎ *787/823– 2323* ⊕ *www.islandwestrentals.com* ⤸ *6 bedrooms, 5 baths* ⚟ *In-room: no a/c, Wi-Fi. In-hotel: pool, beach, laundry facilities.*

## NIGHTLIFE

Rincón attracts a younger crowd, so there are plenty of options for fun after dark.

**Calypso Café.** On weekends the Calypso Café often has live rock-and-roll bands. The open-air establishment has daily sunset happy hour and is a good place to grab fresh ceviche, grilled fish, or a juicy burger after you've had your fill of the beach. They have the coldest beers in town. ⊠ *Maria's Beach, Rte. 4413* ☏ *787/823–1626.*

**Rock Bottom Bar & Grill.** The Rock Bottom Bar & Grill is the place to be on Thursday night. This circular bar is especially popular with locals, who gather to watch surf flicks throughout the week. ⊠ *Casa Verde Inn, Carr. 413, Puntas* ☏ *787/823–3756* ⊕ *www.enrincon.com.*

**Rum Shack.** The Rum Shack serves a mean bloody mary and something called a "rum shackle" that's made with four types of rum. This poolside bar is the hot spot on Wednesday, when a live reggae band hits the stage. ⊠ *Lazy Parrot Inn, Rte. 413, Km 4.1* ☏ *787/823–0103* ⊕ *www. rumshack.net.*

## SHOPPING

**Playa Oeste.** Playa Oeste has an eclectic collection of surf art, jewelry, clothing, and pottery. Paintings and photographs can be shipped directly to your home. ⊠ *Rte. 413, Km 0.5* ☏ *787/823–4424* ⊕ *www. playaoestegallery.com* ⊙ *Closed Mon.–Wed. June–Aug.*

## SPORTS AND THE OUTDOORS

DIVING AND
SNORKELING

Most of the region's dive operators also run fishing charters around Desecheo Island and whale-watching trips in season.

★ **Taíno Divers.** Taíno Divers has all-day snorkeling and diving trips that cost $89 and $129, including lunch. It also offers daily trips to Desecheo Island, winter whale-watching trips, and scuba certification courses. ⊠ *Black Eagle Marina, Black Eagle Rd., off Rte. 413* ☏ *787/823–6429* ⊕ *www.tainodivers.com.*

HORSEBACK
RIDING

**Pintos R Us.** Pintos R Us has two-hour horseback-riding tours along the beach to the lighthouse, as well as full-moon tours and riding lessons. The horses are spirited but gentle enough for newcomers. Reservations are a must. ⊠ *Rte. 413, Km. 4.7* ☏ *787/516–7090* ⊕ *www.pintosrus. com.*

SAILING

**Katarina Sail Charters.** Set sail in the morning for a day in the sun, or in the late afternoon for unobstructed sunset views, with Katarina Sail Charters. The catamaran sails from Black Eagle Marina, except from mid-August to November 15, during hurricane season. ⊠ *Black Eagle Marina, Black Eagle Rd., off Rte. 413* ☏ *787/823–7245* ⊕ *www. sailrinconpuertorico.com.*

**Rincón Sailing.** Rincón Sailing has introductory courses and race clinics that cover handling, strategy, tactics, and tuning. For those who know how to sail, the shop rents Lasers, Sunfish, and Optimists. Four-hour

*Continued on page 267*

# SURFING
## PUERTO RICO

by Marlise Kast

With turquoise waters, sugary sand, hollow barrels, offshore winds, and arching palm trees, it's no wonder the island has been labeled "Hawaii of the Atlantic." This vision of paradise is a magnet for myriad surfers. Whether you're a beginner or a big-wave rider, there's a break to suit your ability—on the northwest coast near Rincón, along the northern beaches, or off the eastern shores.

# WAVES OF GLORY

Pro surfer Gabriel Escudero conquers the waves at Domes Beach in Rincón.

Puerto Rico is home to more than 70 surf spots with some of the Caribbean's most consistent waves, breaking anywhere between 3 feet (for beginners) and 20 feet (for advanced/professionals). Along 310 miles of ride-able waters are coral reefs, point breaks, hallow barrels, beach breaks, rights and lefts. The downside of surfing in the tropics are jellyfish and sea urchins that cling onto the rocks. Other dangers include shallow reefs, riptides, and territorialism at some local spots. If you're a beginner, enroll in a surf course and learn from someone who knows the environment. Respect the locals, never surf alone, and remember the unwritten law: never drop in on another surfer.

## THE GOOD OLE DAYS

According to local legend, the first surfers to test the northwest waters were Puerto Rico's own Jose Rodriguez, Rafy Viella, and Guille Bermuda. In 1960, American surfer Gary Hoyt opened the island's first surf shop in San Juan. Following in his wake were Johnny Flain and Butch Linden from Malibu, California, who claim that only fifty surfers braved the waters in the mid 60s. It wasn't until 1968, when Rincón hosted the World Surfing Championships, that word spread of epic waves peeling along the north and northwest coasts. Winter waves and a laid-back lifestyle made the island a haven for American surfers and hippies, who took one look at the coastline and never turned back. Since the 1970s, Puerto Rico's roster of talent has featured such legends as Edwin Santos, Juan Ashton, and Pepe Alvarez. Noted for charging monster waves are local big-wave riders like Alberto Lincha, Carlos Cabrero, and Waldo Oliver

Today, the island hosts dozens of competitions and is home to 25,000 surfers and 30 surf shops.

Cresting a wave at the Corona Pro Surfer event

# SURF SEASONS

(clockwise from top left) serene paddle-boarding; a crowded wave at Tres Palmas; competing at Middles Beach

Waves peak during winter, but it's possible to catch one during "off season" due to periodic hurricanes and cold fronts that pass Puerto Rico. Summer is generally flat, except when a hurricane passes (season, July–November) off the coast. The fall is when North Atlantic storms create enough swell to make Puerto Rico a world-class destination. This is when the pros take to the waves, providing a spectacle for beachgoers.

### BEGINNER

For a light splash in the whitewash, the summer months (late May through August) offer playful waves.

### INTERMEDIATE

In springtime (March to mid-May), swells fade but are compensated with offshore winds that hold the wave's barreling shape, averaging between shoulder-to-head high.

### ADVANCED

September through May is ideal for experienced surfers. November through February in particular is when top surfers—mostly locals and East Coasters—crowd the line-up for monster waves that can fire as high as 20-feet.

## WHERE TO RENT

Puerto Rico has dozens of surf shops renting everything from foam longboards and boogieboards for beginners to high-performance shortboards and paddleboards for experts.

Offering the best quiver on the island is **Mar Azul** (☎ 787/823–5692 ⊕ www.puertoricosurfinginfo.com) located on Rincón's Rte 413. **WRV** in Aguadilla (☎ 787/669–3840 ⊕ www.waveridingvehicles.com) is another top spot for beginner board rentals.

6

IN FOCUS SURFING PUERTO RICO

# NORTHWEST BREAKS

**KEY**

-  Right Break
- Left Break
- Point/Beach Break
- Beginner Area
- Intermediate Area
- Advance Area

Pta. Agujereada Jobos
Wilderness Beach
San Antonio
Isabela
Pta. Borinquen 110 Mora 2
Gas Chambers 112
Aguadilla Bahia de Aguadilla
Sandy Beach
Domes Aguada Moca
Maria's Pta. Higüero 115
Tres Palmas Rincón
2 110

When the surf is on in the northwest, it's on. This is the best place to capture the scene, as some breaks here experience 40-foot swells in winter. Aguadilla and Rincón are ideally stationed for off-shore wind conditions, which hold the waves' shape.

## ADVANCED

To witness Puerto Rico's true surfing experience, head north of Rincón to Aguadilla's **Wilderness Beach.** Surrounding jungle landscape makes it worth the drive to this local spot where fast, long rights average 8–15 ft.

Considered the "Sunset Beach" of Puerto Rico, **Tres Palmas** is reserved for kamikaze-surfers who take on the 40-foot waves that only break a few days each year. In summer, however, this deep outer reef is surprisingly calm, making it the perfect place to snorkel.

Head to **Gas Chambers** to watch surfers charge Puerto Rico's most powerful wave. Next to Crash Boat Beach, this spot breaks less than 10 times per year, but is la-

Corona Pro Surfer event, Rincon

beled world-class due to the 15-foot faces and oblong tubes that crash with unbelievable force.

## INTERMEDIATE

At **Domes,** a spot named for the nuclear power dome neighboring the parking lot, peaky right-hand waves average 3 to 10 feet. This break is one of the area's most consistent, even on smaller days. Breaking directly in front of Tamboo Restaurant is a sandbar known as **Sandy Beach.** This intermediate spot still delivers on smaller days, but is not as protected from south winds as the neighboring coves. Although generally void of crowds, the rocky shoreline embedded with urchins isn't good for beginners.

## BEGINNER

When the waves are between 2 to 4 feet, beginners can head just south of Domes to **Maria's.** This break has some fun right- and left-hand peaks, and offers a pleasant beach for photographing surfers when the swell picks up. Once waves reach head-high (Nov. through Feb.), this spot is best reserved for advanced surfers who can handle the shallow reefs and strong currents.

Popular with beginner and intermediate surfers, **Jobos** in Isabela has 4–10 foot rights that break off a reef in a crescent-shaped bay. This section often connects to the inside waves, making for a nice long ride. Because of the food shacks and shallow waters, this spot is often crowded with beachgoers and beginners learning to surf. Those who prefer to watch the action can photograph surfers from the peninsula on the beach's east side.

# NORTH BREAKS

Susceptible to Atlantic storms and their aftermath, the north coast has more than 30 breaks to explore.

**ADVANCED**
Unless you're quite experienced, you may just want to take photographs from the shores of **Chatarras**. This epic wave breaks on a sharp coral reef, creating hollow left-hand tubes fit for the pros. When the 10+ footers are firing, this spot gets crowded with surfers who will do whatever it takes to claim their wave.

**INTERMEDIATE**
Near San Juan, **La Ocho**, is a forgiving wave great for intermediate surfers on medium-size days. Working best at 5 feet, this break is long but usually mushy. It's a long paddle to the break so make sure you're in shape before you head to the line-up.

**BEGINNER**
Near the town of Manati, **Los Tubos** (The Tubes) has a pleasant crowd and is manageable for novices. The best time to come is be-tween September and April, but beware of sea urchins that line the rocky shore. In the town of Luquillo, **La Pared** delivers right and lefts that break on a soft, sandy beach. On a weekday, you may have all the waves to yourself, except after 5 PM when you might be joined by a handful of locals out for a sunset session. This is an excellent beginner's beach, with friendly 3 to 5 foot waves that break 150 days of the year.

# SOUTH BREAKS

Overshadowed by the north, the south rim of Puerto Rico experiences all types of waves from the Caribbean hurricanes and tropical storms. This is most common between August and October when swells hit the southeastern side from Humacao down to Patillas.

**INTERMEDIATE TO ADVANCED**
**Inches,** has the island's longest left-hand barrel. Waves here often peel for 300+ yards. Named for the "inches" separating you from the reef, this spot has powerful waves that spread between three peaks. Trade winds make this the south's most consistent surf break, even in summer when most other spots are flat.

**6**

**IN FOCUS** SURFING PUERTO RICO

# BOARD SHAPES

**Longboard:** Lengthier (about 2.5—3 m/ 9–10.5 feet), wider, thicker, and more buoyant than the often-miniscule shortboards. Offers more flotation and speedier paddling, which makes it easier to get into waves. Great for beginners and those with relaxed surf styles. Skill level; Beginner to Intermediate.

**Funboard:** A little shorter than the longboard with a slightly more acute nose and blunt tail, the Funboard combines the best attributes of the longboards with some similar characteristics of the shorter boards. Good for beginners or surfers looking for a board more maneuverable and faster than a longboard. Skill level; Beginner to Intermediate.

**Fishboard:** A stumpy, blunt-nosed, twin-finned board that features a "V" tail (giving it a "fish" like look, hence the name) and is fast and maneuverable. Good for catching small, steep slow waves and pulling tricks. At one point this was the world's best-selling surfboard. Skill level; Intermediate to Expert.

**Shortboard:** Shortboards came on the scene in 1967-70 when the average board length dropped from 9'6" to 6'6" (2.9m to 2m) and changed the wave riding styles in the surf world forever. This board is a short, light, high-performance stick that is designed for carving the wave with a high amount of maneuverability. These boards need a fast steep wave, completely different than a longboard break, which tends to be slower with shallower wave faces. Skill level; Expert.

Beginner                                                                Expert

Fish

Funboards

Shortboards

Longboards

Shallow wave faces, easiest surfing                    Steeper wave faces, difficult surfing

lessons start at $120. Call to reserve a spot in one of their weekly courses. ⊠ *Rincón* ☎ *787/421–4700,* ⊕ *www.rinconsailing.com.*

SURFING **Desecheo Surf & Dive Shop.** Desecheo Surf & Dive Shop rents snorkeling equipment ($15 a day), Boogie boards ($20 a day), and a variety of short and long surfboards ($25–$45 a day). The company also has a small shop with swimwear, sandals, sunglasses, and surf gear. ⊠ *Rte. 413, Km 2.5* ☎ *787/823–0390* ⊕ *www.desecheosurfshop.com.*

**Mar Azul.** Mar Azul has Rincón's best selection of performance surf-boards and stand-up paddleboards to buy or rent. Paddleboard lessons ($40 for 90 minutes) are also available. This is one of the best surf shops on the entire island. ⊠ *Rte. 413, Km 4.4* ☎ *787/823–5692* ⊕ *www. puertoricosurfinginfo.com.*

**Puntas Surf School.** With more than a decade of surf-coaching experi-ence, Puntas is the only surf school in Rincón with female instructors. ⊠ *Rincón* ☎ *787/366–1689, 939/687–8040* ⊕ *www.puntassurfschool. com.*

# MAYAGÜEZ

6

*15 miles (24 km) southeast of Rincón.*

"Me encanta" is what most people from Puerto Rico say when you ask them about Mayagüez. But you are likely to be less than enchanted by the grungy city, home to 12,000 university students and several casinos. With more charming communities in every direction, there's no real reason to stop in this traffic-clogged area. But if you have some spare time, the city known as the "Sultan of the West" has some worthwhile attractions. Its tree-lined main square, called Plaza Colón, is dominated by a large statue of Christopher Columbus. On the surrounding streets you'll find the domed Teatro Yagüez, which dates from 1902, and a mishmash of buildings that run the gamut from neoclassical to baroque to art deco. You'll also find the largest shopping mall on the west coast.

## GETTING HERE AND AROUND
### AIR TRAVEL
The small Aeropuerto Eugenio María de Hostos (MAZ), just north of Mayagüez on Highway 2, has flights between San Juan and Mayagüez on American Eagle and Cape Air. If you are not flying into San Juan, you can rent a car at the airport. Prices vary from $35 to $65 per day.

**Airport Information Aeropuerto Eugenio María de Hostos** ⊠ *Off Rte. 2* ☎ *787/833-0148.* **Aeropuerto Internacional Rafael Hernández** ⊠ *Hwy. 2, Km 148.7, Carretera 110 & 107 Borinquen/Ramey, Aguadilla* ☎ *787/891-2286, 787/890-6075.*

### CAR TRAVEL
Driving in Mayagüez can be complicated, especially in the high-trafficked center of town where one-way streets compose the city grid. Nevertheless, a rental car is your best option for getting around town. From Highway 2 you can reach downtown by taking Route 105 (Calle McKinley) or Route 106 (Calle Méndez Vigo). Either route will take you to the heart of the city.

**Car Rental Avis** ⏻ *975 Av. Hostos 00680* 🕾 *787/890–3311.* **Budget** ✉ *Aeropuerto Eugenio María de Hostos, Off Rte. 200610* 🕾 *800/527–0700.* **Enterprise** ✉ *505 Calle Post Sur, www.enterprise.com00681* 🕾 *787/805–3722* ⊕ *www.enterprise.com.* **Hertz** ✉ *Aeropuerto Eugenio María de Hostos, Off Rte. 200610* 🕾 *787/890–5650.* **Leaseway of Puerto Rico.** 🕾 *787/833–1140 in Mayagüez.* **Thrifty** ✉ *Aeropuerto Eugenio María de Hostos, Off Rte. 200610* 🕾 *787/834–1590 in Mayagüez.*

### TAXI TRAVEL

In Mayagüez, taxis charge flat rates—no meters—by location. Fares to or from San Juan are steep: for example, service is $120 from Mayagüez.

**Taxis Arecibo Taxi Cab** 🕾 *787/878–2929.*

## EXPLORING MAYAGÜEZ

**Estación Experimental de Agricultura Tropical** (*Tropical Agriculture Research Station*). Founded in 1901 on a 235-acre farm on the outskirts of Mayagüez, the Estación Experimental de Agricultura Tropical is run by the U.S. Department of Agriculture and contains a tropical plant collection that has been nurtured for more than a half century. More than 2,000 plant species from all over the tropical world are found here, including teak, mahogany, cinnamon, nutmeg, rubber, and numerous exotic flowers. Free maps are available for self-guided tours. ✉ *Hwy. 2 at Rte. 108* 🕾 *787/831–3435* 🎟 *Free* ⊙ *Weekdays 7–4.*

**Teatro Yagüez.** The Teatro Yagüez is an extravagant yellow-and-white theater dating from 1902 that's famed throughout the island for its lavish, columned facade and domed roof. The structure, a little over the top, is still the main venue for theater in Mayagüez. ✉ *Calle McKinley, 1 block from Plaza Colón* 🕾 *787/834–0523* 🎟 *Free* ⊙ *Weekdays 8–4:30.*

☉ **Zoológico de Puerto Rico.** Puerto Rico's only zoo, the 45-acre Zoológico de Puerto Rico, is just north of downtown. After $13 million in renovations, it's looking pretty spiffy. New on the scene is a 45-foot-tall aviary, which allows you to walk through a rain-forest environment as tropical birds fly freely above your head. There's also a new butterfly park where you can let brilliant blue morphos land on your hand, and an arthropodarium where you can get up close and personal with spiders and their kin. Video monitors are built into the floor to show off the bugs that normally get trampled underfoot. The older section of the park has undergone an extensive renovation, so most of the cages have been replaced by fairly natural-looking environments. One of the most popular residents is Mundi, a female elephant who arrived as a baby more than two decades ago. There are also plenty of lions, tigers—and even bears. There is a $3 charge for parking. ✉ *Rte. 108, north of Rte. 65, Miradero* 🕾 *787/834–8110* ⊕ *www.parquesnacionalespr.com* 🎟 *$13* ⊙ *Wed.–Sun. 8:30–4.*

## WHERE TO EAT

$$ ✕ **Laissez Faire.** A much-needed addition to the Mayagüez dining scene, EUROPEAN this loftlike bistro has cement floors, black leather chairs, and a glass wall that showcases chef Christian Quiñones at work. The lunch menu

is creatively broken into food categories like "proteins," "sides," "salads," and "desserts" that you can mix and match. Midday selections vary but might include lobster risotto or rabbit wrapped in bacon. The tapas are perfect if you want to sample a small variety. By night, white linens, smooth jazz, and candlelight set the scene for such entrées as seared foie gras with poached pear purée, mussels with lemongrass and coconut curry, or ahi tuna with seaweed and spiced mango. The wine list is extensive and the cocktails are refreshingly clever—the blueberry mojito is a house favorite. ⊠ *Calle McKinley 98* ☎ *787/805–2400* ⊗ *Closed Sun.*

¢ ✕ **Ricomini Bakery.** This popular bakery, open daily from 5 am to midnight, is a good spot to try one of the city's trademark delicacies, a *brazo gitano* ("gypsy arm"). These gigantic jellyrolls are filled with anything from guava to sweet cheese. You can also find another famous local product here, Fido's Sangría, made from the closely guarded secret recipe of Mayagüez resident Wilfredo Aponte Hernández. There are also tasty pastries like flan, tres leches, and cheesecake, as well as freshly baked bread and a selection of sandwiches. ⊠ *101 Calle Méndez Vigo* ☎ *787/833–1444.*

CAFÉ

¢ ✕ **Siglo XX.** This busy restaurant has an enormous menu of chicken, steak, and seafood dishes prepared every way imaginable. Meals come in a basket with rice, beans, or plantains. Sandwiches, displayed behind the glass counter, are served lightly toasted with the traditional mayo-ketchup "secret sauce." Booths at the diner setting are packed with locals, especially during the midweek lunch hour. This Spanish-speaking eatery is a great place to practice your language skills. ⊠ *9 Calle Peral* ☎ *787/832–1370* ⊗ *Closed Sun.*

PUERTO RICAN

## WHERE TO STAY

*For expanded hotel reviews, visit Fodors.com.*

$$ 🛏 **Holiday Inn Mayagüez & Tropical Casino.** Everything seems shoehorned into this big box on the northern edge of Mayagüez—the sound of slot machines is impossible to escape in the extremely popular casino, which is adjacent to the lobby, as well as the bar and restaurant. **Pros:** Great staff; pretty pool area. **Cons:** Not on the beach; motel-style rooms; free continental breakfast for executive rooms only. ⊠ *2701 Hwy. 2, at Km 149.9* ☎ *787/833–1100* ⊕ *www.hidpr.com* ⥲ *141 rooms* ᐸ *In-room: a/c, Wi-Fi. In-hotel: restaurant, bar, pool, gym, laundry facilities, business center, parking* ⦶ *No meals.*

HOTEL

$ 🛏 **Howard Johnson Downtown Mayagüez.** Set in a former monastery, this downtown hotel still has stained-glass windows in some rooms and a stone cross on the roof. **Pros:** Interesting building; rooms designed for families and business people. **Cons:** Far from the beach; on an uninteresting block, Wi-Fi only in common areas. ⊠ *70 Calle Méndez Vigo* ☎ *787/832–9191* ⊕ *www.hojo.com* ⥲ *50 rooms* ᐸ *In-room: a/c, safe. In-hotel: restaurant, bar, pool, laundry facilities, parking* ⦶ *Breakfast.*

HOTEL

$$ 🛏 **Mayagüez Resort & Casino.** The center of the city's social life, this old-fashioned hotel is packed with elegantly dressed men and women all weekend. **Pros:** Lovely pool area; best casino on this coast. **Cons:** Not

RESORT

on the beach; must pay for parking even to visit the casino; guests must wear identity wristbands. ⊠ *Rte. 104, Km 0.3, off Hwy. 2* ☎ *787/832–3030, 888/689–3030* ⊕ *www.mayaguezresort.com* ⤶ *140 rooms* ⚛ *In-room: a/c, safe, Wi-Fi. In-hotel: restaurant, bar, pool, tennis court, gym, spa, business center, parking* ⊺◉⌐ *No meals.*

## NIGHTLIFE

**Dom Pepe.** A block from Plaza Colón, Dom Pepe has live eclectic music upstairs. ⊠ *54 Calle Méndez Vigo Este* ☎ *787/298–4069, 939/630–1769.*

**Karma Lounge.** The coolest bar in Mayagüez has Latin jazz played as videos are projected onto a large screen. This trendy spot is known for its blueberry mojotos and fruit martinis. ⊠ *Laissez Faire, Calle McKinley 98* ☎ *787/805–2400.*

## SHOPPING

Small stores and pharmacies dot downtown Mayagüez.

**Mayagüez Mall.** For heavy-duty shopping, Mayagüez Mall has local stores, a food court, movie theaters, and stateside chains such as JCPenney, Walmart, and Marshalls. ⊠ *Hwy. 2, Km 159.4* ☎ *787/834–2760.*

# CABO ROJO

Named for its pinkish cliffs, "Red Cape" was used in the late 18th century as a port for merchant vessels—and for the smugglers and pirates who inevitably accompanied oceangoing trade. Today the miles of coastline to the west and north of this tiny curl of land jutting into the Caribbean are a destination for families. Many small, inexpensive hotels can be found in the communities of Joyuda, Boquerón, and El Combate. Outdoor activities are quite popular, from sailing out of Boquerón to hiking to the lighthouse near El Combate.

## JOYUDA

*14 miles (21 km) south of Mayagüez.*

Known as the Milla de Oro (Golden Mile) because of its string of more than 15 seaside restaurants, the community of Joyuda is a must for seafood lovers. The same can't be said for those in search of a beautiful beach, as erosion has taken a terrible toll, leaving in some places only a sliver of sand. But that doesn't stop hordes of local families from making a beeline to the bit of beach that's left.

### GETTING HERE AND AROUND

From Mayagüez, take Highway 2 south to Route 100 south toward Cabo Rojo. Head west on Route 102 until you hit the coastal town of Joyuda. Most of the area's restaurants and hotels are staggered along a 2-mile (3-km) stretch on Route 102, making this a convenient town to explore by foot.

Surrounded by rugged coastline, the Cabo Rojo Lighthouse is best reached by a four-wheel drive vehicle.

## EXPLORING

★ **Mona Island.** About 50 miles (80 km) off the coast of Cabo Rojo, Mona Island sits brooding in the Caribbean Sea. Known as the Galápagos of the Caribbean, the 14,000-acre island has long been a destination for adventurous travelers. It's said to have been settled by the Taíno and visited by both Christopher Columbus and Juan Ponce de León. Pirates were known to use the small island as a hideout, and legend has it that there is still buried treasure to be found here. Today, however, Mona's biggest lure is its distinctive ecosystem. It is home to a number of endangered species, such as the Mona iguana and leatherback sea turtle. A number of seabirds, including red-footed boobies, also inhabit the island. Off its coast are reefs filled with 270 species of tropical fish, black coral, and purple seafans. There are plenty of places to explore, such as the 200-foot cliffs on the north side of the island or the abandoned lighthouse that once protected ships off the southern coast. Travelers must reach the island by boat—planes aren't permitted to land. Several tour operators in Joyuda and Boquerón, as well as companies in Mayagüez and Rincón, offer overnight camping trips to the island; they will help you with the camping permits from the Department of Natural and Environmental Resources. You need to reserve at least a few weeks ahead for an overnight stay. ☎ 787/722–1726 *Department of Natural and Environmental Resources.*

## WHERE TO EAT

$$ ✕ **El Bohío.** Watch seagulls dive for their food while you dine on a cov-
SEAFOOD ered deck extending out into the bay. The long list of seafood is prepared in a variety of ways: Shrimp comes breaded, stewed, or skewered;

conch is served as a salad or cooked in a butter-and-garlic sauce; and the lobster can be prepared just about any way you can imagine. This restaurant, on stilts above the water, is about the most charming setting in Joyuda. ⊠ *Rte. 102, Km 13.9* ☎ *787/851–2755* ⊕ *www. restauranteelbohiojoyuda.com* ⊙ *Closed Oct.*

$$    ✕**Raito's.** Specializing in croquette-encrusted seafood, this waterfront
SEAFOOD    fish house is reminiscent of the '70s with its linoleum speckled floors and clear vinyl tablecloths. Mozzarella tops most house favorites, including the baked lobster and snapper. For the seafood-weary, pork chops and filet mignon are on the menu, but be sure to leave room for the mango-, guava-, or coconut-flavored flan. Two inviting gazebos overlook the water, but sadly the view is somewhat obstructed by a chain-link fence. ⊠ *Carr. 102, Km 13.7, Joyuda* ☎ *787/851–4487* ⊙ *Closed Mon.*

$$    ✕**Tino's.** The colorful neon sign outside this restaurant touts its sig-
SEAFOOD    nature dish of mofongo as: "An earthenware goblet overflowing with
★    mashed plantains and seafood." It comes in two sizes, but the smaller one is usually enough to satisfy all but the biggest appetites. There are plenty of other seafood dishes on the menu, from red snapper in a spicy sauce to lobster with butter. Although most come here for the fish, the restaurant also serves beef, pork, and chicken. There's no ocean view, but the elegant dining makes up for it. ⊠ *Rte. 102, Km 13.6* ☎ *787/851– 2976* ⊙ *Closed Tues.*

$$    ✕**Tony's.** Serving locals since 1978, this authentic Puerto Rican fish
SEAFOOD    house specializes in lobster, shrimp, and red snapper. The menu features seven varieties of mofongo as well as steak, chicken, and pasta. Every wall is emblazoned with autographed images of Puerto Rican pop stars and politicians. Not for the cholesterol-challenged, this eatery fries nearly everything, including cheese, fish, and vegetables. Sit outside for an ocean view or stop by on Saturday for live music and karaoke. ⊠ *Carr. 102, Km 10.9* ☎ *787/851–2500* ⊕ *www.tonyspr.com* ⊙ *Closed Tues.and Wed.*

## WHERE TO STAY
*For expanded hotel reviews, visit Fodors.com.*

$    ▒**Parador Joyuda Beach.** Talk about truth in advertising: The beach in
HOTEL    question is so close to this place that the water laps against the seawall. **Pros:** Waterfront location; friendly staff; Wi-Fi in common areas. **Cons:** Motel-style rooms; no elevator; ugly plastic chairs in pool area, bar, and restaurant. ⊠ *Rte. 102, Km 11.7* ✉ *Box 18410, Joyuda 00623* ☎ *787/851–5650, 800/981–5464* ⊕ *www.joyudabeach.com* ⇆*41 rooms* ⚇ *In-room: a/c. In-hotel: restaurant, bar, pool, beach, parking* ▯◯▯ *Multiple meal plans.*

¢    ▒**Parador Perichi's.** Joyuda isn't packed with luxury accommodations,
HOTEL    but this comfortable hotel is the best in town. ⊠ *Carr 102, Km 14.3* ☎ *787/851–3131* ⊕ *www.hotelperichi.com* ⇆ *58* ⚇ *In-room: a/c, safe. In-hotel: restaurant, pool, parking* ▯◯▯ *No meals.*

## SPORTS AND THE OUTDOORS
DIVING AND    Several reef-bordered cays lie off the Cabo Rojo area near walls that
SNORKELING    drop to 100 feet. A mile-long reef along Las Coronas, better known as Cayo Ron, has a variety of hard and soft coral, reef fish, and lobsters.

**Tour Marine Adventures.** You can arrange snorkeling and scuba-diving trips with Captain Elick Hernández Garciá, who runs Tour Marine Adventures. Trips cost between $35 and $75 per person. He'll also arrange trips out to Mona Island for around $200 per person. ⊠ *Rte. 101, Km 14.1* ☎ *787/255–2525* ⊕ *www.tourmarinepr.com.*

GOLF **Club Deportivo del Oeste.** Get in 18 holes at the Club Deportivo del Oeste. Jack Bender incorporated the region's rolling hills in his design to provide golfers with panoramic views. The nicely tended course is open daily, as are the tennis courts on the same property. Greens fees are $50, and half price after 3 pm. ⊠ *Rte. 102, Km 15.1* ☎ *787/254–3748* ⊕ *www.clubdeportivodeloeste.com.*

# BOQUERÓN

*3 miles (5 km) south of Joyuda.*

Once a quiet fishing village, Boquerón still has its share of seaside shanties. Its narrow streets are quiet during the week but come alive on the weekend, when vendors appear with carts full of clams and oysters you can slurp down on the spot—wedges of lemon are provided, of course. Bars and restaurants throw open their doors—if they have any, that is. Many of the establishments here are open to the breeze, making this a Puerto Rican party spot where the music (and the people) can be heard until 2 in the morning. Boquerón is also a water-sports center; many companies operate from or near the docks of the imposing Club Náutico de Boquerón, which is easy to find at the end of Route 100.

**GETTING HERE AND AROUND**

To reach Boquerón from Mayagüez, head south on Highway 2 to Route 100 south. After bypassing Cabo Rojo, take Route 101 and follow the signs southwest to Boquerón. The small town can easily be explored on foot.

**EXPLORING**

**Refugio de Vida Silvestre de Boquerón** (*Boquerón Wildlife Refuge*). The Refugio de Vida Silvestre de Boquerón encompasses three tracts of land at the island's southern tip. The first is about 1 mile (2 km) south of Boquerón. There is a trail that leads through three different types of mangroves to picnic areas and a dock where you can launch a canoe or kayak. Note: Hunting is allowed in the reserve between November and January. ⊠ *Rte. 101, Km 1.1* ☎ *787/851–4795* ⊠ *Free* ☉ *Weekdays 7:30–4.*

**WHERE TO EAT AND STAY**

*For expanded hotel reviews, visit Fodors.com.*

$$ ✕ **Brasas Steak House.** Offering a refreshing alternative to seafood, this
STEAKHOUSE is Boquerón's most upscale eatery. It's also one of the island's few restaurants serving certified Angus beef, including T-bone, sirloin, and filet mignon. Equally notable are the grilled chicken, pork, and pastas. Set back from the main strip, this restaurant lacks an ocean view but is quieter and more intimate than others in the area. For a livelier vibe, check out its waterfront sister property, Brasas Beach Pub, just around the corner. ☉ *Closed Mon.–Tues.*

Locals flock to the pretty beaches of Boquerón on weekends.

**$$** ✕ **Galloway's.** From a covered deck overlooking Bahía Boquerón, you
SEAFOOD can catch the sunset while enjoying some seafood—caught fresh from
local waters, of course. Steak, ribs, chicken, and pasta are available, but
the red snapper and dorado—prepared breaded, sautéed, or grilled—
are by far the best options. There's a lively happy hour and occasional
live music. This place is along the main drag but is set back from the
street, so you don't have to be a part of the passing parade. One major
plus in this traffic-choked town: There's a large free parking lot. ⊠ *12
Calle José de Diego* ☎ *787/254–3302* ⊕ *www.gallowaysrestaurant.com*
⊗ *Closed Wed. and Oct.*

**$** ⊡ **Aquarius Beach Resort.** As Boquerón's largest property, this high-rise
RESORT resort offers one-, two-, and three-bedroom suites, each with a private
balcony. **Pros:** Family-friendly; calm beach; prime location. **Cons:** No
Internet in rooms; hotel is often full; blocked double parking. ⊠ *Carr.
101, Km 18* ☎ *787/254–5400* ⊕ *www.aquariusvacationclub.com* ⤳ *88
rooms* ⎘ *In-room: a/c, safe, kitchen. In-hotel: restaurant, bar, pool,
gym, beach, parking* ⦿ *No meals.*

**$** ⊡ **Cofresí Beach Hotel.** A favorite with families, this place puts you a few
HOTEL blocks from the hustle and bustle of Boquerón. **Pros:** Best value in the
area; family-friendly environment; walking distance to many restau-
rants. **Cons:** Not on the beach; some traffic noise; additional $15 daily
cleaning fee; no Wi-Fi. ⊠ *57 Calle Muñoz Rivera* ⌂ *Box 120900622*
☎ *787/254–3000* ⊕ *www.cofresibeach.com* ⤳ *12 apartments* ⎘ *In-
room: kitchen. In-hotel: pool, parking* ⦿ *No meals.*

**$** ⊡ **Parador Boquemar.** Even though it's a hike from Balneario Boquerón,
HOTEL families flock to this friendly parador on weekends. **Pros:** Near plenty
of dining and nightlife options; family-friendly environment; discount

packages available. **Cons:** Ugly building; rusty tins roofs undermine ocean view; can get very noisy. ⊠ *Calle Gill Buyé* ⌑ *Box 133, 00622* ☎ *787/851–2158* ⊕ *www.boquemar.com* ⇄ *75 rooms* ⚿ *In-room: safe, Wi-Fi. In-hotel: restaurant, bar, pool* ⦿ *No meals.*

## NIGHTLIFE

**Boquerón Bay.** A curvy bar distinguishes Boquerón Bay from its straight-forward neighbors. The open-air establishment has a second floor where you can catch a glimpse of the sunset, listen to live music, and sample some tapas. ⊠ *Calle Jose de Diego* ☎ *787/638–5459* ⊗ *Closed Mon.–Thurs.*

## SPORTS AND THE OUTDOORS

DIVING AND SNORKELING **Mona Aquatics.** Snorkeling and scuba-diving trips are the specialty at Mona Aquatics. Night dives are available as well. You'll find the crew in a wooden shack painted an eye-popping shade of blue next to the Club Nautico de Boquerón. The company has weekly trips to Mona Island. ⊠ *Calle Jose de Diego* ☎ *787/851–2185* ⊕ *www.monaaquatics.com.*

FISHING **Light Tackle Adventure.** You can arrange fishing trips with Captain Francisco "Pochy" Rosario, who runs Light Tackle Adventure. His specialty is tarpon, which are plentiful in these waters. ☎ *787/849–1430* ⊕ *www. lighttackleadventure.8k.com.*

# EL COMBATE

*2 miles (3 km) south of Boquerón.*

This is the end of the earth—or the end of the island, anyway. El Combate sits on the southwest corner of Puerto Rico, a bit removed from everything. The travel industry hasn't figured out how to market this place, so they've left it mostly to the locals, who have built small but elaborate weekend homes—some with grandiose touches like fountains—along the narrow streets. On the road closest to the beach, which for some reason is called Calle 3, is a cluster of seafood shacks. The more prosperous ones have added second stories.

If you're wondering about the town's odd name, which literally means "The Combat," it seems that long ago some unscrupulous characters were eyeing the salt flats just outside town. But they were repelled by machete-wielding villagers who were to live forever in local lore. Is it a true story? Residents of El Combate swear it is.

## GETTING HERE AND AROUND

To reach the coastal town of El Combate from the 101, take Route 301 south to km 7.8, where the road intersects with Route 3301. The five-minute drive west on Route 3301 ends at El Combate Beach, where a cluster of restaurants and hotels line the main strip, Calle 3. To reach Cabo Rojo Lighthouse and the salt flats, bypass Route 3301 and continue south on Route 301 until the road ends. This paved road soon turns into a bumpy one with potholes dotting the dusty course. The trek is well worth the effort, however, as jutting mangroves and crystal waters welcome travelers to Puerto Rico's southwestern tip.

It's a good idea to rent a four-wheel-drive vehicle from Mayagüez airport if you are heading to Cabo Rojo Lighthouse, as it is reached via a truly terrible dirt road.

## EXPLORING

★ **Cabo Rojo Lighthouse.** The area's most popular attraction is the neoclassical Cabo Rojo Lighthouse, dating from 1881. The magnificent structure is open to the public, and you are free to hike around the rugged terrain or relax on La Playuela or one of the other pink-sand beaches nearby. ■**TIP→** There are no facilities here, so bring water, food, and sunscreen. ⊠ *End of Rte. 301* ☎ *787/851–7260* 🖃 *Free* 🕘 *Wed.–Sun. 9:30–5.*

**Centro Interpretativo Las Salinas de Cabo Rojo** (*Cabo Rojo Salt Flats Interpretive Center*). The Centro Interpretativo Las Salinas de Cabo Rojo has two-hour guided tours along the nature trails and a small display about the salt flats. (Remember that the name of the town comes from a battle over control of the salt flats.) The best part of the center is a massive observation tower that lets you scan the outline of Cabo Rojo itself. Next to the main building is an audiovisual center where presentations on marine ecosystems and bird migration are offered. ⊠ *Rte. 301, Km 11* ☎ *787/851–2999* ⊕ *proambientepr.org* 🖃 *Center free, tours $3* 🕘 *Thurs.–Sat. 8:30–4:30, Sun. 9:30–5:30, tours at 9:30 and 1:30.*

**Refugio de Vida Silvestre de Cabo Rojo** (*Cabo Rojo Wildlife Refuge*). Home to six different ecosystems, the Refugio de Vida Silvestre de Cabo Rojo has an interpretive center with exhibits of live freshwater fish and sea turtles. You can see as many as 100 species of birds along the trails, even the elusive yellow-shouldered blackbird. The entrance is about 1 mile (2 km) north of the turnoff for El Combate. ⊠ *Rte. 301, Km 1.2* ☎ *787/851–7260* 🖃 *Free* 🕘 *Weekdays 8–4.*

## WHERE TO EAT AND STAY

*For expanded hotel reviews, visit Fodors.com.*

**$$**
PUERTO RICAN

✕ **Annie's.** A dining room facing the ocean is a fitting place to try some of the southwest coast's best seafood. You can snack on *empanadillas* (deep-fried fritters), then move on to red snapper with rice and beans or mofongo *relleno* (stuffed with seafood). This place, in an unmistakable lime-colored building on the main drag, has festive music and great views. ⊠ *Rte. 3301, Km 3.0, at Calle 3* ☎ *787/254–2553* ⊕ *www.anniesplacepr.com.*

**$$**
INTERNATIONAL

✕ **Xabores.** At Combate Beach Resort, this restaurant flaunts the most contemporary menu in town. Specializing in tapas, the family-owned eatery puts a new spin on Puerto Rican cuisine with steak medallions stuffed with plantains or mahimahi turnovers served with a spicy sauce. The starters are meals in themselves, but if you need something else to satisfy your appetite, try the chicken fajitas or mini *pizzetas* (personal pizzas) with a side salad or bowl of soup. For such a small establishment, there is a surprisingly large wine selection and outstanding cocktails. ⊠ *Carr. 3301, Km 2.7* ☎ *787/254–2358* ⊕ *www.combatebeachresort. com* 🕘 *Closed Mon.–Wed.*

**$$**
HOTEL
Fodor'sChoice
★

🏨 **Bahía Salinas Beach Hotel.** With the Cabo Rojo Lighthousein view, you can wander along the boardwalk or down the garden paths, bask in the sun on a deck or terrace, or relax in the infinity pool at this resort. **Pros:** Near interesting sites; good dining options; all-inclusive rate available.

**Cons:** Beach is extremely narrow; stray dogs roam property, sulfur odor from nearby salt flats. ✉ *End of Rte. 301* 🖃 *Box 2356, 00622* ☎ *787/254–1212* ⊕ *www.bahiasalinas.com* ➷ *30 rooms* ♿ *In-room: a/c, safe, Wi-Fi. In-hotel: restaurant, bar, pool, spa* ⑩ *Multiple meal plans.*

**$**  🏨 **Combate Beach Resort.** On a quiet side street near the beach, this
HOTEL nicely renovated little hotel is one of the best in the area. **Pros:** Good value; quiet neighborhood; recently remodeled. **Cons:** Isolated location; patios face the parking lot. ✉ *Rte. 3301, Km 2.7* 🖃 *Box 1138, 00622* ☎ *787/254–2358* ⊕ *www.combatebeachresort.com* ➷ *18 rooms* ♿ *In-room: a/c, kitchen, Wi-Fi. In-hotel: restaurant, bar, pool, spa, parking* ⑩ *Breakfast.*

**¢**  🏨 **Combate Guest House.** This simple property—across the street from
HOTEL El Combate Beach—is centrally located just off Calle 3. **Pros:** Centrally located; good value **Cons:** Noise from beach crowds; cash only; no Wi-Fi. ✉ *Rte. 3301 and Calle 2, across from Combate Beach* ☎ *787/254–0001* ⊕ *www.combateguesthouse.com* ➷ *19 rooms* ♿ *In-room: a/c, kitchen, no TV. In-hotel: beach* ▭ *No credit cards* ⑩ *No meals.*

### NIGHTLIFE

**12 Rounds.** Filling a nightlife void, this sports bar is the newest (and hippest) place in town. There are massive TVs and a drink menu that will knock you out. (Try the the locally famous *cocotini*.) A DJ spins music on Saturday until 1 am. If you're not in the mood for sports, you can simply relax on one of the glowing leather sofas. ✉ *Combate Beach Resort, Carr. 3301, Km 2.7* ☎ *787/254–2358* ⊕ *www. combatebeachresort.com* ☾ *Closed Mon.–Wed.*

# THE NORTHWESTERN COAST

North of Rincón there is a string of beaches that have yet to be discovered. You won't find much large-scale development along this stretch of shoreline, other than the new Royal Isabela Golf Club and Resort. Instead, the area is populated with modest hotels that cater to local families. Many surfers say the waves here are better than those in Rincón itself.

## AGUADILLA

*12 miles (18 mi) north of Rincón.*

Resembling a fishing village, downtown Aguadilla has narrow streets lined with small wooden homes. Weathered but lovely, the faded facades recall the city's long and turbulent past. Officially incorporated as a town in 1775, Aguadilla subsequently suffered a series of catastrophes, including a devastating earthquake in 1918 and strong hurricanes in 1928 and 1932. Determined to survive, the town rebuilt after each disaster, and by World War II it had become known for the sprawling Ramey Air Force Base. The base was an important link in the U.S. defense system throughout the Cold War. Ramey was decommissioned in 1973; today the former base has an airport, a golf course, a university, and some small businesses. As a result of tourism, the north end of town is budding with international restaurants, surf shops, and even an outdoor mall. Additions such as a children's water park and ice-skating rink make Aguadilla a family-friendly destination, too.

Perhaps the town's greatest draw is its surfing at local spots like Wilderness Beach, Table Tops, Playa Crash Boat, and Gas Chamber. Famous for their right-hand barrels, these beaches have hosted a variety of amateur and professional surfing events, including the 1968 and 1988 ISA World Championships and the 2010 ASP World Tour.

### GETTING HERE AND AROUND

Most people arrive in Aguadilla either by car from San Juan or by flying directly into Aguadilla's Aeropuerto Internacional Rafael Hernández. Continental Airlines offers daily flights from Newark to Aguadilla, and JetBlue has service from Orlando or New York. Rental cars ($35–$65 per day) are available from companies operating out of the Aguadilla airport, located at the old Ramey Air Force Base. To reach Aguadilla by car from San Juan, head west on toll road Highway 22, which turns into Highway 2. Continue on Highway 2 until it intersects with Route 111, leading to the center of town.

**Airport Information Aeropuerto Internacional Rafael Hernández** ⊠ *Hanger Rd., reached via Rte. 110 or Rte. 107* ☎ *787/890–6075.*

**Car Rental Avis** ⊠ *Aeropuerto Internacional Rafael Hernández, Hanger Rd.* ☎ *787/890–3311.* **Enterprise** ⊠ *Aeropuerto Internacional Rafael Hernández, Hanger Rd.* ☎ *787/890–3732.* **Hertz** ⊠ *Aeropuerto Internacional Rafael Hernández, Hanger Rd.* ☎ *787/890–5650.* **L & M Rent a Car** ⊠ *Aeropuerto Internacional Rafael Hernández, Hanger Rd.* ☎ *787/890–3010* ⊕ *www.alliedcarrentalpr.com.*

### EXPLORING

**Aguadilla Ice Skating Arena.** As you might imagine, this is the only ice-skating complex in the Caribbean. ⊠ *Rte. 442, Km 4.2, Aguadilla Centro* ☎ *787/819–5555* ⊕ *www.miaguadilla.com* ☎ *$10* ⊘ *Daily 10 am–11 pm.*

**La Ponderosa.** Along Route 107—an unmarked road crossing through Punta Borinquen Golf Club—you'll find the ruins of La Ponderosa, an old Spanish lighthouse, as well as its replacement Punta Borinquen at Puerto Rico's northwest point. The original was built in 1889 and destroyed by an earthquake in 1918. The U.S. Coast Guard rebuilt the structure in 1920. Just beyond the ruins is a local surf spot, Playa Wilderness. ⊠ *Rte. 107.*

**Museo de Arte de Aguadilla.** Built in 1925, the building that houses this small museum was listed on the National Register of Historic Places in 1985. Inside, you will find a collection of oil paintings by local artists. ⊠ *Calle Betances, between Calle San Carlos and Calle Corchado* ☎ *787/882–4336* ⊕ *www.museodeartedeaguadilla.com.*

**Parque Acuático las Cascadas.** Parque Acuático las Cascadas has a large wave pool, giant slides, and the "Crazy River," a long, free-flowing river pool. It's strictly kid stuff. ⊠ *Hwy. 2, Km 126.5* ☎ *787/819–1030* ⊘ *Mar.–Aug., weekdays 10–5, weekends 10–6.*

## WHERE TO EAT

¢  ✕ **Cocina Creativa.** At first glance, you might mistake this place for a
ECLECTIC  vegetarian restaurant with its organic greens, homemade hummus, and
fresh breads. In fact, the menu includes such meat dishes as chicken lemongrass lollipops, jerk chicken with mango chutney, and churrasco with
caramelized onions. The chalkboard-inscribed menu changes weekly
but always features the in-house flan, torte, and cheesecake. With a
Bohemian ambience, this is the type of place you could hang out for
a while to enjoy the outdoor patio, local artwork, and free Internet—
while savoring one of their fruit smoothies or specialty coffees. ⊠ *Carr.
110, Km 9.2, Aguadilla* ☎ *787/890–1861.*

¢  ✕ **D'Rose Chocolate Factory.** This truffle treasure camouflaged in a non-
CAFÉ  descript strip mall is acclaimed for having the "best coffee in Puerto
Rico." The owner, Jose Rivera, refuses to disclose the secret source of
his specialty beans or the technique that produces his mysterious blend.
The aroma of chocolate entices passersby into the sweet shop with its
candy-striped pink walls and chocolate-toned tables. Rotating glass
towers display rich cakes and pastries, while endless rows of candy jars
further tempt the palate. Chocolate-covered strawberries and gourmet
truffles are all made in-house and are served by adorable grandmothers in their Little Miss Muffet–like uniforms topped with lace bonnets.
⊠ *Carr. 107, Km 2.1* ☎ *787/891–0552.*

$  ✕ **One Ten Thai.** This restaurant, which started with the owner's experi-
THAI  ments at home with Thai cuisine, has blossomed into Aguadilla's most
popular eatery. The menu includes lettuce wraps, curry bowls, and pad
Thai noodles with tofu, beef, chicken, or shrimp. The owner's passion
for cooking ultimately took him around the world, resulting in such signature dishes as lime-peanut stir-fry with cilantro and chili sauce served
over your choice of meat. Despite the restaurant's name, the cuisine is
Pan-Asian, utilizing authentic flavors and ingredients. Most herbs and
vegetables are grown on-site or are supplied by local organic farmers.
A next-door microbrew-bar has the largest beer selection in Porta del
Sol. The bar usually has live music on weekends. Seating is limited, so
expect to wait awhile. ⊠ *Rte. 110, Km 9.2* ☎ *787/890–0113* ☉ *Closed
Mon. and Tues. No lunch.*

## WHERE TO STAY

*For expanded hotel reviews, visit Fodors.com.*

$$  ⛺ **Courtyard Marriott.** This former military hospital has been trans-
HOTEL  formed into a hotel attracting both business executives and vacationing families. **Pros:** Near airport; nice pool area **Cons:** Airplane noise
pollution; no beach; Wi-Fi in lobby only. ⊠ *West Parade, off Cliff Rd.*
☎ *787/658–8000* ⊕ *www.marriott.com/bqncy* ⇲ *146 rooms, 4 suites*
⛄ *In-room: safe, Internet. In-hotel: restaurant, bar, pool, gym, parking*
⛶ *No meals.*

$  ⛺ **El Faro Parador.** This family-friendly hotel isn't very close to the light-
HOTEL  house from which it takes its name, but it's a good place to keep in
☉  mind if you're driving along the coast and need a place to stop for
the night. **Pros:** Reasonable rates; pretty pool areas, children's playground. **Cons:** No beach; rather secluded location. ⊠ *Rte. 107, Km
2.1* ☎ *787/882–8000* ⊕ *www.farohotels.net* ⇲ *69 rooms* ⛄ *In-room:*

*a/c. In-hotel: restaurant, pool, tennis court, laundry facilities, parking* ⦿ *No meals.*

$ **El Pedregal.** In what looks like a tropical forest, El Pedregal is a great
HOTEL place to stay on the island's northwestern tip. **Pros:** Family-friendly
environment; game area, kids under 12 stay free. **Cons:** Noise from
nearby housing development; not on beach; isolated location. ⊠ *Rte.
111, Km. 0.1, Cuesta Nueva* ☎787/891–6068 ⊕ *www.elpedregalpr.
com* ⤳*29 rooms, 3 villas* ⚭ *In-room: Wi-Fi. In-hotel: restaurant, bar,
pool, gym, laundry facilities* ⦿ *No meals.*

$ **Hotel Cielo Mar.** Just north of Aguadilla, this massive hotel is perched
HOTEL on a bluff high above the water. **Pros:** Reasonable rates; great views.
**Cons:** No beach; far from other dining options; no elevator. ⊠ *84 Av.
Montemar, off Rte. 111* ☎787/882–5959, 787/882–5961 ⊕ *www.
cielomar.com* ⤳*72 rooms* ⚭ *In-room: a/c, Internet. In-hotel: restau-
rant, bar, pool, parking* ⦿ *No meals.*

¢ **JB Hidden Village.** This family-friendly hotel is in Aguada, about half-
HOTEL way between Aguadilla and Rincón. **Pros:** Close to several beaches;
good base for exploring the area. **Cons:** No beach; bland architecture; difficult to locate. ⊠ *Rte. 4416, Km 9.5, after 416 split, Aguada*
☎787/868–8686 📠787/868–8701 ⤳*42 rooms* ⚭ *In-room: a/c. In-
hotel: restaurant, bar, pool, parking* ⦿ *No meals.*

## SPORTS AND THE OUTDOORS

DIVING AND **Aquatica.** Near Gate 5 of the old Ramey Air Force Base, Aquatica
SNORKELING offers scuba-diving certification courses, as well as snorkeling, paddle
boarding, and surfing trips. There's a great selection of surfboards and
paddleboards for rent. For a memorable adventure, try the two-hour
paddleboard tour down the Rio Guajataca. Along the peaceful river,
you'll visit an old train tunnel from 1906. Aquatica also rents bikes.
⊠ *Rte. 110, Km 10* ☎787/890–6071 ⊕ *www.aquaticadive-surf.com.*

GOLF **Punta Borinquen Golf Club.** The 18-hole Punta Borinquen Golf Club, on
the former Ramey Air Force Base, was a favorite of President Dwight
D. Eisenhower's. Now a public course, the beachfront course is known
for its tough sand traps and strong crosswinds. It is open daily. ⊠ *Rte.
107, Km 2* ☎787/890–2987 ⊕ *www.puntaborinquengolf.com.*

SURFING **Wave Riding Vehicles.** Surfboard rentals ($20 for 4 hrs) and one-hour
surfing lessons ($35) are offered through Wave Riding Vehicles, a surf
shop and board factory. They also rent paddleboards and bodyboards.
⊠ *Carr. 4466, Jobos Beach, next to Happy Belly's Restaurant, Isabela*
☎787/669–3840 ⊕ *www.waveridingvehicles.com* ⊙ *Mon.–Fri. 10–6;
Sat & Sun 9–6.*

# ISABELA

*13 miles (20 km) east of Aguadilla.*

Founded in 1819 and named for Spain's Queen Isabella, this small,
whitewashed town on the northwestern tip of the island skirts tall
cliffs that overlook the rocky shoreline. Locals have long known of the
area's natural beauty, and lately more offshore tourists have begun coming to this niche, which offers secluded hotels, sprawling golf courses,

fantastic beaches, excellent surf, and, just inland, hiking through one of the island's forest reserves.

**GETTING HERE AND AROUND**

Flying into Aguadilla's airport (BQN) is the fastest way to reach Isabela and will eliminate the two-hour drive from San Juan. Direct flights to Aguadilla from Newark are available through Continental Airlines, and from Orlando or New York through JetBlue. Several rental-car companies are on-site at Aguadilla's Aeropuerto Internacional Rafael Hernández, only 15 minutes from Isabela. If you are driving to the town of Isabella from San Juan, take Highway 2 west to Route 112 north. The 1120 will intersect with Route 4466, Isabella's coastal road.

**Airport Information Aeropuerto Internacional Rafael Hernández** ⊠ *Hwy. 2, Km 148.7, Aguadilla* 🕾 *787/891–2286, 787/890–6075.*

**Car Rental Avis** ⊠ *Rafael Hernández Airport, Aguadilla* 🕾 *787/890–3311* ⊕ *www.avis.com.* **Budget** ⊠ *Rafael Hernández Airport, Aguadilla* 🕾 *787/890– 1110.* **Hertz** ⊠ *Rafael Hernández Airport, Aguadilla* 🕾 *787/890–5650.*

**EXPLORING**

**Bosque Estatal Guajataca** (*Guajataca State Forest*). Explore karst topography and subtropical vegetation at the 2,357-acre Bosque Estatal Guajataca between the towns of Quebradillas and Isabela. On more than 46 walking trails you can see 186 species of trees, including the royal palm and ironwood, and 45 species of birds—watch for red-tailed hawks and Puerto Rican woodpeckers. Bring a flashlight and descend into the **Cueva del Viento** (Cave of the Wind) to find stalagmites, stalactites, and other strange formations. At the entrance to the forest there's a small ranger station where you can pick up a decent hiking map. (Get here early, as the rangers don't always stay until the official closing time.) A little farther down the road is a recreational area with picnic tables and an observation tower. ⊠ *Rte. 446, Km 10* 🕾 *787/872–1045* 🎟 *Free* ⊙ *Ranger station weekdays 8–5.*

**OFF THE BEATEN PATH**

**Palacete Los Moreau.** In the fields south of Isabela toward the town of Moca, a French family settled on a coffee and sugar plantation in the 1800s. The grand two-story house, trimmed with gables, columns, and stained-glass windows, was immortalized in the novel *La Llamarada*, written in 1935 by Puerto Rican novelist Enrique A. Laguerre. In Laguerre's novel about conditions in the sugarcane industry, the house belonged to his fictional family, the Moreaus. Although it doesn't have many furnishings, you can walk through the house and also visit Laguerre's personal library in the mansion's basement. On the grounds is an old steam engine once used to transport sugarcane. ⊠ *Rte. 2, Km 115.9* 🕾 *787/830–4475* 🎟 *Free* ⊙ *Wed.–Sun. 9–5.*

**WHERE TO EAT**

$$
CARIBBEAN

✕ **Ocean Front Restaurant.** True to its name, this seaside restaurant overlooks Playa Jobos, the area's most popular surf break. Outdoor seating is appropriately decorated with surfboards hanging from the rafters and a boat-shaped bar in the center of the rough-hewn patio. To take a break from the salty air, step into the air-conditioned comfort of the more formal dining area. Whatever your appetite, you'll find something to please your palate with a menu offering everything from tropical ceviche and salmon wraps to garlic mahimahi and Porterhouse steaks. Drop by on the weekend to enjoy live music on an outdoor stage. ✉ *Playa Jobos, Rte. 4466, Km 0.1* ☎ *787/872–3339* ⊕ *www.oceanfrontpr.com* ⊗ *Closed Mon.–Tues.*

¢ ✕ **Ola Lola's.** Boasting "the friendliest wave on the island," the owners
BISTRO have maximized their private residence by converting their garage into overflow seating for this garden bistro. With fairy lights, beach chairs, and Latin music, the no-frills setting complements the simple menu of burgers, sandwiches, and signature dips. Flavorful creations include chipotle chicken, the peanut-butter burger (just try it!), and for dessert, the grilled banana split. Owners John and Elaine Cosby refuse to reveal the secret of their rum punch recipe, which draws in a large clientele. The "Piña Lo-Lada" is the smoothest you'll ever taste. For an interesting keepsake, buy one of the souvenir T-shirts from each of the island's top surf spots. ✉ *Playa Shacks, Rte. 4466, Km 2.1* ☎ *787/872–1230* ⊕ *www.ola-lolas.com* ▭ *No credit cards* ⊗ *Closed Tues.–Thurs.*

$$ ✕ **Olas y Arena.** This restaurant, whose name means "Waves and Sand,"
PUERTO RICAN is the best place to admire both while you're enjoying traditional Puerto Rican cuisine. Grab a seat on the open-air terrace where live fish serve as the table centerpiece. After a glass of sangria, start with fried cheese dribbled with guava sauce before indulging in the plentiful mofongo stuffed with chicken, steak, octopus, shrimp, or seafood. The paella for two is a good option, as is the fresh fish served with plantains and rice and beans. Some of the dishes tend to be heavy on the salt, so tell the chef if you prefer otherwise. Bring insect spray, since mosquitoes can be a nuisance. ✉ *Villas del Mar Hau, Carr. 466, Km. 8.3* ☎ *787/830–8315.*

## WHERE TO STAY
*For expanded hotel reviews, visit Fodors.com.*

$ 🏨 **Pelican Reef.** Although in need of a facelift, this place is great for bud-
HOTEL get travelers. **Pros:** Great location; good value. **Cons:** Some traffic noise; musty smell in a few of the units. ✉ *Rte. 4466, Km 0* ☎ *347/804–7505* ⊕ *www.pelicanreefapartments.com* ➪ *14 apartments* ⌂ *In-room: a/c, kitchen, Wi-Fi. In-hotel: beach* ¶○¶ *No meals.*

$$$$ 🏨 **Royal Isabela.** The island's newest luxury property, this 2,200-acre
RESORT paradise is a must for anyone remotely interested in golf. **Pros:** best golf course in Puerto Rico; chefs use organic foods; great views. **Cons:** casitas are pricey; 15 minutes from other dining options. ✉ *396 Av. Noel Estrada* ☎ *949/940–4150* ⊕ *www.royalisabela.com* ➪ *20* ⌂ *In-room: a/c, safe, Wi-Fi. In-hotel: restaurant, bar, golf course, pool, tennis court, gym, beach, parking* ¶○¶ *No meals.*

$$$ 🏨 **Villa Montaña.** This secluded cluster of villas, situated on a deserted
RESORT stretch of beach between Isabela and Aguadilla, feels like a little town.
Fodor's Choice **Pros:** Bikes and playground for children; on a secluded beach; great
★ food. **Cons:** A bit pricey; far from other dining options; airplane noise. ✉ *Rte. 4466, Km 1.9* ☎ *787/872–9554, 888/780–9195* ⊕ *www.villamontana.com* ➪ *38 rooms, 41 villas* ⌂ *In-room: a/c, safe, kitchen, Wi-Fi. In-hotel: restaurant, pool, tennis court, gym, beach, water sports, laundry facilities, parking* ¶○¶ *No meals.*

6

$$ ☒ **Villas del Mar Hau.** One-, two-, and three-bedroom cottages—painted
HOTEL  in cheery pastels and trimmed with gingerbread—are the heart of this
beachfront hotel. **Pros:** Laid-back vibe; protected swimming cove great
for children; good restaurant. **Cons:** Very basic rooms; may be too
kitschy for some, 5 pm check-in. ☒ *Rte. 466, Km 8.3* ☎ *787/872–2045*
⊕ *www.hauhotelvillas.com* ↩ *46 cottages* ⚒ *In-room: a/c, kitchen,
Wi-Fi. In-hotel: restaurant, bar, pool, tennis court, beach, water sports,
laundry facilities, parking, some age restrictions* ⎮○⎮ *No meals.*

## SPORTS AND THE OUTDOORS

HORSEBACK **Tropical Trail Rides.** Tropical Trail Rides has two-hour morning and
RIDING  afternoon rides (9 and 3:30) along the beach and through a forest
of almond trees. Groups leave from Playa Shacks, one of the region's
prettiest beaches. At the end you have a chance to take a dip in the
ocean. The company also offers hiking trips to the limestone caves
at Survival Beach. ☒ *Rte. 4466, Km 1.9* ☎ *787/872–9256* ⊕ *www.
tropicaltrailrides.com.*

DIVING AND  **La Cueva Submarina Dive Shop.** Beginning and advanced divers can
SNORKELING  explore the submerged caves off Playa Shacks through La Cueva Sub-
marina Dive Shop, which also offers certification courses and snorkeling
trips. ☒ *Rte. 466, Km 6.3* ☎ *787/872–1390.*

SURFING  **Hang Loose Surf Shop.** For surf lessons, Hang Loose Surf Shop offers a
two-hour basic course and has board rentals. Lessons are usually held
at Playa Jobos, a great surfing spot where you can reward yourself with
a refreshing drink from one of the beach shacks. ☒ *Rte. 446, Km 1.2*
☎ *787/872–2490* ⊕ *www.hangloosesurfshop.com* ☉ *Tues.–Sun. 10–5.*

**Wave Riding Vehicles.** Surfboard rentals ($20) and one-hour surfing les-
sons ($35) are offered through Wave Riding Vehicles, a surf shop and
board factory. They also rent paddleboards and bodyboards. ☒ *Jobos
Beach, Rte. 4466, next to Happy Belly's* ☎ *787/669–3840* ⊕ *www.
waveridingvehicles.com.*

# Ruta Panorámica

## AN EXHILARATING DRIVE ON THE PANORAMIC ROUTE

### WORD OF MOUTH

"The Ruta Panorámica is a drive through the Cordillera Central. The interior mountainous area is my favorite part of Puerto Rico, even more than the beaches. It's generally about 5–10 degrees cooler and so lush. It's where you really here the coquis, at night, too."

— nirosa

The Ruta Panorámica, or Panoramic Route, is an unforgettable overland journey that reveals rugged beauty and tranquil woodlands not found anywhere else on the island. It's an unruly road that clambers its way through the forests of Puerto Rico's mountainous interior. Towering trees create canopies over the narrow roads, and in their shade pink and purple impatiens bloom in profusion. You'll drive through sleepy colonial villages named for their Taíno ancestors, discover trails leading to secret waterfalls, and behold one breathtaking vista after another.

7

The grandiose name may lead you to think that the Ruta Panorámica is a highway, but it's actually a network of mountain roads that snakes through the central region, or Cordillera Central. Some are nicely maintained, others are little more than gravel. But the Panoramic Route certainly lives up to its name, rewarding travelers with sprawling scenery around every bend of the road.

## DRIVING THE HIDDEN HEART OF PUERTO RICO

You can explore the Ruta Panorámica in chunks, alternating rural and urban charms. Or you can plan an extended road trip, taking time to fully explore Puerto Rico's interior. Bring your sense of adventure, and on your journey perhaps you'll try *lechon asado*, mouthwatering pork, slow-roasted over open pits. Did we mention that these are whole pigs? You may decide to cool off with a cup of cold maví, a local drink made of fermented tree bark. The beaches and the city recede from memory here, and you begin to adopt new, unhurried rhythms, allowing serendipity to be your guide. Tropical flora, like birds of paradise, beg to be photographed. On foggy stretches of road, umbrella-sized *yagrumo* leaves laden with water brush the roof of your car. Puerto Rico's highest mountain is tucked into the Toro Negro Forest, and lookout points afford views all the way to the ocean.

## THREE JOURNEYS

We've divided the Ruta into three discrete trips, each requiring a full day. Trip 1 takes you from Yabucoa to Aibonito; Trip 2, from Aibonito to Adjuntas; and Trip 3, from Adjuntas to Mayagüez. Put them together for the complete journey, which you can start from the east or the west (Yabucoa or San Juan for eastbound journey; Mayagüez for a west coast departure).

### RUTA PANORÁMICA DRIVING TIPS

**Rent from a nationally recognized rental car agency.** Should you break down on the Ruta or need a tire change, the national chains are more able than local agencies to dispatch assistance or provide a replacement vehicle. Ensure your rental has a spare tire and a jack and have the roadside assistance number handy in the event that you need it.

**Fuel up at each opportunity.** There are few gas stations on the Ruta; don't get down to a quarter tank before you fill up.

**Avoid driving after dark.** The Ruta isn't lit and driving after dark can be dangerous. Occasional patches of washed-out road aren't uncommon, and they're sometimes impossible to see at night. Also, there are few, if any, food or gas services available once the sun goes down.

**Pack drinks and snacks.** Because services are limited along most of the route, your options may be limited when hunger strikes. Bring your own drinks and snacks in case you can't wait for the roadside stands, where men sell just-picked fruits and vegetables from the backs of their trucks. These make a great snack option; just be sure to wash all produce thoroughly.

**Invest in a good map.** Most hotels have free maps, courtesy of the tourism board; these are highly detailed maps worth picking up. If they don't have one, invest in a good one. Although it may not include all the numbered roads that make up the Ruta, it's better than nothing.

San Cristóbal Canyon near Aibonito

# YABUCOA TO AIBONITO

To start exploring the Ruta Panorámica from San Juan, make your way south to the town of Yabucoa, picking up Route 901 Oeste (901 West). Don't be discouraged by all the traffic lights, fast-food outlets, pharmacies, and shops you'll first encounter (in fact, you may want to stock up on supplies here). The road will soon give way to the com-

**THE PLAN**

Distance: 48 miles (77 km)

Time: Six hours

Breaks: Roadside fruit stands and roadside restaurants such as El Tenedor Dorado

parative isolation that characterizes the rest of the Ruta. ■TIP→ Gas up at the Gulf station less than a mile into Yabucoa at the start of the Ruta; it's the last service station for a while.

The landscape from Yabucoa to Aibonito is stunning in its variety. From trees typical of the tropics—mango, almonds, palms, and the lush, leafy tree fern—to cedar and bamboo, this stretch offers a preview of the Ruta's diversity.

Don't let your eyes get too carried away by the scenery, though. The Ruta is notorious for its poor signage. Though brown and white "Ruta Panorámica" signs are more plentiful on this stretch of the road, they're easy to miss, often covered over by plants or obscured by filmy drippings from the flora. If you're in doubt about your direction, don't hesitate to stop and ask a local. Even if you have road numbers and detailed directions, the Ruta's twists and turns can be puzzling, but going off course and getting back again is all part of the adventure!

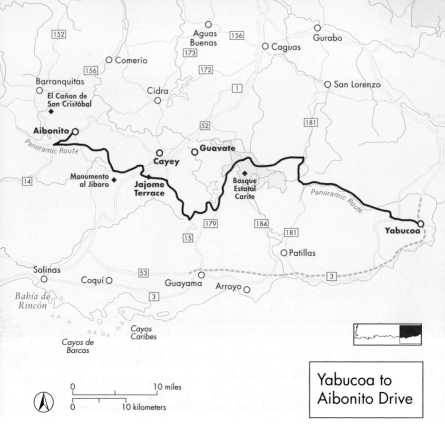

Aguas
Buenas

Gurabo

Caguas

Comerío

173

Barranquitas

156

172

San Lorenzo

El Cañon de
San Cristóbal

Cidra

1

181

52

Aibonito

Guavate

Panoramic Route

Cayey

14

Monumento
al Jíbaro

Jajome
Terrace

Bosque
Estatal
Carite

Panoramic Route

Yabucoa

179

184

181

15

Patillas

Salinas

53

Coquí

Guayama

Arroyo

3

Bahía de
Rincón

3

Cayos
Caribes

Cayos de
Barcas

**Yabucoa to
Aibonito Drive**

0                    10 miles

0                    10 kilometers

Once you're out of Yabucoa proper, there's little more than the flora to capture your attention—that and the road itself—until you reach Aibonito. Legend has it that Aibonito got its name when a Spaniard exclaimed *"¡Ay, que bonito!"* ("Oh, how pretty!") upon seeing the valley where the town now stands. Puerto Rico's highest city, Aibonito is known as the "Queen of Flowers" because flowering plants thrive in its temperate climate. The city hosts a flower festival every year, usually in late June or July, and gives awards for blossoms and garden design. Live music and craft stalls add to the festivities. A double-steepled cathedral graces the charming town square, which is surrounded by shops and restaurants. Local guides organize outings to nearby Cañón de San Cristóbal.

ROAD WATCH   This stretch of the Ruta is demanding of the driver; with no shoulder for most of the way, there's little, if any, opportunity to stop for a rest or pull over to take photos. Be patient; if you tack on trips 2 and 3, you'll find plenty of places to satisfy both needs.

## WHERE TO EAT AND STAY

*For expanded hotel reviews, visit Fodors.com.*

$$   ✕ **El Toro de Piedra.** Near the Mirador Piedra Degetau, this hilltop restau-
PUERTO RICAN   rant has a stunning panoramic view of Aibonito. At night you can see the lights of the city through the floor-to-ceiling windows, and dinner guests frequently remark how romantic it is. Servings of the *comida*

*criolla* (homestyle Puerto Rican food) are generous. Try one of the *mofongos rellenos* (mashed plantains, stuffed with your choice of meat, chicken, or seafood), or a churrasco steak, served with fried plantains on the side. ⊠ *Rte. 7718, Km 0.8, Aibonito* ☎ *787/735–1034* ⊘ *Closed Mon. and Tues. No dinner Mon.–Wed.*

**$$** ⚜ **Jajome Terrace.** This is the only lodging in Cayey, and it nestles itself
HOTEL cozily into its mountain surroundings. Rooms are basic but clean; there are no TVs or phones, but Wi-Fi is available. Be advised that the hotel no longer has a restaurant, though it does offer a continental breakfast daily. ⊠ *Carr. 15, Km 18.6, Cayey* ☎ *787/738–4016* ⊕ *www.jajometerrace.com* ⇴ *10 rooms* ⦿ *Breakfast.*

# AIBONITO TO ADJUNTAS

Quite possibly the prettiest part of the Ruta Panorámica, the section running from Aibonito to Adjuntas takes you through Puerto Rico's mountain region and the Toro Negro Forest. The views from Aibonito to the midway point of this route open up onto sweeping panoramas of valleys; from the vantage point of your high elevation, the houses below look like tiny dots.

Be sure to stop at the **Mirador Villalba-Orocovis** at Km 39.7 for some of the most spectacular views. This state-run overlook has ample parking and is open from 9 am until

> ### THE PLAN
>
> **Distance:** 46 miles (74 km) direct from Aibonito to Adjuntas; approximately 19 miles (30 km) for side trip south to Ponce
>
> **Time:** One day without side visit to Hacienda Buena Vista and Ponce; two days for full itinerary
>
> **Breaks:** Mirador Villalba-Orocovis, Doña Juana Recreational Area of the Toro Negro Forest, Hacienda Buena Vista

5 pm, Wednesday to Sunday. In addition to the view, there's a playground and sheltered picnic areas. Don't worry if your visit doesn't coincide with the overlook's hours; there's plenty of room to pull over on the side of the road and you can still enjoy the view, surrounded by mountains on either side. It tends to be windy up here at 2,000 feet, so bring an extra layer.

After the Mirador, the next stop is the **Toro Negro Forest.** Climbing to an elevation of more than 4,000 feet, the forest has the distinction of being home to the highest point in Puerto Rico, Cerro de Punta, which tops out at 4,390 feet. Outdoor enthusiasts should stop by the ranger station at Km 32.4 to inquire about trails, request maps, or obtain camping permits. For those who enjoy their scenery within easy reach, pull over at the **Area Recreativa Doña Juana** (the Doña Juana Recreational Area). Just a short walk across from the parking area is a natural pool; feel free to dip your feet in!

From the forest, you can drive through to Adjuntas, picking up either Route 10 South or Route 123 South. Both will lead you to Ponce, Puerto Rico's second largest city, after San Juan, but 10 is faster and less scenic. It's also newer and somewhat less treacherous than 123.

If time allows, don't miss **Hacienda Buena Vista,** one of the historic sites operated by the Fideicomiso de Conservación de Puerto Rico (the

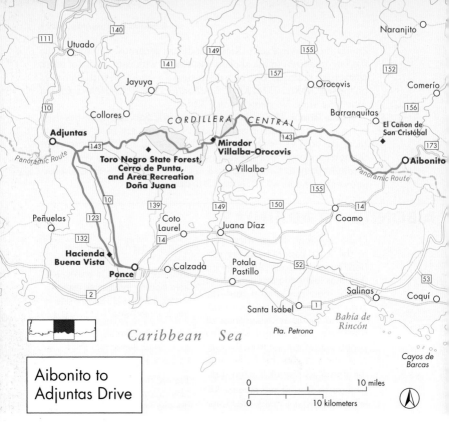

Aibonito to
Adjuntas Drive

Conservation Trust of Puerto Rico). This 79-acre property was once one of the island's most important agricultural hubs; today the Fideicomiso maintains the restored hacienda and invites you to explore coffee and cacao production on tours with knowledgeable guides. You'll need to make reservations to visit. Be sure to ask if any special activities—such as the cacao or coffee harvests—coincide with the dates of your visit. Four general tours are offered each day: 8:30 am, 10:30 am, 1:30 pm, and 3:30 pm. Guides also offer a four-hour "long trail" tour Friday to Saturday and two, two-hour short-trail tours Wednesday to Sunday.

From Buena Vista, it's just a 20-minute drive to Ponce. Start your visit at the **Plaza de las Delicias** (Plaza of Delights), Ponce's main square. Here you'll see a historic firehouse, a church, and decorative fountains, all rich with history. Guides and brochures are available at the firehouse. Along the side streets radiating from the square you'll notice Ponce's distinctive architecture, quite different from that of San Juan. If you extend your visit another day, visit the town's cemetery, where many of the island's prominent politicians are buried in elaborate mausoleums. Alternatively, you can scale the hillside for a tour of **Castillo Serrallés**, the former home of the Serralles family, Puerto Rico's rum barons, and the Cruceta La Vigía, a cross-shaped observatory that provides views straight to the Caribbean Sea.

Hiking the Toro Negro Forest

## WHERE TO EAT AND STAY

*For expanded hotel reviews, visit Fodors.com.*

You won't find much food along this stretch of the Ruta, so it's best to time your meal around your arrival in Ponce, where dining options are abundant. Unless you plan to camp in the Toro Negro Forest (and if you do, you'll need a permit), you'll have to detour off this section of the Ruta Panorámica to find a place to rest. Ponce offers many places to stay. *For a complete list of our recommended hotels and restaurants in Ponce, see Where to Eat and Where to Stay sections in chapter 5.*

Take Route 10 North out of Adjuntas to get to Utuado.

**$** ✕**Casa Grande.** From the café tables on Casa Grande's towering balcony PUERTO RICAN or deck, you feel as if you've been painted into the landscape. Lunch is served only on weekends, though you can request sandwiches in advance during the week. Dinner consists of typical Puerto Rican dishes, though vegetarians will be pleased to learn that Casa Grande offers viable alternatives to the meat-heavy local diet. Unless you're arriving for breakfast or dinner, you'll need reservations for lunch. ⊠ *Rte. 612, Km 0.3, Utuado* ☎ *787/894–3939* ⊕ *www.hotelcasagrande.com.*

**$$** ⌂**Casa Grande Mountain Retreat.** Here you'll come as close as you can HOTEL to sleeping in a tree house. **Pros:** unspoiled setting with spectacular Fodor's Choice views; accessible for people with disabilities; outdoor activities. **Cons:** ★ no air-conditioning; long drive to other sights/restaurants. ⊠ *Rte. 612, Km 0.3, Utuado* ⌂ *P.O. Box 1499, Utuado 00641* ☎ *787/894–3939* ⊕ *www.hotelcasagrande.com* ⌁ *20 rooms* ⌂ *In-room: no a/c, no TV. In-hotel: restaurant, pool* ⓘ⦿*No meals.*

Tram to Cueva Clara, the cave network of Río Camuy Cave Park

## ADJUNTAS TO MAYAGÜEZ

This is a journey through unspoiled nature. There are few places or reasons to stop from the starting point to the stopping point, but one exception is the **Torre de Piedra** (Stone Tower), an observation tower in Maricao with breathtaking views. On a clear day you can see almost the entire western coast of the island from this vantage point.

**THE PLAN**

**Distance:** 69 miles (111 km)

**Time:** Eight hours without side visits to Camuy Caverns; two days for full itinerary

**Breaks:** Torre de Piedra, Camuy Caverns

⚠ This section of the Ruta is perhaps the most treacherous—the road from Adjuntas to Maricao is in bad shape, pocked with potholes and the occasional sinkhole that's eaten away part of the road—so take it slow. It's also poorly marked; signage is scarce to nonexistent in some areas.

From this section a nice detour is available; veer off the Ruta and steer north on Route 129 toward Lares and Arecibo. This road is no less scenic, but leads through more pueblos until you end up north of Lares at the **Parque de las Cavernas del Río Camuy** (Río Camuy Cave Park).

Fodor's Choice ★ **Parque de las Cavernas del Río Camuy.** The 268-acre Parque de las Cavernas del Río Camuy contains one of the world's largest cave networks. After watching an introductory film, a tram takes you down a trail shaded by bamboo and banana trees to Cueva Clara, where the stalactites and stalagmites turn the entrance into a toothy grin. Hour-long

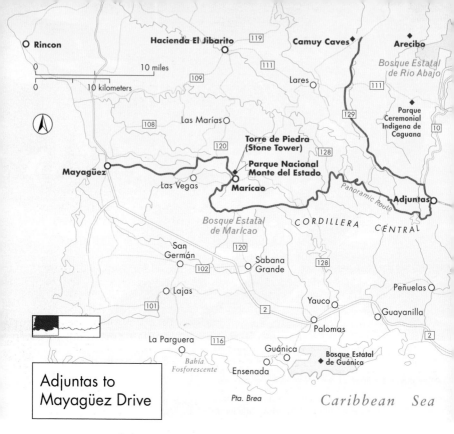

Adjuntas to
Mayagüez Drive

guided tours in English and Spanish lead you on foot through the 180-foot-high cave, which is teeming with wildlife. You're likely to see the blue-eyed river crabs and long-legged tarantulas. More elusive are the bats that make their home here. They don't come out until dark, but you can feel the heat they generate at the cave's entrance. The visit ends with a tram ride to the Tres Pueblos sinkhole, where you can see the third-longest underground river in the world passing from one cave to another. Tours are first-come, first-served; plan to arrive early on weekends, when locals join the crowds. There's a picnic area, cafeteria, and gift shop. ⊠ *Rte. 129, Km 18.9, Camuy* ☎ *787/898–3100* ⊕ *www. parquesnacionalespr.com* ⊠ *$15* ⏱ *Wed.–Sun. 8:30–5; last tour at 3:30.*

Once you arrive in Mayagüez, you have numerous options. Go north on Highway 2 toward Rincón, a popular town for surfers and mainland U.S. expats, or south toward Cabo Rojo, a charming town with lots of open-air seafood restaurants, houses poised on stilts in the water, and unfailingly beautiful sunsets. Still another option is to head back inland toward the town of San Sebastián (a reasonable drive to or from Arecibo or Camuy), where numerous activities await at **Hacienda El Jibarito**.

## WHERE TO EAT AND STAY

*For recommended lodgings in Rincón, see Where to Stay in Rincón, Chapter 6.*

*For expanded hotel reviews, visit Fodors.com.*

**\$\$**
ECLECTIC
✕ **Hacienda Luz de Luna.** This is one restaurant where you can't show up unannounced, nor would you ever recognize it from a sign outside, simply because there isn't one. That's the intrigue of this "underground restaurant" where guests are invited to dine at the home of renowned-chef Ventura Vivoni Rivera. In 2008 he had a dream to cook for strangers in the historic hacienda built in 1887. Three weekends per month, Ventura prepares a 10-course meal for a maximum of 35 guests, served during two daily seatings (at 1 and 6 pm). Hosted by the chef's father, Edric, the evening begins with a tour of property, starting at the orchard where lemons grow the size of coconuts. Sprawling 374 acres is the family's farm and small factory where soap, jam, candy, and coffee are produced. Each unique menu (emailed to guests in advance) is never repeated, but might include coffee-crusted pork with mango puree or grilled fish with crunchy rice. This dining *experience* generally takes up to five hours and costs a flat \$60; bring cash, since they don't accept credit cards. Be sure to reserve well in advance. ✉ *Carretera 135, Km. 73.3, Barrio Yahuecas, Adjuntas* ☎ *787/829–9096* ⌂ *Reservations essential* ▭ *No credit cards.*

**\$\$**
B&B/INN
⌂ **Hacienda El Jíbarito, San Sebastián.** Designated the island's first "agrotourism" inn, Hacienda El Jíbarito is an attractive parador hidden in the mountains of San Sebastián. **Pros:** ideal for couples and families; variety of activities; attentive service. **Cons:** distance from off-site services, including restaurants. ✉ *Rte. 445, Km 6.5, San Sebastián* ☎ *787/280–4040* ⊕ *www.haciendaeljibarito.com.* ¶〇¶ *No meals.*

**\$\$**
RESORT
⌂ **Parador Villas Sotomayor.** If you're looking for a place to relax in nature and forget about the stress of city life, then look no further. **Pros:** friendly staff; great for kids; gym offers spin and dance classes; mountain scenery. **Cons:** tons of bugs; noise from neighboring villas; not very luxurious. ✉ *Carr. 123 Km 36.6, Int. 522 Km 0.2, Adjuntas* ☎ *787/829–1717* ⊕ *www.paradorvillassotomayor.com.*

# Travel Smart
# Puerto Rico

**WORD OF MOUTH**

"Driving in PR in general is easy, it's just slow. We didn't encounter any crazy drivers. The rules of the road are the same as in the continental US, and the roads are in pretty good condition. The challenge is that it will take you twice the amount of travel time due to traffic."

—Continental_Drifter

# GETTING HERE AND AROUND

■ **TIP**→ Ask the local tourist board about hotel and local transportation packages that include tickets to major museum exhibits or other special events.

## ■ AIR TRAVEL

Nonstop flights to San Juan from New York are 3¼ hours; from Miami, 2½ hours; from Atlanta, 3½ hours; from Boston, 4 hours; from Chicago, 4¾ hours; from Los Angeles, 8 hours; from Spain, 8¾ hours; from the United Kingdom, 11 hours.

There are dozens of daily flights to Puerto Rico from the United States, and connections are particularly good from the East Coast, although there are a few nonstop flights from the Midwest as well. San Juan's international airport is a major regional hub, so many travelers headed elsewhere in the Caribbean make connections here. Because of the number of flights, fares to San Juan are among the most reasonably priced to the region.

**Airlines and Airports Airline and Airport Links.com.** Airline and Airport Links.com has links to many of the world's airlines and airports. ⊕ www.airlineandairportlinks.com.

**Airline Security Issues Transportation Security Administration** ⊕ www.tsa.gov.

### AIRPORTS

The island's main airport is Aeropuerto Internacional Luis Muñoz Marín (SJU), 20 minutes east of Old San Juan in the neighborhood of Isla Verde. San Juan's secondary airport is the small Fernando L. Ribas-Dominicci Airport (SIG), also called Isla Grande, near the city's Miramar section. From either airport you can catch flights to Culebra and Vieques, and from SJU you can also connect to other destinations in Puerto Rico and throughout the Caribbean.

Other Puerto Rican airports include Aeropuerto Internacional Rafael Hernández (BQN) in the northwestern town of Aguadilla, Aeropuerto Eugenio María de Hostos (MAZ) in the west-coast community of Mayagüez, Mercedita (PSE) in the south-coast town of Ponce, José Aponte de la Torre (RVR) in the east-coast town of Ceiba; Antonio Rivera Rodríguez (VQS) on Vieques, and Aeropuerto Benjamin Rivera Noriega (CPX) on Culebra.

**Airport Information Aeropuerto Antonio Rivera Rodríguez** ⊠ *Vieques* ☎ *787/741–8358.* **Aeropuerto Benjamin Rivera Noriega** ⊠ *Culebra* ☎ *787/742-0022.* **Aeropuerto Eugenio María de Hostos** ⊠ *Mayagüez* ☎ *787/833-0148.* **Aeropuerto Fernando L. Ribas-Dominicci** ⊠ *Isla Grande, San Juan* ☎ *787/729-8711.* **Aeropuerto Internacional Luis Muñoz Marín** ⊠ *Isla Verde, San Juan* ☎ *787/791-3840.* **Aeropuerto José Aponte de la Torre** ⊠ *Ceiba* ☎ *787/534-4100.* **Aeropuerto Mercedita** ⊠ *Ponce* ☎ *787/842-6292.* **Aeropuerto Rafael Hernández** ⊠ *Aguadilla* ☎ *787/890-6075.*

### GROUND TRANSPORTATION

Before arriving, check with your hotel about transfers: some hotels and resorts provide transport from the airport—free or for a fee—to their guests; some larger resorts run regular shuttles. Otherwise, your best bets are *taxis turísticos* (tourist taxis). Uniformed officials at the airport can help you make arrangements. They will give you a slip with your exact fare to hand to the driver. Rates are based on your destination. A taxi turístico to Isla Verde costs $10. It's $15 to Condado and $19 to Old San Juan. There's a $1 charge for each bag handled by the driver.

### FLIGHTS

San Juan's busy Aeropuerto Internacional Luis Muñoz Marín receives flights from all major American carriers. AirTran offers direct flights from Atlanta, Baltimore, Orlando, and Tampa. American Airlines flies nonstop from Chicago, Dallas, Hartford, Miami, Newark, New York–JFK, and Philadelphia. Continental

Airlines flies nonstop from Houston and Newark. Delta flies nonstop from Atlanta, New York–LGA, and New York–JFK. JetBlue flies nonstop from Boston, Fort Lauderdale, Orlando, Tampa, and New York–JFK. Spirit Air flies nonstop from Fort Lauderdale and Orlando. United flies nonstop from Chicago and Washington, D.C.–Dulles. US Airways flies nonstop from Baltimore, Charlotte, and Philadelphia.

It used to be that travelers arriving at San Juan's international airport had to transfer to nearby Aeropuerto Fernando L. Ribas-Dominicci (close to Old San Juan and Condado) to take a flight to Vieques or Culebra. These days, all the carriers servicing the islands also have flights from the international airport. Air Flamenco and Vieques Air Link offer daily flights from both airports in San Juan to Vieques and Culebra. Cape Air flies between the international airport and Vieques.

Puerto Rico is also a good spot from which to hop to other Caribbean islands. American Eagle serves many islands in the Caribbean from San Juan; Cape Air connects San Juan to St. Thomas, St. Croix, Tortola, Anguilla, and Nevis. Seaborne Airlines departs from San Juan International to St. Thomas and St. Croix. JetBlue now flies to St. Thomas, St. Croix, and St. Maarten from SJU.

San Juan is no longer the only gateway into Puerto Rico. If you're headed to the western part of the island, you can fly directly into Aguadilla. Continental flies here from Newark, JetBlue flies here from New York–JFK and Orlando, and Spirit Air flies nonstop from Fort Lauderdale. If the southern coast is your goal, JetBlue flies to Ponce from New York–JFK and Orlando.

**Airline Contacts American Airlines** ☎ 800/433-7300 ⊕ www.aa.com. **AirTran** ☎ 800/247-8726 ⊕ www.airtran.com. **Continental Airlines** ☎ 800/523-3273 for U.S. and Mexico reservations, 800/231-0856 for international reservations ⊕ www.continental.com. **Delta Airlines** ☎ 800/221-1212 for U.S. reservations, 800/241-4141 for international reservations ⊕ www.delta.com. **JetBlue** ☎ 800/538-2583 ⊕ www.jetblue.com. **Spirit Airlines** ☎ 800/772-7117 ⊕ www.spirit.com. **United Airlines** ☎ 800/864-8331 for U.S. reservations, 800/538-2929 for international reservations ⊕ www.united.com. **US Airways** ☎ 800/428-4322 for U.S. and Canada reservations, 800/622-1015 for international reservations ⊕ www.usairways.com.

**Regional Airlines Air Flamenco** ☎ 787/724-1818, 877/535-2636 ⊕ www.airflamenco.net. **Cape Air** ☎ 866/227-3247 ⊕ www.capeair.com. **Seaborne Airlines** ☎ 888/359-8687, 787/294-6161 ⊕ www.seaborneairlines.com. **Vieques Air Link** ☎ 787/741-8331, 888/901-9247 ⊕ www.viequesairlink.com.

# ▌BUS TRAVEL

The Autoridad Metropolitana de Autobuses (AMA) operates buses that thread through San Juan, running in exclusive lanes on major thoroughfares and stopping at signs marked *parada*. Destinations are indicated above the windshield. Bus B-21 runs through Condado all the way to Plaza Las Américas in Hato Rey. Bus A-5 runs from San Juan through Santurce and the beach area of Isla Verde. Service starts at around 6 am and generally continues until 9 pm. Fares are 75¢ and are paid in exact change upon entering the bus. Most buses are air-conditioned and have wheelchair lifts and lockdowns.

There's no bus system covering the rest of the island. If you do not have a rental car, your best bet is to travel by *públicos*, which are usually shared 17-passenger vans. They have yellow license plates ending in "P" or "PD," and they scoot to towns throughout the island, stopping in each community's main plaza. They operate primarily during the day; routes and fares are fixed by the Public Service Commission, but schedules aren't set, so you have to call ahead.

Bus Information **Autoridad Metropolitana de Autobuses** ☎ *800/981–0097, 787/294–0500* ⊕ *sashto.dtop.gov.pr/AMA.*

# ▌ CAR TRAVEL

Several well-marked, multilane highways link population centers. Route 26 is the main artery through San Juan, connecting Condado and Old San Juan to Isla Verde and the airport. Route 22, which runs east–west between San Juan and Camuy, and Route 52, which runs north–south between San Juan and Ponce, are toll roads. Route 2, a smaller highway, travels west from San Juan toward Rincón, and Route 3 traverses east toward Fajardo. Route 3 can be mind-numbingly slow, so consider taking Route 66, a toll road that bypasses the worst of the traffic.

Five highways are particularly noteworthy for their scenery and vistas. The island's tourism authorities have even given them special names. Ruta Panorámica (Panoramic Route) runs east–west through the central mountains. Ruta Cotorra (Puerto Rican Parrot Route) travels along the north coast. Ruta Paso Fino (Paso Fino Horse Route, after a horse breed) takes you north–south and west along the south coast. Ruta Coquí, named for the famous Puerto Rican tree frog, runs along the east coast. Ruta Flamboyán, named after the island tree, goes from San Juan through the mountains to the east coast.

## GASOLINE

All types of fuel—regular, super-premium, and diesel—are available by the liter. Most stations are self-service. Hours vary, but stations generally operate daily from early in the morning until 10 or 11 pm; in metro areas many are open 24 hours. Stations are few and far between in the Cordillera Central and other rural areas, so plan accordingly. In cities you can pay with cash and bank or credit cards; in the hinterlands cash is occasionally your only option.

## ROAD CONDITIONS

Puerto Rico has some of the Caribbean's best roads, but potholes, sharp turns, speed bumps, sudden gradient changes, and poor lighting can sometimes make driving difficult. Be especially cautious when driving after heavy rains or hurricanes; roads and bridges might be washed out or damaged. Many of the mountain roads are very narrow and steep, with unmarked curves and cliffs. Locals are familiar with such roads and often drive at high speeds, which can give you quite a scare. When traveling on a narrow, curving road, it's best to honk your horn as you take any sharp turn.

Traffic around cities—particularly San Juan, Ponce, and Mayagüez—is heavy at rush hours (weekdays from 7 am to 10 am and 3 pm to 7 pm).

| FROM | TO | RTE./ DISTANCE |
|------|-----|----------------|
| San Juan | Aguadilla | Rte. 22 81 miles (130 km) |
| San Juan | El Yunque | Rte. 3 35 miles (55 km) |
| San Juan | Fajardo | Rte. 3 34 miles (54 km) |
| San Juan | Mayagüez | Rte. 22 98 miles (160 km) |
| San Juan | Ponce | Rte. 52 70 miles (112 km) |

## ROADSIDE EMERGENCIES

In an emergency, dial 911. If your car breaks down, call the rental company for a replacement. Before renting, make sure you investigate the company's policy regarding replacement vehicles and repairs out on the island, and ask about surcharges that might be incurred if you break down in a rural area and need a new car.

## RULES OF THE ROAD

U.S. driving laws apply in Puerto Rico, and you'll find no problem with signage or directionals. Street and highway signs are most often in Spanish but use international symbols; brushing up on a few key Spanish terms before your trip will help. The following words and phrases are especially useful: *calle sin salida* (dead-end street), *cruce de peatones* (pedestrian crossing), *cuidado* (caution), *desvío* (detour), *estación de peaje* (tollbooth), *no entre* (do not enter), *prohibido adelantar* (no passing), *salida* (exit), *tránsito* (one way), *zona escolar* (school zone).

Distances are posted in kilometers (1 mile to 1.6 km), but speed limits are posted in miles per hour. Speeding and drunk-driving penalties are much the same here as on the mainland. Police cars often travel with their lights flashing, so it's difficult to know when they're trying to pull you over. If the siren is on, move to the right lane to get out of the way. If the lights are on, it's best to pull over—but make sure that the vehicle is a *marked* police car before doing so.

## ▌ FERRY TRAVEL

The Autortidad de Transporte Marítimo (Maritime Transportation Authority) runs passenger ferries from Fajardo to Culebra and Vieques. Service is from the ferry terminal in Fajardo, about a 90-minute drive from San Juan. Advance reservations are not accepted. There are a limited number of seats on the ferries, so get to the terminal in plenty of time. This means arriving an hour or more ahead of the departure time in Fajardo, somewhat less in Vieques and Culebra. In Fajardo the ticket counter is in the small building across the street from the actual terminal. In Vieques and Culebra the ticket counters are at the entrance to the terminals. There are food kiosks at Fajardo and Vieques that are open even for the early-morning departures. Culebra doesn't have any eateries nearby.

The Fajardo–Vieques passenger ferry departs from Vieques weekdays at 9:30 am, 1 pm, 4:30 pm, and 8 pm, returning at 6:30 am, 11 am, 3 pm, and 6 pm. On weekends ferries depart from Vieques at 9 am, 3 pm, and 6 pm, returning at 6:30 am, 1 pm, and 4:30 pm. Tickets for the 90-minute journey are $2 each way. The Fajardo–Culebra ferry leaves Culebra daily at 9 am, 3 pm, and 7 pm, returning at 6:30 am, 1 pm, and 5 pm. The 90-minute trip is $2.25.

Information **Autortidad de Transporte Marítimo** ☎ *800/981–2005, 787/723–2260* ⊕ *www.prpa.gobierno.pr.*

# ESSENTIALS

## ■ ACCOMMODATIONS

San Juan's high-rise hotels on the Condado and Isla Verde beach strips cater primarily to the cruise-ship and casino crowd, though some also target business travelers. Outside San Juan, particularly on the east coast, you'll find self-contained luxury resorts that cover hundreds of acres. In the west, southwest, and south—as well as on the islands of Vieques and Culebra—smaller inns, villas, condominiums, and government-sponsored *paradores* are the norm.

| CATEGORY | COST |
|---|---|
| $$$$ | over $350 |
| $$$ | $250–$350 |
| $$ | $150–$250 |
| $ | $80–$150 |
| ¢ | under $80 |

All prices are for a standard double room in high season, meals not included, and excluding tax and service charges.

Most hotels and other lodgings require you to give your credit-card details before they will confirm your reservation. If you don't feel comfortable emailing this information, ask if you can fax it (some places even prefer faxes). However you book, get confirmation in writing and have a copy of it handy when you check in.

Be sure you understand the hotel's cancellation policy. Some places allow you to cancel without any kind of penalty—even if you prepaid to secure a discounted rate—if you cancel at least 24 hours in advance. Others require you to cancel a week in advance or penalize you the cost of one night. Small inns and B&Bs are most likely to require you to cancel far in advance. Most hotels allow children under a certain age to stay in their parents' room at no extra charge, but others

charge for them as extra adults; find out the cutoff age for discounts.

### APARTMENT AND HOUSE RENTALS

**Local Agents Island West Properties.** Island West Properties can help you rent condos in Rincón by the week or the month. ⌂ Box 700, Rincón ☎ 787/823–2323 ⊕ www.island-wes.com. **Puerto Rico Vacation Apartments.** Puerto Rico Vacation Apartments represents some 200 properties in Condado and Isla Verde. ⌂ Calle Marbella del Caribe Oeste S-5, Isla Verde ☎ 787/727–1591, 800/266–3639 ⊕ www.sanjuanvacations.com. **Rainbow Realty.** Rainbow Realty rents condos and villas on Vieques. ⌂ 278 Calle Flamboyán, Esperanza, Vieques ☎ 787/741–4312 ⊕ www. viequesrainbowrealty.com.

### HOTELS

In the most expensive hotels your room will be large enough for two to move around comfortably, with two double beds or one queen- or king-size bed, air-conditioning, a phone, Wi-Fi or other Internet access, a private bath, an in-room safe, cable TV, a hair dryer, iron and ironing board, room service, shampoo and toiletries, and possibly a view of the water. There will be a concierge and at least one hotel restaurant and lounge, a pool, a shop, and an exercise room or spa. In Puerto Rico's smaller inns, rooms will have private baths, air-conditioning or fans, a double to king-size bed, possibly room service, and breakfast (continental or full) included in the rates. Most also have Wi-Fi or other Internet access in the rooms, though some have Wi-Fi in public areas only. In some smaller hotels several rooms share baths—it's a good idea to ask before booking. All hotels listed in this guide have private baths unless otherwise noted.

In Puerto Rico smoking is prohibited in public places, including restaurants, bars, cafes, casinos, and hotel common areas.

## PARADORES

Some *paradores* are rural inns offering no-frills apartments, and others are large hotels; all must meet certain standards, such as proximity to an attraction or beach. Most have a small restaurant that serves local cuisine. They're often good bargains (usually from $85 to $125 for a double room). You can make reservations by contacting the Puerto Rico Tourism Company. Small Inns of Puerto Rico, a branch of the Puerto Rico Hotel & Tourism Association, is a marketing arm for some 25 small hotels island-wide. The organization occasionally has package deals including casino coupons and LeLoLai (a cultural show) tickets.

**Contacts Puerto Rico Tourism Company**
☎ *787/721–2400, 800/866–7827* ⊕ *www. seepuertorico.com.* **Small Inns of Puerto Rico** ⊕ *www.puertoricosmallhotels.com.*

# ▮ ADDRESSES

Addresses in Puerto Rico, especially in and around San Juan, can be confusing because Spanish terms like *avenida* and *calle* are used interchangeably with English terms like avenue and street. This means that the shopping strip in Old San Juan may be called Calle Cristo or Cristo Street. (And it might just be called Cristo, as it is on many maps.) A highway is often called an *expreso,* and an alley or pedestrian-only street is labeled a *paseo.*

Outside a metropolitan area, addresses are most often given by the kilometer mark along the road. That means that the address for Parque de las Cavernas del Río Camuy, south of Arecibo, is given as Route 129, Kilometer 18.9.

# ▮ COMMUNICATIONS

## INTERNET

Internet access in Puerto Rico is as widespread as it is on the U.S. mainland. You can expect rooms in large hotels or resorts to have plug-in Ethernet access or Wi-Fi—or, more likely, both. Many hotels also have business centers; these may be quite sophisticated or merely a computer terminal or two for guest use. In smaller B&Bs and inns Wi-Fi is occasionally limited to common areas only, but this is the exception rather than the rule. If it's important to you, call ahead to double-check that the hotel you want to stay in can meet your needs. Wi-Fi is also available in many chain restaurants, including Burger King and Starbucks, as well as some local cafés.

**Cybercafes.** Cybercafes lists more than 4,000 Internet cafés worldwide. ⊕ *www.cybercafes. com.*

## PHONES

All Puerto Rican phone numbers consist of a three-digit area code and a seven-digit local number, just like those in the United States. Puerto Rico's area codes are 787 and 939. Toll-free numbers, with the prefixes 800, 888, or 877, are widely used in Puerto Rico, and most can be accessed from North America. By the same token, you can also access most North American toll-free numbers from the island.

Most major American cell-phone companies consider Puerto Rico as part of regular nationwide calling, so it's unlikely that those with U.S calling plans will incur roaming charges during a visit. However, it's always best to call your provider to confirm before you travel. Companies that offer service in Puerto Rico include AT&T, T-Mobile, and Sprint. Verizon customers use the local Claro network.

Note that calling from a hotel is almost always expensive; hotels usually add huge surcharges to all calls, particularly international ones. Locally purchased calling cards can help keep costs to a minimum.

### CALLING CARDS

Phone cards are widely available. The Puerto Rico Telephone Company sells its "Ring Card" in various denominations that can be used for both local and international calls. They're available in shops, supermarkets, and drugstores, as well as from the phone company.

Information **Ring Cards** ☎ *800/781–1314* ⊕ *www.telefonicapr.com.* **Cellular Abroad.** Cellular Abroad rents and sells GMS phones and sells SIM cards that work in many countries. ☎ *800/287–5072* ⊕ *www.cellularabroad. com.* **Mobal.** Mobal rents mobiles and sells GSM phones (starting at $29) that will operate in 170 countries. Per-call rates vary throughout the world. ☎ *888/888–9162* ⊕ *www.mobal. com.* **Planet Fone.** Planet Fone rents cell phones, but the per-minute rates are expensive. ☎ *888/988–4777* ⊕ *www.planetfone.com.*

# ▮ CUSTOMS AND DUTIES

Puerto Rico is considered a part of the United States for customs purposes, so you will not pass through customs on arrival if you're coming from the mainland. When leaving Puerto Rico, you must pass your bag through a checkpoint of the U.S. Department of Agriculture's (USDA) Animal and Plant Health Inspection Service (APHIS). The list of organic products that can be transported from Puerto Rico to the States includes avocados, bananas, breadfruits, citrus fruits, ginger, papayas, and plantains.

U.S. Information **U.S. Department of Agriculture** ⊕ *www.aphis.usda.gov.*

# ▮ EATING OUT

Throughout the island you can find everything from French haute cuisine to sushi bars, as well as superb local eateries serving *comidas criollas,* traditional Puerto Rican meals. Note that the *mesón gastronómico* label is used by the government to recognize restaurants that preserve culinary traditions. By law, every menu has a written warning about the dangers of consuming raw foods; therefore, if you want something medium rare, you need to be specific about how you'd like it cooked. *For information on food-related health issues see Health, below.* The restaurants we list are the cream of the crop in each price category.

## MEALS AND MEALTIMES

Puerto Ricans' eating habits mirror those of their counterparts on the mainland United States: They eat breakfast, lunch, and dinner, though they don't tend to drink as much. Instead, islanders like a steaming, high-test café con leche in the morning and another between 2 and 4 pm. They may finish a meal with coffee, but they never drink coffee *during* a meal.

People tend to eat dinner late in Puerto Rico. Many restaurants don't open until 6 pm. You may find yourself alone in the restaurant if you eat before 7 pm; from 8 pm onward, it may be quite busy.

Unless otherwise noted, the restaurants listed in this guide are open daily for lunch and dinner.

## RESERVATIONS AND DRESS

Regardless of where you are, it's a good idea to make a reservation if you can. In some places, it's expected. We mention them specifically only when reservations are essential (there's no other way you'll ever get a table) or when they are not accepted. For popular restaurants, book as far ahead as you can (often 30 days), and reconfirm as soon as you arrive. (Large parties should always call ahead to check the reservations policy.) We mention dress only when men are required to wear a jacket or a jacket and tie.

Puerto Ricans generally dress up to go out, particularly in the evening. And always remember: beach attire is only for the beach.

## WINES, BEER AND SPIRITS

Puerto Rico isn't a notable producer of wine, but it does make several well-crafted local beers and, of course, lots of rum. Legends trace the birthplace of the piña colada to any number of San Juan establishments. Puerto Rican rum is popular mixed with cola (known as a *cuba libre*), soda, tonic, juices, or water, or served on the rocks or even straight up. Look for Bacardí, Don Q, Ron Rico, Palo Viejo, and Barrilito. The drinking age in Puerto Rico is 18.

# ELECTRICITY

Puerto Rico uses the same 110-volt AC (60-cycle), two-prong-outlet electrical system as in North America. Plugs have two flat pins set parallel to each other. European visitors should bring adapters and converters, or call ahead to see whether their hotel has them on hand.

Consider making a small investment in a universal adapter, which has several types of plugs in one lightweight, compact unit. Most laptops and mobile phone chargers are dual voltage (i.e., they operate equally well on 110 and 220 volts), so require only an adapter. These days the same is true of small appliances such as hair dryers. Always check labels and manufacturer instructions to be sure. Don't use 110-volt outlets marked for shavers only for high-wattage appliances such as hair dryers.

# EMERGENCIES

Emergencies are handled by dialing 911. You can expect a quick response by police, fire, and medical personnel, most of whom speak at least some English. San Juan's Tourist Zone Police are particularly helpful to visitors.

**General Emergency Contacts Ambulance, police, and fire** ☎ *911.* **Air Ambulance Service** ☎ *787/756–3424.* **Fire Department** ☎ *787/343–2330.* **Medical Emergency** ☎ *787/754–2222.* **Police** ☎ *787/343–2020.* **Tourist Zone Police** ☎ *787/726–7020 for Condado, 787/728–2981 for Isla Verde.*

## GAY AND LESBIAN TRAVEL

In sophisticated San Juan, gays and lesbians will find it easy to mingle. Many gay-friendly hotels, restaurants, and clubs are scattered throughout the city, and the beaches at Condado and Ocean Park tend to attract a gay crowd. On the first Sunday in June a gay pride parade takes place in Condado and is preceded by a week of events. The bohemian Old San Juan crowd is particularly friendly and—just as in Ocean Park and Condado—many

businesses there are owned by gays or lesbians. Some clubs and bars also host a weekly "gay night." Other welcoming areas include Ponce in the south, Rincón in the west, and the out-islands of Vieques and Culebra in the east.

# HEALTH

The most common types of illnesses are caused by contaminated food and water. You should even consider using bottled water to brush your teeth. Make sure food has been thoroughly cooked and is served to you fresh and hot; avoid vegetables and fruits that you haven't washed (in bottled or purified water) or peeled yourself. If you have problems, mild cases of traveler's diarrhea may respond to Imodium (known generically as loperamide) or Pepto-Bismol. Be sure to drink plenty of fluids; if you can't keep fluids down, seek medical help immediately.

Infectious diseases can be airborne or passed via mosquitoes and ticks and through direct or indirect physical contact with animals or people. Some, including Norwalk-like viruses that affect your digestive tract, can be passed along through contaminated food. Condoms can help prevent most sexually transmitted diseases, but they aren't absolutely reliable and their quality varies from country to country. Speak with your physician and/or check the CDC or World Health Organization Web sites for health alerts, particularly if you're pregnant, traveling with children, or have a chronic illness.

## SPECIFIC ISSUES IN PUERTO RICO

An outbreak of dengue fever, a mosquito-borne disease, hit the island in both 2007 and 2010. Virulent forms of the virus can cause high fever, joint pain, nausea, rashes, and occasionally death, but the strain that spread through the island's urban areas was mild, causing mostly flu-like symptoms. Most cases were reported in urban areas far from the usual tourist destinations. As a precaution, the U.S. Centers for Disease Control and Prevention advises the use of an insect repellent with DEET and clothing that covers the arms and legs.

Health care in Puerto Rico is among the best in the Caribbean, but expect long waits and often a less-than-pleasant bedside manner. At all hospitals and medical centers you can find English-speaking medical staff, and many large hotels have an English-speaking doctor on call.

Tap water on the island is generally fine for drinking, but avoid drinking it after storms (when the water supply can become mixed with sewage). Thoroughly wash or peel produce you buy in markets before eating it.

Do not fly within 24 hours of scuba diving.

### OVER-THE-COUNTER REMEDIES

All the U.S. brands of sunscreen and over-the-counter medicines (for example, Tylenol, Advil, Robitussin, and Nyquil) are available in pharmacies, supermarkets, and convenience stores.

## ▮ HOURS OF OPERATION

Bank hours are generally weekdays from 9 to 5, though a few branches are also open Saturday from 9 to noon or 1. Post offices are open weekdays from 8:00 to 4:30 and Saturday from 8 to noon. Government offices are open weekdays from 9 to 5.

Most gas stations are open daily from early in the morning until 10 or 11 pm. Numerous stations in urban areas are open 24 hours.

As a rule, San Juan–area museums are closed on Monday and, in some cases, Sunday. Hours otherwise are 9 or 10 am to 5 pm, often with an hour off for lunch between noon and 2. Sights managed by the National Parks Service, such as Castillo San Felipe del Morro and San Cristóbal, are open daily from 9 to 5.

In cities, pharmacies are generally open weekdays and on Saturday from 9 to 6 or 7. Walgreens operates numerous pharmacies around the island; some are open 24 hours.

Street shops are open Monday through Saturday from 9 to 6; mall stores tend to stay open to 9 or sometimes even later. Count on convenience stores staying open late into the night, seven days a week. Supermarkets are often closed on Sunday, although some remain open 24 hours, seven days a week.

## ▮ MAIL

Puerto Rico uses the U.S. postal system, and all addresses on the island have ZIP codes. The rates to send letters and postcards from Puerto Rico are the same as those everywhere else in the United States.

**Main Branches U.S. Post Office** ⊠ *100 Paseo Colón, Old San Juan, San Juan* ⊠ *113 West Calle Garrido Morales, Fajardo* ⊠ *60 Calle McKinley, Mayagüez* ⊠ *2340 Av. Eduardo Ruperte, Ponce.*

### SHIPPING PACKAGES

Many shops—particularly those in Old San Juan and Condado—will ship purchases for you. Shipping services are especially common at art galleries. Pay by credit card, and save your receipts. Make sure the proprietor insures the package against loss or damage and ships it first-class or by courier. Grab a business card with the proprietor's name and phone number so you can readily follow up with him or her if needed.

Post offices in major Puerto Rican cities offer express mail (next-day) service to the U.S. mainland and to Puerto Rican destinations. In addition, you can send packages via FedEx or UPS. Ask at the concierge desk of your hotel; most have regular courier pickups or can call for one. Hotels that offer business services will take care of the entire ordeal for you. Note that courier delivery and pickup is not available on Saturday, and even "overnight" packages often take two to three days to reach the U.S. mainland.

**Express Services FedEx** ☎ *800/463–3339* ⊕ *www.fedex.com.* **UPS** ☎ *800/PICK–UPS* ⊕ *www.ups.com.*

# ▌ MONEY

Puerto Rico, which is a commonwealth of the United States, uses the U.S. dollar as its official currency. Prices for most items are stable and comparable to those in the States, and that includes restaurants and hotel rates. As in many places, city prices tend to be higher than those in rural areas, but you're not going to go broke staying in the city: soft drinks or a cup of coffee run about $1–2; a local beer in a bar, $3–5; museum admission, $2–5.

Prices listed here are for adults. Substantially reduced fees are almost always available for children, students, and senior citizens.

## ATMS AND BANKS

Your own bank will probably charge a fee for using ATMs abroad; the foreign bank you use may also charge a fee. Nevertheless, you'll usually get a better rate of exchange at an ATM than you will at a currency-exchange office or even when changing money in a bank. And extracting funds as you need them is a safer option than carrying around a large amount of cash.

▐ **TIP**→ PIN numbers with more than four digits are not recognized at ATMs in many countries. If yours has five or more, remember to change it before you leave.

Automated Teller Machines (or ATMs, known here as ATHs) are as readily available and reliable as on the U.S. mainland; many are attached to banks, but you can also find them in gas stations, drugstores, supermarkets, and larger hotels. Just about every casino has one—to keep people in the game—but these can carry large surcharges, so check the fee before withdrawing money. ATMs are found less frequently in rural areas, but there's usually at least one in even the smallest village. Look to local banks, such as Banco Popular.

## CREDIT CARDS

It's a good idea to inform your credit-card company before you travel, especially if you're going abroad and don't travel internationally very often. Otherwise, the credit-card company might put a hold on your card owing to unusual activity—not a good thing halfway through your trip. Record all your credit-card numbers—as well as the phone numbers to call if your cards are lost or stolen—in a safe place, so you're prepared should something go wrong. Both MasterCard and Visa have general numbers you can call (collect if you're abroad) if your card is lost, but you're better off calling the number of your issuing bank, since Master-Card and Visa usually just transfer you to your bank; your bank's number is usually printed on your card.

**Reporting Lost Cards American Express** ☎ *800/528–4800 in U.S., 336/393–1111 collect from abroad* ⊕ *www.americanexpress. com.* **Diners Club** ☎ *800/234–6377 in U.S., 303/799–1504 collect from abroad* ⊕ *www. dinersclub.com.* **Discover** ☎ *800/347–2683 in U.S., 801/902–3100 collect from abroad* ⊕ *www.discovercard.com.* **MasterCard** ☎ *800/627–8372 in U.S., 636/722–7111 collect from abroad* ⊕ *www.mastercard.com.* **Visa** ☎ *800/847–2911 in U.S., 303/967–1096 collect from abroad* ⊕ *www.visa.com.*

# ▌PASSPORTS AND VISAS

U.S. citizens don't need passports to visit Puerto Rico; any government-issued photo ID will do. Nor is there passport control either to or from Puerto Rico; in this respect, flying here is just like traveling on any domestic flight. Nevertheless, it's always wise to carry some form of identification that proves your citizenship, and we still recommend that you carry a valid passport when traveling to Puerto Rico; it's a necessity if you're making any other trips around the Caribbean, except to the U.S. Virgin Islands, where you will pass through customs but not passport control.

# ▌SAFETY

San Juan, Mayagüez, and Ponce, like most other big cities, have their share of crime, so guard your wallet or purse in markets, on buses, and in other crowded areas. Avoid beaches at night, when muggings have been known to occur even in Condado and Isla Verde. Don't leave anything unattended on the beach. If you must keep valuables in your vehicle, put them in the trunk. Always lock your car. The exception is at the beaches of Vieques, where rental-car agencies advise you to leave the car unlocked so thieves don't break the windows to search for valuables. This happens extremely rarely, but it does happen.

We recommend that women carry only a handbag that closes completely and wear it bandolier style (across one shoulder and your chest). Open-style bags and those allowed to simply dangle from one shoulder are prime targets for pickpockets and purse snatchers. Avoid walking anywhere alone at night.

# ▌TAXES

You must pay a tax on your hotel room rate: For hotels with casinos it's 11%, for other hotels it's 9%, and for government-approved paradores it's 7%. Ask your hotel before booking. The tax, in addition to each hotel's discretionary service charge (which usually ranges from 5% to 16%), can add a hefty 12% to 27% to your bill. There's a 7% sales tax in Puerto Rico.

# ▌TIPPING

Some hotels—usually those classified as resorts—automatically add a 5%–16% service charge to your bill. Check ahead to confirm whether this charge is built into the room rate or will be tacked on at checkout. Tips are expected, and appreciated, by restaurant waitstaff (15%–20%), hotel porters ($1 per bag), maids ($1–$2 a day), and taxi drivers (10%–15%).

# ▌VISITOR INFORMATION

In addition to the Puerto Rico Tourism Company's ¡Qué Pasa!, pick up the Puerto Rico Hotel and Tourism Association's Bienvenidos and Places to Go. Among them you can find a wealth of information about the island and its activities. All are free and available at tourism offices and hotel desks. The Puerto Rico Tourism Company has information centers at the airport, Old San Juan, Ponce, Aguadilla, and Cabo Rojo. Most island towns also have a tourism office, usually in the city hall.

**Contacts Puerto Rico Tourism Company** ⬢ *La Princesa Bldg. #2, Paseo de la Princesa, San Juan 00902* ☎ *787/721–2400, 800/866–7827* ⊕ *www.gotopuertorico.com* ✉ *3575 W. Cahuenga Blvd., Suite 560, Los Angeles, California, USA90068* ☎ *323/874–5991, 800/874–1230.*

# ▌VACATION PACKAGES

Packages *are not* guided excursions. Packages combine airfare, accommodations, and perhaps a rental car or other extras (theater tickets, guided excursions, boat trips, reserved entry to popular museums, transit passes), but they let you do your own thing. During busy periods packages may be your only option, as flights and rooms may be sold out otherwise.

Packages will definitely save you time. They can also save you money, particularly in peak seasons, but—and this is a really big "but"—you should price each part of the package separately to be sure. And be aware that prices advertised on websites and in newspapers rarely include service charges or taxes, which can up your costs by hundreds of dollars.

■ TIP→ Some packages and cruises are sold only through travel agents. Don't always assume that you can get the best deal by booking everything yourself.

Each year consumers are stranded or lose their money when packagers—even large ones with excellent reputations—go out of business. How can you protect yourself?

First, always pay with a credit card; if you have a problem, your credit-card company may help you resolve it. Second, buy trip insurance that covers default. Third, choose a company that belongs to the United States Tour Operators Association, whose members must set aside funds to cover defaults. Finally, choose a company that also participates in the Tour Operator Program of the American Society of Travel Agents (ASTA), which will act as mediator in any disputes.

You can also check on the tour operator's reputation among travelers by posting an inquiry on one of the Fodors.com forums.

Organizations **American Society of Travel Agents** ☎ 703/739–2782 ⊕ www.travelsense. org. **United States Tour Operators Association** (USTOA). ☎ 212/599–6599 ⊕ www.ustoa. com.

# INDEX

## A

Abe's Snorkeling and Bio-Bay Tours, *186*
Acacia Boutique Hotel ☷ , *89*
Academia de Baile Julie Mayoral, *100*
Accommodations, 5, *304–305*. ⇨ *See also* Lodging *under specific regions, cities, and towns*
Addresses, *305*
Adjuntas, *291–297*
Adobo, *24*
Agriculture research station, *268*
Aguadilla, *244, 277–280*
Aguadilla Ice Skating Arena, *278*
Aguaviva ✕ , *65*
Aibonito, *288–294*
Aibonito Flower Festival, *11*
Air travel, *300–301*
*El Yunque and the Northeast, 127*
*Ponce and the Porta Caribe, 205*
*Rincón and the Porta del Sol, 246, 250, 267*
*San Juan, 38*
*Vieques and Culebra, 165*
Ajili-Mójili, *24*
Alcaldía, *44*
Alcaldía Antigua, *236*
Alcapurrias, *24*
Alexandra ✕ , *231*
Ali Baba ✕ , *75*
Amarillos, *24*
Andalucia ☷ , *91*
Annie's ✕ , *276*
Antiques shops, *110*
Antojitos Puertorriqueñes ✕ , *135*
Apartment and villa rentals, *304*
*Ponce and the Porta Caribe, 231*
*Rincón and the Porta del Sol, 259*
*San Juan, 86*
*Vieques and Culebra, 182, 192–193*
Aquarius Beach Resort ☷ , *274*
Archaeological sites, *215*
Archipiélago ✕ , *216*
Architecture, *37*

Area Recreation Doña Juana, *291*
Arecibo Lighthouse and Historical Park, *30*
Arecibo Observatory, *13, 64*
Arepas, *24*
Art festivals, *21*
Art galleries and museums, *20–21*
*El Yunque and the Northeast, 155–156*
*Ponce and the Porta Caribe, 214–215, 226, 238*
*Rincón and the Porta del Sol, 278*
*San Juan, 21, 44, 49, 57, 60, 61, 107–108*
*Vieques and Culebra, 185*
Artesania Puertorriqueña, *106*
At Wind Chimes Inn ☷ , *89*
ATMs, *309*
Augusto's ✕ , *75*
Aureola ✕ , *65*

## B

Bacalaitos, *24*
Bahía de Fosforescente, *232*
Bahía Marina ☷ , *193*
Bahía Salinas Beach Hotel ☷ , *276–277*
Ballena Trail, *230*
Balneario Boquerón, *243*
Balneario Caña Gorda, *201*
Balneario de Carolina, *35*
Balneario de Rincón, *243*
Balneario El Escambrón, *35*
Balneario Seven Seas, *148*
Banana Dang ✕ , *251–252*
Banana's ✕ , *173–174*
Banks, *309*
Bar Gitano ✕ , *78*
Bars
*Ponce and the Porta Caribe, 219, 233–234*
*Rincón and the Porta del Sol, 260, 270, 275, 277*
*San Juan, 96, 102–103*
*Vieques and Culebra, 184–185, 194–195*
Barú ✕ , *65*
Baseball, *112*
Batido, *24*
Beaches, *12, 175–179*
*El Yunque and the Northeast, 124–125, 148*

*Ponce and the Porta Caribe, 200–201, 232*
*Rincón and the Porta del Sol, 242–244*
*San Juan, 34–35*
*Vieques and Culebra, 162–163, 170, 173, 190*
Bebo's Café ✕ , *78*
Belz Factory Outlet World, *107*
Ben & Jerry's ✕ , *50*
Beside the Pointe ☷ , *255–256*
Bicycling
*El Yunque and the Northeast, 134*
*San Juan, 112–113*
*Vieques and Culebra, 186, 195*
Bili ✕ , *174*
Bioluminescent Bays, *13, 173, 175–179*
Bistro Rico ✕ , *156*
Blossom's ✕ , *149*
BLT Steak ✕ , *82*
Blue Boy Inn ☷ , *256*
Boat and ferry travel, *303*
*San Juan, 38*
*Vieques and Culebra, 166*
Boating and sailing
*El Yunque and the Northeast, 152–153, 154–155*
*Rincón and the Porta del Sol, 260, 267*
*Vieques and Culebra, 186–187, 195–196*
Bomba, *135*
Boquerón, *243, 273–275*
Bosque Estatal de Boquerón, *233*
Bosque Estatal de Guajataca, *282*
Bosque Estatal de Guánica, *226, 230*
Brasas Steak House ✕ , *273*
Bravo Beach Hotel ☷ , *182*
Budatai ✕ , *78*
Bus and trolley travel, *301–302*
*El Yunque and the Northeast, 127*
*Ponce and the Porta Caribe, 205*
*Rincón and the Porta del Sol, 246, 250*
*San Juan, 38–39*
Business hours, *308*

## C

Cabo Rojo, *270–277*
Cabo Rojo Lighthouse, *276*

Cabo Rojo Salt Flats Interpretive Center, 276
Cabuqui ✕, 216
Café Berlin ✕, 65–66
Café 4 Estaciones ✕, 50
Cafeteria Mallorca ✕, 66
Caficultura ✕, 66–67
Caguana, 14
Caja de Muertos, 201
Calizo ✕, 149
Caparra Ruins, 62
Capilla de Porta Coeli, 235–236
Capilla del Cristo, 44
Capitol building, 15, 60
Cappalli (shop), 109
Car travel and rentals, 302–303
*El Yunque and the Northeast, 123, 127*
*Ponce and the Porta Caribe, 205*
*Rincón and the Porta del Sol, 246, 250, 267–268*
*Ruta Panorámica, 287–288*
*San Juan, 39*
*Vieques and Culebra, 165*
Carambola ✕, 174
Caribbean Paradise ⊠, 259
Caribe Hilton San Juan ⊠, 88–89
Carli's Fine Dining & Piano ✕, 67
Carnival, 11
Carved saints, 228–229
Casa Armstrong-Poventud, 209
Casa Bacardi Visitor Center, 17, 62
Casa Blanca, 14, 43
Casa Cautiño, 225
Casa Cubuy Ecolodge ⊠, 154
Casa Dante ✕, 82
Casa de Amistad ⊠, 182
Casa de Lola Rodríguez de Tío, 236–237
Casa de los Kindy, 237
Casa de Ramón Power y Giralt, 45
Casa Grande ✕, 294
Casa Grande Mountain Retreat ⊠, 294
Casa Isleña ⊠, 256
Casa Morales, 237
Casa Perichi, 237–238
Casa Wiechers-Villaronga, 208
Casablanca Hotel ⊠, 87
Casals, Pablo, 54
Casals Festival, 11, 104–105
Cascada La Coca, 122

Casinos
*El Yunque and the Northeast, 152*
*Ponce and the Porta Caribe, 219*
*San Juan, 101*
Castillo San Cristóbal, 43
Castillo San Felipe del Morro, 14, 17, 43–44
Castillo Serrallés, 212, 292
Catedral de Nuestra Señora de Guadalupe, 209–210
Catedral de San Juan Bautista, 43
Caverns, 12–13, 30
*La Cueva de Maria de la Cruz, 14*
*Rincón and the Porta del Sol, 282*
*Ruta Panorámica, 295–296*
Cayo Caracoles, 201
Cayo Luis Peña, 190
Ceiba Country Inn ⊠, 151
Cementerio Santa María Magdalena de Pazzis, 45
Centro Ceremonial Indígena de Tibes, 215
Centro de Bellas Artes, 226
Centro Interpretivo Las Salinas de Cabo Rojo, 276
Chaparritas ✕, 238
Cherry Blossom ✕, 78–79
Che's ✕, 81
Chez Daniel ✕, 156–157
Chez Shack ✕, 174
Children, attractions for, 30
*El Yunque and the Northeast, 137, 140, 148, 151–152*
*Ponce and the Porta Caribe, 208–209, 212, 214, 218, 224, 231*
*Rincón and the Porta del Sol, 258, 268, 269–270, 278, 279–280*
*San Juan, 43–44, 45, 49, 50, 65–66, 72, 79–80, 88–89, 91, 92, 94*
*Vieques and Culebra, 172–173, 193*
Chimichurri, 24, 132
Chumar ✕, 154
Churches, 15
*Ponce and the Porta Caribe, 209–210, 223, 226, 235–236, 238*
*San Juan, 43, 44, 48*
CIRCA Art Fair, 21
Climate, 10, 37–38
Clothing shops, 108–110

Club Seaborne ⊠, 193
Coamo, 221–223
Coamo Springs Resort ⊠, 223
Cocina Creativa ✕, 279
Cocina Criolla, 22
Cofresí Beach Hotel ⊠, 274
Combate Beach Hotel ⊠, 277
Combate Guest House ⊠, 277
Communications, 305–306
Concalma (shop), 109
Condado, 54–55, 75–80, 89–91
Conrad San Juan Condado Plaza ⊠, 90
Conuco ✕, 174, 180–181
Copamarina Beach Resort ⊠, 231
Coral Princess ⊠, 90
Courtyard by Marriott Isla Verde Beach Resort ⊠, 92
Courtyard Marriott ⊠, 279
Credit cards, 5, 309
Crispy y Relleno ✕, 132
Cruceta El Vigía, 215–216
Cruises, 16–17
Cuatro Sombras Torrefacción y Café ✕, 67
Cueva del Viento, 282
Cuisine of Puerto Rico, 22–24, 129, 132, 224
Culebra. ⇨ *See* Vieques and Culebra
Culebra Beach Villas , 193
Customs and duties, 306

**D**

Da House ⊠, 87
Dance, 97–100, 135
Dance clubs
*Ponce and the Porta Caribe, 219, 233–234*
*Rincón and the Porta del Sol, 260*
*San Juan, 100, 101–103*
*Vieques and Culebra, 184, 194*
DanzActiva, 100
Das Alpen ✕, 252
Desecheo Island, 250
Designers, 111
Dinghy Dock ✕, 191
Dining, 5, 306. ⇨ *See also* under specific regions, cities, and towns
*cuisine of Puerto Rico, 22–24, 129, 132, 224*
*Fodor's choice, 66*
*price categories, 64, 128, 167, 206, 247*
Domes (beach), 243
Dos Angeles ⊠, 256

**Doubletree by Hilton San Juan** ⬚, 90
**Dragonfly** ✕, 67, 70
**D'Rose Chocolate Factory** ✕, 279
**Duffy's** ✕, 181
**Duties**, 306

**E**

**Ecotourism**, 123
**El Alcázar** (shop), 110
**El Ancla** ✕, 216
**El Balcón de Capitán** ✕, 224
**El Bohío** ✕, 271–272
**El Capitolio**, 15, 60
**El Combate**, 243, 275–277
**El Combate Beach**, 243
**El Conquistador Resort & Golden Door Spa** ⬚, 151, 152
**El Eden** ✕, 191
**El Faro Parador** ⬚, 279–280
**El Faro Punta Mulas**, 171
**El Fortin Conde de Mirasol**, 171–172
**El Patio de Sam** ✕, 70
**El Pedregal** ⬚, 280
**El Pescador** ✕, 80–81
**El Picoteo** ✕, 70
**El Plátano Loco** ✕, 179
**El Portal Rainforest Center**, 140
**El Quenepo** ✕, 181
**El Resuelve** ✕, 181
**El Roble** ✕, 224
**El San Juan Hotel & Casino** ⬚, 92
**El Toro de Piedra** ✕, 290–291
**El Varadero Seaside Grill** ✕, 149–150
**El Yunque and the Northeast**, 8, 12, 17, 118–157
beaches, 124–125, 148
children, attractions for, 137, 140, 148, 151–152
dining, 128, 129, 132, 135–136, 140–141, 143, 146, 149–150, 154, 156–157
the eastern coast, 154–157
emergencies, 140
flora and fauna, 121, 123
itineraries, 122, 131
lodging, 121, 123, 128, 136–137, 146, 151–152, 154, 157
nightlife, 133, 137–138, 152, 157
the northeastern coast, 129–153
outdoor activities and sports, 122–123, 124, 129, 134,

138–139, 147, 152–153, 154–155, 157
packing, 128
price categories, 128
safety, 128
shopping, 133–134, 139, 141–142
tours, 139–140, 178
transportation, 123, 127
visitor information, 121, 129
when to tour, 120, 126–127
**Electricity**, 307
**Embassy Suites San Juan Hotel & Casino** ⬚, 92
**Emergencies**, 307
and car travel, 302
El Yunque and the Northeast, 140
**Empanadillas**, 24
**English Rose, The** ✕⬚, 253, 256
**Espacio 1414**, 21
**Esperanza**, 172–173
**Estación Experimental de Agricultura Tropical**, 268

**F**

**Factory outlets**, 107
**Fajardo**, 125, 147–153, 178
**Fajardo Inn** ⬚, 151–152
**Fajardo Lighthouse**, 149
**Fern Restaurant** ✕, 135–136
**Ferry travel.** ⇨ See Boat and ferry travel
**Festival de los Máscaras**, 11
**Festivals and seasonal events**, 11, 21, 37, 60, 100, 104–105, 111
**Fiestas de la Calle San Sebastián**, 11
**Fishing**
El Yunque and the Northeast, 134, 157
Ponce and the Porta Caribe, 234
Rincón and the Porta del Sol, 275
San Juan, 114
Vieques and Culebra, 187–188
**Flavors of San Juan** (tours), 43
**Fodor's choice**, 5
dining, 66
lodging, 88
**Forests.** ⇨ See Natural wonders
**Fortresses**
San Juan, 14, 17, 43–44, 48–49
Vieques and Culebra, 171–172
**Fuerte Trail**, 230

**Fundación Nacional Para la Cultura Popular**, 48
**Furniture shops**, 110

**G**

**Galería Botello**, 107
**Galería Nacional**, 21, 44
**Gallery Inn, The** ⬚, 87
**Galloway's** ✕, 274
**Gambling.** ⇨ See Casinos
**Gardens**, 60–61
**Gay and lesbian bars and clubs**, 102–103
**Gay Puerto Rico**, 19, 307
**Gift shops**, 110
**Gilligan's Island**, 230–231
**Golf**
El Yunque and the Northeast, 129, 138, 152, 157
Ponce and the Porta Caribe, 221, 223, 226
Rincón and the Porta del Sol, 273, 280
San Juan, 114, 115
**Gozalandia Waterfalls**, 251
**Gran Meliá Puerto Rico** ⬚, 136
**Guánica**, 201, 226, 230–232
**Guayama**, 225–226
**Guided tours**
El Yunque and the Northeast, 139–140, 178
Ponce and the Porta Caribe, 206, 211, 214, 237
Rincón and the Porta del Sol, 247–248
San Juan, 42–43, 61
Vieques and Culebra, 178, 186

**H**

**Hacienda Buena Vista**, 212, 214, 292
**Hacienda El Jibarito, San Sebastion** ⬚, 296, 297
**Hacienda Luz de Luna** ✕, 297
**Hacienda Tamarindo** ⬚, 183
**Hampton Inn & Suites San Juan** ⬚, 94
**Handicrafts shops**, 110–111
**Hatillo**, 203
**Hato Rey**, 55
**Health concerns**, 10, 307–308
**Heather's Pizza** ✕, 191
**Hector's** ✕, 183
**Heineken JazzFest**, 11, 105
**Hiking**
El Yunque and the Northeast, 122–123

Ponce and the Porta Caribe, 207

San Juan, 115

**Hilton Ponce Golf & Casino Resort** ⊡, 218

**Historical buildings**

El Yunque an the Northeast, 155–156

Ponce and the Porta Caribe, 208, 209, 212, 214, 225, 236–238

Rincón and the Porta del Sol, 282

Ruta Panorámica, 292

San Juan, 14, 15, 17, 43, 44

**History of Puerto Rico**, 14–15

**Hix Island House** ⊡, 183

**Holiday Inn** ⊡, 218

**Holiday Inn Mayagüez & Tropical Casino** ⊡, 269

**Honeymoons**, 18

**Horned Dorset Primavera** ⊡, 256

**Horse racing**, 115

**Horseback riding**

El Yunque and the Northeast, 138

Ponce and the Porta Caribe, 232

Rincón and the Porta del Sol, 260, 284

**Hostería del Mar** ⊡, 92

**Hotel Bélgica** ⊡, 218

**Hotel Cielo Mar** ⊡, 280

**Hotel El Convento** ⊡, 87

**Hotel La Playa** ⊡, 94

**Hotel Meliá** ⊡, 218

**Hotel Milano** ⊡, 87

**Hotel Miramar** ⊡, 91

**Hotel Olimpo Court** ⊡, 90–91

**Hotels**, 5, 304.⇨ See also Lodging under specific regions, cities, and towns

meal plans, 5

Fodor's choice, 88

price categories, 86, 128, 167, 206, 247, 304

**House rentals**, 304

**Howard Johnson** ⊡, 218

**Howard Johnson Downtown Mayagüez** ⊡, 269

**Humacao**, 125, 155–157

**I**

**Ice skating**, 278

**Iglesia Católica San Blás**, 223

**Iglesia de San Germán Auxerre**, 238

**Iglésia de San José**, 48

**Iglesia San Antonio de Padua**, 226

**Il Mulino New York** ✕, 82–83

**Inn on the Blue Horizon** ⊡, 183

**InterContinental San Juan Resort & Casino** ⊡, 94

**International Salsa Congress**, 100

**Internet connection**, 305

**Isabel Segunda**, 170–172

**Isabela**, 244, 280, 282–284

**Isla Culebrita**, 190

**Isla de Ballena**, 231

**Isla Mata de la Gata**, 201

**Isla Verde**, 55, 82–83, 92–94

**Itineraries**, 26–27

for El Yunque and the Northeast, 122, 131

for Ponce and the Porta Caribe, 209

for Rincón and the Porta del Sol, 252

for Ruta Panorámica, 288

for San Juan, 57

for Vieques and Culebra, 170

**It's Yoga Puerto Rico**, 116

**J**

**Jajome Terrace** ⊡, 291

**Jam Rum Bar and Bistro Moderne** ✕, 79

**Jardín Botánico**, 60–61

**JB Hidden Village** ⊡, 280

**Jewelry shops**, 111–112

**Joyuda**, 270–273

**Juanita Bananas** ✕, 191

**K**

**Kasalta** ✕, 81

**Kayaking**

El Yunque and the Northeast, 153

San Juan, 115

Vieques and Culebra, 186–187, 195–196

**King's Cream Helados** ✕, 211

**L**

**La Bombonera** ✕, 70

**La Casita** ✕, 233

**La Casona** (historic home), 236

**La Ceiba** ✕, 223

**La Chiva**, 163

**La Coca Falls**, 122

**La Concha – A Renaissance Resort** ⊡, 91

**La Cucina di Ivo** ✕, 70–71

**La Cueva de Maria de la Cruz**, 14

**La Estación** ✕, 150

**La Finca Caribe** ✕, 183

**La Fonda del Jibarito** ✕, 71

**La Fortaleza**, 48–49

**La Guancha**, 201

**La Guancha Promenade**, 214

**La Madre** ✕, 71

**La Mallorquina** ✕, 72

**La Parguera**, 201, 232–234

**La Parrilla** ✕, 143, 146

**La Playita** ✕, 83

**La Playuela**, 244

**La Ponderosa**, 278

**Laguna Grande**, 149

**Laissez Faire** ✕, 268–269

**Las Cabezas Nature Reserve**, 178

**Las Croabas**, 148

**Las Mercedes Cemetery**, 15

**Latin music clubs**, 100, 103

**Laurel Kitchen | Art Bar** ✕, 81

**Lazy Parrot** ⊡, 256

**Lazy Parrot Restaurant** ✕, 253

**Le Lo Lai** (festival), 104

**Lechón**, 24

**Lemongrass** ✕, 75

**Lemontree Oceanfront Cottages** ⊡, 258

**Lighthouses**

El Yunque and the Northeast, 149

Rincón and the Porta del Sol, 250, 276, 278

Ruta Panorámica, 30

Vieques and Culebra, 171

**Lodging**, 5, 304–305.⇨ See also under specific regions, cities, and towns

Fodor's choice, 88

meal plans, 5

price categories, 86, 128, 167, 206, 247, 304

**Loíza**, 14–15, 203

**Lola** ✕, 216

**Lolita's** ✕, 146

**Luquillo**, 125, 142–147

**M**

**Mail and shipping**, 308–309

**Malecón**, 172

**Malecón House** ⊡, 183

**Malls**, 106–107

**Mamacitas** ✕⊡, 191–192, 193–194

**Manatee Eco Resort** ✕, 224

**Mar Azul Villas** ⊡, 258

**Maria's** (beach), 243

Marina de Salinas ⊡, *225*
Marina Puerto Chico, *148*
Marina Puerto del Rey, *148*
Marisquería Atlántica ✕, *75*
Markets, *106–107*
Mary Lee's by the Sea ⊡, *231*
Mask-makers, *11, 202–203*
Mayagüez, *267–270, 295–297*
Mayagüez Resort & Casino ⊡, *269–270*
Meal plans, *5*
Metropol ✕, *83*
Mirador Villaba-Orocovis, *291*
Miramar, *55*
Miró ✕, *79*
Mix on the Beach ✕, *181–182*
Mofongo, *23, 24*
Mojito Isleño, *24*
Mojo, *24*
Mona Island, *271*
Mosquito Bioluminescent Bay, *13, 173, 177*
Mundo Taino (shop), *110*
Money matters, *309*
Muralla ✕, *140–141*
Museo Casa Roig, *155–156*
Museo de Arte Contemporáneo de Puerto Rico, *21, 57, 60*
Museo de Arte de Aguadilla, *278*
Museo de Arte de Ponce, *20, 214–215*
Museo de Arte de Puerto Rico, *20, 60*
Museo de Arte y Casa de Estudio, *238*
Museo de Historia, Antropología y Arte, *20, 61*
Museo de la Conquista y Colonización de Puerto Rico, *62*
Museo de la Historia de Ponce, *210*
Museo de la Universidad de Puerto Rico, *21*
Museo de las Américas, *49*
Museo de San Juan, *49*
Museo del Niño, *30, 49*
Museo Felisa Rincón de Gautier, *49–50*
Museo Histórico de Coamo, *223*
Museo la Casa del Libro, *50*
Museums. ⇨ *See also* Art galleries and museums
*African heritage, 49*
*anthropology, 20, 61*
*architecture, 208*

*art, 20–21, 44, 49, 57, 60, 61, 155–156, 214–215, 226, 238, 278*
*books, 50*
*for children, 30, 49*
*conservation, 172–173*
*in El Yunque and the Northeast, 155–156*
*fire-fighting, 208–209*
*history, 20, 44, 49–50, 61, 62, 155–156, 171–172, 210, 223, 225, 236–238*
*lighthouse, 30*
*music, 45, 210–211*
*in Ponce and the Porta Caribe, 20, 208–209, 210–211, 214–215, 223, 225, 226, 236–238*
*Puerto Mosquito, 172–173*
*in Rincón and the Porta del Sol, 278*
*in San Juan, 20–21, 44, 45, 49–50, 57, 60, 61, 62*
*Taíno Indians, 210*
*Tibes Indians, 215*
*in Vieques and Culebra, 171–173*
Music, *37, 54, 97–100, 103, 104–105*
Music clubs
*Ponce and the Porta Caribe, 233–234*
*Rincón and the Porta del Sol, 260, 270*
*San Juan, 100, 101–103*
*Vieques and Culebra, 194–195*

**N**

Naguabo, *125, 154–155*
Natural wonders, *12–13, 17*
*El Yunque and the Northeast, 120–123, 139–142, 148–149, 156*
*Ponce and the Porta Caribe, 226, 230, 233*
*Rincón and the Porta del Sol, 250, 273, 276, 282*
*Ruta Panoracmica, 291, 295–296*
*Vieques and Culebra, 173, 177, 178, 190*
Next Course ✕, *182*
Nightlife and the arts, *20–21*
*El Yunque and the Northeast, 133, 137–138, 152, 157*
*Ponce and the Porta Caribe, 219, 224–225, 233–234*

*Rincón and the Porta del Sol, 260, 270, 275, 277*
*San Juan, 37, 95–106*
*Vieques and Culebra, 184–185, 194–195*
Nono Maldonado (shop), *109*
Northeast, The. ⇨ *See* El Yunque and the Northeast
Numero Uno Guest House ⊡, *92*
Nuyorican Café (Latin music club), *100, 103*

**O**

Observatorio de Arecibo, *13, 64*
Ocean Front Restaurant ✕, *282–283*
Ocean Park, *55, 81–82, 91–92*
Ola Lola's ✕, *283*
Olas Spa, *90*
Olas y Arena ✕, *283*
Old San Juan, *17, 40–54, 65–74, 87–88*
One Ten Thai ✕, *279*
Outdoor activities and sports. ⇨ *See also* specific activities
*El Yunque and the Northeast, 122–123, 124, 129, 134, 138–139, 147, 152–153, 154–155, 157*
*Ponce and the Porta Caribe, 206, 221, 223, 226, 232, 234*
*Rincón and the Porta del Sol, 247, 260–267, 272–273, 275, 280, 284*
*San Juan, 112–116*
*Vieques and Culebra, 186–188, 195–196*

**P**

Package deals, *310–311*
Paddleboarding, *116*
Palacete Los Moreau, *282*
Palio ✕, *136*
Palmas del Mar Country Club, *157*
Pamela's ✕, *81–82*
Pancho Villa Mexican Grill ✕, *243*
Pandeli ✕, *192*
Parador Boquemar ⊡, *274–275*
Parador Guanica 1929 ⊡, *231*
Parador Joyuda Beach ⊡, *272*
Parador Perichi's ⊡, *272*

Parador Villas Sotomayor ⊤, 297
Paradores, 305
*Ponce and the Porta Caribe, 231*
*Rincón and the Porta del Sol, 272, 274–275*
*Ruta Panorámica, 297*
*San Juan, 86*
Parque Actuático las Cascades, 278
Parque Ceremonial Indígena de Caguana, 20
Parque Ceremonial Indígena de Tibes, 20
Parque de Bombas, 208–209
Parque de las Cavernas del Río Camuy, 12–13, 30, 295–296
Parque de las Palomas, 50
Parque Histórico Juan Ponce de León (Ruinas de Caparra), 62
Parque Pasivo El Faro, 250
Parrot Club, The ✕, 72
Parrots, 146
Paseo de la Princesa, 44
Paseo Piñones, 132
Pasión por el Fogón ✕, 150
Passports and visas, 310
Pasteles, 24
Pastelillos, 24
Pata Prieta, 163
Pelican Reef ⊤, 283
Picadillo, 24
Pikayo ✕, 79
Piña Colada wars, 102
Pinky's ✕, 79–80
Piñones, 125, 130–134
Pique, 24
Piratos del Toro Al' Diente ✕, 224
Pirilo ✕, 104
Piscinas Aguas Termales, 223
Pito's Seafood ✕, 216–217
Planetariums and observatories, 13, 64
Playa Buyé, 243
Playa Caracas, 170
Playa Córcega, 243
Playa de Guajataca, 244
Playa de Jobos, 244
Playa de Ocean Park, 35
Playa de Piñones, 125
Playa del Condado, 35
Playa Flamenco, 12, 163
Playa Jaboncillo, 201
Playa La Pared, 125
Playa Luquillo, 125
Playa Media Luna, 163
Playa Melones, 163

Playa Montones, 244
Playa Santa, 201
Playa Shacks, 244
Playa Sun Bay, 163
Playa Zoni, 163
Playita Rosada, 201
Plaza de Armas, 50
Plaza de Colón, 50, 54
Plaza de Humacao, 156
Plaza de las Delicias, 292
Plaza del Mercado, 61
Plaza Las Américas, 107
Plazuela de la Rogativa, 54
Ponce and the Porta Caribe, 9, 198–238
*beaches, 200–201*
*children, attractions for, 208–209, 212, 214, 218, 224, 231*
*dining, 200, 206, 211, 216–218, 223, 224, 225–226, 231, 233, 238*
*exploring, 208–216, 223, 225, 226, 230–234, 232–233, 235–238*
*itineraries, 209*
*lodging, 206, 218, 223, 231, 233, 238*
*nightlife and the arts, 219, 224–225, 233–234*
*outdoor activities and sports, 206, 221, 223, 226, 232, 234*
*price categories, 206*
*safety, 206*
*shopping, 202–203, 219–221, 234*
*southeastern coast, 221–226*
*southwestern coast, 226, 230–238*
*tours, 206, 211, 214, 237*
*transportation, 205*
*visitor information, 206–207*
*when to tour, 205*
Ponce Centro, 211
Pool Bar Sushi, The ✕, 243
Porta Caribe. ⇨ See Ponce and the Porta Caribe
Porta del Sol. ⇨ See Rincón and the Porta del Sol
Posada La Hamaca ⊤, 194
Price categories
*dining, 64, 128, 167, 206, 247*
*El Yunque and the Northeast, 128*
*lodging, 86, 128, 167, 206, 247, 304*
*Ponce and the Porta Caribe, 206*
*Rincón and the Porta del Sol, 247*

*San Juan, 64, 86*
*Vieques and Culebra, 167*
Puerta de San Juan, 54
Puerta de Tierra, 54, 75, 88–89
Puerto Mosquito Bioluminescent Bay, 13, 173, 177
Puerto Rican green parrots, 146
Puerto Rico Heineken Jazzfest, 11, 105
Puerto Rico Premium Outlets, 107
Puerto Rico Restaurant Week, 11
Puerto Rico Symphony Orchestra, 11

**R**

Raices ✕, 72–73
Raito's ✕, 272
Ramada Inn Ponce ⊤, 218
Reef Bar and Grill, The ✕, 132
Refugio de Vida Silvestre de Boquerón, 273
Refugio de Vida Silvestre de Cabo Rojo, 276
Refugio de Vida Silvestre de Culebra, 190
Refugio de Vida Silvestre de Humacao, 156
Reggaetón, 103
Reserva Natural Las Cabezas de San Juan, 148–149
Restaurant Aaron at the Horned Dorset Primavera ✕, 243, 255
Restaurants, 5, 306. ⇨ See also Dining under specific regions, cities, and towns
*cuisine of Puerto Rico, 22–24, 129, 132, 224*
*Fodor's choice, 66*
*price categories, 64, 128, 167, 206, 247*
Rex Cream ✕, 225
Richie's Café ✕, 136
Ricomini Bakery ✕, 269
Rincón and the Porta del Sol, 9, 240–284
*beaches, 242–244*
*Cabo Rojo, 270–277*
*children, attractions for, 258, 268, 269–270, 278, 279–280*
*dining, 246–247, 251–255, 268–269, 271–272, 273–274, 276, 279, 282–283*
*exploring, 250–251, 268, 271, 273, 276, 278, 282*
*itineraries, 252*

lodging, 247, 255–259, 269–270, 272, 274–275, 276–277, 279–280, 283–284
Mayagüez, 267–270
nightlife and the arts, 260, 270, 275, 277
northwestern coast, 277–284
outdoor activities and sports, 247, 260–267, 272–273, 275, 280, 284
price categories, 247
safety, 247
shopping, 260, 270
tours, 247–248
transportation, 246, 250, 267–268
visitor information, 248
when to tour, 245–246
Rincón Argentina ✕, 217
Rincón Beach Resort ☶, 258
Rincón Ocean Villa ☶, 259
Rincón of the Seas ☶, 258
Rincón Tropical ✕, 255
Río Grande, 135–139
Río Mar Beach Resort & Spa, a Wyndham Grand Resort ☶, 137
Río Mar Country Club, 138
Río Piedras, 55
Ritz-Carlton, San Juan, The ☶, 94
Ritz Carlton Spa, The, 90
Royal Isabela ☶, 283
Ruinas de Caparra, 62
Rum, 23–24
Rum distilleries, 17, 62
Ruta Panorámica, 9, 13, 287–297
Adjuntas to Mayagüez, 295–297
Aibonito to Adjuntas, 291–294
dining, 290–291, 294, 297
itineraries, 288
lodging, 291, 294, 297
packing, 288
safety, 288, 290, 297
transportation, 287, 288
Yabucoa to Aibonito, 289–291

S

Saborea Puerto Rico, 11
Safety, 10, 310
El Yunque and the Northeast, 128
Ponce and the Porta Caribe, 206
Rincón and the Porta del Sol, 247

Ruta Panorámica, 288, 290, 297
San Juan, 42
Vieques and Culebra, 167
Sailing. ⇨ See Boating and sailing
St. Germain Bistro & Café ✕, 73–74
St. Regis Bahia Beach Resort Golf Course, 138
St. Regis Bahia Resort ✕, 137
Salinas, 224–225
Salsa, 97–100
San Germán, 234–238
San Jacinto ✕, 231
San Juan, 8, 32–116
architecture, 37
beaches, 34–35
children, attractions for, 43–44, 45, 49, 50, 65–66, 72, 79–80, 88–89, 91, 92, 94
climate, 37–38
Condado, 54–55, 75–80, 89–91
dining, 50, 64–83, 103
exploring, 40–64
festivals and seasonal events, 11, 37, 60, 100, 104–105, 111
greater San Juan, 54–61
Hato Rey, 55
Isla Verde, 55, 82–83, 92–94
itineraries, 57
lodging, 83–94, 100
Miramar, 55
music, 37, 54, 97–100, 103
nightlife and the arts, 37, 95–106
Ocean Park, 55, 81–82, 91–92
Old San Juan, 17, 40–54, 65–74, 87–88
outdoor activities and sports, 112–116
price categories, 64, 86
Puerta de Tierra, 54, 75, 88–89
Río Piedras, 55
safety, 42
San Juan environs, 62–64
Santurce, 55, 80–81
shopping, 17, 106–112
spas, 90
tours, 42–43, 50, 51–53, 61
transportation, 38–39, 41–42, 56, 62
visitor information, 39–40
when to tour, 37–38
San Juan Fashion Week, 111
San Juan Marriott Resort & Stellaris Casino ☶, 91, 100

San Juan National Historic Site, 12
San Juan Water & Beach Club ☶, 94
San Patricio, 15
San Sebastián Street Festival, 11
Santorini ✕, 217–218
Santos, 228–229
Santurce, 55, 80–81
Scuba diving and snorkeling
El Yunque and the Northeast, 124, 134, 153
Ponce and the Porta Caribe, 207, 221, 232, 234
Rincón and the Porta del Sol, 260, 272–273, 275, 280, 284
San Juan, 113–114
Vieques and Culebra, 187, 196
Seagate Hotel ☶, 184
Sheraton Old San Juan Hotel & Casino ☶, 87
Shipwreck Bar & Grill ✕, 255
Shopping, 228–229
El Yunque and the Northeast, 133–134, 139, 141–142
Ponce and the Porta Caribe, 202–203, 219–221, 234
Rincón and the Porta del Sol, 260, 270
San Juan, 17, 106–112
Vieques and Culebra, 185, 195
Siddhia Hutchinson Fine Art Studio & Gallery, 185
Siglo XX ✕, 269
Snorkeling. ⇨ See Scuba diving and snorkeling
Sofia Italian Kitchen & Bar ✕, 73
SoFo Culinary Festival, 11
Sol Creation (shop), 185
Soleil Beach Club ✕, 132
Spas, 90
Sports. ⇨ See Outdoor activities and sports; specific sport
Steps (beach), 243
Stingray Cafe ✕, 150
Surfing, 261–266
El Yunque and the Northeast, 147
Rincón and the Porta del Sol, 247, 267, 280, 284
San Juan, 115–116
Susie's ✕, 192
Symbols, 5

# T

Tamarindo Estates ⊞, *194*
Tamboo ✕, *255*
Tapas Café ✕, *238*
Taxes, *310*
Taxis
*El Yunque and the Northeast,*
*127*
*Ponce and the Porta Caribe,*
*205*
*Rincón and the Porta del Sol,*
*246, 268*
*San Juan, 39*
Teatro La Perla, *211*
Teatro Yagüez, *268*
Telephones, *305–306*
Tembleque, *24*
Tennis, *116, 139*
Theater buildings
*Ponce and the Porta Caribe,*
*211*
*Rincón and the Porta del Sol,*
*268*
Thermal springs, *223*
Tibes, *14*
Tino's ✕, *272*
Tipping, *310*
Tony's ✕, *272*
Toro Negro Forest, *291*
Toro Salao ✕, *74*
Tostones, *24*
Tours
*El Yunque and the Northeast,*
*139–140, 178*
*Ponce and the Porta Caribe,*
*206, 211, 214, 237*
*Rincón and the Porta del Sol,*
*247–248*
*San Juan, 42–43, 51–53, 61*
*Vieques and Culebra, 178, 186*
Trade Winds ⊞, *184*
Transportation, *300–303*
*El Yunque and the Northeast,*
*123, 127*
*Ponce and the Porta Caribe,*
*205*
*Rincón and the Porta del Sol,*
*246, 250, 267–268*
*Ruta Panorámica, 287, 288*
*San Juan, 38–39, 41–42, 56, 62*
*Vieques and Culebra, 165–166*
Travel agencies, *19*
Tres Palmas, *243*
Tres Sirenas ⊞, *258*
Trolley travel. ⇨ *See Bus and*
*trolley travel*

# U

Uvva ✕, *82*

# V

Vacation packages, *310–311*
Verde Mesa ✕, *74*
Via Appia ✕, *80*
Vieques and Culebra, *8,*
*160–196*
*beaches, 162–163, 170, 173,*
*190*
*children, attractions for,*
*172–173, 193*
*dining, 166, 167, 173–174,*
*180–182, 191–192*
*exploring, 169–173, 190*
*itineraries, 170*
*lodging, 166, 182–184,*
*192–194*
*nightlife and the arts, 184–185,*
*194–195*
*outdoor activities and sports,*
*186–188, 195–196*
*packing, 167*
*price categories, 167*
*safety, 167*
*shopping, 185, 195*
*tours, 178, 186*
*transportation, 165–166*
*visitor information, 167*
*when to tour, 165*
Vieques Conservation & Historical Trust, *172–173*
Vieques National Wildlife Refuge, *173*
Villa Boheme ⊞, *194*
Villa Cofresí ⊞, *258–259*
Villa del Rey ⊞, *238*
Villa Herencia Hotel ⊞, *88*
Villa Marina, *149*
Villa Montaña ⊞, *283*
Villa Parguera , *233*
Villa rentals. ⇨ *See Apartment*
*and villa rentals*
Villa Tres Palmas ⊞, *259*
Villas del Mar Hau ⊞, *284*
Visas, *310*
Visitor information, *11, 310*
*El Yunque and the Northeast,*
*121, 129*
*Ponce and the Porta Caribe,*
*206–207*
*Rincón and the Porta del Sol,*
*248*
*San Juan, 39–40*
*Vieques and Culebra, 167*

# W

W Retreat & Spa ⊞, *184*
Waffle-era Tea Room ✕, *74*
Water sports, *139*
Waterfalls
*El Yunque and the Northeast,*
*122*
*Rincón and the Porta del Sol,*
*251*
Weather, *10, 37–38*
Weddings and honeymoons,
*18*
What to pack, *11*
*El Yunque and the Northeast,*
*128*
*Ruta Panorámica, 288*
*Vieques and Culebra, 167*
When to go, *10*
*El Yunque and the Northeast,*
*120, 126–127*
*Ponce and the Porta Caribe,*
*205*
*Rincón and the Porta del Sol,*
*245–246*
*San Juan, 37–38*
*Vieques and Culebra, 165*
Wildlife preserves
*El Yunque and the Northeast,*
*120–123, 139–142, 148–149,*
*156*
*Ponce and the Porta Caribe,*
*226, 230, 233*
*Rincón and the Porta del Sol,*
*250, 273, 276, 282*
*Vieques and Culebra, 173, 177,*
*178, 190*
Windsurfing, *116*
Wyndham Garden at Palmas
del Mar ⊞, *157*

# X

Xabores ✕, *276*

# Y

Yabucoa, *288–291*
Yerba Buena ✕, *80*
Yoga, *116*
Yuque Mar ⊞, *146*
Yuquiyú Delights ✕, *141*

# Z

Zaco's Tacos ✕, *192*
Zen Spa, *90*
Ziplining, *123*
Zoológico de Puerto Rico, *30,*
*268*
Zoos, *30, 268*

## PHOTO CREDITS

1, Katja Kreder / age fotostock. 3, Franz Marc Frei / age fotostock. Chapter 1: Experience Puerto Rico: 6-7, Katja Kreder / age fotostock. 8, Christian Wheatley/Starwood Hotels & Resorts. 9 (left), Lori Froeb/Shutterstock. 9 (right), John Frink/iStockphoto. 12 (left), Jacom Stephens/Avid Creative, Inc./ iStockphoto. 12 (center), Diueine/Flickr. 12 (right),Ksaraf/wikipedia.org. 12 (bottom), Jorge González. 13 (top left), Nick Hanna /Alamy. 13 (bottom left), Frank Llosa. 13 (right), imagebroker / Alamy. 15 (left), Jbermudez/wikipedia.org. 15 (right), MissChatter/wikipedia.org. 16, Danny Lehman/Celebrity Cruises. 17 (left), Tomás Fano/Flickr. 17 (right), Charles Harris/Royal Caribbean International. 18, Hotel El Convento. 19, Hotel El Convento. 20, Museo de Arte de Puerto Rico. 21 (left), Museo de Arte de Puerto Rico. 21 (right), wikipedia.org. 22, Lynn Watson/Shutterstock. 23 (left), The Ritz-Carlton. 23 (right), The Ritz-Carlton. 25Aleksandar Kolundzija/iStockphoto. 30, Oquendo/Flickr. Chapter 2: San Juan: 31, Katja Kreder / age fotostock. 32 (top), John Rodriguez/iStockphoto. 32 (bottom), Lori Froeb/Shutterstock. 33 (left), Miguel A. Alvarez/Shutterstock. 33 (right), Adam Bies/Shutterstock. 34, Katja Kreder / age fotostock. 35 (top right), mysticchildz/Flickr. 35 (bottom left), Stinkie Pinkie/Flickr. 36 (left), DU BOISBERRANGER Jean / age fotostock. 41, Heeb Christian / age fotostock. 45, Tomás Fano/Flickr. 48, George Oze / Alamy. 51 (left), Franz Marc Frei / age fotostock. 51 (top right), Lawrence Roberg/Shutterstock. 51 (bottom right), Franz Marc Frei / age fotostock. 52 (top right), iStockphoto. 52 (bottom left), Oquendo/Flickr. 53 (top left), runneralan2004/Flickr. 53 (top middle), runneralan2004/ Flickr. 53 (top left), Franz Marc Frei / age fotostock. 53 (bottom), Prknlot/Flickr. 55, Atlantide S.N.C. / age fotostock. 56, Oliver Gerhard / age fotostock. 63, imagebroker / Alamy. 71, Wendell Metzen / age fotostock. 73, steve bly / Alamy. 84-85, Ken Welsh / age fotostock. 89, DU BOISBERRANGER Jean / age fotostock. 93 (top), Thomas Hart Shelby 2007. 93 (bottom left), The Ritz-Carlton. 93 (bottom right), Hotel El Convento. 97, Lawrence Manning/photolibrary.com. 98, Craig Lovell / Eagle Visions Photography / Alamy. 99 (top), Pietro Scozzari / age fotostock. 99 (second from top), Julie Schwietert. 99 (third from top), Julie Schwietert. 99 (bottom), STEPHANE - FOTODECLIC / age fotostock. 100 (left), Julie Schwietert. 100 (right), Julie Schwietert. 108, Martin Florin Emmanuel / Alamy. 113, Wendell Metzen / age fotostock. Chapter 3: El Yunque and the Northeast: 117, Ken Welsh / age fotostock. 118, Diana Lundin/Shutterstock. 119 (left), Joseph/Shutterstock. 119 (right), Thomas Hart Shelby. 120, Robert Fried / Alamy. 121 (left), John Frink/iStockphoto. 121 (right), iStockphoto. 122, Doug Schneider/ iStockphoto. 123, Joseph/Shutterstock. 124, Julie Schwietert. 125 (left), Pavelsteidl/wikipedia.org. 125 (right), Ryan Bonneau / Alamy. 126, Luis César Tejo/Shutterstock. 133, Kreder Katja / age fotostock. 137, Katja Kreder / age fotostock. 142, Rolf Nussbaumer / age fotostock. 144-45, Ken Welsh / age fotostock. 147, Katja Kreder / age fotostock. 151, Scott Wiseman. 155, Larry Lambrecht. Chapter 4: Vieques and Culebra: 159, Katja Kreder / age fotostock. 160 (top and bottom), underwhelmer/Flickr. 161 (top left), plizzba/Flickr. 161 (top right), Jjankechu/wikipedia.org. 161 (bottom), underwhelmer/ Flickr. 162, Katja Kreder / age fotostock. 163 (left), kkaplin/Shutterstock. 163 (right), blucolt/Flickr. 164, Michele Falzone / age fotostock. 171, Michele Falzone / age fotostock. 172, SuperStock/age foto- stock. 175, Frank Llosa. 176 (top), Frank Llosa. 176 (bottom), kayakingpuertorico.com. 177, Starwood Hotels & Resorts. 178 (top), Frank Llosa. 178 (bottom), Sue Braden. 179, Starwood Hotels & Resorts. 187, jasonsager/Flickr. 193, Kim Karpeles / Alamy. Chapter 5: Ponce and the Southern Coast: 197, Ken Welsh / age fotostock. 198 (top), Capricornis Photographic Inc./Shutterstock. 198 (bottom), Oquendo/ wikipedia.org. 199 (top), Oquendo/Flickr. 199 (bottom), Jmoliver/wikipedia.org. 200, Oliver Gerhard / Alamy. 201 (bottom left), Oquendo/Flickr. 201 (top right), Greg Vaughn / Alamy. 202, Jim Zuckerman / Alamy. 203 (left), Jim Zuckerman / Alamy. 203 (right), Nicholas Gill. 204, Oquendo/Flickr. 212, Franz Marc Frei / age fotostock. 215, Greg Vaughn / Alamy. 217, Eric Fowke / Alamy. 220, Nicholas Gill. 228, Julie Schwietert. 229 (left), Museo de los Santos / Richard Holm. 229 (right), Tony Amador. 230, DU BOISBERRANGER Jean / age fotostock. 233, giulio andreini / age fotostock. 236, Morales / age foto- stock. Chapter 6: Rincón and the Porta del Sol: 239, Marlise Kast. 240, Hiram A. Gay/wikipedia.org. 241 (top), Oquendo/Flickr. 241 (bottom), Oquendo/Flickr. 242, Katja Kreder / age fotostock. 243 (left), cogito ergo imago/Flickr. 243 (right), Marlise Kast. 244, BlueMoon Stock / Alamy. 245, SuperStock/ age fotostock. 251, Juerg Heinimann / Alamy. 257 (top), Tres Sirenas Beach Inn. 257 (bottom), Horned Dorset Primavera. 261, Marlise Kast. 262 (top and bottom), Eric Rivera Vázquez/Shutterstock. 263 (top left), Marlise Kast. 263 (bottom left), Eric Rivera Vázquez/Shutterstock. 263 (right), Marlise Kast. 264, Eric Rivera Vázquez/Shutterstock. 271, Israel Pabon/Shutterstock. 274, Nicholas Pitt / Alamy. 281, Ken Welsh / age fotostock. Chapter 7: Ruta Panorámica: 285, Nick Hanna / Alamy. 286, Michele Falzone / age fotostock. 287, Casa Grande Mountain Retreat. 289, Robert Fried / Alamy. 293, Nick Hanna / Alamy. 294, Oliver Gerhard / Alamy. 295, Jorge González.

# NOTES

# NOTES

# NOTES

# NOTES

# NOTES

# NOTES

# ABOUT OUR WRITERS

Julie Schwietert Collazo is a bilingual writer interested in overlooked people and places, especially in Latin America. She has written about Chinese Cubans in Havana, Generation Y in Colombia, workers' and indigenous movements in Mexico City, and environmental issues in Chile and Puerto Rico. She was one of only a handful of journalists to visit the Joint Detention Facility at Guantanamo Bay in Cuba in 2008. Julie has lived in Mexico City and San Juan, Puerto Rico. She currently calls New York City home.

As a freelance journalist and author, Marlise Elizabeth Kast has contributed to over 50 publications including *Forbes, Surfer, San Diego Magazine* and the *New York Post*. Her passion for traveling has taken her to 65 countries with short-term residency in Switzerland, the Dominican Republic, Spain, and Costa Rica. Following the release of her memoir, *Tabloid Prodigy*, Marlise coauthored *Fodor's Mexico* (2009–2013), *San Diego* (2009), *Panama* (2nd Edition), *Peru* (4th Edition), *Puerto Rico* (6th Edition) and *Corsica & Sardinia* (2010). She has also written *Day & Overnight Hikes on California's Pacific Crest Trail*. Marlise recently completed a 13-month surfing and snowboarding expedition through 28 countries. Now based in San Diego, she is currently working on her next full length manuscript.

A New York City-based travel, food, and lifestyle writer, Marie Elena Martinez has contributed to a host of publications including *Newsday, Boston Globe, Wall Street Journal, Miami Herald, Women's Adventure*, MensFitness.com, and CNTraveler.com. A regular blogger for The Huffington Post, she left her corporate PR job in 2005 and has been traveling the world ever since.

Heather Rodino traded the island of Manhattan for the island of Puerto Rico, leaving behind a career in book publishing that included editorial positions at Barnes & Noble's publishing division and the Times Books imprint of Henry Holt. Now a freelance editor and writer, she has contributed to *Fodor's Puerto Rico* (6th and 7th eds.) and *Caribbean* (2011–2013). She lives in the Condado neighborhood of San Juan and doesn't miss those long New York winters.